明德百獻

HKU Memories
from the Archives

香港大學檔案中心文物

明德百獻
香港大學檔案中心文物
HKU Memories from the Archives

香港大學美術博物館
University Museum and Art Gallery
The University of Hong Kong

本書配合香港大學檔案中心與香港大學美術博物館合辦的《明德百獻：香港大學檔案文物》展覽出版，展覽日期為二零一一年十二月七日至二零一二年三月十八日。

Published after the exhibition 'HKU Memories from the Archives' presented by the University Archives and the University Museum and Art Gallery of the University of Hong Kong from 7th December 2011 to 18th March 2012.

策展	*Curator of the Exhibition*
張慕貞	Cheung Mo-ching
作者	*Authors*
古達詩	Stacy Belcher Gould
彭綺雲	Tina Yee-wan Pang
中文編輯	*Chinese Editors*
施君玉	Jane Sze Kwan-yuk
黃燕芳	Anita Wong Yin-fong
楊春棠	Yeung Chun-tong
資料搜集及中文翻譯	*Research and Chinese translation*
鄭秀珍	Hemans Cheng
張慕貞	Cheung Mo-ching
蔡筱雯	Angela Choy
江麗春	Lily Kong Lai-chun
林建勳	Garfield Lam
劉家瑜	Michelle Lau Ka-yu
施君玉	Jane Sze Kwan-yuk
黃燕芳	Anita Wong Yin-fong
設計	*Design*
李建華	Li Kin-wah
葉駿濠	Edmund Ip
攝影	*Photography*
潘榮健	Ricky Poon
羅森	Sam Law

印刷：中華商務彩色印刷有限公司
Printed by: C & C Offset Printing Co., Ltd.
© University Museum and Art Gallery, The University of Hong Kong 2013
ISBN: 978-988-19021-6-0

版權所有。如未經香港大學美術博物館書面許可，任何人士不得翻印或發放本圖錄之任何內容或資料。
All rights reserved. No part of this publication may be reproduced or transmitted in any form or by any means, electronic or mechanical, including photocopying, recording, or any information storage or retrieval system, without permission in writing from the publisher.

香港大學美術博物館
香港般咸道九十號
University Museum and Art Gallery
The University of Hong Kong
90 Bonham Road
Hong Kong
www.hku.hk/hkumag

目錄 Contents

鳴謝	**Acknowledgements**	ii
前言	**Foreword**	iv
	香港大學美術博物館總監　羅諾德	
	Florian Knothe, Director of the University Museum and Art Gallery	
引言	**Introduction**	vi
	香港大學檔案中心總監　古達詩	
	Stacy Belcher Gould, Director of the University Archives	
	香港大學美術博物館館長　彭綺雲	
	Tina Yee-wan Pang, Curator of the University Museum and Art Gallery	
編者的話	**Notes to the Reader**	ix
時序	**Timeline**	xi
章節	**Chapters**	
1	香港大學初期的檔案文物 In the Beginning: Early Records of the University	1
2	香港大學創建期的檔案文物 The Establishment Years: Treasures of the University	19
3	早期大學生生活 Early Student Life	81
4	香港大學一九三零至四零年代 The University in the 1930s and 1940s	109
5	二次大戰與日治時期 The War Years	147
6	戰後復元 The University after the War	169
7	金禧誌慶 Celebrating the First 50 Years	205
8	收藏香港大學的歷史檔案 Collecting for the Future	225
附錄	**Appendices**	
	I 「呈盧督頌詞」華人捐獻名冊 　List of Chinese subscribers to the Lugard Tribute	232
	II 香港大學學生會組織架構 　Students' Union Organizational Chart	240
	III 香港大學校長名錄及簽署 　List of Vice-Chancellors with signatures	242
	IV 學位、文憑及證書 　List of degrees (by faculty)	247
參考書目	**Selected Bibliography**	257

鳴謝 Acknowledgements

本展覽能夠順利舉行，香港大學檔案中心與香港大學美術博物館衷心感謝杜鵑基金 (1972)，並向下列機構及賢達人士，深表謝忱。

The University Archives and University Museum and Art Gallery of the University of Hong Kong would like to thank the Azalea Fund (1972), and the following individuals and parties, without whose generous support the exhibition and publication would not have been possible.

Ms Lisa Ride Bailey, Australia (澳洲)

Ms Jody Beenk, Preservation and Conservation Librarian 周貞德女士 (館藏維護主任)

Mrs Muriel Blandford, United Kingdom (英國)

陳慶恩博士 (音樂系) Dr H. Y. Chan, Department of Music

陳國蘭小姐 (圖書館特藏部) Ms Edith Kwok-lan Chan, Special Collections, Libraries

陳桂英女士 (圖書館特藏部) Ms Iris Kwai-ying Chan, Special Collections, Libraries

陳樹衡先生 Mr Chan Shu-hang

陳光先生 (皇家香港軍團(義勇軍)協會) Mr Tony K. Chan, The Royal Hong Kong Regiment, The Volunteers Association

張敏莉小姐 (檔案中心) Ms Lily Man-lee Cheung, University Archives

周肇平副校長 Pro-Vice-Chancellor S. P. Chow

蔡寬量教授 (音樂系) Dr Daniel K. L. Chua, Department of Music

Dr Peter Cunich, Department of History 管沛德博士 (歷史系)

馮陳善奇女士 Mrs Sydney S. K. Fung

郭大江博士 (土木工程系) Dr Guo Dajiang, Department of Civil Engineering

Dr Otto Heim, School of English (英文學院)

何屈志淑醫生 Dr Faith C. S. Ho, Australia (澳洲)

邢廣生女士 Mdm Hsin Kweon-shing, Kuala Lumpur (吉隆坡)

胡世昌夫人 (周妙坤女士) Mrs Dorcas Hu (Chau Miu-kwan)

賴恬昌教授 Professor Lai Tim-chang

劉志雄先生 (英文學院) Mr Franky Lau, School of English

李鴻烈先生 Mr Lee Hong-lie

連浩鋈教授 (歷史系) Dr Alfred Lin, Department of History

劉蜀永教授 Professor Liu Shuyong

馬楚堅教授 (中文學院) Professor Ma Chor-kin, School of Chinese

馬靄媛小姐 Ms Velentina Ma

Mrs Shelagh Meade, United Kingdom (英國)

錢世俊先生 (香港大學職員協會) Mr Qin S. T., HKU Staff Association

Mr David Ride

Ms Elizabeth M. Ride, Norway (挪威)

Mrs Alethea Rogers, United Kingdom (英國)

Mr John Rux-Burton, United Kingdom (英國)

宋以朗博士 Dr Roland Y. L. Soong

蕭文強教授 (數學系) Prof Siu Man-keung, Department of Mathematics

施偉庭夫人 (程德智女士) Mrs Sansan Sweeting

Mr Ronald Taylor, The Royal Hong Kong Regiment, The Volunteers Association 泰萊先生 (皇家香港軍團(義勇軍)協會)

譚靄勵夫人 (鄭碧蓮女士) Mrs Lily Thomas, Australia (澳洲)

譚美瑜女士 Ms Audrey Thomas, Australia (澳洲)

丁新豹博士 Dr Joseph S. P. Ting

謝天錫先生 Mr Michael Tse

謝榮滾伉儷 Mr & Mrs Tse Wing-kwon

徐佩乾先生 Mr Lawrence Tsui, Canada (加拿大)

邱清娜小姐 Ms Cécile Tu

韋永庚先生(教務長) Mr Henry Wai, Registrar

黃保傑先生 Mr Jeffrey Wong

黃月妙小姐 (總監 (發展)) Ms Kitty Wong, Director of Development

黃用諏夫人 (陳桑蓮女士) Mrs Shong-lin Bow Wong

黃玉瑩博士 Dr Wong Yuke-ngan, Kuala Lumpur (吉隆坡)

Mr Jason Wordie 謝偉德先生

楊永安博士 (中文學院) Dr Yeung Wing-on, School of Chinese

葉承耀醫生 Dr Yip Shing-yiu

香港大學文學院 Faculty of Arts

香港大學中文學院 School of Chinese

香港大學英文學院 School of English

香港大學人文學院 School of Humanities

香港大學歷史系 Department of History

香港大學傳訊及公共事務處 Community and Public Affairs Office (CPAO)

香港大學發展及校友事務處 Development and Alumni Affairs Office (DAAO)

香港大學工程學院 Faculty of Engineering

香港大學百周年秘書處 HKU 100 Secretariat

香港大學學生會 University of Hong Kong Students' Union (HKUSU)

香港大學圖書館 University Libraries

香港大學李嘉誠醫學院 Li Ka Shing Faculty of Medicine

香港大學教務處 General Records, Registry

香港大學理學院 Faculty of Science

雍仁會館及大學分會3666團 Zetland Hall and the University Lodge No. 3666

前言 Foreword

本書輯錄了香港大學百年檔案資料，內容不是平鋪直敘地介紹學校的歷史，而是透過記述校園的興建和發展過程中的人物軼事，追尋大學在過去一個世紀多元的發展軌跡。這圖錄結集了本土不少傑出人士的故事，同時收錄了大學隨著時代的變遷和需要而擴展的珍貴文獻，見證了大學與香港在政治社會方面的共同成長歷程。

檔案中心和美術博物館致力為香港大學這所本地歷史最悠久的高等學府庋藏豐富多樣的文物史料。在二零零六年檔案中心創建以前，香港大學美術博物館（一九五三年成立）專門收藏中國藝術品外，還蒐集與大學歷史有關的相片、文物、畢業袍、紀念文集、外界餽贈、具悠久歷史價值的印刷品等。美術博物館更步教務處的後塵，將與港大歷史相關的文物檔案移交至檔案中心集中處理、悉心保管，有助日後研究大學的歷史。

《明德百獻：香港大學檔案文物》的出版不僅讓讀者追溯大學的往昔時光，亦讓我們在慶祝百周年校慶之餘，仔細思考如何為學生、學者及參觀者保存、記錄及展示這批儲藏於美術博物館及檔案中心的歷史文物 — 我們需要持續研究及保存這些珍貴的文獻，積極改善藏品的管理，並進一步將師生職工的校園回憶承傳下去。

保存大學檔案並非為了個人建功立業，而是大學在發展到某個階段的時候，校園大家庭成員開始回顧過去，思索如何保留學校的歷史，透過歷史學及人類學的角度，記下多年來一代接一代出類拔萃的學生、精明能幹的管理人員與高瞻遠矚的教師共同努力的豐碩成果。新近成立的檔案中心確保了歷史文獻能妥善保存，並提供機會讓研究員閱覽與港大今昔有關的資料；而美術博物館則致力舉辦關於傳統、現代及當代藝術的展覽，教育及啟迪大眾，同時收藏及受贈藝術品，為下一代建構一所'博古通今'的校園。

香港大學美術博物館 總監
羅諾德 博士

This publication of archival material is not an institutional history but a multi-faceted account of some of the individuals who played an important part in the making and development of the University of Hong Kong (HKU). A human story, this account preserves the memories of some outstanding members of our community, and it showcases selected regalia and ephemera, which document the growth of a beloved institution by focusing on key moments in the political and social history of both the University and Hong Kong, for one would not have gained its importance without the other.

The University Archives and University Museum and Art Gallery serve as guardians of the rich and diverse history of Hong Kong's oldest tertiary institution, the University of Hong Kong. Until the foundation and subsequent development of the Archives from 2006, the Museum (est. 1953) housed the University's collections of Chinese art, and numerous photographs, artefacts, graduation robes, commemorative publications, gifts and ephemera, which document the long life of the University. The University Museum and Art Gallery, leading by example along with the offices of the Registry, has been transferring its HKU-related artefacts and collections to the University Archives, thus centralizing the research materials for the history of the school in one main repository for the ease of future research and preservation efforts.

HKU Memories from the Archives offers a glimpse into our institution's past and it is published at a time when the University has just celebrated its centenary, and is carefully re-thinking where individual HKU history-related items are most advantageously kept—in the Museum or the Archives—and how they can be best catalogued, preserved and displayed, for current and future generations of University students, scholars and visitors alike. The past century has bestowed upon us a wealth of historically important documents, and our ongoing and future research and preservation work will not only strive to achieve the most suitable and accessible storage methods for present and future collections, but further to interpret the 'memories' we hold.

The preservation of University records and artefacts is neither a self-fulfilling prophecy nor a self-aggrandising or promotional exercise, but a normal result of the age and growing self-awareness of the University and the HKU family. The life of the institution has reached a point at which we recognise the need for proper accounting of our history that requires the professional discipline that follows archival principles to register the achievements, decision-taking, and culture of generations of successful students, able administrators and visionary educators. The recently established Archives ensures the safe-keeping and consultation of our historic documents and guarantees the continuous study of present and future collections, whereas the Museum promises to enlighten and educate with historic, modern and contemporary artworks, and to build up—through acquisitions and donations—collections that inform the coming generations that will shape the future of the University and its constituency.

Dr Florian Knothe
Director, University Museum and Art Gallery, HKU

引言 Introduction

香港大學檔案中心已踏入第五年，成立的目的緣於大學管理層和各學院在籌辦港大九十周年活動時所意識到的需要，就是'建立一個統一儲存庫，收集關於大學歷史的資料……而對這計劃有莫大裨益的，莫過於建立一所正式的大學檔案中心。'當時歷史系曾將歷史學家就大學成立及早期發展撰寫的文章結集出版，該書編輯陳劉潔貞、管沛德也注意到'很多著名學府都著手籌辦檔案館，把資料公開予大學社群和廣大公眾使用，因為他們都與這些學校部門息息相關。'[1]

檔案中心便由此成立，負責保存具持久深遠價值的大學紀錄。我們的工作是蒐集、保存和闡釋各種歷史檔案，提供給港大和港大成員使用。我們會協助大學各部門學系審定和轉移所儲存的資料予檔案中心。此外，我們亦處理個人或家庭捐贈出來的文獻文物。簡單來說，我們的寶庫就是港大的集體回憶。

過去數年我們幫助各大學部門、校外的研究人員和傳媒機構，進行各項關於港大歷史和百周年慶典的籌劃、出版、展覽等工作。而'明德百獻'展覽與別不同的地方就是展品都從本檔案中心精選出來的。當然，我們不可能把港大一百年的歷史搬進展廳，但參觀者所看到的藏品種類眾多，包括文獻、相片、文物、紀錄、藝術品、紀念品。我們也展出新增的收藏，顯示檔案中心所收藏的範圍涵蓋過去和現在，以提供資料給未來參考。我們希望您喜歡這個展覽，更期待您會和我們分享您和港大的故事。

最後我須深切感謝香港大學美術博物館前總監楊春棠先生和各博物館同事，以及教務長韋永庚先生，他們給予很大幫助。我也對杜鵑基金的慷慨資助，深表謝意。因此本書並不作為展覽圖冊，而是配合展覽出版。它雖然不能收錄每件展品，卻加進文物、文獻背後蘊藏的相關歷史資料。本書與展覽同樣展示了香港大學檔案中心所藏豐富的港大歷史資料，讓觀眾領略不同藏品之間千絲萬縷的關係。

香港大學檔案中心 總監 古達詩
香港大學美術博物館 館長 彭綺雲

---

[1] Chan Lau Kit-ching and Peter Cunich (eds), *An Impossible Dream: Hong Kong University from Foundation to Re-establishment 1910–1950* (Hong Kong, Oxford University Press, 2002).

During the preparations for the University's 90th anniversary celebrations in 2001, the 'need to collect in a central repository as much material relating to the University's history as is practicable…' was immediately recognised.[1] And so the idea for the formal establishment of a University Archives was seeded. Five years later, this idea was finally realised. As part of the 90th anniversary celebrations, the Department of History published a collection of essays by historians focusing on the University's founding and early development. The editors of *An Impossible Dream*, Chan Lau Kit-ching and Peter Cunich, noted in their introduction that, 'many other great universities have taken this step [of establishing a university archive] as a means of opening their records to both their own university communities and the wider public, who also have a stake in those institutions…' Dr Cunich became one of the driving forces behind the establishment of the University Archives, and has since acted as an advisor.

The University Archives was established with a mandate to be the central repository for records of enduring value to the University. Its charge is to identify, collect, preserve, describe and make available records of historical value to the University and its alumni in all their various formats. An important part of its work is to assist University departments and faculties in identifying which records are of value and in arranging the transfer of these records to the Archives. It also works with individuals, alumni and their families who wish to donate their records to the Archives. In short, the Archives are the collective memory of the University of Hong Kong.

In recent years the Archives have helped numerous University departments, researchers, and media outlets with research and planning for publications and exhibitions for the Centenary of the University. The 'HKU Memories from the Archives' exhibition was a chance for the Archives to share some of the highlights of the University's history through documents, photographs, artefacts, memorabilia, and artworks in its unique collections. The exhibition and this book have included artefacts that have recently entered the Archives, documenting the present as well as the past in order to inform the future.

The exhibition project began with the encouragement of Professor S. P. Chow, Pro-Vice-Chancellor of University Relations, the former Director of the University Museum and Art Gallery, Mr Yeung Chun-tong, and the support of Mr Henry Wai, the University's Registrar. It was realised with the generous support of the Azalea Fund. While this volume is not a catalogue of the exhibition, its purpose remains the same: to provide a taste of the rich and complex history of the University of Hong Kong through the diverse materials collected by the University Archives.

Stacy Belcher Gould
Director, University Archives, HKU
Tina Yee-wan Pang
Curator, University Museum and Art Gallery, HKU

編者的話
Notes to the reader

本書作者衷心感謝眾多歷史學家及作家對港大歷史的研究心得，這些著作可見於參考書目。

除非另外註明，本書所載檔案文物皆為香港大學檔案中心藏品。

The authors wish to acknowledge the great debt they owe to the many historians and writers whose research has informed the writing of this text. The main publications consulted are listed in the selected bibliography.

Unless otherwise stated, the archival materials and collections included in this book are from the University Archives.

Chinese names are romanised according to Cantonese or pinyin romanisation, whichever the person was more widely recognised by, or other forms of romanisation where they have been used in existing documents. Where known, the Chinese characters will always be given in the Chinese version of the text. Original romanisations will be retained where quotations are used. Chinese place names will appear in pinyin romanisation except where they appear in quotations, in which case the original romanisation will be retained.

香港大學與
世界時序
TIMELINE

19th Century
1840

The University of Hong Kong: Events and developments
香港大學：主要事件及發展

1872
英國教會傳道會赫清臣牧師提出在香港興建一所大學
Reverend A. B. Hutchison of the Church Missionary Society initiated a plan to build a university for Hong Kong

1878
港督軒尼詩擬議在港興建醫學院
John Pope Hennessy (Governor 1877-1882) proposed a medical school for Hong Kong

1880
港督軒尼詩成立委員會研究提升中央書院為大學的可行性
John Pope Hennessy set up a committee to study the feasibility of upgrading the Central School into a college

1887.08.30
會議通過創辦西醫書院
The Hong Kong College of Medicine was formed at Alice Memorial Hospital

Social events of Hong Kong
香港社會重要事件

1842.08
港督批准馬禮遜教育協會在港建校，同年11月馬禮遜書院由澳門遷港，名為馬禮遜書院
Establishment of Morrison College – the first English language school in Hong Kong

1843
倫敦傳道會將英華書院從馬六甲遷港，由中英國教會人士主辦
London Missionary Society relocated Ying Wah College from Malacca, Malaysia to Hong Kong

1847
在九龍城寨開辦由華人主辦的龍津義學
Chinese-run Lung Tsun Free School opened in Kowloon Walled City

1847
成立「教育調查小組」，調查維多利亞城、香港仔及赤柱的8間中文學塾。是年8月資助其中3間及任命「教育委員會」監督
An Education Investigation Team was formed to examine the eight Chinese language schools in Victoria city, Aberdeen and Stanley; three schools were subsequently subsidised and an Education Commissioner was appointed in August

1849
在中環鐵崗開辦聖保羅書院
Opening of St Paul's College in Glenealy, Central

1855
資助的中文學塾改為「皇家書館」，由政府直接管理
Conversion of the subsidised Chinese language schools to 'royal schools' directly administered by Government

1860
改組「教育委員會」，成立教育局
Re-organisation of Education Commission to Education Bureau

1862
皇仁書院的前身「中央書院」成立，1889年易名「皇后書院」，1894年改稱「皇仁書院」
Establishment of the Government Central School, renamed Victoria College in 1889 and Queen's College in 1894

1865
教育局改為「教育司署」，教育司首長直接向港督負責
Education Bureau was renamed the Education Department with expanded functions, with the head reporting directly to the Governor

1873
補助書館計劃獲政府批准，1879年修訂，教會在教育的壟斷結束
Grant-in-aid Scheme was approved by the Government and later revised in 1879, ending church domination of schooling

1880
第一間免費私立學校「文武廟義學」成立
Man Mo Free School, the first free private school was founded

1881
首所開辦英文老師範學堂
Setting up of the first school for training English language teachers

1863
香港第一個水塘「薄扶林水塘」啟用
Opening of the first reservoir in Hong Kong at Pokfulam

1862
香港發行第一套郵票
Issuance of the first Hong Kong postage stamps

1866
爆發全球金融危機，導致全港11間銀行中有6間倒閉
Global financial crisis leading to the collapse of 6 out of 11 banks

1869-1871
海底電纜鋪設於薄扶林，大大加速香港與歐洲的聯繫
Debut landing of submarine telegraph cables at Pokfulam to hasten communications between Europe and Hong Kong

1872.02.14
東華醫院啟用
Opening of Tung Wah Hospital

1880
伍廷芳被委任為首位立法局華人議員
Wu Tingfang was appointed the first Chinese Legislative Councillor

1883
香港天文台成立
Opening of the Hong Kong Observatory

1888
香港九龍渡海小輪公司（今天星小輪）及山頂纜車啟用
Opening of the HK & Kowloon Ferry Co. and the Peak Tram

China and the World
中國及世界大事

1841.01
英軍占領香港
The landing of British forces in Hong Kong

1842.08
簽訂《南京條約》，香港島被割讓成為英國殖民地
Treaty of Nanjing, Hong Kong Island was ceded to the British Government as a colony

1860
簽訂《北京條約》，九龍半島今界限街以南割讓給英國。Kowloon Peninsula was ceded to the British
Convention of Peking. Kowloon Peninsula was ceded to the British

1839 – 1842
第一次鴉片戰爭
First Opium War

1851-1864
太平天國運動
Taiping Rebellion

1856-1858
第二次鴉片戰爭
Second Opium War

1858
簽訂《天津條約》，清政府開放更多貿易港口
Treaty of Tianjin, greater number of treaty ports opened for trade

1866
因英國上市銀行歐沃倫格尼倒閉，爆發金融危機，並蔓延至歐洲及其他地方
Spread of the world financial crisis following the collapse of Overend Gurney & Co. in Britain

1866.11.12
孫中山誕生
Birth of Sun Yat-sen

1884
中法戰爭
Sino-French War

1900 – 1920s 20th Century

1908.01.17
港督盧吉提出在香港創辦大學
Governor Frederick Lugard proposed setting up a university in Hong Kong

1908.03
港督盧吉宣布香港西醫書院將納入香港大學醫學院
Governor Lugard proposed that the Hong Kong College of Medicine would become a part of the new University

1908.03
確定大學選址
Confirmation of the site for the University

1908
麼地捐款15萬元作大學建設
Hormusjee Naorojee Mody donated $150,000 for a university building

1909
為興建香港大學發動勸募籌款
Fund-raising campaigns for the University began

1910
政府撥出薄扶林青草山地段為香港大學建校地址
Green Grass Mountain in Pokfulam was designated as the site for the University of Hong Kong

1910.03.16
本部大樓奠基
Laying of the foundation stone of the Main Building

1911.03.30
香港大學註冊成立
The University of Hong Kong was incorporated by ordinance

1912.09
醫學院，工學院，文學院正式授課，學生共有71人
First semester commenced with a total of 71 students admitted to the Faculties of Medicine, Engineering and Arts

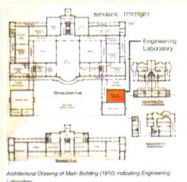

Engineering Building

1912.03.11
本部大樓啟用
Opening of the Main Building

1912
聖約翰宿舍建成
Completion of the construction of St John's Hall

1913
解剖學系和解剖館大樓成立
Opening of the School of Anatomy and the Anatomy Building

1913
馬禮遜堂和大學堂（後易名盧吉堂）啟用
Morrison Hall and University Hall (later renamed Lugard Hall) opened

1914
儀禮堂啟用
Opening of Eliot Hall

1915
梅堂和薄扶林運動場啟用
Opening of May Hall and Pokfulam Athletic Ground

1902.17
...ng of the Alice Memorial ...tal

1910.01
...uration ceremony of Hong ... College of Medicine for ...se held at City Hall

1910.01
...入讀香港西醫書院
...at-sen was admitted to the ...Kong College of Medicine for ...se

1894.05
香港爆發鼠疫
Outbreak of the bubonic plague, also known as the Black Death, in Hong Kong

1894
中日戰爭
Sino-Japanese War

1900
義和拳／義和團事件，八國聯軍入京
Boxer Rebellion and Eight-Nation Alliance

1890.03.30
創辦官立女子中央書院，後易名為庇利羅士女子公立學校
Central School for girls opened, later renamed Belilios Public School

1892.07.23
西醫書院首兩屆畢業生包括孫中山及江英華
Sun Yat-sen and Kong Ying-wah among the first graduates of the Hong Kong College of Medicine for Chinese

1898
滿清簽訂《拓展香港界址專條》，把新界租借予英國99年
Second Convention of Peking when the Qing government leased the New Territories to Britain for 99 years

1900
印僑嘉道理及港紳劉鑄伯等組成「育才書社」
Sir Elly Kadoorie and Lau Chu-pak established Elly Kadoorie School

1905.12.15
《德臣西報》編輯唐納在社評再次鼓吹香港設立大學
Australian editor, William Henry Donald, re-iterated the idea of a university for Hong Kong in the *China Mail*

1904
電車開始服務，行走堅尼地城至銅鑼灣一帶
Tram services from Kennedy Town to Causeway Bay commenced

1904
通過《山頂區保留條例》，將山頂區劃為歐人住宅區，至1945年廢除
'Peak District Reservation Ordinance' was enacted whereby residence on the Peak was restricted to Westerners. The Ordinance was lifted in 1945

1904.06.07
雅麗氏母嬰醫院啟用，開設首屆婦產科護理課程
Opening of the Alice Memorial Maternity Hospital and the launch of a course for midwives

1906
何妙齡醫院啟用
Opening of the Ho Miu-ling Hospital

1905
愛因斯坦發現相對論
Albert Einstein expounds the Theory of Relativity

1905
滿清廢除科舉考試，推行新式教育制度，促使更多學生出國留學，西方國家紛紛在中國辦大學
Abolition of the Qing Civil Service Examination by the Chinese Government. The establishment of a modern school system led to an increase in students studying abroad, and the establishment of universities by Western powers

1906
創立香港工業訓練校，1907年改為香港工學院
Establishment of an industrial technical training school. This became the Technical Institute of Hong Kong in 1907

1907.05.23
香港西醫書院英文易名，刪除「for Chinese」字眼，並作註冊
The Hong Kong College of Medicine for Chinese was renamed Hong Kong College of Medicine and legally incorporated

1910
約5174名中國學生精英往日本留學，400人則往英美深造
Approximately 5174 Chinese students went to study in Japan; 400 students went to Britain and the United States

1910.10
九廣鐵路香港段啟用
The Kowloon-Canton Railway begins operation

1913
公布1913年教育條例，規定所有學校要經教育司署註冊
All schools were required to be registered under the Education Department as stated in the Education Ordinance

1911.10.10
辛亥革命
October Tenth Revolution

1911
中華民國成立
Founding of the Republic of China

xiii

1900 – 1920s 20th Century

The University of Hong Kong: Events and developments / 香港大學：主要事件及發展

1912 聖士提反書院校長查詢香港大學是否招收女生
Principal of St Stephen's Girls' College enquired if the University would accept women students

1912 史密夫教授被委任為工學院太古講席，是首位講座教授
Professor Cades Alfred Middleton Smith became the first appointed Chair at HKU (Taikoo Professor of Engineering)

1915 香港西醫書院正式解散
Hong Kong College of Medicine was dissolved

1916.12.23 大學首屆畢業禮，共有23名來自八省的畢業生獲頒學位
First University Congregation with 23 graduates coming from 8 provinces

1918 朱光潛在港大講課
Zhu Guangqian lectured at HKU

1918 國內師範學生獲送到香港大學就讀
Students from teachers' colleges in Mainland China admitted to HKU

1920 港府撥款100萬元給香港大學基金
Hong Kong Government allocates $1 million to the HKU endowment fund

1920.02.12 香港大學生於大會堂首度演出舞台劇，演繹英國名家丹塞尼的劇作
Debut theatrical performance of plays by Lord Dunsay performed by HKU students at City Hall

1921 首名大學女生伊惠珠入讀香港大學文學院
Admission of the first female student, Rachel Irving, into the Faculty of Arts, HKU

1921 首名本地女生何艾齡入讀香港大學文學院
Admission of the first local female student, Irene Ho Tung, into the Faculty of Arts, HKU

1922 首期《學生會會刊》出版
Publication of the first volume of Union Magazine

1923.02.20 孫中山應學生會邀請在港大大禮堂演講
Sun Yat-sen delivered a speech at the University's Great Hall

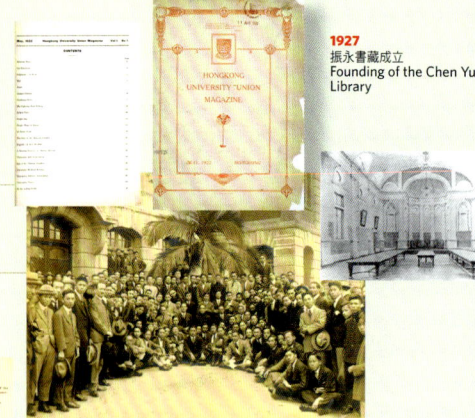

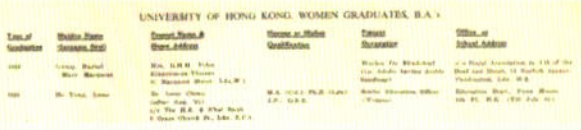

1927 振永書藏成立
Founding of the Chen Yung Library

1927 中文學系成立
Institute of Chinese Studies founded

1929 中文學院成立
School of Chinese established

1913 文學院成立
Faculty of Arts established

1916 開辦首屆碩士學位課程
Masters degrees offered for the first time

1918 生理學系成立
Establishment of the School of Physiology

1918.05 香港大學醫學院開幕
Opening of the Faculty of Medicine

1916.05.03 大學體育亭啟用
Opening of the University Sports Pavilion

1917 增建病理學館大樓和發電站
Addition of Pathology Building and power station

1919.11 學生會大樓（今孔慶熒樓）啟用
Opening of the University Union Building (Hung Hing Ying Building)

1919 熱帶病與病理學館大樓啟用
Opening of the Schools of Pathology and Tropical Medicine Building

1922.09 佐敦紀念圖書館啟用
Jordan Memorial Library established

1923 女生宿舍聖士提反堂建成
Establishment of St Stephen's Hall for women

1925 何東機械實驗所成立
Ho Tung Engineering Workshop established

1928 生物樓建成
Completion of Biology Building

1929.12.16 利瑪竇宿舍建成
Completion of Ricci Hall

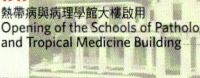

Social events of Hong Kong / 香港社會重要事件

1914 第一次世界大戰爆發，大量國內學生到港求學
Outbreak of the First World War brought an influx of Mainland students to Hong Kong

1919.05.04 五四運動
May Fourth Movement

1920 成立「教育諮詢委員會」以制訂教育政策
Formation of the education policy-making committee

1920 國內大學首次招收女生
Woman students were admitted into universities in China

1921 中國首間國立大學「中央大學」在南京成立
First National Central University was founded in Nanjing

1924 位於廣州的廣東大學（現中山大學）成立
Foundation of University of Guangdong (Zhongshan University) in Guangzhou

1925–1926 省港大罷工，長達16個月，遍及各行各業，引發港穗各地成立勞工團體和工會
Strikes in Hong Kong and Guangzhou spread into different sectors over 16 months resulting in the founding of many labour associations and trade unions

1925 回應學生罷課及響應工人運動，港督金文泰強調傳統儒家思想和價值觀
Governor Clements (1925–1930) publicly emphasised the importance of Confucianism in response to student support for the labour strikes

1925.03.12 孫中山逝世
Death of Sun Yat-sen

1926.03 官立漢文中學成立
Opening of Government Vernacular (Hon Mun) Middle School

1927 魯迅訪港，在香港青年會演講
Lu Xun delivered a speech at the YMCA in Hong Kong

1928 香港中文學校實施「六三三學制」
Adoption of the '6-3-3 Study Scheme' by Chinese schools

1928 1928年開始興建啟德機場，並於1959年擴建
Construction of Kai Tak Airport began in 1928; expansion works were conducted in 1959

1928 香港電台啟播
Launch of radio broadcasting

1926 周壽臣獲任為首位行政局華人議員
Shouson Chow was appointed the first Chinese Executive Councillor

China and the World / 中國及世界大事

1911.12.23 孫中山獲委任為臨時大總統四日後旋即訪港
Sun Yat-sen visited Hong Kong four days after he was elected provisional President

1912.05.20 孫中山辭去總統職務後訪港，在香港酒店接受《南華早報》訪問
Sun Yat-sen resigned from the presidency and was interviewed by the South China Morning Post in the Hong Kong Hotel

1914–1918 第一次世界大戰
World War I

1917 俄國革命
Russian Revolution

1929–30 華爾街崩潰，導致經濟大蕭條
Wall Street Crash followed by the Great Depression

xiv

1930s – 1940s
War Time

1933
劇作家蕭伯納訪問香港大學作演講
Playwright George Bernard Shaw visited HKU

1935
許地山受聘為首任中文系教授
Hsu Ti-shan (1893-1941) was appointed as the first Professor of the Chinese Department

1937.05
馮平山圖書館舉行徐悲鴻畫展
Exhibition of paintings by Xu Beihong was held at the Fung Ping Shan Library

1937
香港大學學生會組成「香港學生賑濟會」供應物資予中國軍隊
Formation of HKU Students' Union China Medical Relief Association to support the Chinese army

1938.11
嶺南大學借用港大校舍辦學
Lingnan University borrowed HKU campus to hold classes

1938
馮平山圖書館安置中國各地圖書館逃避戰鎬的藏書
Fung Ping Shan Library received various collections from mainland libraries to escape destruction

1938
黃麗松讀香港大學
Rayson Huang was admitted to HKU

1939.08.29
張愛玲入讀香港大學文學院
Eileen Chang was admitted into HKU

1940
陳寅恪在香港大學講課
Chen Yinke lectured at HKU

1941
本科學生中女性約佔兩成
Female undergraduates comprise approximately 20% of the student body

1931.09.28
鄧志昂樓啟用
Opening of the Tang Chi Ngong Building

1932.12.14
馮平山中文圖書館啟用，1934年1月對外開放
Opening of the Fung Ping Shan Library to the public in January 1934

1935.01.07
外科學院校舍啟用，1977年拆卸
School of Surgery Building was opened. It was demolished in 1977

1935.12.07
貝璐工程實驗室啟用
Opening of Peel Laboratory

1936
余東璇運動場啟用，1952年拆卸
Opening of the Eu Tong Sen Gymnasium. It was demolished in 1952

1931
據人口統計顯示，5至10歲兒童有119,008人，其中學生佔68,953人
Census records show that 69,953 of 119,008 children between the ages of 5 and 10 were enrolled as students

1932
港督會同議政局修訂「1913年教育條例」，加添「規則25條」
The Legislative Council added amendment 25 to Education Ordinance of 1913

1934
香港教師會成立
Establishment of the Hong Kong Teachers' Association

1935
發表「賓尼報告書」
Publication of the Burney Report on education

1937
教育司署舉辦全港中學畢業會考
Education Department organised examinations for all secondary school graduates

1937
香港人口突破160萬
Hong Kong population reached 1.6 million

1937.09
颱風襲港，傷亡逾萬
Typhoon killed over ten thousand people

1938
日軍佔領廣州，嶺南大學、廣州大學、廣東國民大學被迫遷港復課
Japanese occupation of Guangzhou, forced Lingnan, Guangzhou, and Guangdong Guomin universities to relocate to Hong Kong

1939
開辦一年的教師學院改名為羅富國師範學院，1967易名為羅富國教育學院
Opening of the Northcote Training College, renamed Northcote College of Education in 1967

1934
紅軍長征
Long March of the Red Army

1939
歐戰爆發
Outbreak of war in Europe

1939-1945
第二次世界大戰
Second World War

1937-1945
日本侵華
Japanese invasion of China

XV

The University of Hong Kong: Events and developments / 香港大學：主要事件及發展

1941.12.08-1945.08
港大停課，停課前共有四個學院，包括醫學、工程、文學、理學，學生共516人；同時收容嶺南大學和中國軍事學院學生共500人。日軍入侵香港後，逾200名港大學生進入中國
Classes suspended due to Japanese occupation. Prior to that, the University had 516 students in 4 faculties, including Medicine, Engineering, Arts and Sciences. It also hosted 500 students from Lingnan University and the Chinese Maritime School. 200 HKU students escaped to Free China

1941.12.04
受戰況影響，港大考試被迫撤銷，部份學生參與義勇軍
HKU examinations were abandoned. Many students joined the Volunteer Defence Force

1942.01
校園被徵調作臨時集中營，本部大樓充當醫院
Campus was used as a temporary internment camp, and the Main Building served as a relief hospital

1942
王國棟教授避走重慶，安排在中國避難的醫科生繼續上課
Professor Gordon King fled to Chongqing and conducted medical classes for students exiled in China

1942
賴廉士教授組織「英軍服務團」
Professor Lindsay Ride organised the British Army Aid Group (BAAG)

1946.03.22
在大禮堂頒授戰時學位
Wartime degrees were conferred in the Great Hall

1946.10.23
復課
Classes resumed

1948
大學重開
Re-opening of the University

1948
侯寶璋教授獲委任為醫學院講師，直到1961年榮休
Hou Pao-chang appointed lecturer of Medicine until retirement in 1961

1939
理學院成立，脫離於文理學院
Establishment of the Faculty of Science, separate from the Faculty of Arts.

1949
開設普通話課程，為1951年成立的語文學院基石，1953年2月易名「東方文化研究院」
Mandarin courses offered, forming the foundation of a Language School in 1951. This evolved into the Institute of Oriental Studies in February 1953

1939.08.30
聖母堂啟用
Opening of Our Lady's Hall

1941.09
羅富國科學大樓啟用
Opening of Northcote Science Building

1937.06
瑪麗醫院啟用
Opening of Queen Mary Hospital

War Time
1930s – 1940s

Social events of Hong Kong / 香港社會重要事件

1941
全港共有645間學校，包括官立學校9間，津貼學校20間，補助學校91間，私立學校529間，學生人數為118,000人
The total number of schools was 645 with 118,000 students, this included 9 Government schools, 20 subsidised schools, 91 aided schools and 529 private schools

1945
二次大戰時，香港學生人數只有4000人
Approximately 4000 students were enrolled in Hong Kong during war time

1946.10
達德學院開辦，李濟深為董事
Opening of Ta Teh Institute, chaired by Li Jishen

1947
全港學校復課大致完成，統計學生人數為112,368人
Education in Hong Kong resumed with around 112,368 students enrolled

1949
新亞書院創立
Establishment of New Asia College

1941.12.08-1945.08.15
日軍占領香港
Japanese Occupation of Hong Kong

1945
二戰前香港人口約160萬，到二戰結束時人口只有60萬，次年回升至100萬
At the end of the War, the population had fallen to 0.6 million but quickly rose to 1 million by 1946

1949
開始簽發香港居民身份證
Issuance of identity cards to Hong Kong residents

China and the World / 中國及世界大事

1945
聯合國成立
Formation of the United Nations

1946
第一代電腦出現
Appearance of the first generation of computers

1949.10.01
中華人民共和國成立，國民政府遷往台灣
Establishment of the People's Republic of China. The Nationalist government moved to Taiwan

1952
學生人數千人，當中95%為本地生
Student numbers reached 1,000 with 95% local students

1952.10
根德公爵夫人訪問大學
Duchess of Kent visited the University

1952
中文系由鄧志昂樓遷往本部大樓
Relocation of the Chinese Department from the Tang Chi Ngong Building to Main Building

1952
本科生首次穿著綠袍
Undergraduate green gowns were worn for the first time

1952
香港大學出版社成立
Founding of the HKU Press

1953
香港大學出版社首部著作《明器圖錄》面世
HKU Press' first publication is *Chinese Tomb Pottery Figures*

1954.03
東方文化研究院首次出版期刊
Publication of the first journal volume of the Institute of Oriental Studies

1956
大學醫療保健處成立
Establishment of the University Health Service

1958
大學議會成立
Establishment of Convocation

1959.04.02
大學議會首次會議
The first Convocation

1950
建築學院成立
Establishment of the Faculty of Architecture

1951.01
語文學院成立
Founding of the Language School

1952
生物學院設置漁業研究所
Fisheries Research Unit established under the Department of Biology

1953
中國藝術及考古學陳列所成立，於1964年改為馮平山博物館
Museum of Chinese Art and Archaeology established. Later named the Fung Ping Shan Museum in 1964

1953.02
東方文化研究院成立
Institute of Oriental Studies was established

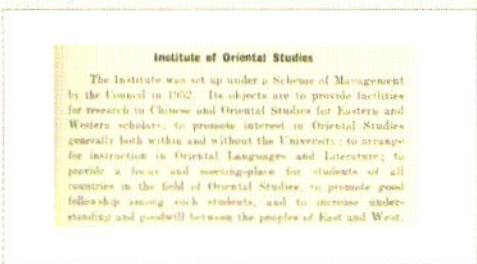

1956
大學考古組成立
An Archaeology Unit was established

1956
香港大學校外課程部成立，現為香港大學專業進修學院
Department of Extra-mural Studies was founded (now the School of Professional and Continuing Education)

1950.03.01
史羅司樓啟用，並於1959年擴建
Opening of the Duncan Sloss Building with extension works conducted in 1959

1950
新校長寓所建成
A new Vice-Chancellor's lodge was built

1952
本部大樓擴建完成
Extension works on the Main Building were completed

1952
何東夫人紀念堂建成，1957年擴建
Lady Ho Tung Hall was completed and later extended in 1957

1952
兩所非寄宿舍堂「根德公爵夫人堂」和「康寧堂」成立
The first two non-residential halls, Duchess of Kent Hall and Hornell Hall were founded

1953
化學大樓啟用
Chemistry Building was opened

1953
香港大學接管「拿撒勒堡」，於1956年命名為「大學堂」
HKU acquired the Nazareth House. It was renamed University Hall in 1956

1955
聖約翰學院啟用，1979年擴建
St John's College opened, and extended in 1979

1956
本部大樓的大禮堂易名「陸佑堂」
The Great Hall in Main Building was renamed Loke Yew Hall

1958
新病理學大樓啟用
New Pathology Building was opened

1958
本部大樓再次擴建
Main Building was further extended

1950s – 1960s

1950
教育署擬定「十年建校計劃」
The Education Department proposed the 'Draft Ten-Year Plan'

1951
崇基學院創立
Establishment of Chung Chi College

1952
中文和英文中學會考舉行
Hong Kong Certificate of Examination (Chinese and English) took place

1956
聯合書院成立
Establishment of Union College

1956
香港浸會學院成立
Establishment of Baptist College

1950.04
關閉香港與中國的邊界
Hong Kong-China border closed

1953.12.25
石硤尾大火，導致5萬3千人無家可歸，港府推行徙置計劃
Shek Kip Mei Squatter Fire left 53,000 people homeless. The Government to proposed a public housing policy

1957
有線電視「麗的映聲」開辦
Introduction of Rediffusion Television

1950-1953
韓戰時期，聯合國對中國實施貿易禁運
Korean War. The United Nations placed an embargo against China

1958
大躍進
Great Leap Forward in China

The University of Hong Kong: Events and developments
香港大學：主要事件及發展

1961
慶祝金禧
Golden Jubilee Celebrations

1962.02
馮平山圖書館搬往圖書館大樓三樓
The Fung Ping Shan Library relocated to the third floor of the University's Main Library

1964.01.31
馮平山博物館易名
Museum of Chinese Art and Archaeology renamed the Fung Ping Shan Museum

1966.01.14
位於白文信樓的醫學圖書館開幕
Medical Library opened in Patrick Manson Building

1967.07.01
實施大學教職員保健計劃
Launching of medical benefits scheme for University staff

1967
香港大學納入大學資助委員會架構
HKU came under the University Grants Committee

1968
語文研習所啟用
Opening of the Language Centre

1969
電腦中心啟用
Opening of Computer Centre

1969
大學生宿舍改為非強制性
Requirement for undergraduate students to be resident at University was lifted

1969
學生資助計劃開始
Introduction of financial assistance for students

1967
亞洲研究中心成立
Centre of Asian Studies established

1967
社會科學學院成立
Faculty of Social Sciences established

1969
社會科學學院法律系成立
Department of Law was established within the Faculty of Social Sciences

1961.11.06
雅麗珊郡主為新學生會大樓啟用儀式進行揭幕
New Students' Union Building was opened by Princess Alexandra

1961
圖書館大樓建成
The Main Library was opened

1963
賴廉士體育中心啟用
Lindsay Ride Sports Centre was opened

1965.10.28
柏立基學院奠基，1982年擴建
Foundation stone for Robert Black College was laid with extension added in 1982

1965.04.05
李樹芬樓啟用
Li Shu Fan Building was inaugurated

1965
白文信樓啟用，1972年擴建
Patrick Manson Building was opened and later expanded in 1972

1967.01.19
柏立基學院啟用
Robert Black College was opened

1967.12.08
利瑪竇堂重建後啟用
Ricci Hall was opened after reconstruction

1969.02.09
盧吉堂、儀禮堂、梅堂合併為明原堂
Lugard, Eliot and May Halls were combined as Old Halls

1950s – 1960s

Social events of Hong Kong
香港社會重要事件

1963.10.17
香港中文大學成立，由崇基、新亞、聯合三間書院合併而成
Formation of Chinese University of Hong Kong incorporating three post-secondary colleges: New Asia College, Chung Chi College and United College of Hong Kong

1962
颱風溫黛襲港，造成130人傷亡和千艘船被毀
Typhoon Wanda caused 130 casualties and widespread destruction in Hong Kong

1963
因水荒實施制水
Water shortages and water rationing

1966
中文大學開辦研究院
Opening of the Graduate School, Chinese University of Hong Kong

1965
港府發表「教育政策白皮書」
Announcement of the 1965 White Paper

1967
三間師範學院易名教育學院
Three teacher training colleges renamed the College of Education

1965
港府選定洋紫荊為市花
Selection of bauhinia as Hong Kong's city flower

1966
天星小輪事件
Riots due to fare increases on the Star Ferry

1967
受文革影響，香港出現示威及恐怖活動
Demonstrations and terrorist activities prompted by the Cultural Revolution

China and the World
中國及世界大事

1961
太空人加加林首次乘坐太空船環繞地球一周
Yuri Gagarin became first man to orbit the earth

1962
古巴導彈危機
Cuban Missile crisis

1963
美國總統甘迺迪遭刺殺
Assassination of US President John Fitzgerald Kennedy

1963-1975
越南戰爭
Vietnam War

1966–1976
中國經歷文化大革命
Cultural Revolution in China

1969
美國太空人岩士唐及奧爾德林首次登陸月球
Neil Armstrong and Buzz Aldrin were the first men on the moon

1970s
港大學生人數約4千
HKU student population reached 4000

1970
大學開始男女職員同工同酬
HKU established equal pay for male and female employees

1971.2.28
保衛釣魚台事件
Defending Diaoyu Island movement

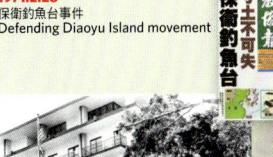

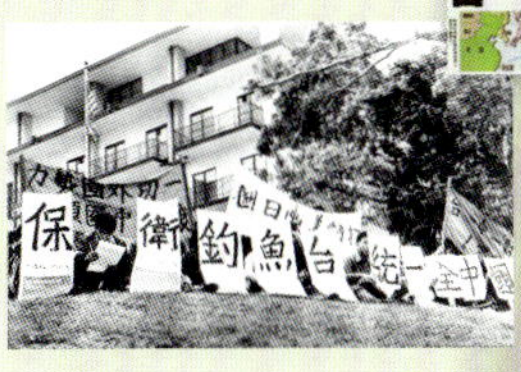

1972
黃麗松獲委任為首位華人校長
Rayson Huang became the first Chinese Vice-Chancellor of the University

1974
香港特藏易名「孔安道紀念圖書館」
Hong Kong Collections renamed Hung On To Memorial Library

1974.10.22
包兆龍保健中心啟用
Opening of the Pao Siu Loong Health Centre

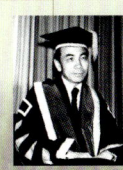

1975.05.06
英女皇伊莉莎伯二世訪問港大
Queen Elizabeth II visited the University

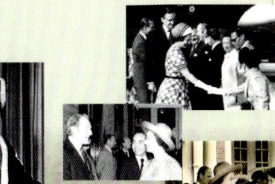

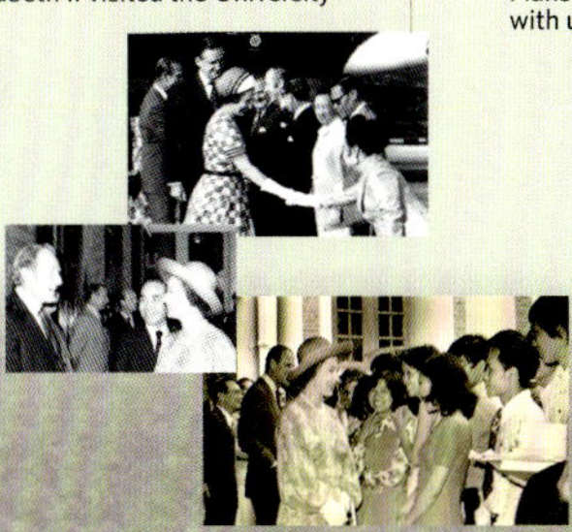

1979
大學計劃與中國內地大學作學術交流
Plans were made for academic exchange with universities in China

1980s
港大延續發展，師生人數增至逾萬，累積畢業生總數逾4萬
The University expanded further, student population over 10,000 and the total number of graduates since the first Congregation reached 40,000

1981.09.25
位於太古樓的方樹泉文娛中心啟用
Opening of the Fong Shu Chuen Amenities Centre in Swire Building

1982
牙醫學院成立，校舍設在菲臘牙科醫院
Opening of the Faculty of Dentistry located at the Prince Philip Dental Hospital

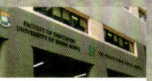

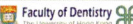

1971
艾蒙樓建成，後易名任白樓
Completion of Redmond Building, later renamed Yam Pak Building

1971.07.27
賴廉士體育中心內的史密夫游泳池啟用
Stanley Smith Swimming Pool opened at the Lindsay Ride Sports Centre

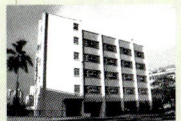

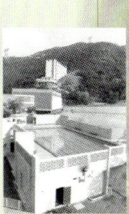

1973. 10.12
鈕魯詩樓啟用
Opening of the Knowles Building

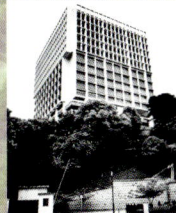

1979.10.18
實驗動物中心啟用
Opening of the Laboratory Animal Building

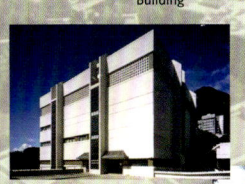

1980.11.11
太古樓啟用，內設太古堂
Opening of the Swire Building housing Swire Hall

1980.10.31
陳蕙琴樓啟用，1986年擴建
Pauline Chan Building opened and later extended in 1986

1980
物業處大樓建成，並於1986年擴建
Estates Office Building was opened and later extended in 1986

1981.12.10
許愛周科學館啟用
Opening of Hui Oi Chow Science Building

1982.02.11
厲樹雄科學館啟用
Opening of James Hsioung Lee Science Building

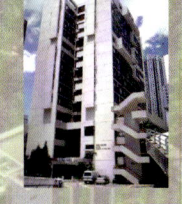

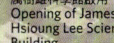

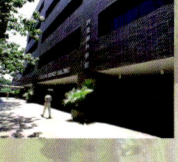

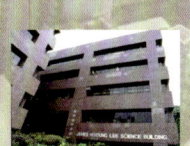

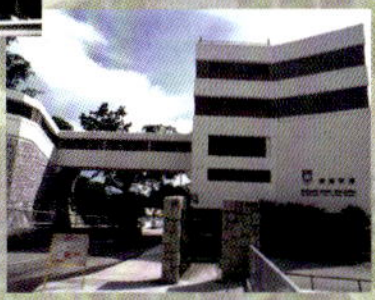

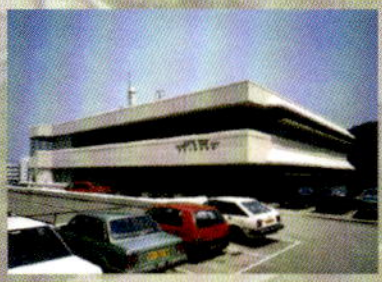

1970s – 1980s

1971
推行六年免費教育，1978年改為九年免費教育
Free six-year compulsory education introduced. This was extended to nine years in 1978

1971.05
保釣事件
Protest against the Japanese over the Diaoyu Islands

1977
金禧事件
Golden Jubilee Secondary School Incident

1978
寶血金禧中學罷課事件
Precious Blood Golden Jubilee Secondary School students strike

1980
香港高級程度會考由香港大學轉交香港考試局主辦
HK advanced level examinations, formerly organised by HKU, were taken over by the Hong Kong Examinations Authority

1970s
香港經濟由製造業發展為多元化經濟模式
Evolution from manufacturing to a more diversified economy

1972
首條海底隧道通車
Opening of the first Cross-Harbour Tunnel

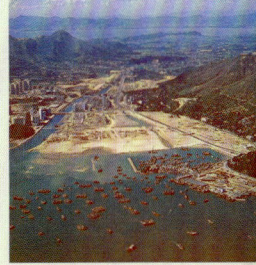

1973
港府展開新市鎮計劃以配合人口迅速增長
Initiation of New Town Programme to meet rapid population growth

1973.03
股災 — 恒生指數暴跌
Stock market crash, Hang Seng Index drops from 1774 to 150

1974
廉正公署成立
Establishment of the Independent Commission Against Corruption (ICAC)

1974
中英文同列為法定語文
Chinese and English became statutory languages

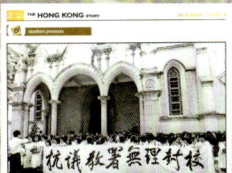

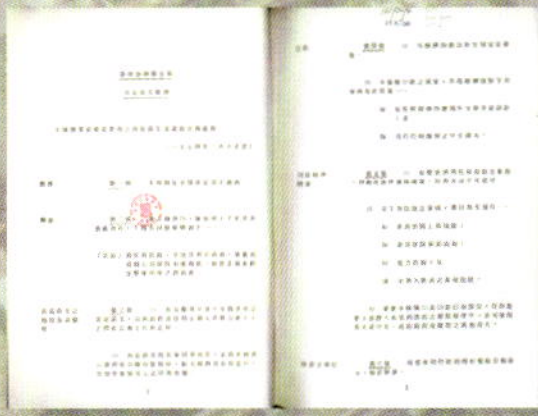

1979
地下鐵路通車
Mass Transit Railway service began

1979
全港最大水庫 — 萬宜水塘落成
Hong Kong's largest reservoir, High Island Reservoir, opens

1982
中英展開香港前途談判
Sino-British talks on the resumption of Hong Kong's sovereignty began

1982–1986
經濟泡沫爆破，出現一連串金融危機
Series of monetary and banking crises

1983.09
香港前途談判僵持，港人信心急挫
Confidence plunges as Sino-British talks reach deadlock

1972
美國總統尼克遜訪問北京
US President Nixon visits Beijing

1972
水門事件
Watergate scandal

1973–1974
阿拉伯產油國停止向美國、歐洲及日本輸送石油
Oil Crisis. Arab countries proclaimed an oil embargo against USA, Europe and Japan

1976
毛澤東及周恩來逝世，四人幫下台
Death of Mao Zedong and Zhou Enlai, fall of Gang of the Four

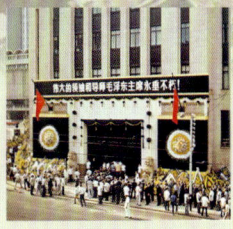

1978
鄧小平成為中國共產黨的主要策劃人/領導人
Deng Xiaoping became paramount leader of the Chinese Communist Party

1978
中國實行四個現代化
The Four Modernisations of China

1979
中國實施門戶開放政策，規劃深圳、珠海、汕頭、廈門四個經濟特區
China's open-door policy. Creation of four 'special economic zones' comprising Shenzhen, Zhuhai, Shantou and Xiamen

1979
成立歐洲貨幣體系
Creation of the European Monetary System

The University of Hong Kong: Events and developments / 香港大學：主要事件及發展

1983.10.06 黃克競樓啟用 Opening of Haking Wong Building

1983 邵氏大樓竣工 Completion of the Shaw Buildings

1984 建築學院成立 Foundation of the Faculty of Architecture

1984 教育學院成立 Establishment of the Faculty of Education

1984 法律學院成立 Foundation of the Faculty of Law

1984.04.18 何世光夫人體育中心啟用 Opening of the Flora Ho Sports Centre

1985 新綜合大樓啟用，大樓內設有新學生會會址，於11月24日開幕的李國賢堂，以及於翌年3月16日開幕的徐朗星文娛中心 A composite building housing the Students' Union, the Simon K Y Lee Hall opened on 24 November, and the Hsu Long Sing Amenities Centre opened on 16 March 1986

1985.08.19 位於大口環的何鴻燊體育中心啟用 Stanley Ho Sports Centre was opened at Sandy Bay

1986.05.13 利希慎醫科圖書館啟用 Opening of the Lee Hysan Medical Library

1986.06.07 嘉道理農業研究所啟用 Opening of Kadoorie Agricultural Research Centre

1986.06.20 黃麗松講堂啟用 Opening of the Rayson Huang Theatre

1986 首座學生會大樓易名為「孔慶熒樓」 The University Union Building renamed the Hung Hing Ying Building

1987 醫學院慶祝成立百週年 Centenary celebrations of the Faculty of Medicine

1989.09.19 梁銶琚樓啟用 Opening of K K Leung Building

1970s – 1980s

Social events of Hong Kong / 香港社會重要事件

1984 教育統籌委員會成立 Establishment of the Education Commission

1984.12.19 中英兩國簽署「聯合聲明」 Sino-British Joint Declaration signed

1986.08.13 香港政府成立土地基金信托 Establishment of the Land Fund Trust

1987 宣布「科技大學」為第三間大學 Plans to establish the Hong Kong University of Science and Technology announced

1989.06.07 港人示威支持參與國內六四運動的學生 Mass demonstrations in Hong Kong in support of the June Fourth student movement in China

China and the World / 中國及世界大事

1987 全球股災 World stock market crashed

1989.06.04 天安門事件 Tiananmen Square Incident

1989 東歐各國共產政權瓦解 Collapse of Communist regimes in Eastern Europe

1996.01.22
李志雄堂啟用
Opening of Lee Chi Hung Hall

1996
艾蒙樓易名「任白樓」
Redmond Building was renamed Yam Pak Building

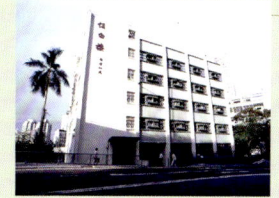

1992
專業進修學院（前校外課程部）成立
School of Professional and Continuing Education (SPACE) established, formerly the Extra-Mural Studies Department

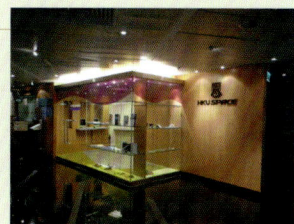

1995
商學院成立
School of Business established

The University of Hong Kong
School of Business
Breeds the Future Business Leader

1991.01.23
何善衡夫人宿舍啟用
Opening of Madam S H Ho Residence Hall

1991
圖書館大樓在學生會舊會址上擴建新翼
Main Library extension built on the site of the Students' Union Building

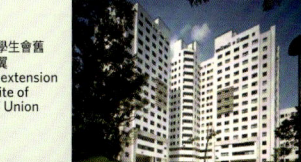

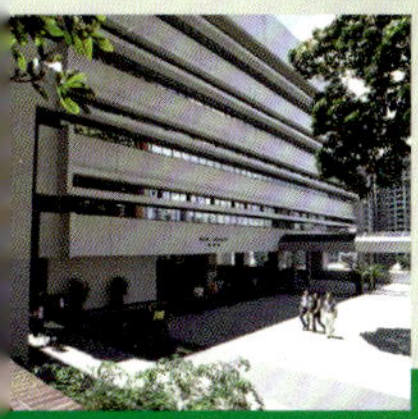

1992
何鴻燊體育中心加建霍英東游泳池
Henry Fok Swimming Pool was built at the Stanley Ho Sports Centre

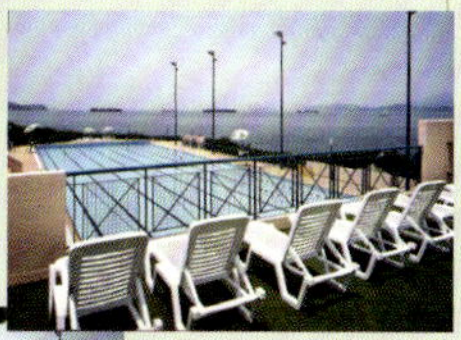

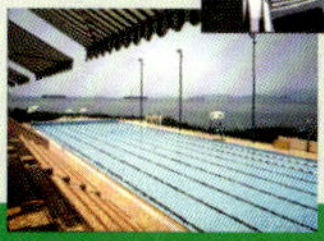

1993
利銘澤堂和利希慎堂啟用
Lee Hysan Hall and R C Lee Hall built

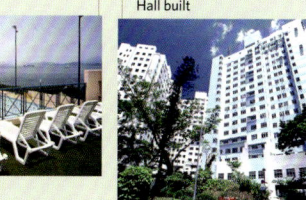

1994.12.13
莊月明綜合大樓啟用
Chong Yuet Ming Amenities Centre opened

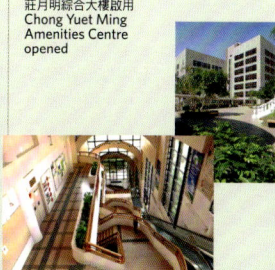

1996.06.13
文洪礎樓啟用
Opening of the Dexter H C Man Building

1996.11.08
徐展堂樓啟用
T T Tsui Building was opened

1990s – 2000s

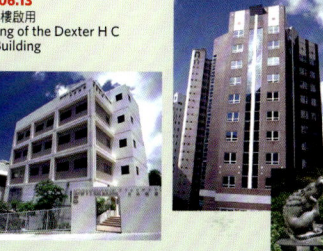

1990s
香港專上學院增至8所
The number of higher education institutions in HK increased to eight

1990.04.04
中華人民共和國通過香港特別行政區《基本法》
The Basic Law of the HKSAR was adopted

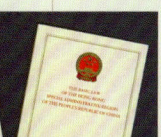

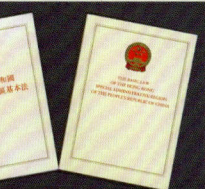

1991
國際商業信貸銀行倒閉，引發多間銀行擠提
Collapse of the Bank of Credit and Commerce International (BCCI) led to a run on banks

1992
彭定康成為第二十八任，亦是最後一任港督
Chris Patten became the 28th and last colonial Governor

1993.04.01
香港金融管理局成立
Establishment of the Hong Kong Monetary Authority

1993
中環半山行人電梯啟用，是全球最長的室外有蓋電梯系統
Central-Mid-Levels escalator begins service as the longest outdoor covered escalator system in the world

1993
港府推出洋紫荊硬幣設計取代英女皇頭像
Government launched a new coin design replacing Elizabeth II's profile with the bauhinia flower

1994
中國銀行首次發行港元紙幣
Bank of China issued its first Hong Kong bank notes

1990
德國統一
Reunification of East and West Germany

1991
蘇聯解體
Dissolution of the Soviet Union

1991
波斯灣戰爭
Gulf War

1993
江澤民出任中華人民共和國主席
Jiang Zemin became the President of the People's Republic of China

1995
世界貿易組織成立
World Trade Organisation established

The University of Hong Kong: Events and developments
香港大學：主要事件及發展

1997.09
位於聖約翰學院的王植庭堂啟用
Opening of Wong Chik Ting Hall at St John's College

1998
本科課程改組
Undergraduate curriculum reform

1998.11.30
位於研究生堂的王賡武講堂啟用
Opening of Wang Gungwu Lecture Hall at Graduate House

1999
位於圖書館大樓新翼的許磐卿堂命名
Naming of the Hui Pun Hing Hall in the New Wing of Main Library

2000.09
鄭耀宗校長因民意調查事件辭職
Resignation of Vice Chancellor Cheng Yiu-chung due to public opinion polling controversy

2001-2002
慶祝大學九十周年，學生人數達1萬4千人，校友逾9萬
HKU celebrates 90th Anniversary with over 14,000 students and over 90,000 alumni

2005-2006
慶祝大學九十五周年
The University celebrates its 95th Anniversary

2006.07.01
成立香港大學檔案中心
Establishment of the University Archives

1998.06.19
研究學院成立
Foundation of the Graduate School, formerly known as the School of Research Studies

2000.01
商學院和經濟金融學院合併「經濟及工商管理學院」
School of Business, and School of Economics and Finance combined to become the Faculty of Business and Economics

2001.09
香港大學舊生會首間直接資助小學「港大同學會小學」啟用
Establishment of the first direct subsidised primary school by the Hong Kong University Graduates Association (HKUGA)

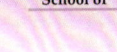

2000.01.17
嘉道理生物科學大樓啟用
Opening of the Kadoorie Biological Sciences Building

2001.08
賽馬會學生村建成，舍堂包括施德堂、何添堂及重建的何東夫人紀念堂
Completion of the Jockey Club Student Village including Starr Hall, Ho Tim Hall and a rebuilt Lady Ho Tung Hall

2002
位於沙宣道的新醫學院綜合大樓啟用
Opening of the Faculty of Medicine Building on Sassoon Road

1998.04
研究生堂竣工
Completion of Graduate House

1999.09.15
賽馬會樓啟用
Opening of the Jockey Club Building

1990s - 2000s
21th Century

Social events of Hong Kong
香港社會重要事件

1997.07.01
香港回歸祖國成為特別行政區
Hong Kong sovereignty returned to China creating the Hong Kong Special Administrative Region

1997
八達通卡面世
Octopus card introduced

1998
位於赤鱲角的香港國際機場啟用
Opening of the Hong Kong International Airport at Chek Lap Kok

2003.03.06
爆發非典型肺炎疫症，近1700名市民受感染，約299人死亡
Outbreak of Severe Acute Respiratory Syndrome (SARS) affecting about 1,700 people and leading to 299 deaths

China and the World
中國及世界大事

1997.02.19
鄧小平逝世
Deng Xiaoping dies

1997
英國科學家成功培殖出複製羊
British scientists cloned Dolly the sheep

1997-1998
多個亞洲國家爆發金融危機
Asian Financial crisis

1999
歐元面世
European common currency (Euro) introduced

2000
南北韓高峰會簽訂「南北共同宣言」
Inter-Korea summit and signature of the North-South Joint Declaration

2001
美國911恐怖襲擊
September 11th Attacks

2001
中國加入世界貿易組織
China admitted to the World Trade Organisation

2002.07
港府改組
HKSAR government restructured

2003
中國太空人楊利偉首次飛行太空
First Chinese astronaut, Yang Liwei, sent into space

2003-2004
伊拉克戰爭
Iraq war

2004.12.26
印度洋海嘯
Indian Ocean tsunami

xxii

08.04
ablishment of the Lung Fu
an Environmental Education
ntre

03-2008, 2009-2014
mulation of the University's
ategic Development Plan

2010
港大位處世界頂級大學之列；亞
洲大學排名榜及泰晤士高等教育
亞洲大學排名榜列席首位、世界
大學排名榜及泰晤士高等教育世
界大學排名榜分別排名第23及21位
Outstanding University Rankings:
Quacquarelli Symonds-no. 1 in
Asia and no. 23 in World rankings,
Times Higher Education-no. 1 in
Asia and no. 21 in World rankings

2010
中央政府指派在港大設立兩所
省級肝病實驗室
HKU chosen by the Chinese
Government to establish
two key state laboratories
of Liver Diseases and
Synthetic Chemistry

2010.03.16
百周年校園奠基
Foundation stone-laying
Ceremony of Centennial
Campus

2010
港大成立知識轉移辦事處，負責推廣及
技術交流發展
Knowledge Exchange Office established
to promote the development of
knowledge exchange activities

2011.01.09
百周年啟動禮
Centennial kick off ceremony

2011.08.18
李克強在香港大學的818事件
August 18th incident during a visit to the
University by then-Vice Premier of China,
Li Keqiang

2011–2012
慶賀香港大學百周年
HKU 100 Celebrations

2012
四年學制實施
Introduction of four-
year curriculum

2010
理學院慶祝七十周年
Faculty of Science celebrated its 70th
Anniversary

2011.09
開辦五年制法律文學雙學位課程
Launch of 5-year double major in
Law and Literary Studies

2010
建築學院慶祝六十周年
Faculty of Architecture celebrated its
60th Anniversary

2005–2012
百周年校園
Centennial Campus

2010s

2008.09.14
雷曼兄弟破產
Bankruptcy of Lehman Brothers

2009.12
香港舉辦第五屆東亞運動會
The 5th East Asian Games were
held in Hong Kong

2008.05.12
中國四川省汶川大地震
Sichuan earthquake

2008.08
北京舉辦第二十九屆奧運會和第十三屆
殘奧會，香港舉行奧運馬術項目
Beijing held the 29th Olympic Games
and the 13th Paralympics Games;
Hong Kong hosted the Equestrian
events

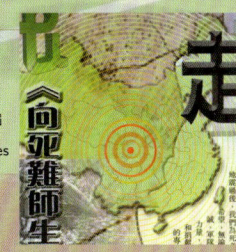

2011.01
埃及反政府運動
Anti-government protests in Egypt

2011.03.09
日本仙台福島地震，引發沿岸海嘯和核電廠爆漏
Japan earthquake and explosion at
Fukushima nuclear plant

xxiii

宣統元年元月廿五日即西歷一千九百零
十五號　盧制軍請香港大學堂名勸捐
　　香港大學堂總理會議於督憲府是日在塲
　　芳名列下

何沃生　韋寶珊
蕭遠輝　吳理卿　陳春泉
區澤民　陳雲翹　源雲翹　高聲琴
黎潤生　陳啟明　陳雲翹　劉緯卿　潘寅存
梁健安　郭少流　　　　　郭耀垣　李右泉
莫藻泉　莫若廉　蔣士楷　容翼廷　李芳軒
譚子劉　胡菁雲　　　　　何澤生　何葵樓
黃永兆　關心焉　何星儔　黃兆棠　何祿生
溫俊居　　　陸慶南　杜關臣　黃金福　周少岐
盧制軍云　顏恒甫　黎乙真　曹善允　冼德芬
　　何君沃生　（冼君德芬傳譯）　周雨亭
經費　何君沃生與陳君少伯　譯　擬創建大學堂
　　　　　　　　　　　　　　以華文課育

香港大學初期的檔案文物
IN THE BEGINNING
Early Records of The University of Hong Kong

1

香港大學初期
盧吉勳爵參與籌建計劃

盧吉勳爵
香港總督（一九零七至一九一二年）
香港大學校監（一九一一至一九一二年）

盧吉（一八五八至一九四五年）早年入伍，自一八七八年起在印度英軍第二營服役，至一八八九年加入英國皇家東非公司為止。後加入英國政府殖民部，一九零零至一九零六年出任北尼日利亞高級專員。一九零七年到任香港總督，直至一九一二年重返尼日利亞出任總督。

盧吉在尼日利亞所作功績不少，更建立新政府，他躊躇滿志地轉任香港總督，得悉籌辦大學的計劃，雖遇英政府殖民部冷淡對待，自己也缺乏辦學經驗，但他對這計劃態度十分積極。一九零八年一月他於聖士提反書院致詞呼籲興建大學，演說其後刊登於《德臣西報》，深深打動了巴斯商人麼地。後來在盧吉夫人游說下，麼地率先響應捐款十五萬元。[1]

盧吉擬定新大學最先設立醫學和工程兩院，吸納當時的香港西醫書院和香港官立技術專科學校，為中國培育醫科和工程人材，但並未實現；[2] 不久再加設文學院，以取得英國皇家特許的資格。大學雖已開設中國語文及文學課程，但盧吉堅持其他學科一律以英文教學，以在校內維持西方教育體制，並鞏固英國對香港的管治。

可惜麼地於港大建成以前逝世，而盧吉也於一九一二年三月十一日主持港大開幕禮後不久離開香港。二人對大學的貢獻卻長存。

盧吉爵士銅像
一九六零年
Sir Frederick Lugard
Bronze
1960
刻字 Inscribed:
PILKINGTON JACKSON ARSA FRBS
EDINBURGH 1960
H: 90 cm W: 61 cm

---

1 Peter Cunich, *A History of the University of Hong Kong, Volume 1, 1911–1945*, pp. 90–92.
2 Cunich, pp. 152–153.

In the Beginning Lord Frederick Lugard and The University Project

Lord Frederick Lugard
Governor of Hong Kong (1907–1912)
Chancellor of the University (1911–1912)

Frederick Lugard (1858–1945) spent the early part of his life (1878–1889) in military service with the second battalion in India. He joined the Imperial British East Africa Company in 1889, later entering colonial service as High Commissioner of the Protectorate of Northern Nigeria (1900–1906). He was appointed Governor of Hong Kong in 1907, a position that he held until 1912 when he returned to Nigeria as Governor.

Lugard's professional achievements in Nigeria had included the establishment of a new government. Hong Kong by comparison proved a less challenging posting. Once he learned of the proposal for a university, he undertook it with vigour, despite a lack of enthusiasm on the part of the Colonial Office, and his own limited experience in education. In January 1908 Lugard delivered an impassioned address at St Stephen's College on the subject of the university. Published soon afterwards in the China Mail, Lugard's ideas were brought to the attention of the Parsee merchant Hormusjee Naorojee Mody who was already favorably impressed by Lugard. He was also fond of Lady Lugard who he later credited with persuading him of the importance of the project. A month later, he offered Lugard $150,000 for the University scheme.[1]

Lugard intended for the new university to have two faculties incorporating the existing Hong Kong College of Medicine and Hong Kong Technical Institute, to train doctors and engineers for China, although this was not realised.[2] A third Faculty of Arts was added to qualify the new university for a royal charter. The teaching of Chinese language and literature was to be offered but Lugard stressed the importance of English as the medium of instruction. This was both to maintain the integrity of a Western education in a Western language, but also to ensure British influence.

Although Mody did not live to see the University completed, and Lugard left Hong Kong shortly after the opening on 11th March 1912, their legacies live on.

---

1 Peter Cunich, *A History of the University of Hong Kong, Volume 1, 1911–1945*, pp. 90–92.
2 Cunich, pp. 152–153.

慈善家
The Philanthropist

麼地爵士[1]（一八三九至一九一一年）為著名商人及慈善家。他出生於印度孟買，在當地曾為報紙督印人。一八六零年代初他移居香港，一八六八年與亞美利亞商人遮打合夥創立證券公司。他們隨後在九龍半島投資房地產，更參與一八九零至一九零四年的中環海旁填海計劃，遂累積了巨富。麼地投資股票市場無往而不利，亦喜愛收藏藝術品及古董。一八九七年為紀念英女皇登基六十周年誌慶，他捐造了一座維多利亞女皇像，該像現放於銅鑼灣維多利亞公園。一九零八年在港督盧吉的游說及盧吉夫人的號召下，捐出十五萬元予香港大學興建本部大樓。最終建築費用上升至三十六萬五千元，但麼地仍堅守誠諾，不計成本出資捐建。[2]

Sir Hormusjee Noarojee Mody[1] (1839–1911) was a prominent businessman and philanthropist. Born in Bombay where he was a newspaper publisher, he settled in Hong Kong in the early 1860s. By 1868 he had set up a brokerage company with the Armenian businessman, Catchick Paul Chater. Mody's fortune was built on their subsequent real estate developments on the Kowloon peninsula, and the success of the Praya Reclamation of 1890–1904. He was a highly successful investor in the stock market and developed a taste for collecting art and antiques. In 1897 he donated a statue of Queen Victoria to Hong Kong to celebrate the Diamond Jubilee, which is now in Causeway Bay's Victoria Park. In 1908, persuaded in equal measure by Lugard's arguments for the founding of a university for Hong Kong, and Lady Lugard's charm, he promised $150,000 for the construction of the University. In the end, the costs for completing the Main Building would rise to $365,000, which Mody paid for to honour his commitment to pay for the University building, regardless of the cost.[2]

麼地爵士 Sir Hormusjee Mody

1 *Dictionary of Hong Kong Biography*, pp. 322–323.
2 Cunich, p. 134.

約一八九一年德輔道海旁
The Des Voeux Road Praya, *c.* 1891

海旁填海工程在中環增闢了五十九英畝土地以興建樓宇、公園、道路。左方的大建築物是第一代的大會堂，內設皇家劇院、圖書館、博物館。其右鄰為第二代的香港上海匯豐銀行。海旁豎立的界標始於填海工程開始後翌年。

The Praya Reclamation Scheme provided 59 acres of land for the development of buildings, gardens and roads in Central district. The large building to the left is Hong Kong's first City Hall, which housed a Theatre Royal, library and museum. Right of City Hall is the second Hong Kong and Shanghai Bank Building. The structures in the harbour mark the limits of the praya reclamation begun a year earlier.

籌款建校
Fundraising for the New University

籌建大學的經費由麼地捐出十五萬元而展開。港督盧吉熱切準備建樓，但輔政司梅含理卻擔憂大學貿然在捐贈基金未穩健下而開校，日後將難以獲得更多經濟支持。麼地有見及此，亦訂下捐款條件，聲明必須獲得總數一百二十五萬元捐款後才能啟動他所捐款項建樓。[1]

因此盧吉成立了十二人組成的籌款監督委員會，由他出任主席。同時何啟爵士領導另一組勸捐籌款支會，負責管理華人捐款，其中五十三名捐款人亦贊助'呈盧督頌詞'絹軸（參看第24頁）。[2]

香港大學華人勸捐支會會議紀錄（墨書原稿）
一九零九年
香港大學圖書館特藏部藏品
Minutes of the Chinese fund-raising sub-committee
1909
H: 24.5 cm W: 27 cm
Special Collections, The University of Hong Kong Libraries

Having secured Hormusjee Mody's initial donation of $150,000 for the University, Lugard was eager to begin building. Colonial Secretary Henry May cautioned, however, that further financial support would be hard to raise if the University were built without a sufficient endowment. Mody was also of the same mind and separately made it a condition of his donation that building did not start until an endowment of $1,250,000 was raised. He also included a condition that the sum needed to be raised within six months.[1]

Consequently, Lugard formed a Management Committee of twelve that he chaired to supervise the collection of subscriptions. Sir Kai Ho Kai chaired a separate Chinese Fund-Raising Sub-Committee to manage Chinese subscriptions, fifty-three members of which also subscribed to the Tribute made in honour of Lugard (p. 24).[2]

1 Cunich, p. 113.
2 Alfred H. Y. Lin, 'The Founding of the University of Hong Kong: British Imperial Ideals and Chinese Practical Common Sense', in Chan Lau Kit-ching and Peter Cunich (eds), *An Impossible Dream: Hong Kong University from Foundation to Re-establishment, 1910–1950*, pp. 7–11.

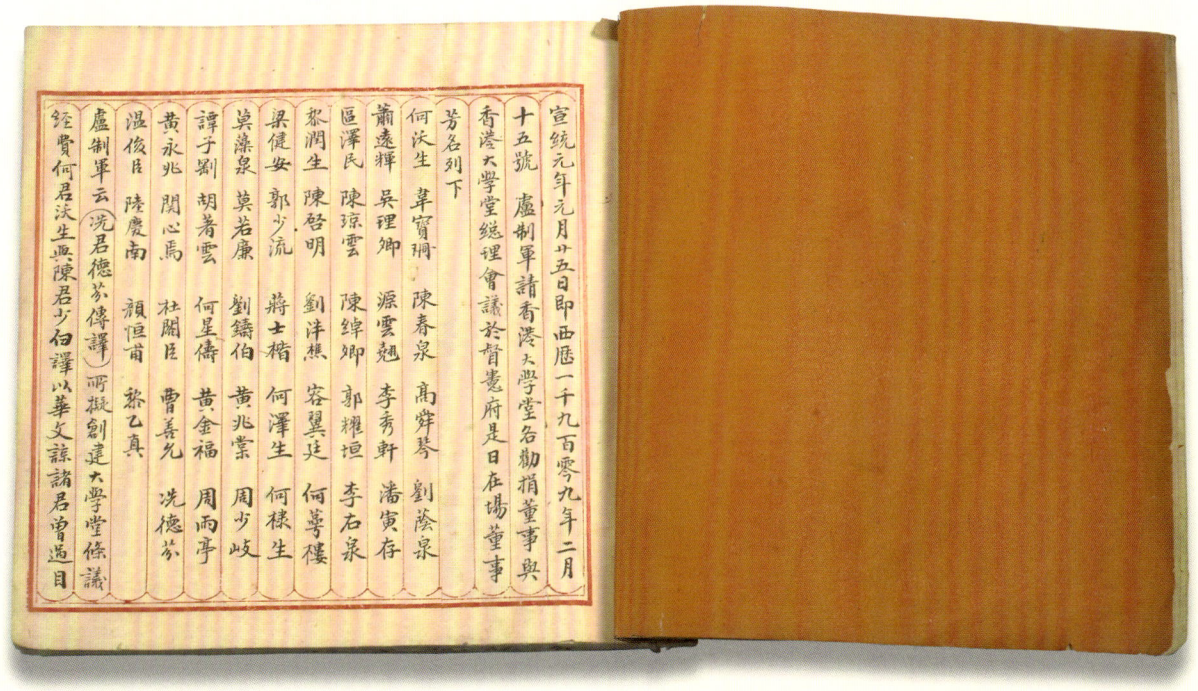

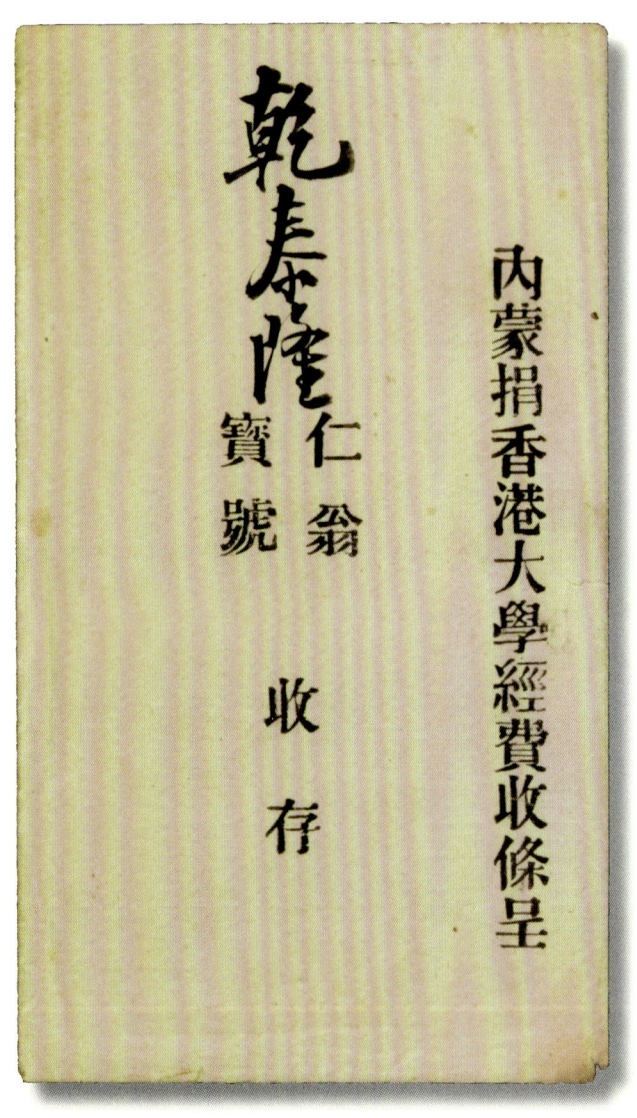
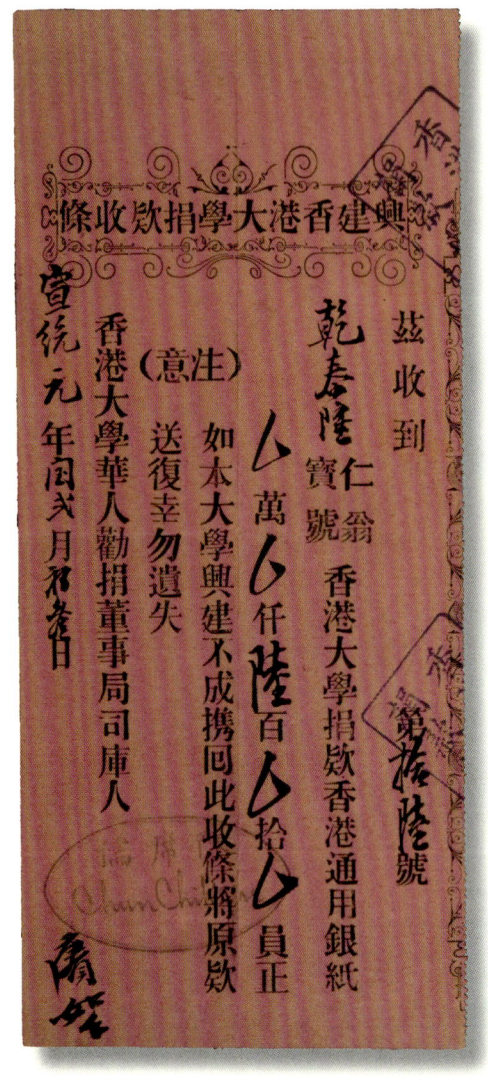

乾泰隆捐款陸佰圓興建香港大學收條第拾陸號（連信封）
宣統元年閏貳月初叁日（一九零九年三月二十四日）
墨書：賡如手（由陳賡如經手）
鈐印：陳席儒* Chun Chik yu（橢圓）
林準祥博士捐贈
A receipt for a donation of $600 from 'Qian Tai Long' towards the establishment of the University of Hong Kong (with envelope)
24th March 1909
Signature in ink: 'Geng yu shou' (Received by [Chen] Geng-yu)
Stamp: 'Chun Chik yu' *
H: 24.7 cm W: 11.3 cm
Gift of Dr Otto Lam Chun-cheung

收據上註明 '如本大學興建不成，携回此收條，將原款送復'
The University scheme was by no means certain to succeed. The receipt includes a note that if the University failed to be established, the sum donated would be returned.

*陳席儒為香港大學華人勸捐支會司庫。陳席儒與陳賡如為親兄弟。
Chun Chik-yu was treasurer of the Chinese fund-raising sub-committee. Chun Chik-yu and Chun Geng-yu were brothers.

香港大學畢業生名冊
一九二五/一九二六年學位名錄中可見金文泰的名字
Clementi listed in the Register of Graduates at the 1925/1926 Congregation

金文泰爵士與香港大學
Sir Cecil Clementi and the New University

金文泰爵士（一八七五至一九四七年），香港總督（一九二五至一九三零年），為傑出的殖民地行政官、學者兼語言學家。一八九九年他選擇香港作為首次出任殖民地官員之地，到任後並很快精通粵語和國語。他於任內擢升連連，一九一二年已當上署理輔政司。

一九零九年金文泰還是助理輔政司兼任立法局秘書，已獲港督盧吉委任作香港大學管理委員會十二委員之一，監督籌募建校經費。[1] 當香港大學正式組建時，盧吉曾邀請金文泰出任首任校長，但被婉拒。然而金文泰對港大建校出力不少。一九一二年他撰寫了拉丁文本港大校歌，校歌並於為期一週的本部大樓開幕誌慶兼籌款園遊會及義賣會上首度演奏。

金文泰於一九一三至一九二二年間轉往英屬圭亞納出任輔政司，後來更到錫蘭就任，直至一九二五年重返香港出任第十七任港督（任期為一九二五至一九三零年）。一九一六年港大頒授名譽法學博士學位予身處英屬圭亞納的金文泰，以表揚他於港大創建的關鍵歲月所付出的貢獻，但延至一九二六年畢業禮上才由校長康寧爵士把學位頒給他。[2] 金文泰就任港督後，曾牽頭推動了港大於一九二七年正式成立中文系；以及一九三零年再為校歌譜上較簡單的歌詞。

Sir Cecil Clementi (1875–1947), Governor of Hong Kong (1925–1930), was a talented colonial administrator, scholar and linguist who mastered both Cantonese and Mandarin dialects after choosing Hong Kong to be his first colonial posting in 1899. He rose quickly through the administration, and by 1912 had assumed the position of Acting Colonial Secretary.

In 1909, when Clementi was Assistant Colonial Secretary and Clerk of Council, Governor Frederick Lugard appointed him to the 12-member Management Committee to supervise the collection of subscriptions for the University scheme.[1] When the University was built, Lugard invited him to be its first Vice-Chancellor, a position that Clementi declined. Nevertheless, his support for the University was evident. In 1912, Clementi penned the Latin verses for the Anthem, or Alma Mater, which was performed for the first time at the week-long fête and bazaar held to celebrate the opening of the new Main Building, and to raise further funds.

From 1913 to 1922 Clementi was appointed Colonial Secretary first of British Guiana and then Ceylon. In 1925 he returned to Hong Kong as its 17th Governor (1925–1930). In 1916, while he was in British Guiana, the University conferred Clementi with an honorary Doctor of Laws in recognition of his service to the University during 'the critical days of its infancy.' This was eventually presented to him in 1926 by the Vice-Chancellor, Sir William Hornell, at that year's Congregation.[2] After returning to Hong Kong, Clementi was instrumental in the formal establishment of a Chinese Department in 1927, and wrote a simpler version of the Alma Mater in 1930.

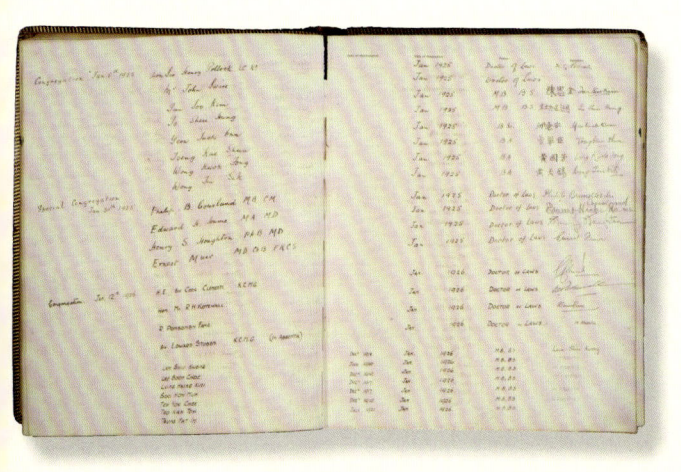

---

1 Lin, pp. 7–8.

2 這頗不尋常，港大的名譽學位應由港督兼港大校監頒授。但當時金文泰本身已是港督，其名譽法學博士學位須由港大校長康寧爵士打破常規代為頒發。

   This represented a departure from usual practice as Honorary Degrees are presented by the University's Chancellor, the Governor of Hong Kong. As Clementi was Governor at the time, it was the Vice-Chancellor, Sir William Hornell who had to break with protocol to present him with his Doctor of Laws Degree.

香港大學與香港西醫書院

何啟爵士[1]（一八五九年至一九一四年）為香港的改革派領袖及政府官員。他自香港中央書院畢業，後出國到英國鴨巴甸大學醫學院修讀醫科，一八七九年畢業並獲取西醫資歷，繼而到林肯律師學院進修法律，一八八一年取得律師執照。同年他與雅麗氏結婚。翌年他返回香港，決心提倡中醫學習西方醫學。一八八四其妻雅麗氏逝世，何啟再婚，仍將一手創建的醫院命名雅麗氏紀念醫院。一八八七年他和白文信爵士協助創辦香港西醫書院，並負責教授生理學及法醫學。孫中山入讀後，深受何啟參與的中國革命活動影響。

何啟亦與麼地同樣，深受盧吉夫人的聰明慧詰感染，他投身於創立香港大學的工作，並擔任華人勸捐支會主席。

何啟的胞姐何妙齡與伍才（伍廷芳）（一八四二至一九二二年）於一八六二年結婚。伍廷芳與李鴻章、袁世凱及孫中山活躍於同一時代。他是香港首位取得外國律師資格的華人，也是出色的政治家、香港首名華人立法局非官守議員。一八九六年他更出任中國駐美大使，並以東方外交家角度撰寫《美國觀察記》。他支持辛亥革命，曾出任革命軍的外事代表，以及擔任孫中山內閣的司法部長。一九一二年退休後，他續任民國總統黎元洪（參看56頁）的外交部長。

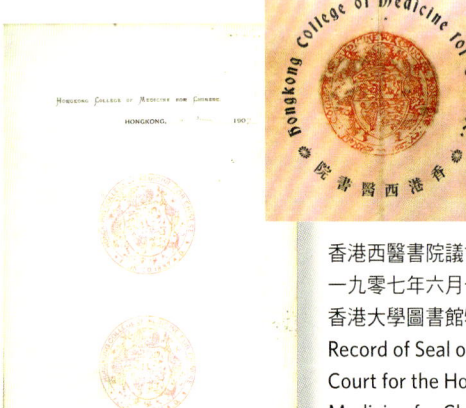

香港西醫書院議會訂製印章的紀錄
一九零七年六月十四日
香港大學圖書館特藏部藏品
Record of Seal ordered by the Court for the Hongkong College of Medicine for Chinese
14th June 1907
H: 33 cm W: 20 cm
Special Collections, The University of Hong Kong Libraries

Sir Kai Ho Kai[1] (1859–1914) was a leading reformer and public servant in Hong Kong. He was educated at the Central School in Hong Kong, and St Thomas' Medical and Surgical College at Aberdeen University where he qualified in Western medicine. Following his graduation in 1879, he went on to study law at Lincoln's Inn and was called to the bar in 1881, which was also the year in which he married Alice Walkden. He returned to Hong Kong the following year, determined to encourage Chinese doctors to learn about Western medicine. Alice died in 1884, and though he later remarried, he established the Alice Memorial Hospital in her memory. In 1887, he and Sir Patrick Manson were instumental in founding the Hongkong College of Medicine where Ho Kai's involvement with the Chinese revolutionary movement influenced student Sun Yat-sen. Ho Kai taught physiology and medical jurisprudence.

Like Hormusjee Mody, Ho Kai was persuaded by Flora Lugard's intelligence and charm to take a leading role in the University project and chair the Chinese Fund-raising Sub-Committee for the University of Hong Kong.

Ho Kai's sister, Ho Miu-ling married Ng Choy (Wu Tingfang (1842–1922) in 1862. Ng was a contemporary of Li Hongzhang, Yuan Shikai, and Sun Yat-sen. He was Hong Kong's first Chinese barrister, and a prominent political figure, becoming the first Chinese to be appointed a member of the Legislative Council. In 1896 he became Chinese Minister to the USA. He recorded his impressions of those years in America in *Through the Spectacles of an Oriental Diplomat*. He served as foreign-affairs representative for the revolutionaries, and as Minister of Justice in Sun Yat-sen's cabinet. He retired in 1912, but continued to serve as Foreign Minister to Li Yuanhong, the President of the Republic of China (see also p. 56).

1   *Dictionary of Hong Kong Biography*, pp. 188–190; 337–338.

HKU and the Hongkong College of Medicine

白文信爵士（一八四四年至一九二二年）原籍蘇格蘭，一八六六年自英國鴨巴甸大學醫科畢業，何啟稍後亦入讀同系。他於畢業當年到台灣擔任中國清廷海關醫官，並開設熱帶醫學的研究。他後來調往廈門工作十三年，一八八三年轉到香港行醫。

一八八七年他出任香港西醫書院創立委員會主席，康德黎（亦是鴨巴甸大學畢業生）擔任秘書，何啟等列席委員。翌年康德黎即為西醫書院院長，孫中山是首批學生之一。

白文信並設立薄扶林乳牛場，後成為牛奶公司。一八八九年他返回倫敦定居。一八九六年孫中山在倫敦被清大使館人員誘捕拘禁時，幸得他奔走營救才能脫險。

一八九九年白文信協助創辦倫敦衛生及熱帶醫學學院。該院現已成為世界知名的公共及全球衛生研究教育中心。

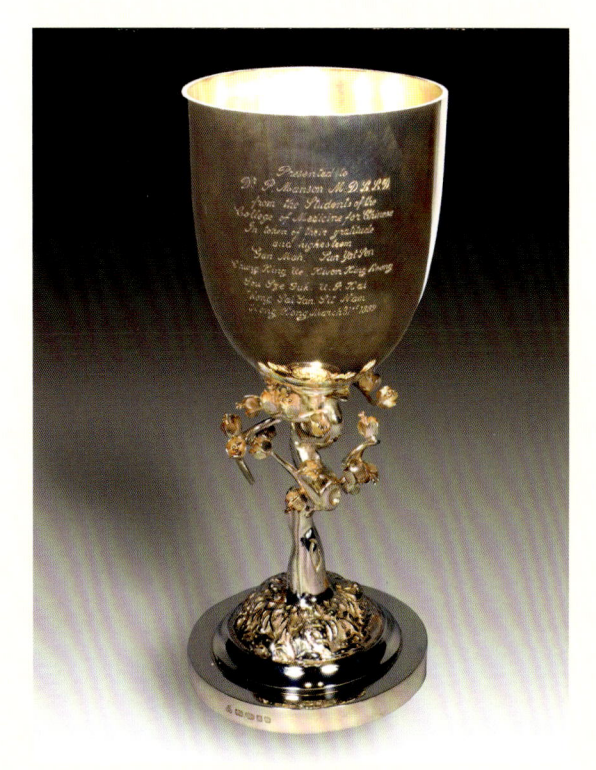

一八八九年三月三十一日孫中山及同學贈送給白文信教授的銀盃（複製品）
李嘉誠醫學院藏品
Silver Cup presented to Patrick Manson by Sun Yat-sen and his classmates on 31st March 1889 (replica)
H: 24 cm W: 10 cm Diameter of cup: 9.5 cm
Li Ka Shing Faculty of Medicine Collection

Sir Patrick Manson (1844–1922) was born in Scotland and received his medical doctorate from Aberdeen University in 1866, where Ho Kai would also later study. That same year Manson went to Taiwan (then Formosa) as a medical officer for the Chinese Imperial Maritime Customs. There he founded the study of tropical medicine. After 13 years in Xiamen (Amoy), he arrived in Hong Kong in 1883.

In 1887, Manson chaired a committee with James Cantlie as secretary (also a graduate of Aberdeen University), Ho Kai and others for the founding of the Hongkong College of Medicine. Cantlie would become the dean of the college the following year.

Manson also established a dairy farm in Pokfulam, which later became the Dairy Farm company. He returned to London in 1889. One of Manson's earliest students was Sun Yat-sen. In 1896, when Sun was kidnapped by Chinese officials in London, Manson worked to secure his release.

Manson was instrumental in establishing the London School of Hygiene and Tropical Medicine in 1899. Now part of the University of London, it is a world centre for research and education in public and global health.

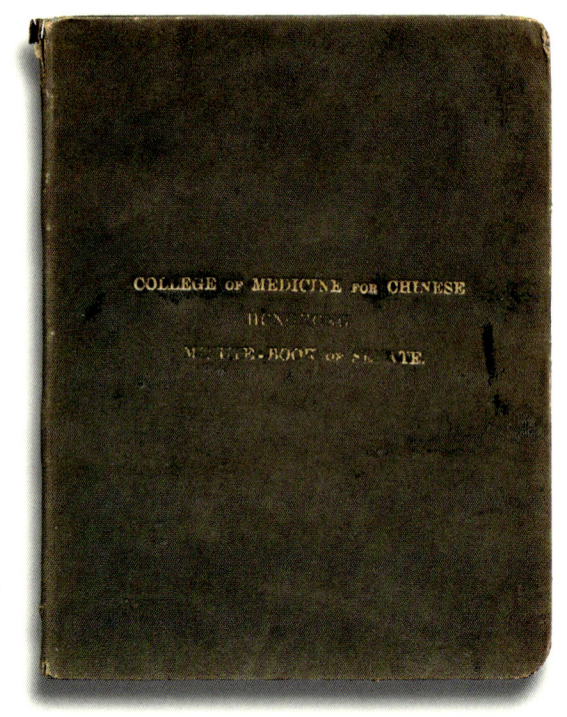

香港西醫書院會議紀錄（一八八七至一九零二年）
一八九三年二月二十七日主席湛約翰、榮譽秘書周壽臣簽署
Minutes of the Hongkong College of Medicine (1887-1902)
Page signed and dated by Chairman John Chalmers and
Secretary John C. Shouson [Shouson Chow], 27th February 1893

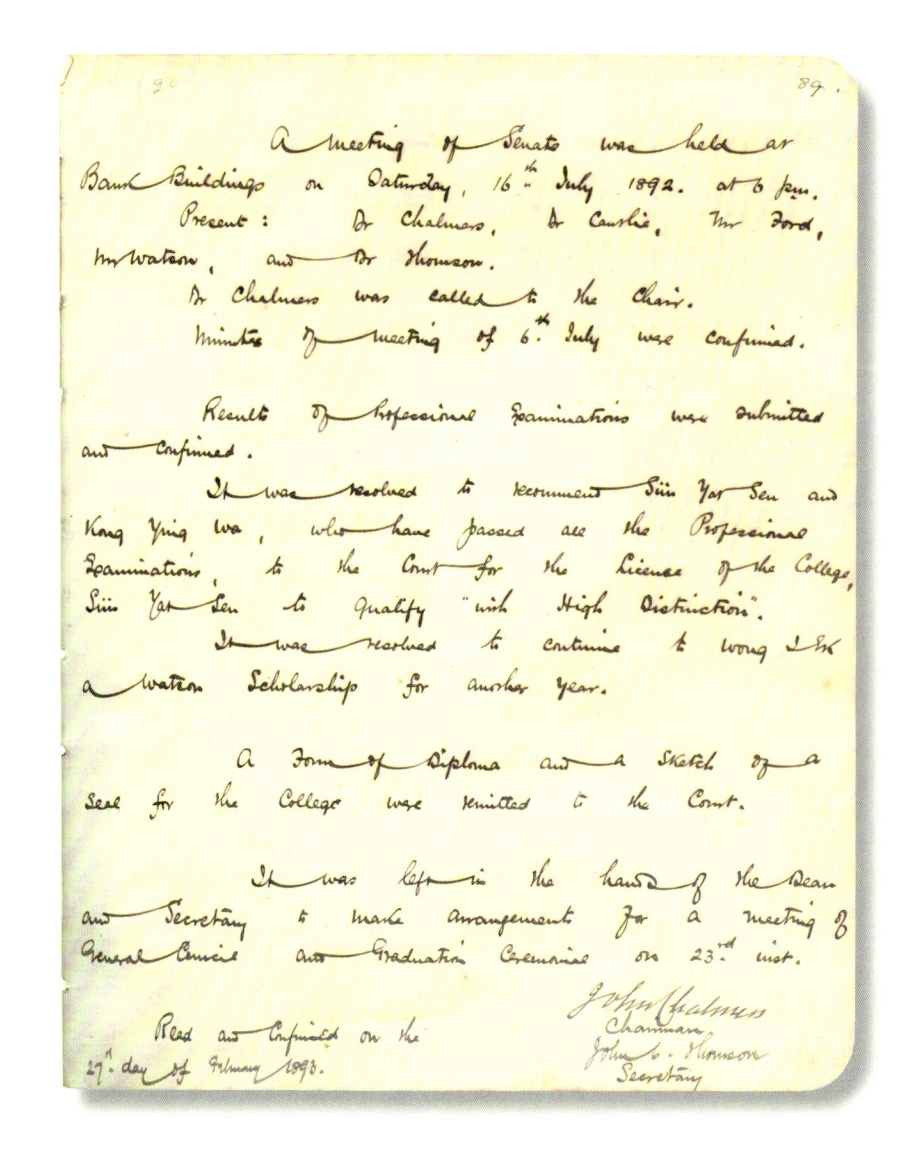

A meeting of Senate was held at Bank Buildings on Saturday, 16th July 1892 at 6 p.m.

Present: Dr Chalmers, Dr Cantlie, Mr Ford, Mr Watson, and Dr Thomson.

Dr Chalmers was called to the Chair.

Minutes of meeting of 6th July were confirmed.

Results of Professional Examinations were submitted and confirmed.

It was resolved to recommend Sun Yat Sen and Kong Ying Wa, who have passed all the Professional Examinations, to the Court for the Licence of the College, Sun Yat Sen to qualify "with High Distinction".

It was resolved to continue to Wong I Ek a Watson Scholarship for another year.

A Form of Diploma and a Sketch of a Seal for the College were remitted to the Court.

It was left in the hands of the Dean and Secretary to make arrangements for a meeting of General Council and Graduation Ceremonial on 23rd inst.

Read and Confirmed on the 27th day of February 1893.

John Chalmers
Chairman.
John C. Thomson
Secretary

一八八八年四大寇（楊鶴齡、孫中山、陳少白、尢列）
與關心焉（關景良）攝於西醫書院
（香港大學檔案中心複件，原來相片不詳）
The 'Four Bandits' (Yeung Hok-ling, Sun Yat-sen, Chen Siu-pak, Yau Lit)
with Kwan Sam-yin (Kwan King-leung) at the Hongkong College of
Medicine for Chinese, 1888
(Origin of image unknown, HKUA copy)

孫中山手書大元帥令
一九二四年十一月八日
Letter written by Sun Yat-sen as Commander-in-chief
Dated 8th November 1924
H: 31.5 cm W: 21 cm

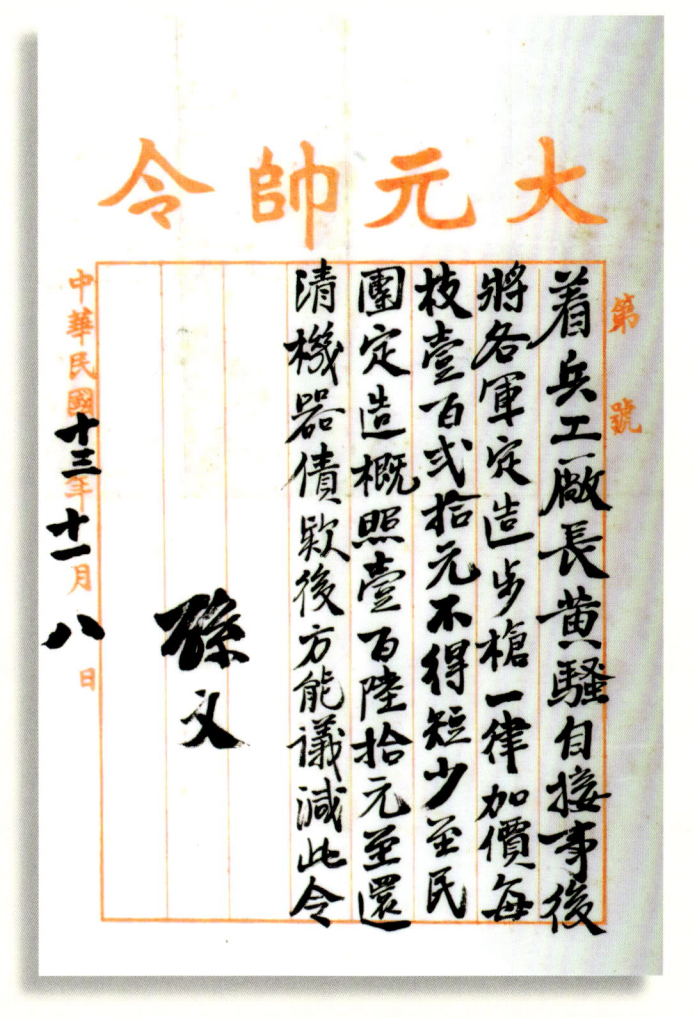

HKU Memories | from the Archives

一九二三年二月二十日孫中山於
大禮堂演說後與港大學生合照
香港大學聯會相簿
香港大學檔案中心「香港大學學生會特藏」
Dr Sun Yat-sen with students following his speech
at the Great Hall on 20th February 1923
Hong Kong University Union Album
Collection of the Hong Kong University Union, HKUA

一九二三年二月，國父孫中山由上海轉抵香港，獲香港大學聯會邀請於二十日到香港大學大禮堂（今陸佑堂）公開演說，當日到會嘉賓超過四百名。國父的演講題目是《革命思想的誕生》，翌日經傳媒廣泛報導。

演講後，學生將國父連籐椅抬到本部大樓外與眾師生合照。國父的右方坐著香港大學聯會會長何東之子何世儉，而相片最右方坐地者是香港大學最早的工程系畢業生之一趙今聲。

In 1923 Sun Yat-sen was invited to deliver a speech at the University by the University Union. Arriving from Shanghai, he addressed over four hundred guests in the Great Hall on 20th February 1923. His speech was titled, 'Why I became a Revolutionist?', and widely reported throughout Hong Kong the following day.

Following the speech, the students carried Sun outside for this historic group photograph. Sitting to Sun's right is Edward Ho Tung, President of the University Union and son of Sir Robert Ho Tung. The first student seated on the ground to the far right is one of the University's earliest civil engineering graduates, Zhao Jinsheng.

HKU Memories | from the Archives

李樹芬醫生（一八八七年至一九六六年）出生於廣東台山。後入讀香港西醫書院，一九零八年獲頒內外科醫學執照。一九一零年再獲英國愛丁堡大學內科、外科醫學士學位。一九一一年孫中山委任他為中華民國衛生部長。一九二六年他回港主持養和療養院，後改名養和醫院。日治時期李樹芬出走桂林，其後輾轉抵達美國。戰後他於一九四五年十一月自美國返港。

李樹芬於一九五八年自醫務退休。一九六一年他將八萬呎土地捐贈香港大學擴建院舍，後命名為香港大學醫學院李樹芬樓。同年他獲頒授名譽法學博士。

Dr Li Shu-fan (1887–1966) was born in Taishan district, Guangdong province. He studied medicine at the Hongkong College of Medicine and was awarded a Licentiate in Medicine and Surgery in 1908 and the degrees of Bachelor of Medicine and Bachelor of Surgery from the University of Edinburgh in 1910. In 1911, Sun Yat-sen, a fellow alumnus from the Hongkong College of Medicine, appointed Li to the position of Minister of Health. In 1926 he was appointed to head the Yeung Wo Nursing Home, which he transformed into the Hong Kong Sanatorium and Hospital. During the Japanese occupation, Li escaped first to Guilin and from there eventually to the United States. He remained there until the end of the war, returning to Hong Kong in November 1945.

Li retired from medical practice in 1958. In 1961, he presented 80,000 square feet of land to the University on Sassoon Road where a building was named in his honour. That year he was also conferred an Honorary Doctor of Laws.

一九六三年三月十六日《南華早報》執行董事庇雅斯致函香港大學校長賴廉士爵士（任期一九四九至一九六四年），內容有關一幅香港西醫書院全體師生在雅麗氏紀念醫院拍攝的相片（見對頁）

Letter dated 16th March 1963 from T. G. N. Pearce, the Managing Director of the *South China Morning Post* to Sir Lindsay Ride, Vice-Chancellor of the University (1949-1964) regarding a photograph of members of the Hongkong College of Medicine taken at Alice Memorial Hospital (see opposite page)

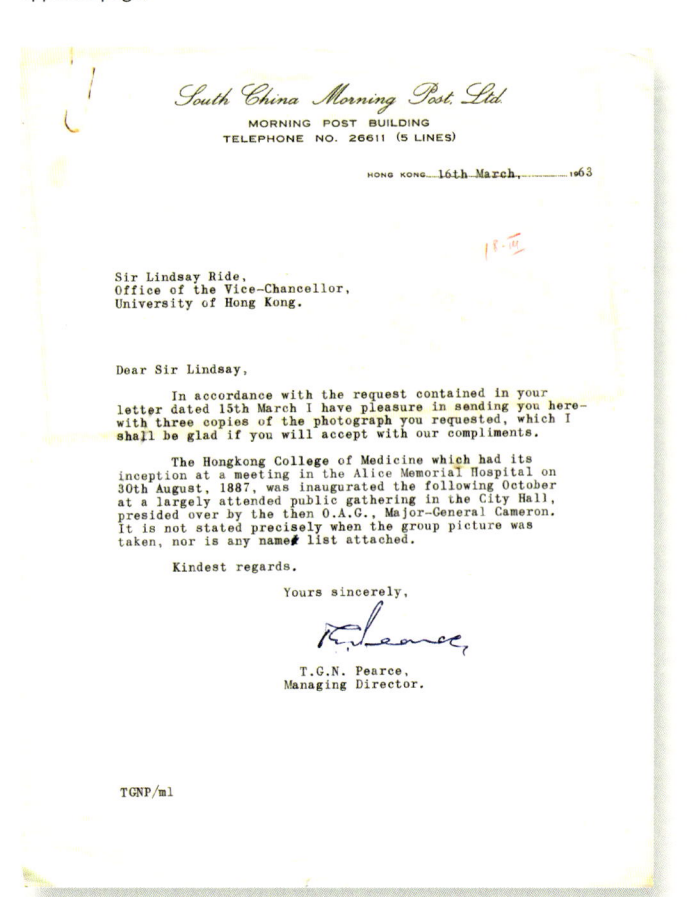

DR. LI SHU-FAN
J.P., LL.D. (Hon.), F.I.C.S. (Hon.), F.R.C.S. (Edin.)

TELEPHONES:
HOSPITAL (9-10.30 A.M.) — 762911
OFFICE (4- 4.30 P.M.) — 35258

301, BANK OF EAST ASIA BUILDING
HONG KONG

21st March, 1963.

Sir Lindsay T. Ride, C.B.E.,
Vice-Chancellor,
University of Hong Kong,
Hong Kong.

Dear Sir Lindsay,

It is indeed kind of you to send me the photograph of the Hong Kong College of Medicine group, for which I must thank you. It will be a precious reminder of my medical student days.

As far as I can remember, the attached sheet contains the list of names of all but one shown in the photograph, which was probably taken about 1903-4 (since I was a junior student standing in the very last row).

Reiterating my thanks and with best personal regards,

Yours sincerely,

Li Shu-fan

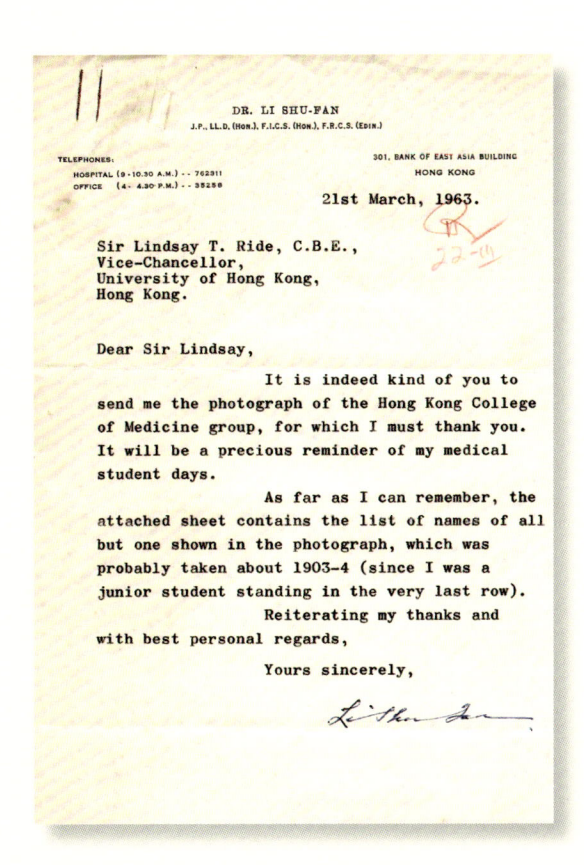

Seated, front row, left to right:	Mr. A.H. Crook, Lecturer in Biology, and later Headmaster of Queen's College.
	Dr. G.R.D. Black
Seated, 2nd row:	Dr. G.E. Aubrey
	Dr. W.V.M. Coch
	Dr. R.M. Gibson
	Dr. Noble (Dentist)
	Sir Henry May
	Sir Kai Ho Kai
	Dr. J.C. Thomson
	Dr. Heenley
	Dr. Belilios
	Dr. Moore, P.C.M.O.
Standing, 3rd row:	Dr. Lee Yin-Sze (deceased)
	Dr. Coxian To (deceased)
	Dr. Chan Hin-Fun
	Dr. Lo Nai-Lun
	Dr. Kwan Sum-Yin (deceased)
	Dr. Ma Luk (deceased)
	Dr. Chung Yik-Shun
	Dr. Au Sze-Cham
	Dr. Kwan
	Dr. Chan
	Dr. Wong Sai-Yan (deceased)
	Dr. Wang Chung-Yik (deceased)
Standing, 4th row:	Dr. Y.Y. Chan (deceased)
	Dr. Tam Cheung-Wah (deceased)
	Dr. Benjamin Wong (deceased)
	Dr. Leung To-Yat
	Dr. C.H. Wan
	Dr. Lam Tze-Fung
	Dr. Yim Yee-Lun
	Dr. Leung Chik-Fan
	Dr. P.F. Woo
Standing, 5th row:	Dr. Wong Ka-Cheong
	Dr. Li Shu-Fan
	Dr. Lee Ying-Yau (deceased)
	?
	Mr. Otis King
	Mr. Lau Yiu-Chung
	Dr. Graca Ozorio (deceased)
	Mr. Au Sze-Sum
	Dr. Lam Yun-Hei

Photograph probably taken about 1903-4.

一九六三年三月二十一日李樹芬醫生致函賴廉士爵士，內容有關該幅香港西醫書院師生在雅麗氏紀念醫院拍攝的相片（下圖），附頁記錄了大約拍攝日期（一九零三至一九零四年），並列出相片中人的名字

Letter dated 21st March 1963 from Dr Li Shu-fan to Sir Lindsay Ride including a separate sheet identifying members of the Hongkong College of Medicine in a photograph taken at Alice Memorial Hospital (below), and the date it was taken (1903-04)

西醫書院與香港大學的協議書
Agreement between
the Hongkong College of Medicine
and
the University of Hongkong

西醫書院與香港大學的協議書
一九一一年
Agreement between
the Hongkong College of Medicine and
the University of Hong Kong
1911

W H E R E A S an arrangement was come to on March 13th. 1908 between the Court of the College of Medicine on the one hand and the Governor on the other hand together with Mr. A. H. Rennie representing the Donor of the University buildings Now Therefore the following agreement dated the   day of   One thousand nine hundred and eleven is hereby made in pursuance of the arrangement aforesaid between the University of Hongkong (hereinafter called "The University") of the one part and the Hongkong College of Medicine incorporated under Ordinance No.2 of 1907 (hereinafter called "The College") of the other part whereby it is agreed as follows :-

1. Up to the date on which the University is declared to be open the Hongkong College of Medicine shall continue to issue its diplomas etc. under its present style and title and upon the said day the College shall be dissolved and shall be merged in the University to which all the property of the College shall be transferred.

2. (a.) The members of the Court of the College named in the First Schedule to the Ordinance shall be life members of the Court of the University.

(b.) All Lecturers of the College at the date of this agreement shall be offered lectureships in the University so far as the funds of the University permit and so far as the subjects in which they lecture are retained as part of the cirriculum of the University Provided that if owing to the appointment of Professors or Lecturers whose services are exclusively at the disposal of the University any such lectureship shall in the opinion of the Council and Senate become unnecessary it may be discontinued.

(1)

HONGKONG
UNIVERSITY
BAZAAR
-MARCH 11TH TO 16TH-
-UNDER THE PATRONAGE OF-
-HIS EXCELLENCY SIR FREDERICK LUGARD. G.C.M.G. C.B. D.S.O.
-& LADY LUGARD-
SOUTH CHINA MORNING POST

香港大學創建期
的檔案文物
THE ESTABLISHMENT YEARS
Treasures of the University of Hong Kong

2

首任校長
The First Vice-Chancellor

儀禮（一八六二至一九三一年）於一九一二年獲委任為香港大學首任校長。他是一位學識淵博的學者兼語言學家，畢業於牛津貝利奧爾學院，名列前茅繼而獲選為該校聖三一學院院士。一八八七年他選擇離開學術界，轉投外交事業，成為傑出的殖民地執行官，連連晉升，相繼出任俄羅斯、巴爾幹（一八九三至一八九八年）、美國首都華盛頓等地要職，官至桑給巴爾總領事兼英屬東非專員（一九零一至一九零四年）。一九零五年他轉職英國謝菲爾德大學首位校長。由於他醉心鑽研佛學，每年夏天都會到亞洲考察研究。

儀禮於港大的事蹟極少記載，惟見一九六零年英國詩人布蘭敦引述史密夫在一九四九年十一月大學工程系學報所撰：'他是備受敬仰的牛津大學學者，精通中文等二十七種語言；略懂另外數種。他是著名外交家……有趣的是，儀禮爵士雖才智過人，卻不懂加算英鎊、先令、便士。'[1] 無論如何，史密夫讚揚儀禮爵士憑藉外交手腕及影響力，為港大籌得馬來亞及香港的捐款，包括一九一五年陸佑提供的免息貸款五十萬元，幫助大學安然渡過破產危機。儀禮聘請原任職於東倫敦大學的史密夫為太古工程學講座教授，藉此紀念太古集團對香港大學捐贈基金的首次捐獻。[2]

港大創校初年財政緊絀，在校長儀禮任內，只有他本人、史密夫（一九一二至一九三四年工程系主任）、軒頓（一九一二至一九一三年教務長、經濟學講師、一九一四至一九二三年文學院院長）為大學全職僱員。

一九一八年，儀禮重返外交仕途，出任西伯利亞高級專員，一九二零年轉任駐東京英國大使。一九二六年他在退休後繼續留日生活，至一九三一年因健康問題需回國治療，卻在返英途中不幸逝世，遺體海葬於馬六甲海峽。

儀禮的著作包括首本英文版芬蘭語法（一八九零年），一九二一年出版一套三冊巨集《印度教與佛教》，以及一九三五年出版《日本佛教》遺作。其他還有關於海洋生物的研究，可算是他鮮為人知的興趣。

1　Edmund Blunden, 'Sir Charles Eliot' in Brian Harrison (ed), *University of Hong Kong: The First 50 Years 1911–1961*, pp. 41–42.
2　Cunich, pp. 150, 168.

Sir Charles Eliot (1862–1931) was appointed the first Vice-Chancellor of the University of Hong Kong in 1912. He was an accomplished scholar and linguist who achieved a first at Balliol College, Oxford, and was subsequently elected a fellow at Trinity College, Oxford. He left academia in 1887 for a career in the diplomatic service. He proved a talented colonial administrator and rose quickly through successive posts first in Russia, the Balkans (1893–1898), Washington, DC and finally concurrent positions as Consul General for Zanzibar and Commissioner for British East Africa (1901–1904). In 1905, he became the first Vice-Chancellor of the University of Sheffield. However, a lifelong interest in Buddhism saw him travel every summer to Asia to conduct research.

Few accounts of Eliot's time at the University have been recorded, but writing in 1960 Edmund Blunden cited C. A. Middleton Smith in the University's *Engineering Society Journal* of November 1949: 'He had made a great reputation as a scholar at Oxford University; he spoke twenty-seven languages fluently [including Chinese]; he had a knowledge of several others and he had been famous as a diplomat... It was curious that, although Sir Charles had a giant intellect, he had great difficulty in adding up a column of figures of pounds, shillings and pence.' Nevertheless, Middleton Smith attributed the success of the University in attracting contributions from Malaya and Hong Kong as being 'largely due to the diplomacy and great influence of Sir Charles Eliot.'[1]

This included an interest-free loan of $500,000 from Loke Yew in 1915 that rescued the University from bankruptcy. Eliot appointed C. A. Middleton Smith from East London College to the Taikoo Chair of Engineering. This was the first academic appointment to be made as outlined in the University Ordinance in recognition of the Swire donation to the endowment fund.[2]

A measure of the difficulties that the University struggled with in its early years was that Eliot, Middleton Smith (Dean of Engineering 1912–1934) and W. J. Hinton (Registrar 1912–1913, Economics lecturer, and Dean of Faculty of Arts 1914–1923) were the only full-time staff working during Eliot's tenure.

In 1918, Eliot returned to diplomatic service when he was seconded to Siberia as High Commissioner. Following that he was posted to Tokyo as Ambassador to Japan in 1920. He remained in Japan following his retirement in 1926, but was forced to return to England in 1931 due to ill health. He did not survive the passage and was buried at sea in the Straits of Malacca.

Eliot's publications included the first grammar of Finnish in the English language (1890), with his greatest work being a three-volume publication on *Hinduism and Buddhism*, published in 1921, and *Japanese Buddhism* published posthumously in 1935. His passion for marine biology was less well known.

---

1 Edmund Blunden, 'Sir Charles Eliot', in Brian Harrison (ed), *University of Hong Kong: The First 50 Years 1911–1961*, pp. 41–42.
2 Cunich, pp. 150, 168.

港大創校初年
The Early Decades of the University

港大創校初年，雄心萬丈，可是財政緊絀。當年雖然有遮打爵士的熱心捐獻，但仍存在經營危機，成因包括校園擴建涉及巨款，以及教職員和學生住宿等設備所需資金。

陸佑（一八四六至一九一七年）是大學最早的捐獻者之一。他是來自馬來亞的錫礦大亨及慈善家，亦是一九一二年已認捐五萬五千港元作為大學捐贈基金的何啟爵士之朋友。大學成立初年面臨破產危機，基金委員會司庫遮打爵士建議再向陸佑募捐。一九一五年陸佑回應願意提供二十一年期五十萬元免息貸款，資助四個獎學金予英屬海峽殖民地及馬來亞聯邦的學生就學。一九一七年陸佑逝世前不久，獲港大頒授名譽法學博士學位，並於一九一六年獲選為大學校董會終身委員。

一九一八年，校長儀禮離港重投外交事業，他先調職到西伯利亞，後進駐日本，由佐頓出任署理校長。由於校長職位懸空，加上有大學為誰而立的問題一直困擾，一九二零年遂成立沙普委員會，成員包括律師曹善允。他們對大學的運作進行評估，開啟了研究大學事務的先河。沙普委員會提出大學必須擁有充足的運作資金，以改善其教學及設備質素，達成創校的目的；並建議大學既服務大英帝國與本港，應獲得更多政府及私人的資助。

一九二一年大學向個別人士呼籲籌款的活動迅即展開，其中惠贈香港大學捐贈基金包括內梅茲、莫乾生等，其他善長則捐款予特別項目。何東爵士捐建富有裝飾藝術風格的工程學實驗所（一九二六至一九七七年），由利安建築師樓承建。太古集團則資助工科課程。而工程學系工場撤離本部大樓，正好騰出更多空間使用。另有專款捐獻予中文教育（參看第112頁）。遮打爵士作為香港大學捐贈基金司庫，他的捐助較為實際，為職員設立薪酬遞升表。

一九二一年大學第三任校長William Brunyate爵士上任，宣布洛克菲勒基金慷慨捐款贊助醫療系教授職位。一九二四年初他辭職之際，該基金再捐出一個產科教席。

對於部份庚子賠款不能討回，亦成為很大的隱憂（參看第104頁）。美國積極利用賠款提供獎學金予中國學生赴美留學，並在中國創辦清華預備學堂（清華大學前身），在當地影響力不斷增加。英國政府亦寧願把庚子賠款投予中國的教育項目，以作制衡。

一九一九年的五四運動加劇了中國人民反英國、反殖民化的情緒。舉足輕重人士如胡適更反對大學接受賠款，認為應由廣州申請。沙普委員會提議部份賠款應提前支付給大學，但延至一九三一年，其中二十六萬五千英鎊才獲償還。

至於William Brunyate的繼任人康寧爵士則要面對不同的挑戰，就是如何使港大為中國服務。

貝璐工程實驗室 Peel Engineering Laboratory

一九三四年貝璐工程實驗室由利安建築師樓承建，建築採用裝飾藝術風格，與何東機械實驗所的設計一致，並取代本部大樓成為工程系的實習工場。二次大戰時貝璐工程實驗室、何東機械實驗所全部教學及實驗器材皆被搜掠一空。至一九四八年復建工程才開始。一九八一年大樓拆卸。

Like the Ho Tung Engineering Workshop, the Peel Engineering Laboratory was designed in Art Deco style by Leigh & Orange and opened in 1934. This allowed for the Engineering Faculty to be relocated from the University's Main Building. During the war, the Laboratory and the Ho Tung Engineering Workshop were looted of all teaching and workshop equipment. Restoration work began in 1948. The building was eventually demolished in 1981.

The University opened with high expectations and even higher ambitions in 1912, yet its early decades were characterised by uncertainty and an acute financial need. Treasurer Sir Paul Chater was prudent in his management of the University's endowment fund. Nevertheless a lack of investment from the Colonial Office in London, difficulties raising further funds following the 1911 Revolution, as well as the University's physical expansion of buildings and facilities, including staff and student accommodation, contributed to the University's poor financial circumstances.

One of the earliest donors to the University was Loke Yew (1846–1917), a wealthy Malayan tin magnate and philanthropist. A friend of Ho Kai's, in 1912 Loke Yew donated $55,000 to the endowment fund. Later, when the University was threatened with bankruptcy in its early years, Chater suggested approaching Loke Yew again. He responded in 1915 by offering an interest-free loan of $500,000 for a period of twenty-one years. The only condition was that four annual scholarships would be offered for students of the Straits Settlements and the Federated Malay States. Loke Yew was elected a life member of the University Court in 1916 and died the following year shortly after being awarded an Honorary Doctor of Laws.

In 1918 Vice-Chancellor Sir Charles Eliot took up a posting to Siberia. Intended to be temporary, it effectively represented his return to diplomatic service. G. P. Jordan was appointed Acting Vice-Chancellor in his absence. The leadership vacuum left by Eliot's departure, and ongoing questions regarding the purpose of the University led the government to establish a commission in 1920 to report on the University's viability. Headed by the barrister E. H. Sharp, and including solicitor S. W. Tso (Cao Shanyun), this would be the first of a number of investigative commissions into the University's affairs. The Sharp Commission concluded that in order for the University to fulfill its purposes, it needed to improve both the quality of its teaching, and its facilities. This would require further investment. It also concluded that as it served both imperial and local interests, the University should enjoy both greater government and private support.

Further fundraising efforts were made in 1921 with individual philanthropists, such as H. M. Nemazee and Mok Kon Sang contributing to the endowment, while others donated specific funds. Sir Robert Ho Tung donated funds for the Ho Tung Engineering Workshop (1926–1977), an Art Deco style building designed by Leigh & Orange. A further donation from Messrs. John Swire and Sons supported studies in engineering. This was in addition to the earlier establishment of a chair in the subject. The relocation of the engineering workshops freed up much needed space in the Main Building. There were also specific funds for the development of Chinese studies (see page 112). As Treasurer, Sir Paul Chater's donation was more pragmatic and aimed at establishing a salary scale for staff.

The University's third Vice-Chancellor, Sir William Brunyate, began his term in 1921, which coincided with a generous donation of $500,000 from the Rockefeller Foundation for Chairs in Medicine and Surgery. During his short term, Brunyate attempted to impose some fiscal discipline onto the University. Although frustrated at not having made more progress, he left the University in 1924 in considerably better shape than he found it. That same year, the Rockfeller Foundation made a further donation for a Chair in Obstetrics.

A source of great frustration was a failure to secure part of the Boxer Indemnity funds (see page 104). The British government favoured allocating the funds to educational projects in China directly to counter the growing influence of the United States. The Americans were viewed favourably in China for using their funds judiciously in offering scholarships for Chinese students to study in the United States and establishing preparatory schools such as Tsing Hua Imperial College (the foundations of the later Tsinghua College and University).

There were also concerns that the May Fourth Movement of 1919 had aroused anti-British and anti-colonial sentiments in China. Influential individuals such as Hu Shih also opposed the University receiving any of the funds, arguing in favour of Canton receiving them instead. The Sharp Commission of 1920 included a recommendation that a portion of the Boxer Indemnity should be given to the University, but it was not until 1931 that the sum of £265,000 was finalised.

Sir William Brunyate's successor, Sir William Hornell would face the challenge of fulfilling the University's role within the context of a changing China.

Notes: Cunich, pp. 220–238; Brian Harrison, 'The Years of Growth', in Harrison, pp. 45–57; Bernard Mellor, 'The American Foundations', Harrison, pp. 159–170; Anthony Sweeting, 'The University by Report' in Chan and Cunich, pp. 213–240.

呈盧督頌詞

'呈盧督頌詞'是一幅刺繡華麗的絹軸，於一九一零年四月二十八日港督盧吉和夫人離港休假六個月前，由一眾雲集在港督府的本港華商，向這位港督暨首任港大校監呈上。這份禮物原本計劃在當年三月十六日港大奠基儀式上送贈，但因製作未能如期完成而押後。

'呈盧督頌詞'由韋寶珊(韋玉)和何啟爵士代表八十四位贊助這份禮物的捐贈者向港督呈獻。[1] 送贈儀式上的演辭，讚揚盧吉爵士於任內解決了公共衛生方面有關屍體處理的問題，以及促成香港大學的成立。絹軸上所繡頌詞如下：

惟一千九百一十年四月吉日

制府盧公，遄返祖國，以六閱月為假期，我中華紳商士庶，以祖道之儀文，為尊者之頌禱，典至隆也。

公下車香海，已數易星霜。德政仁恩，口碑載道，其所以撫循百姓，安集遠人者，至為懇摯。而於我華人公益善舉，尤為鼎力贊勵，靡不令人稱道。如港中棄屍之事，曩者數見不鮮。

公用殷憂，力謀洗革，乃與公立醫局妥籌辦法，棄屍之陋習，幾絕迹焉。清淨之例，原為公眾衛生起見，然華人則向苦其嚴。

公蒞任後，於清淨則例，通融辦理，而收效且較前尤著，四民便之。教育者，所以陶鑄人才也。中國現方勵志維新，講學尤為當務之急。惟現在各省多未有大學之設，青年有志之士，銳意求學者，多擔簦負笈，以就傅於重洋，或非父兄長者之所願也。

公來撫是邦，雖庶政均已具舉，而尤以興學育才為唯一之首務。殫精會神，籌設大學，今奠基禮成，偉業就緒，他日得英才而教育之，收效定臻美滿也。我華紳商等感

公盛德，永矢弗諼，故於

公之行也，詞以送之，伏願

公一路福星，榮抵故國，無往不利與

公夫人優游娛養，享此休假之期，並將我華紳商等傾慕

公夫人懿德之忱，代為道達，尤望

公惠顧屬土，早日還轅，俾得瞻仰丰儀，時聆雅訓，是則我華紳商等所深為虔祝者矣。

闔港華紳商

周少岐	陳賡虞	韋　玉	何　啟	劉鑄伯	曹善允	何　福
容翼廷	馮華川	冼德芬	何甘棠	伍漢墀	蕭遠輝	源雲翹
胡海籌	容兆譜	黎季裴	招雨田	鄧鑑之	吳理卿	古輝山
陳綽卿	唐麗泉	阮荔村	盧冠廷	蔣士楷	老潔平	梁炳南
李秀軒	梁培之	區澤民	何蕚樓	劉少焯	何　東	容建邦
黃麗川	郭少流	鄧志昂	陳席儒	佘達材	劉伴樵	余彬南
黃耀東	周卓凡	羅雪甫	陳說巖	李瑞琴	梁建安	潘維宣
李榮光	徐愛堂	李右泉	胡著雲	譚鶴坡	陳洛川	陳春泉
曾維謙	曾秉鈞	黃花農	李葆葵	李竹如	林壽廷	周雨亭
馬杏巢	莫若廉	招頌侯	招晝三	招湘生	陳殿臣	崔仲崿
黃德秦	余日初	姚鉅源	蔡曉嵐	李翹拔	陳秩如	余道生
岑伯銘	盧頌舉	胡鼎三	陳雲繡	陳厚卿	胡蘊初	陳鳳臺

恭頌

---

[1] 林亦英、施君玉編：《學府時光：香港大學的歷史面貌》，第57頁文中所提八十七位贊助名字，因包括了別名，實際上重複了何福、何甘棠、韋玉三人，見附錄一'連浩鋆著贊助人名錄'，該名冊以知名度排序。

'呈盧督頌詞'卷軸的刺繡和木匣上很多裝飾，都象徵幸福長久婚姻，隱含著對總督伉儷的祝福。刺繡精巧上乘，尤其是顏色的陰影部份：工匠以暗針繡上不同顏色的陰影，首先在底層繡上較深色，再在上面以較疏落的暗針繡上淺色，形成有層次漸變的色彩效果。這些繡飾由於工序繁複，日久會令刺繡工人喪失視力。存放頌詞的褐紅色檀香木製匣子，外雕精緻的龍、鳳、花卉、竹子、蝴蝶和其他裝飾。匣子的蓋面刻著'德蔭香江'，意謂以德行護蔭香港，而在四個漢字中間刻有港督盧吉英文名的首字母。[2]

'呈盧督頌詞'重返香港的經過，實在是機緣巧合。當年港大社會醫學系教授賀達理獲邀到英國鴨巴甸大學中國研究部演講，議題是香港西醫書院。聽眾席上一位拉姆齊女士原來與盧吉家族甚有淵源。據稱一九四五年盧吉去世，他的妻子早已離世，二人並沒有子嗣，'呈盧督頌詞'便傳給了夏里森氏姊妹，這四姊妹的父親是夏里森上校，母親是拉姆齊女士的姨祖母輩，她們的祖母是盧吉家族的成員。當夏里森氏姊妹中的碧翠絲於一九六五年去世後，這幅卷軸傳到了盧吉的曾侄孫平克少校。經賀達理游說，最後平克少校慷慨同意把'呈盧督頌詞'運返香港。[3]

2　參考《學府時光：香港大學的歷史面貌》，第58-65頁。
3　同上書，第46-48頁。

呈盧督頌詞
絹本絲繡掛軸連檀香木匣
The Lugard Tribute
Embroidered satin scroll housed in a sandalwood casket
Scroll H: 347 cm　W: 116.5 cm

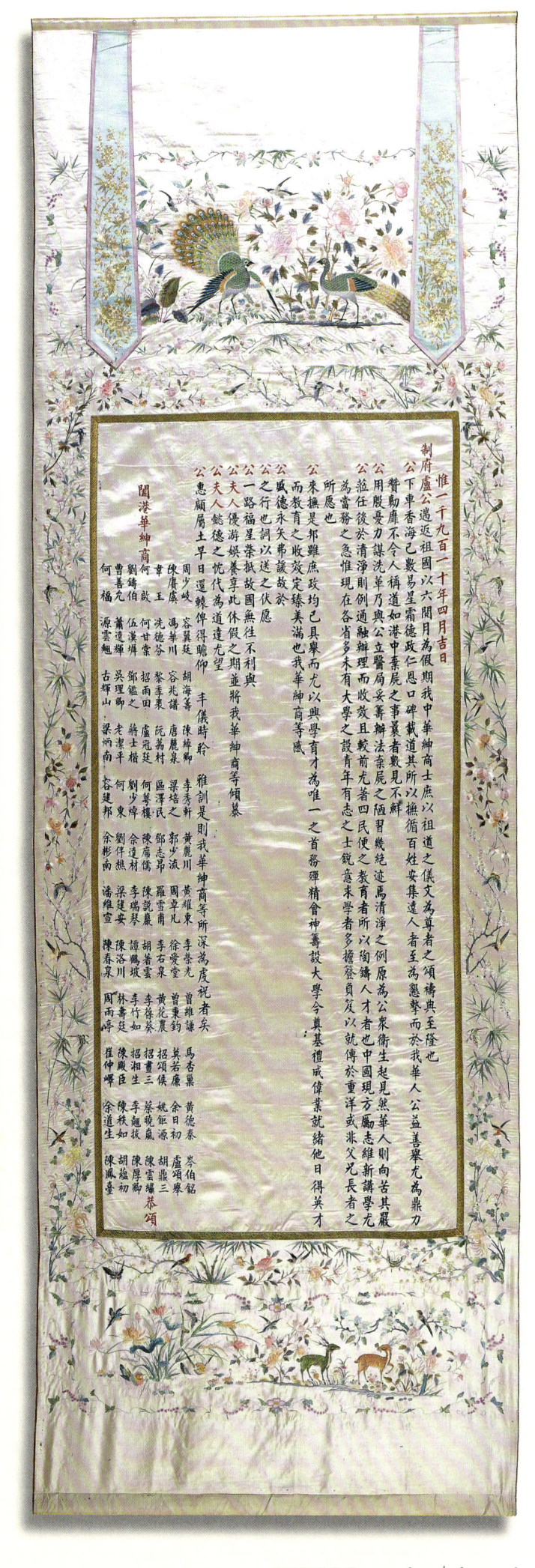

'呈盧督頌詞'絹軸上深藍線繡的八十四位贊助者姓名中，有五十三位曾捐款予港大創校。在典禮當日，何啟爵士讀出他的贊詞如下：

> 總督閣下，無人能及本地華人社區般欣賞你為本殖民地帶來的巨大裨益。我們對你的感激是雙重的，因為我們經歷了一段長期的商業低潮，而你成功地使我們脫離困境。你有廣闊的胸襟，以無比的魄力和熱誠來創立香港大學。這所學府使居於本殖民地或中國境內的華人，都能受惠無窮。因為這項恩惠，我們向你表示最誠摯的感激。總督閣下，我們的後代將對你銘記於心，並像我們現時一樣向你表示最誠摯的謝意。希望閣下回到英國後，能向大不列顛和愛爾蘭胸襟廣闊和有博愛心的人士表達我們急切的需要，好讓我們能為大學基金籌得更多捐款。[4]

創辦港大，盧吉夫人弗洛拉可謂居功不少。她交遊廣闊，婚前是倫敦《泰晤士報》的出色記者，曾擔任《泰晤士報》殖民地版編輯，並積極參與不同的義工服務團。作為當時一位傑出女性，她對於興辦港大的計劃十分雀躍，即使健康出了問題，往英國進行醫療期間，也為籌款出力。在慶祝港大本部大樓開幕時，她更籌備了建校籌款義賣會。雖說盧督推薦麼地封爵，說不定或是盧吉夫人在背後推動玉成。麼地爵士也承認他捐款協助香港大學成立，原因之一便是被弗洛拉的熱誠打動。[5]

匣蓋的外面刻上'德蔭香江'字樣
The inscription 'Tak Yam Heung Kong' (De Yin Xiang Jiang) on the cover of the casket

匣蓋內的絲織畫細部
Detail of the silk painting lining the casket cover

4　原文登於一九一零年四月二十九日《德臣西報》，由韓達理、連浩鋈於'呈盧督頌詞'一文中引述，中譯本摘錄自《學府時光：香港大學的歷史面貌》，第51至53頁。

5　Staci Ford, 'Women, Gender, and HKU', in Chan and Cunich, pp. 121–122.

The Lugard Tribute

The richly-embroidered satin scroll known as The Lugard Tribute was presented to Lord Frederick Lugard, the Governor of Hong Kong and first Chancellor of the University at Government House on 28th April 1910, the day before he and Lady Flora Lugard were to leave Hong Kong for six months. It was originally intended to have been presented to Lugard on 16th March at the foundation-stone-laying ceremony of the new university but was not completed in time.

The Tribute was presented to Lugard by Wei Yuk and Ho Kai on behalf of the eighty-four subscribers[1] who commissioned the Tribute as a formal note of thanks to Lugard for his work in Hong Kong, with particular reference to his leadership in resolving an important matter of public health: the sanitary disposal of the dead; and in the founding of the University.

Translation of the Chinese Address presented to His Excellency the Governor, Sir Frederick John Dealtry Lugard, K.C.M.G., C.S., D.S.O., by the representatives of the Chinese Community.

On a lucky day in April of the year 1910 on the occasion of Your Excellency's returning to your ancestral home on a holiday of six months we Chinese representatives of all classes of the community take the opportunity of your departure to present you with a respectful address in token of our esteem.

More than once have the stars and the boar-frosts returned in their course since Your Excellency came to Hongkong: the benevolence and clemency of your virtuous administration is in the mouth of every passerby in the streets. Your earnest attention has been devoted to everything that would promote the welfare of the people and the comfort of those who have gathered here from afar. More especially has every movement for the benefit of the Chinese received your heartiest support. Not once have your actions failed to call forth the public praise. Your Excellency was moved with great sorrow at the frequency with which bodies have been thrown out into the street in Hong Kong, and with the determination of taking measures to stamp the practice out, you consulted the Public Dispensaries Committee as to the best means of effecting your purpose; and now there is hardly a trace left of the evil practice. The Sanitary laws are made to preserve the public health, but the Chinese have always feared their strictness. Since Your Excellency took up office a compromise has been effected in the administration of the laws while at the same time to the gratification of all classes better results have been achieved.

It is education which moulds and forms men's talents. China is now intent on reform and for this purpose education is the most urgent need. But in few of the provinces is there a University and hence the young men who have the aspirations of a scholar and seek a higher education, much against the wishes of their father their brothers and their elders, have to carry their books and luggage across many an ocean in search of a teacher.

Since Your Excellency came to give peace to this state, all the business of administration has been carried on by you with success, but you have regarded the development of education and the encouragement of talent as your most important duty, and all your energies and faculties have been devoted to the establishment of a University. Now the foundation stone had been duly laid and the magnificent project is on the way to realization. We feel confident that in the future the result of the education given in the University will fulfil all expectations.

Your Excellency's kindness will remain a lasting and grateful memory in the hearts of the Chinese. On your departure therefore we beg to present you with this address, and unite in a prayer that your journey will be made under a lucky star, that you may reach your country in safety and prosper in everything you undertake and that you may spend your holiday in happiness in the society of Her Excellency Lady Lugard, our admiration of whose virtues we pray you to convey to her. We trust that you will remember this Colony in your heart and return soon that we may look again upon the dignity of your countenance and hearken to the grace of your commands.

This is our earnest prayer.

Dated Hongkong the 28th day of April, 1910.

檀香木匣
Sandalwood casket
L: 161 cm H: 54.5 cm D: 38.5 cm

木匣與卷軸
The casket and scroll

Many of the symbols in the embroidery and on the casket refer to long and happy marriages. The high quality of the embroidery, particularly in the shading of the colours, is accomplished using a stitch sometimes known as a blind stitch, in which the thread of a new colour is introduced between the threads of a stronger shade. The fine attention to detail and work on graduating colours can lead to an eventual loss of sight in the embroiderer. The Tribute is stored in a rosewood casket with intricate carvings of dragons, phoenixes, flowers, bamboo, butterflies and other ornamentation. The inscription on the top in silver features four characters flanking Lugard's initials. The inscription 'Tak Yam Heung Kong', which means 'virtue shadows over Hong Kong.'[2]

The existence of the Tribute was uncovered by chance following a lecture Anthony J. Hedley, then professor of Community Medicine at HKU, gave to the Aberdeen University Chinese Studies Group on the subject of the Hongkong College of Medicine. In the audience was Priscilla Ramsay whose maternal great aunt was Annie Florence Martin who had married Colonel John Harrison. Colonel Harrison's mother was a Lugard and it is likely that when Lugard died in 1945 (widowed and childless) he left the Tribute to the Harrison's four daughters. When Beatrice Harrison died in 1965 she left the Tribute to her cousin Major Richard Pinker, a great nephew of Frederick Lugard's. It was with him that Professor Hedley eventually found the Tribute and negotiated its return to the University.[3]

Of the eighty-four subscribers whose names are embroidered on the Tribute, fifty-three had also contributed to the founding of the University, which Ho Kai referred to in his presentation speech that day:

No one, sir, appreciates more than the Chinese community the immense benefits which you have conferred upon this colony and they are doubly grateful to you, for though we have had a long commercial depression you have succeeded by your broadmindedness and by your incomparable energy and enthusiasm in founding the Hongkong University. The vast benefits conferred by such an institution on the colony as a whole, but more especially on the Chinese, whether resident in this colony or throughout China, are incomparable and we thank you, sir, most cordially and most gratefully for such a boon. I am sure, sir, future generations will cherish your memory and thank you as gratefully and cordially as we do now. We hope, sir, when you get to England, you will be able to represent our needs to the large hearted and philanthropic people of Great Britain and Ireland, and be enabled thereby to get further donations, much needed, for our University and its endowment fund. [4]

Lugard's wife, Flora Shaw Lugard, had a leading role in the success of the university project. She was well-traveled and had been a distinguished journalist before she married. She was the colonial editor of *The Times* newspaper and active in helping voluntary aid societies. Unusually accomplished for a woman of her time, Flora took a particular interest in the university project, raising both support and money for it in Britain where she traveled from time to time for medical treatment. She also organised the fund-raising bazaar for the opening of the Main Building. Although it was Lugard who requested a knighthood for Hormusjee Mody, this may also have been at Flora's urging. Mody himself cited Flora's enthusiasm for the project as a factor that influenced him to fund the university.[5]

---

1. In the Museum's 2001 publication, Susan Y. Y. Lam and Jane Sze (eds), *Past Visions of the Future: Some Perspectives on the History of The University of Hong Kong*, the number of subscribers is given as eighty-seven (p. 58), which includes the aliases of three of the named members (Ho Fook, Ho Kam Tong and Wei Yuk). Please refer to the table in Appendix I, prepared by Alfred H. Y. Lin, which lists the subscriber's names in alphabetical order. The names on the Tribute are ordered by significance.
2. For more on the Tribute's features see Hedley and Lin, pp. 58–65.
3. Ibid. pp. 46–48.
4. *China Mail*, 28 April 1910 cited in Anthony J. Hedley and Alfred H. Y. Lin, 'The Lugard Tribute' in Lam and Sze, pp. 46–66.
5. Staci Ford, 'Women, Gender, and HKU', in Chan and Cunich, pp. 121–122.

建校籌款義賣會海報

海報由《南華早報》印刷，向全港市民宣傳香港大學建校籌款義賣會暨本部大樓開幕誌慶。

賣物場為期逾一週，並設有音樂會、舞會、戲劇表演，以及首度表演港大校歌。校歌由富勒作曲，金文泰填詞，管弦協會合唱團及聖約翰大教堂歌詠團演唱，英國皇家輕步兵第一營全體軍樂團伴奏。

義賣場舉行期間，本部大樓開放予公眾參觀，只收酌量門票。公眾進入大樓參觀，可選購盧吉夫人為義賣會在倫敦搜羅的四百件禮品，每件約值二十五元，共值一萬元。參觀人士更可乘義賣會特製的觀光火車，該火車後來由本地商人以一萬元投得。

海報標題：'香港大學堂賣物場籌款 三月十一至十六日 由盧吉爵士與夫人贊助'。

海報採用'新藝術'風格，畫中女神結合了羅馬神話中智慧之神密涅瓦與天文繆思烏拉尼亞的形象。她頭戴象徵勝利的桂冠，手持薪傳火炬，旁置天球儀、羅盤。其身後有自由女神式背光，以及希臘神話中雅典娜女神的橄欖樹。

這張海報多年來一直掛於英文系的會議室，最近由劉志雄發現時已殘破不堪，不宜展出。原稿滿佈水漬，紙面和摺痕處有破損。海報上顏料尤其紅彩明顯褪色，並因造紙時加入硫磺而變褐黃，以及紫外線照射、溫度濕度落差的痕跡。約一九七零年代海報曾經保存處理，以膠水裱托亞麻布後過膠。可惜過膠其實會加速紙張損毀，造成無可挽回和修復的傷害。希望日後能發現另一張保存較好的海報。

《南華早報》印刷的賣物場籌款海報
一九一二年
The Bazaar Poster
South China Morning Post
1912
H: 88.3 cm W: 56.7 cm

University Bazaar Poster

This poster announced the Grand Fête and Bazaar to raise funds for the new University, as well as to celebrate the opening of the Main Building. It was produced by the *South China Morning Post* and distributed across Hong Kong.

The Bazaar lasted just over a week and included musical entertainments, a banquet, theatrical performances, and the first public performance of the University Anthem composed by Denman Fuller with lyrics by Cecil Clementi, by the chorus of the Philharmonic Society, the Choir of St John's Cathedral and the full military band of the 1st Battalion, King's Yorkshire Light Infantry.

The Main Building was opened to members of the public for a small entrance fee. Once inside they could buy one of the 400 items offered for sale that Lady Lugard had personally purchased in London with a budget of $10,000, with each item costing around $25. Visitors to the Bazaar were also able to ride on the scenic railway built specially for the Bazaar and later auctioned off to a local businessman for $10,000.

The poster reads: 'Hongkong University Bazaar – March 11th to 16th – under the patronage of – His Excellency Sir Frederick Lugard G.C.M.G. [Knight Grand Cross] C.B. [Companion] D.S.O. [Distinguished Service Order]– & Lady Lugard'.

The poster is designed in Art Nouveau style and features an allegorical female figure combining the attributes of Minerva, the Roman goddess of wisdom and learning, and Urania, the muse of the stars governing astronomy and astrology. She is shown wearing a laurel wreath symbolising victory, carrying the torch of learning with the celestial globe and compass. Behind her is the radiating sun of the Goddess of Liberty and olive trees associated with the Greek version of Minerva, Athena.

This copy of the poster was discovered by Mr Franky Lau in the University's School of English where it had been displayed for many years in the conference room. It is in such poor condition that it could not be displayed during the exhibition. It has extensive water damage, some loss of paper on the surface and in the folds, and fading, especially of the red colour. It is browned due to the build up of sulphur in the paper from its manufacturing process, exposure to light and fluctuations in temperature and humidity.

At some point in the past, probably in the 1970s when it was considered a valid method of preservation, the poster was backed with linen and glue and laminated with plastic. Unfortunately lamination has accelerated the deterioration of the poster and the resulting damage is both irreversible and irreparable. It is hoped that a better-preserved example of the poster will be found someday.

香港大學建校籌款賣物場出售中國玩偶三款
一九一二年三月十一至十六日
Three Chinese dolls sold during the University Bazaar
11th to 16th March 1912
H: 38 cm W: 13 cm
H: 33 cm W: 13 cm
H: 29 cm W: 10 cm

梅勒在一九八零年記述玩偶回到大學的經過：'中國娃娃家庭相信是由《中國古典文學》（一八六一年於香港出版）著者理雅各的孫女於建校籌款賣物會攤位上購買，隨即送到牛津贈予賴廉士夫人。'
In 1980 Bernard Mellor recorded how the dolls were returned to the University: 'The family of Chinese dolls were bought at one of the stalls, and subsequently presented in Oxford to Lady Ride, she believes by a granddaughter of James Legge, the translator of the *Chinese Classics* published in Hong Kong in 1861.' (*The University of Hong Kong: An Informal History*, Vol. 1, p. 20).

HKU Memories | from the Archives 33

香港大學校歌
University Anthem

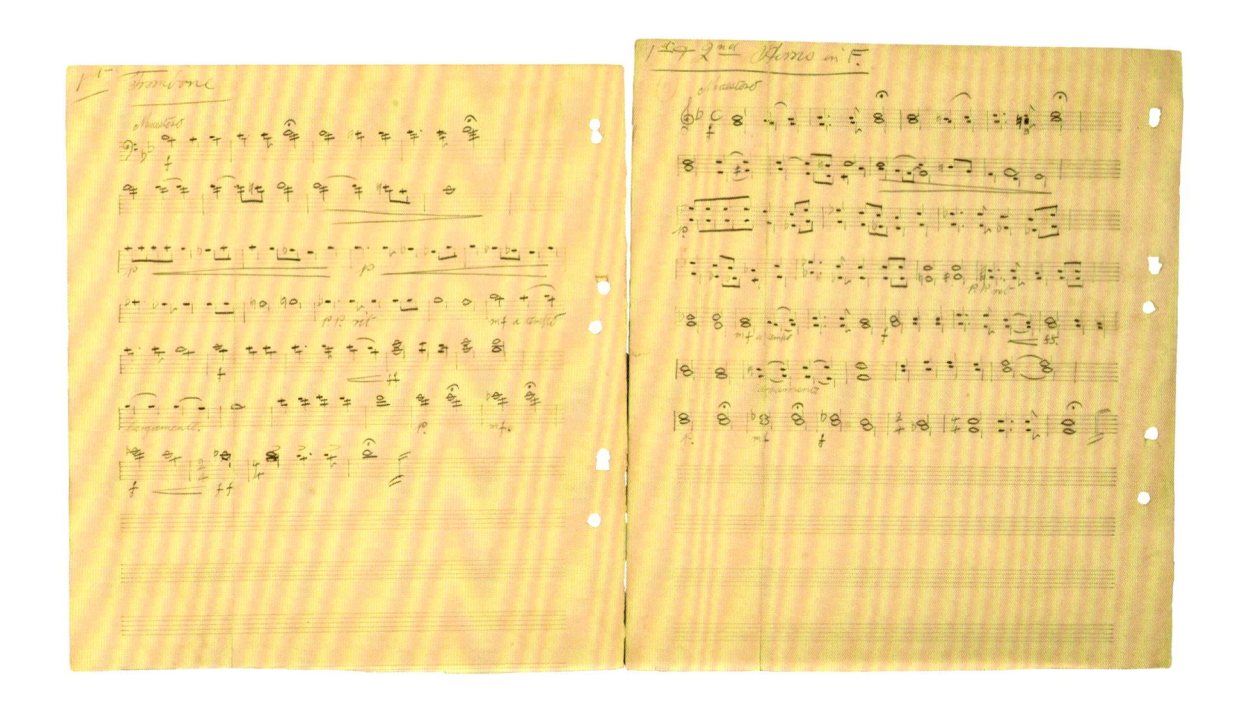

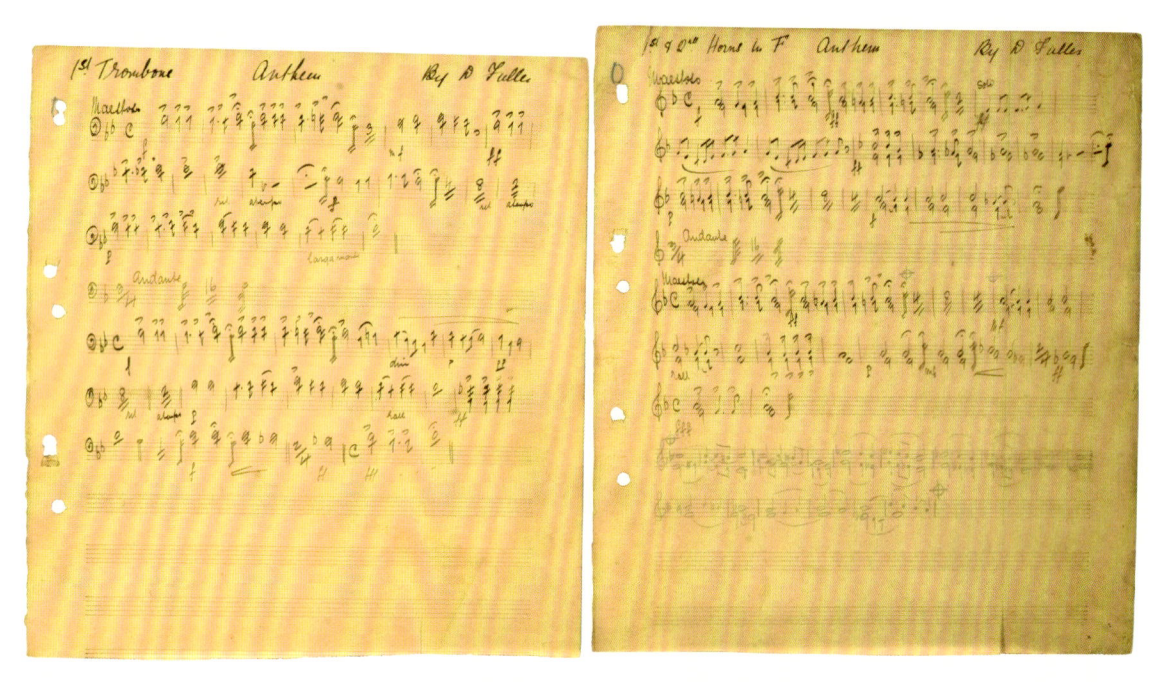

香港大學校歌銅管樂器部原稿,由富勒作曲
Original drafts of the brass sections for the Anthem by Denman Fuller

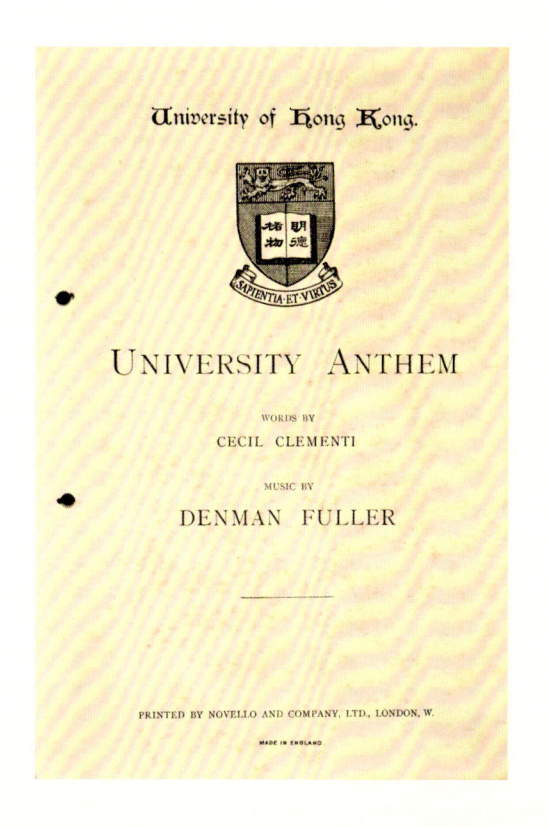

一九一二年節目程序表中的香港大學校歌，由金文泰爵士作詞及富勒作曲，管弦樂團合唱團、聖約翰座堂詩班，以及皇家約克郡輕步兵團第一營全體軍樂隊演出

Program from 1912, featuring the HKU Anthem, with lyrics by Sir Cecil Clementi and music composed by Denman Fuller, performed by the Chorus of the Philharmonic Society, the Choir of the St John's Cathedral, and the full Military Band of the 1st Battalion, King's Own Yorkshire Light Infantry.

香港大學建校籌款義賣會期間臨時成立郵局，一九一二年三月十一至十六日從該處寄出的郵件均戳印 'Hongkong University Post Office' 英文名稱。
During the opening Bazaar a temporary post office issuing mail stamped with a 'Hongkong University Post Office' postmark was in operation for a limited period of six days from 11th to 16th March 1912.

Bonheur 58 Peel Street
Local

HONGKONG UNIVERSITY
13 MAR 12
POST OFFICE
Messrs. GRAÇA & Co.
"Bonheur" 58, Peel Street,
HONGKONG.

HONG KONG
ONE CENT
FOUR CENTS
EIGHT CENTS
Messrs. GRAÇA & Co.
HONGKONG HOTEL BUILDING
HONGKONG UNIVERSITY
14 MAR 12
POST OFFICE
HONGKONG.

港大校園圖則原稿

圖則上雖沒有建築師署名，但推斷利安建築師事務所艾佛烈‧布耶曾參與繪圖，他即麼地暱稱的「我的建築師」。圖則中本部大樓、校長寓所、學院座址各頁均寫上利安建築師事務所，圖則比例為1吋比8呎（約1：96）；而奠基工程之前的地台加固、斜坡和排水管道工程圖則比例則是1吋比30呎（約1：360）。這些圖則顯示本部大樓、各院系、運動場、貯水池在般咸道及薄扶林道上的方位。

盧吉留給外甥女希拉‧米德的遺物除銀製本部大樓模型外，還有鋼筆墨水、水彩所繪大學最早的建築物圖則。她本身是考古學家，曾委託大英博物館將圖則修復，後送贈香港大學，現為大學檔案中心收藏保存。

大學檔案中心接收圖則後將紙張鋪平，再清潔表面，然後以無酸性紙分隔，貯存在地圖抽屜櫃。由於圖則回歸大學前被捲存金屬圓筒內逾八十年，整個修復過程需時數月，而圖則從未受塵染光害、潮濕溫差等影響，畫面的線條色彩得以保存清晰，猶如簇新。

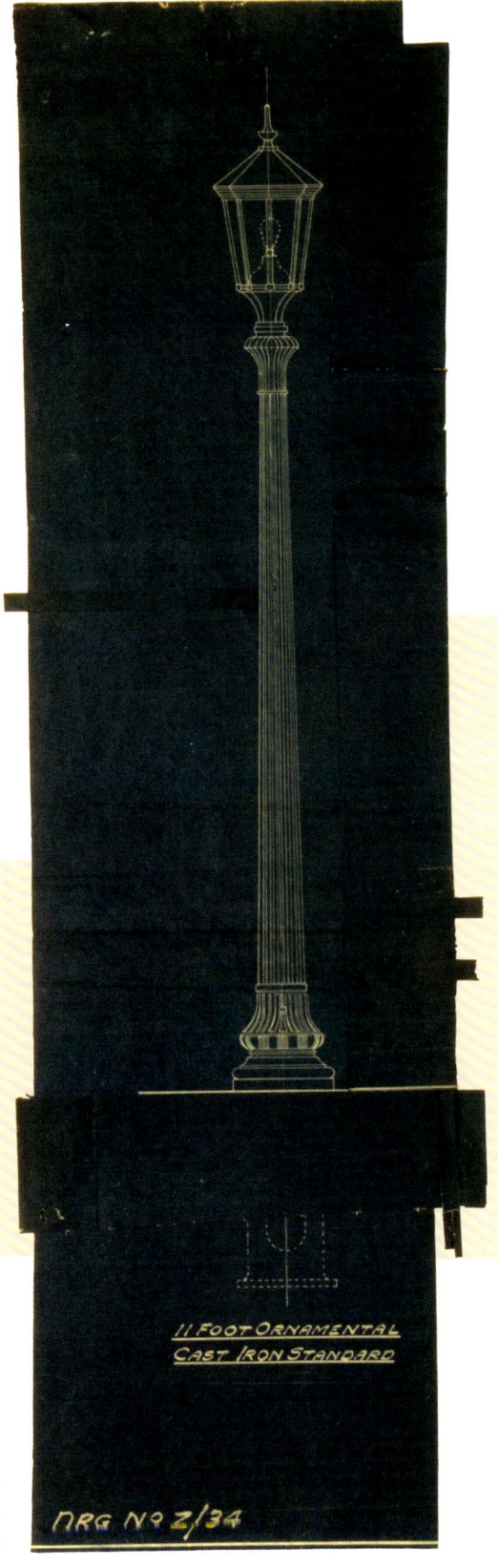

校內初期路燈藍圖
Blueprint of design of campus lamp post
H: 50 cm W: 14.5 cm

The Original Architectural Drawings for the University Campus

Although his signature does not appear on the drawings, Alfred Bryer, whom Hormusjee Mody fondly referred to as 'my architect', is believed to have have drafted these drawings. The firm's name of 'Leigh & Orange, Engineers and Architects, of Hong Kong' is clearly marked on each page depicting the Main Building, the Principal's House and the first Faculty Quarters to a scale of 8 feet to 1 inch. The plans for the building and reinforcement of the foundation, the slope and the drainage work that had to be carried out before the Foundation Stone was laid, are drawn at a scale of 30 feet to 1 inch and show the relationship of the Main Building to the Faculty House, the Playing Fields, the Pumping Station and Bonham and Pokfulam Roads.

Frederick Lugard left the original pen and ink architectural drawings of the earliest University buildings and the silver model to his great niece, Shelagh Meade. As an archaeologist she understood their importance to the history of the University and to Hong Kong. They were restored by the British Museum before being returned to HKU where they are now housed in the University Archives, available for future generations.

The drawings have been relaxed and flattened, their surfaces cleaned, and re-housed in acid free, buffered, tissue-lined folders in a large map case in the Archives. This process took months as the drawings had been rolled up in a tin tube for over 80 years before they were returned to the University. As they were not exposed to light and dust, extreme temperature fluctuations or humidity, they look almost as fresh as the day they were inked.

存放本部大樓原圖則的圓筒
一九一六年
Storage tube for the original drawings of the Main Building
1916
L: 83.5 cm Diam: 8 cm

HONGKONG UNIVERSITY

NORTH

HKU Memories | from the Archives   41

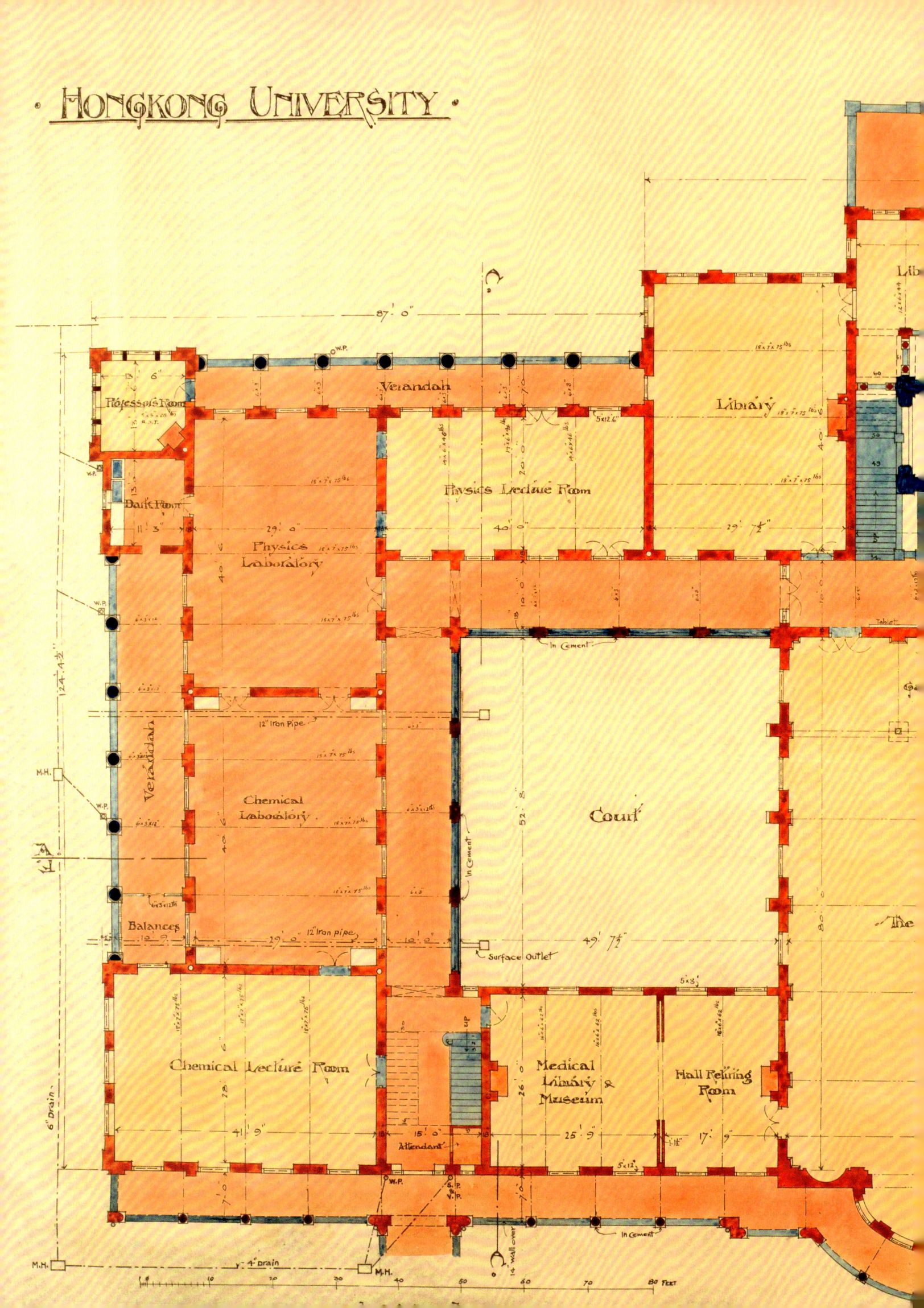

Hongkong University

Ground Floor Plan

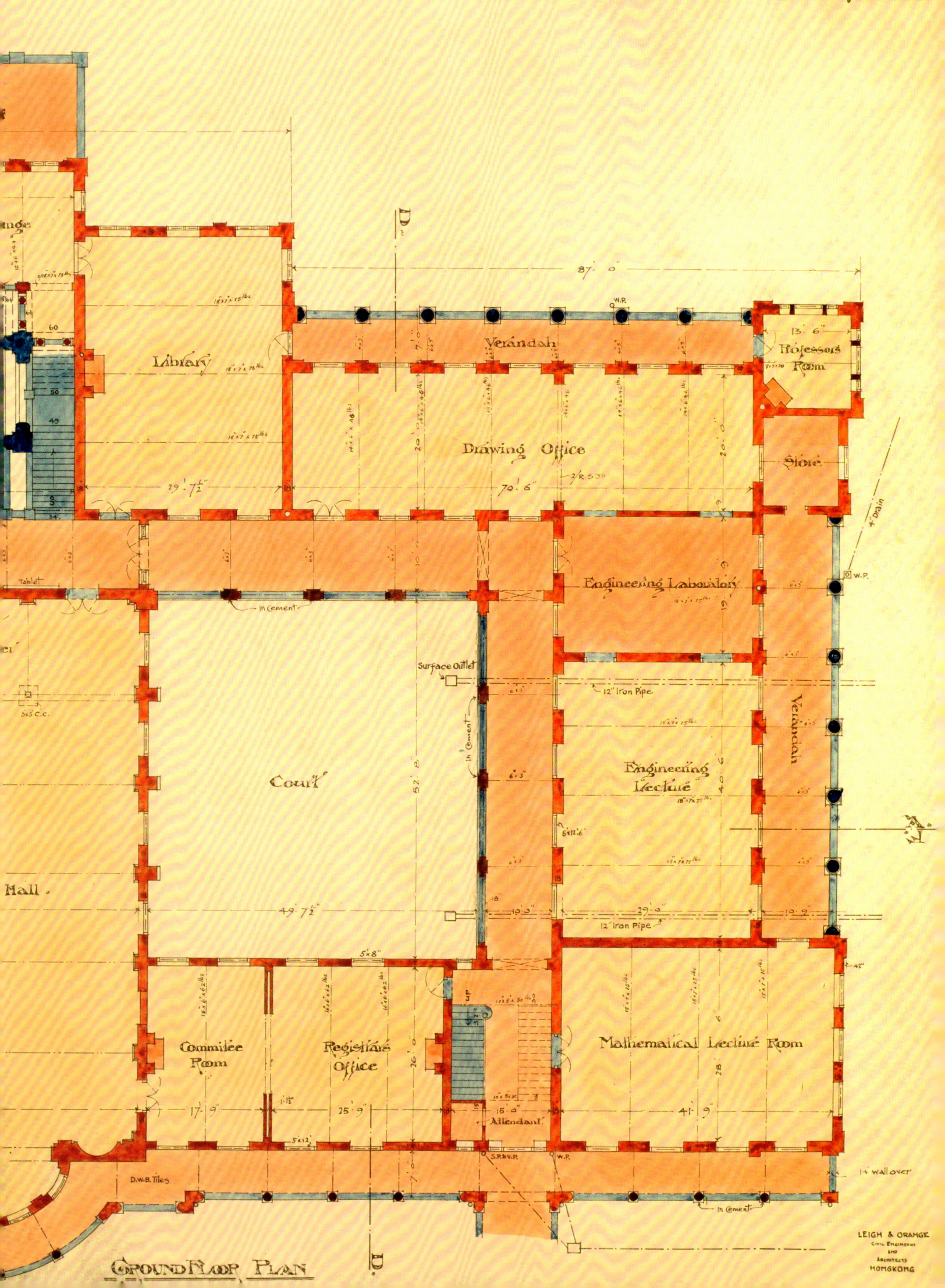

Drawing No.

- Library
- Verandah
- Professor's Room
- Drawing Office
- Store
- Engineering Laboratory
- Engineering Lecture
- Verandah
- Court
- Hall
- Committee Room
- Registrar's Office
- Attendant
- Mathematical Lecture Room

Leigh & Orange
Civil Engineers and Architects
Hongkong

HONGKONG UNIVERSITY

港大校園圖則原稿
紙本鋼筆墨水
約一九零九年
希拉·米德捐贈
The original architectural drawings
for the University campus
Pen and ink on paper
c. 1909
H: 65 cm W: 90 cm
Gift of Shelagh Meade

CONTRACT N°
DRAWING N°

EAST ELEVATION

SECTION B.B.

SCALE 8 FEET = 1 INCH

LEIGH & ORANGE
CIVIL ENGINEERS
AND
ARCHITECTS
HONG KONG

HKU Memories | from the Archives

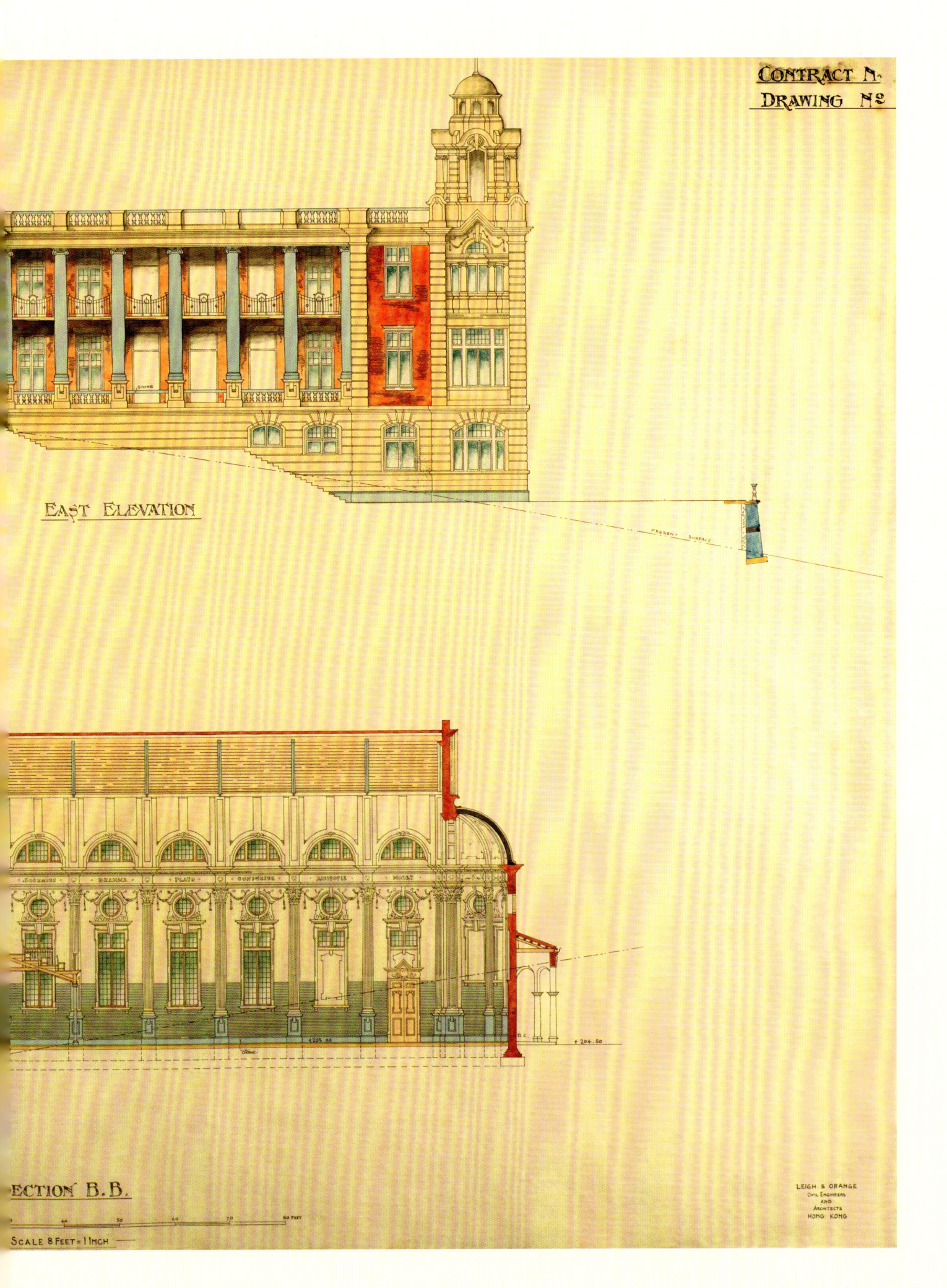

本部大樓銀製模型

本部大樓銀製模型由麽地爵士（一八三八至一九一一年）的兒子訂製，因此刻有他的英文名字 N. H. N. Mody。這是在一九一二年本部大樓開幕典禮時，麽地爵士擬贈送給港督盧吉的模型。麽地爵士率先捐款十五萬元籌建大學，可惜他於港大建成前一年逝世，未能見證與盧吉在香港設立首間專上教育學府的夢想成真。

這模型展示本部大樓落成時的面貌。一九五六年本部大樓擴建至現時的三層規模，後又加進兩個方形部份，將原來的面積增加一倍。大樓最初的格局仿照了當時的單棟式校舍，集結教室、實驗室、辦公室、圖書館等設施。

這件銀器可說是絕無僅有的。同類銀製建築物模型通常在印度製造，用作慶典的賀禮。相信本模型由興旺公司在廣州訂製，該公司早年在中環皇后大道一帶營業多年。香港大學檔案中心收到銀器後，交予金屬品修復專家清潔，然後放進特製的阿加力膠透明箱內，還附設一個提攜外箱。

This model may be the only one of its kind. Models made of important buildings in silver were often made in India as gifts for ceremonial occasions. This example was made in South China, probably Guangzhou, for the Hing Wong Company that had premises on Queen's Road for many years. Since entering the University Archives, the model has been cleaned by a metals conservator and housed within a new custom-made case made of Perspex and an outer traveling case.

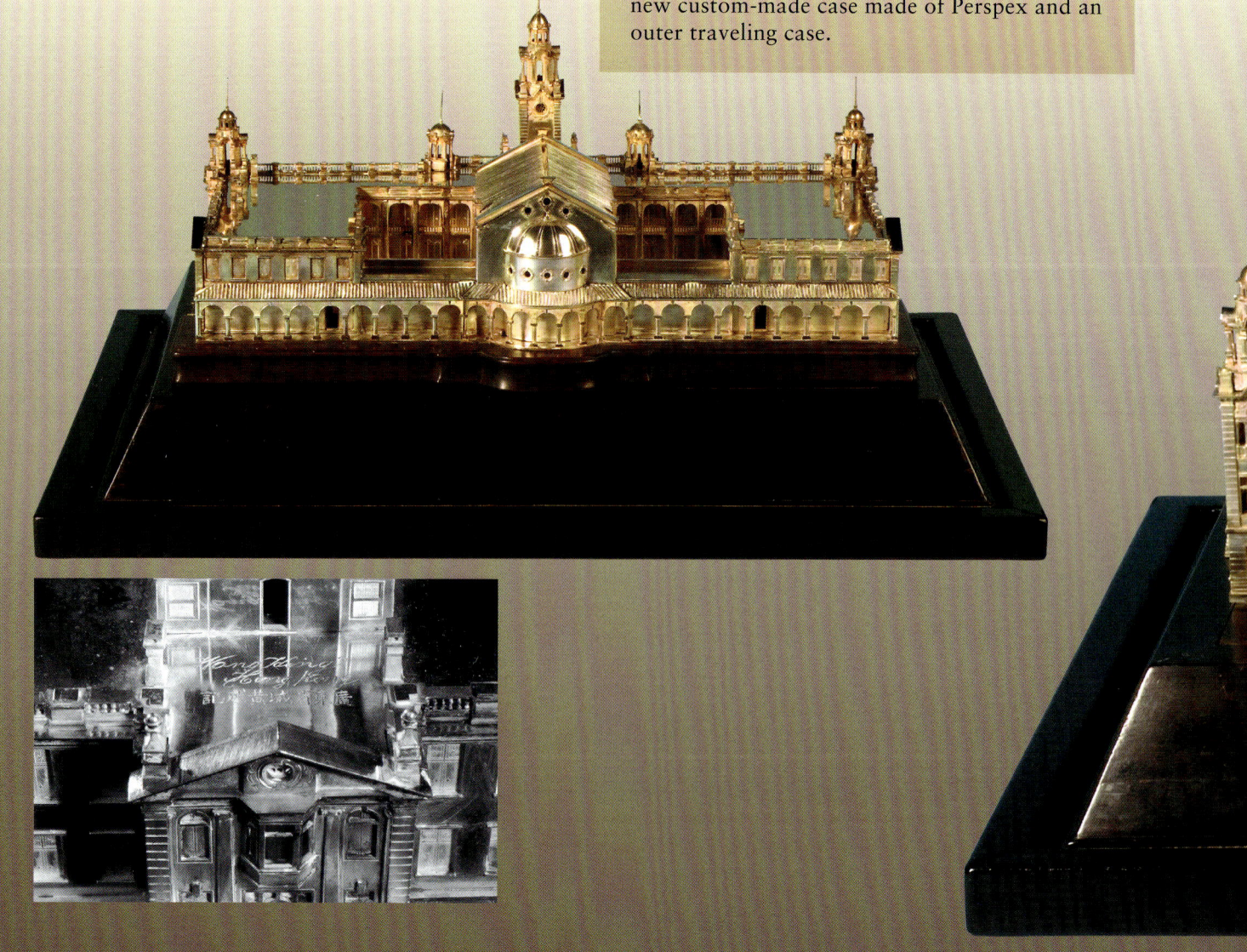

The Silver Model of the Main Building

The silver model of the Main Building was commissioned by the son of Sir Hormusjee Mody (1838–1911), and bears his initials N. H. N. Mody. It was presented to Governor Lugard at the 1912 opening ceremony of the building. Hormusjee Mody, who made the initial donation of $150,000 that kicked off the fundraising for the construction of the University, had sadly passed away the previous year and did not live to see the completion of his and Governor Lugard's dream of having higher education available in Hong Kong.

The model shows how the Main Building looked when it was built. Its current form incorporates a three-storey extension, built in 1956, and two additional quadrangles to increase its original space two-fold. The building was modeled on other single-building campuses of the time and included classrooms, laboratories, offices and a library.

本部大樓銀製模型
一九一二年
希拉・米德捐贈
Model of the Main Building
Sterling silver
1912
H: 21 cm W: 45.5 cm D: 30.5 cm
Gift of Shelagh Meade

一九一零年奠基鏟
1910 Foundation Trowel

港大校園工程奠基鏟作動土儀式的傳統由來已久,可追溯至一九一零年三月十六日本部大樓奠基時首次使用。本金鏟採用14k金製成,柔軟度高,港督盧吉給奠基石塗混凝土時,鏟片被輕微壓彎。

當時另造兩把銀製版本,於儀式上致送兩廣總督張人駿及兩江總督袁樹勛。

鏟面刻龍紋,象牙柄雕龍頭,龍爪抓著鏟片,龍頭前方鑲蛋白石,寶石四周飾光焰,猶如發光。

The tradition of using a ceremonial trowel to mark occasions of significant expansion of the University campus began with the laying of the first foundation stone on the 16th March 1910 at the site of the Main Building. The trowel used for this ceremony was made of solid 14k gold and the joint was so soft that it bent at the handle when used by Governor Frederick Lugard to lay mortar upon stone.

Two replicas of the 1910 trowel were made in sterling silver and given as gifts to the Viceroys of the Two Guangs (Guangdong and Guangxi), Zhang Renjun, and Two Jiangs (Jiangsu and Zhejiang), Yuan Shuxun.

The trowel is engraved with dragons and the ivory handle terminates in a golden dragon head with its front arms and claws appearing to hold the blade of the trowel in place. The dragon faces a single oval cabochon stone, probably a pink tourmaline, surrounded by engraved rays or flames as if the stone were alight.

一九一二年盧吉離任港督後,與夫人返回英國,並把金鏟一併帶走。一九四五年盧吉逝世,他的弟弟 Major Edward Lugard 把金鏟送回香港,自此保存在殖民地部門,直至一九四八年二次大戰後港大重開,金鏟才完璧歸趙。

When Lord Frederick Lugard and Lady Flora left Hong Kong in 1912, they took the 1910 trowel with them. After Lugard's death in 1945, his brother, Major Edward Lugard returned it to Hong Kong where it was kept in the Colonial Office until 1948. It was then returned to the University when it was formally re-opened after the war.

一九一零年鏟（港大奠基用鏟）
14k金嵌象牙
The 1910 Trowel (or the Foundation Trowel)
14 karat gold with ivory
L: 38.5 cm W: 11.5 cm

一九七八年鏟（大學擴建儀式用鏟）
鎳合金
The 1978 Trowel (or the Redevelopment Trowel)
Gold-plated nickel alloy
L: 35.3 cm W: 11.5 cm

一九七八年擴建鏟
1978 Redevelopment Trowel

本鏟用於一九七八年四月二十日港大安放奠基石儀式，以此展開校園的重整工程，包括擴建校園本部、沙宣道分部，在沙灣徑一帶新建體育設施、職員宿舍。當時港督兼校監麥理浩在典禮上致詞：港大作為一間專上學府，畢業生在行政、各科專業、工商各界作出貢獻，對香港社會有著深遠的影響。事實上，港大的成功也同時反映並緊扣著香港的進步，致力為下一代提供最優良的教育。'[1]

一九七三至一九七五年黃麗松履任校長期間，是港大的艱難歲月，當時資金短缺，建築工程被迫凍結，曾一度考慮遷移校園。直至一九七六年，大學決定在原址繼續發展。Sally Lunn 這樣報導當時的奠基儀式：'當天下午儀式的高潮是校長明確表示，展望未來，港大會堅守傳統，本部大樓再不會受到發展商的威脅。'[2]

大學擴建同時配合薄扶林道穿越工科及科學大樓的重鋪工程。該奠基石現放在孫中山廣場階級的右方，上方是邵氏大樓、許愛周樓。該位置當時綠草如茵，稱為化學系草坡。

The development of the University coincided with the rerouting of Pokfulam Road through the existing engineering and science buildings. The foundation stone now stands to the right of the steps that lead from Sun Yat Sen Plaza to the Shaw Buildings and Hui Oi Chow Science Building. At the time this was a grassy knoll referred to as the Chemistry Lawn.

This trowel was used on the 20th April 1978 to lay the new cornerstone marking the redevelopment of the University's Main Estate, the expansion on Sassoon Road, and the new sports facilities and staff accommodation in Sandy Bay. At the ceremony, the Governor and Chancellor of the University, Sir Murray MacLehose said that, 'As a teaching institution [HKU] has deeply influenced Hong Kong through the contribution its alumni have made in every field of administration, the professions, commerce and industry. Indeed our University can rightly see its own success mirrored in the progress of Hong Kong to whose successive generations it has given of its best.'[1]

The University's Vice-Chancellor, Dr Rayson Huang, noted that the years between 1973 and 1975 had been difficult for the University, there was insufficient funding and even a plan to move the University to a new site altogether. It was not until 1976 that a firm decision was made to keep the University in its present location. Sally Lunn, writing of the ceremony noted that, 'In some ways, the high point of the afternoon was the Vice-Chancellor's firm public statement that as well as looking to the future in its building, the University remains also wedded to its traditional heritage: the Main Building is in no danger from would-be developers.'[2]

1, 2   *The Interflow*, May 1978.

二零一零年百周年鏟
2010 Centenary Trowel

用於港大百周年校園奠基儀式上，典禮於二零一零年三月十六日舉行，距創校奠基日剛好一百年。

這是香港設計師丘清娜的作品，她為倫敦皇家藝術學院碩士。其設計參考了一九一零、一九七八年兩時期的金、銀鏟，當年的製作者皆不詳。新鏟的設計圖及創作資料後贈予大學檔案中心。

The Centenary (or Centennial) Trowel was made for the foundation stone-laying ceremony that took place on the 16th March 2010, 100 years after the first ceremony marking the foundation of the University.

Designed by Hong Kong designer Cécile Tu Ching-na, who received her Master of Arts from the Royal College of Art in London, this trowel is a contemporary rendition of the earlier trowels. While very little information is known about the designers of the 1910 or 1978 trowels, Ms Tu has donated her design work, and given an oral account of her experience in designing and making the trowel to the University Archives as documentation of the project.

她的設計意念為：'香港大學踏入第二個世紀，鏟柄由大小不一的長方形組成立體設計，代表不斷變化的校園面貌，如同百周年校園向西面擴建；喻意從一方走向另一方，代表由過去、現在到未來的發展進程……' [1]

In her designer's statement she writes that, 'The University of Hong Kong is moving into its second century. The handle of the trowel is a three-dimensional form presented by a row of irregular rectangles, where they express the ever-changing University landscape – the new Centennial Campus, as an extension of the existing campus to the west. It is expressed by their implicit movement from one end to the other, and that also represents the development from the past to the present, and the future…' [1]

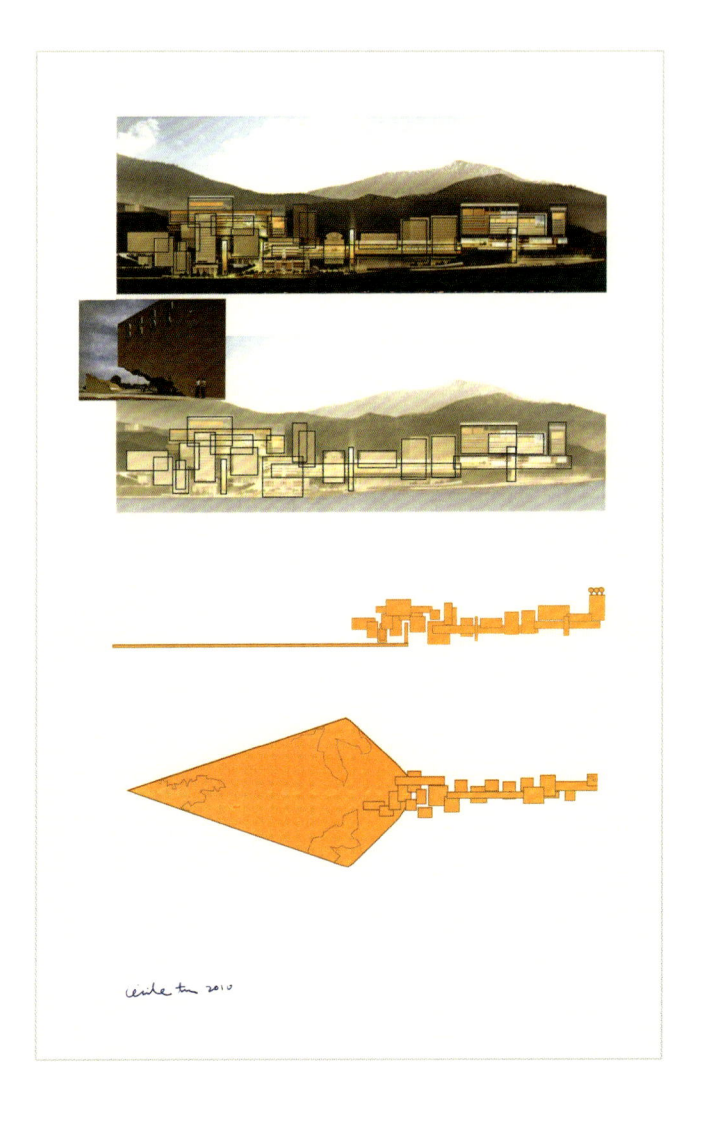

1   Cécile Tu Papers, HKUA

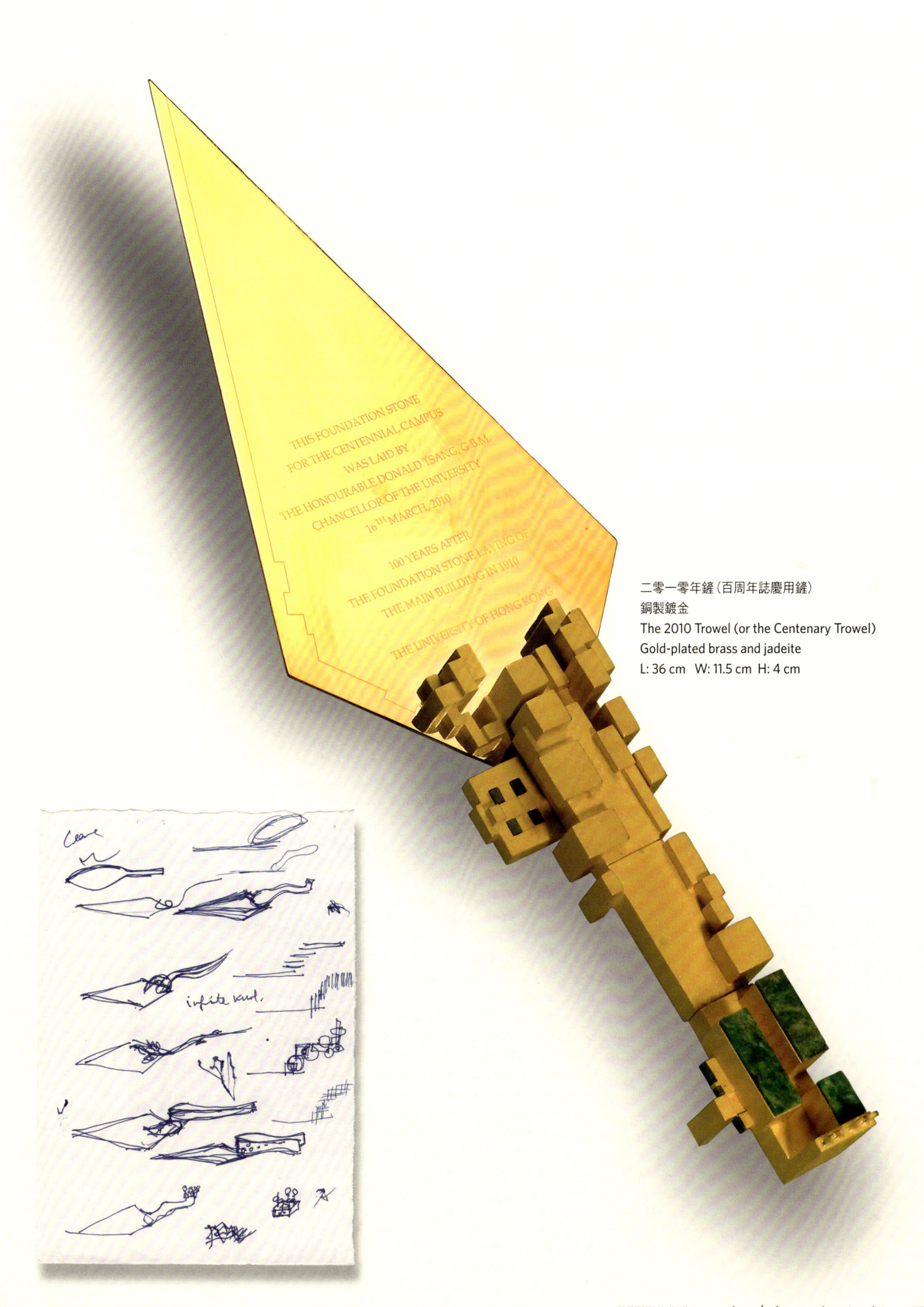

二零一零年鏟（百周年誌慶用鏟）
銅製鍍金
The 2010 Trowel (or the Centenary Trowel)
Gold-plated brass and jadeite
L: 36 cm   W: 11.5 cm   H: 4 cm

HKU Memories | from the Archives

大學印章
The University Seal

大學印章是二次大戰及日治時期後唯一倖存的港大最高權力象徵。印章紋飾包括校盾及校訓，'香港大學'英文字樣圍成圓框。首枚印章為臨時製造。本章自一九一三年起沿用至今，其印鑑廣見於大學的重要文件。

依據一九一一年大學條例，香港大學是'一個永久延續並備有法團印章的政治體及法團'。大學條例章程說明，凡依據英國法律及香港特別行政區基本法所訂立的合約，都必須附有港大印章確立為憑。合約如蓋上大學法團印章，並由大學授權人士簽署及加簽，即當作已妥為簽立，具有法律約束力。[1]

The University Seal is the only symbol of the University's authority to have survived World War II and the Japanese Occupation. The design of the Seal comprises the University shield and motto set in a circle with the name of 'The University of Hong Kong'. The first seal was a temporary stamp. This Seal was made in 1913 and continues to be used today on all important documents.

When the University was established in 1911, it was duly constituted as 'one body politic and corporate with perpetual succession and a common seal'. The University of Hong Kong Ordinance states that any instrument sealed and signed on behalf of the University by a member of the senior management team and countersigned by the Registrar may be executed fully 'under the seal'.[1]

1 *University of Hong Kong Ordinance*, Amended 22 of 1992 s.3.

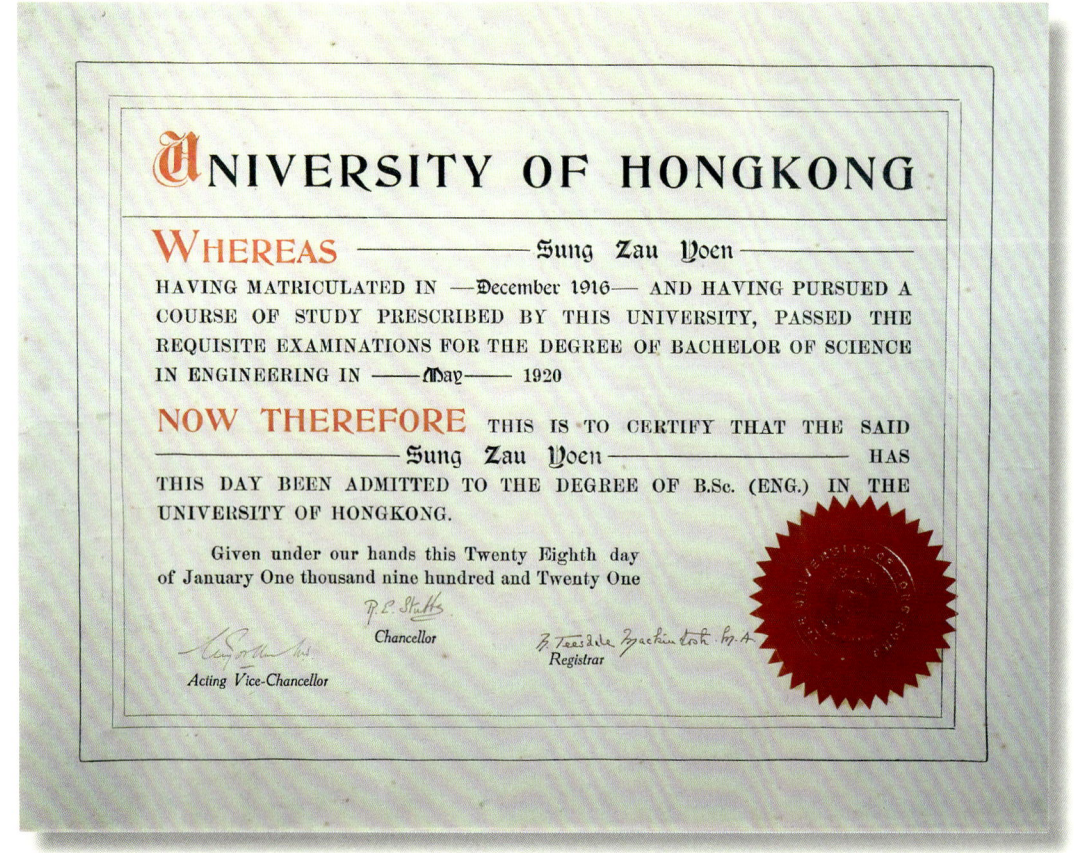

沈肇淵理學士（工程）畢業證書
一九二一年一月二十八日
Bachelor of Science (Engineering) degree certificate awarded to Sung Zau Yoen [Shen Zhaoyuan]
Dated 28th January 1921

這是香港大學現存最早的蓋大學印章工程學院文憑
This is the earliest known B.Sc. (Eng) degree certificate in the University's collections complete with the imprint of the University Seal.

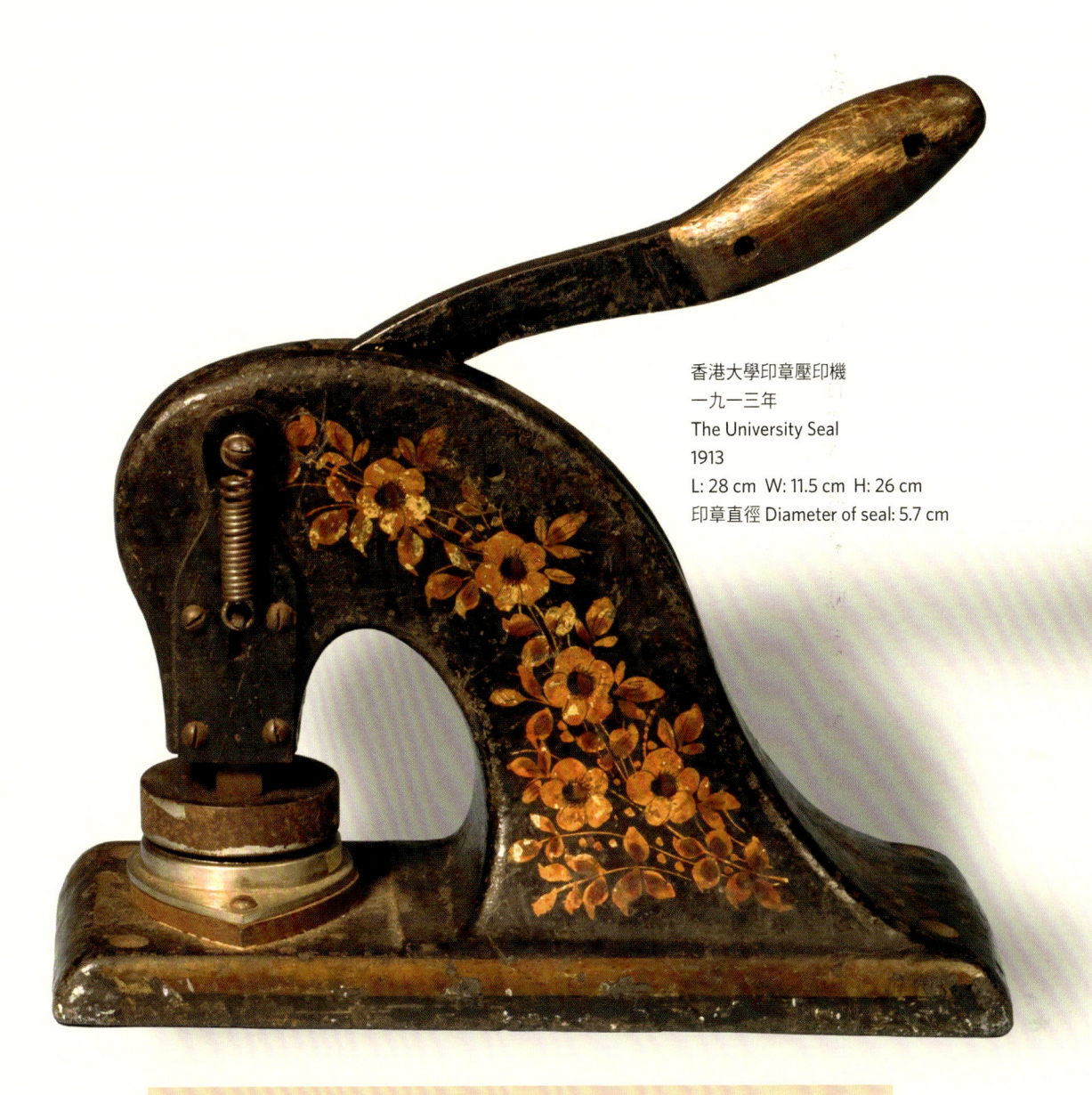

香港大學印章壓印機
一九一三年
The University Seal
1913
L: 28 cm W: 11.5 cm H: 26 cm
印章直徑 Diameter of seal: 5.7 cm

印章可以保存下來，全賴港大病理學系教授羅拔臣的功勞。戰爭爆發時他從手壓印機拆下印章，交給英軍服務團送往重慶保管，後移至英國倫敦；印機則藏於何東機械實驗所。戰後印章從英國運返港大，與一直秘藏的手壓印機重組應用。日治時期羅拔臣被軟禁，至一九四二年逝世。

At the outbreak of war in 1941, the cut-steel dies were detached from the iron hand press and given to Professor R. C. Robertson of Pathology, for safe-keeping until they were collected by an agent of the British Army Aid Group who transported them to Chongqing. From there they were sent to London where they remained until the conclusion of the war. The iron hand press was hidden in the Ho Tung Engineering Workshop until after the war when the dies were returned to Hong Kong and reunited with the press. Professor Robertson was put under house arrest during the Japanese occupation and committed suicide in 1942.

祝賀詞
Congratulatory messages

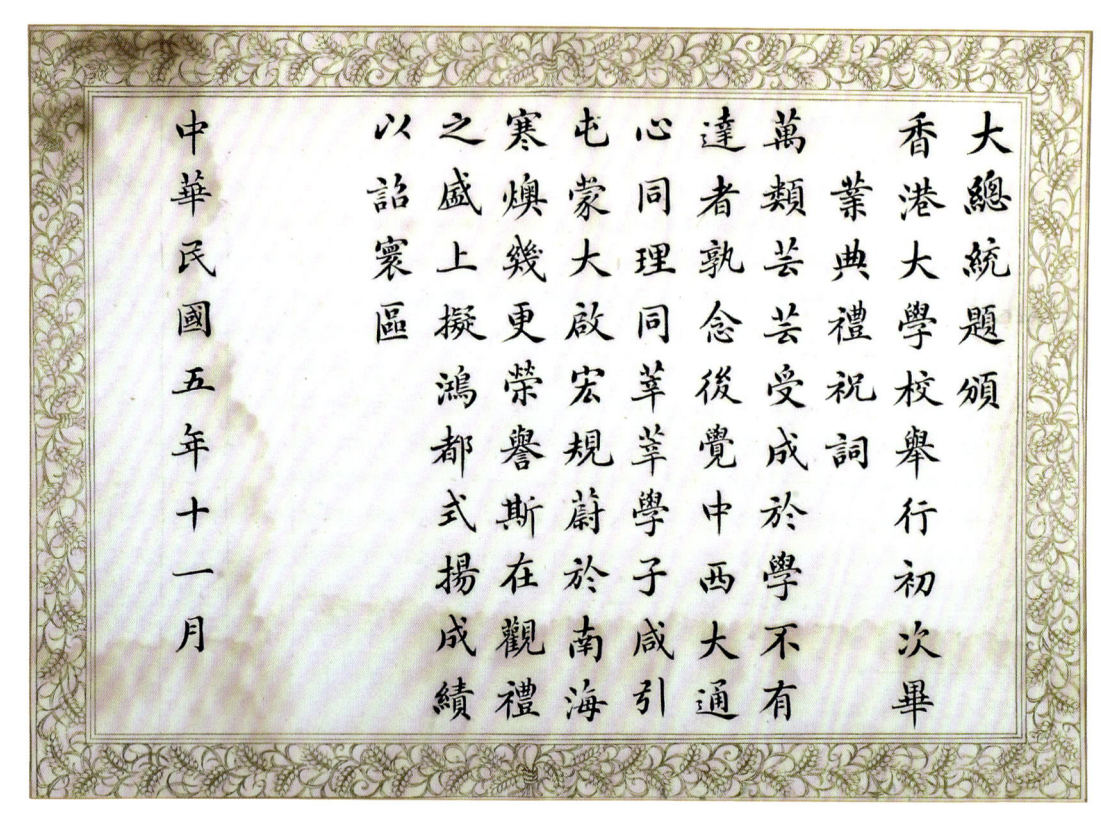

大總統題頒
香港大學校舉行初次畢
業典禮祝詞
萬類芸芸受成於學不有
達者孰念後覺中西大通
心同理同莘莘學子咸引
屯蒙大啟宏規蔚於南海
寒燠幾更榮譽斯在觀禮
之盛上擬鴻都式揚成績
以詔寰區

中華民國五年十一月

中華民國大總統黎元洪題頒香港大學校舉行初次畢業典禮祝詞
一九一六年十一月
Message from His Excellency Li Yuanhong, President of the Republic of China on the occasion of the first congregation for conferring degrees
November 1916
H: 36 cm W: 49 cm

All types of men are here; their gifts diverse:
Plant growths oft mingle, each stem has its root.

Each scholar's competent; his learning show complete,
A boon received through course of study meet.

Were not your teachers versed in wisdom's lore.
Who could awake young manhood's mind to soar?

China and Western lands have now one aim,
One thought and purpose; learning to acclaim.

May scholars throng your portals, there to seek
Training and strength of mind as plants, when weak,
Are trained to grow and thrive.

Your methods, wise and clear, are seen to be
Marks of this learning by the Southern Sea.

Brief through the course of our years,
Achieved is your glorious fame.

Your status is seen to be great
As the Hung To School of Hon days.

Your praises are published to-day,
They will surely be known through the world.

Translation by D. T. W. Pearce in 1916
(*Growing with Hong Kong*, p.72)

Educational institutions have mushroomed throughout Europe and Asia. In China, the idea of education originated with Situ, while in the West its origins can be traced to the ancient Greek cities of Sparta and Athens.

I once studied the history of the education system in the West, where training begins in elementary school and continues to university. The curriculum is well structured, and somewhat parallel with that described in the Xueji [Record of Education] of the Liji, [Book of Rites] in China.

In fact, the intention of educating the younger generation exists everywhere, despite differences in state policies and customs. Great Britain has long traded with China and has accumulated substantial wealth. Through her own universities, she supports education and has therefore been able to continuously cultivate great talent.

A few years ago, Hong Kong founded its very first university to nurture Chinese professionals. The first cohort of students has now completed their studies and their graduation ceremony is certainly a grand occasion.

As the Civil Governor of Guangdong province, I am delighted that talented individuals are valued, as trained personnel play a crucial role in strengthening our nation in various fields such as literature, art and technology.

Universities have already been established in the Chinese capital, but there are none yet in the southeast of the country. Now that the nation has entered a new post-revolutionary era, and the civil war will soon end, it is time that we plan for a better education system and promote the arts and humanities.

Fortunately, the British government has taken the initiative to establish a university in Hong Kong, and train many students from Guangdong province. Funding this significant project, the British have also hired talented personnel to instruct our promising youths. It is a great gesture of friendship that Great Britain has made in doing so.

In the near future, new institutions in southeast China will follow the example of Hong Kong. I hope that the Chinese people, our friends and graduands will not forget the generosity of the British government. Henceforth, we can consolidate the good and peaceful relations between our two nations.

On this momentous occasion, I would like to express the British government's and my own wish to exhort our graduands to carry on the principle of education and foster more able individuals.

廣東省長朱慶瀾香港大學第一次授給學位頌辭
一九一六年十二月十四日
鈐印：廣東省長
馮平山圖書館善本書室藏品
Congratulatory message from His Excellency Chu Ching-lan, Civil Governor of Guangdong province on the occasion of the first congregation for conferring degrees
14th December 1916
Seal: The Civil Governor of Guangdong province
H: 37 cm W: 51 cm unframed /
H: 50 cm W: 66 cm framed
Rare Books Room, Fung Ping Shan Library, University Libraries

金文泰爵士畫像
Portrait of Sir Cecil Clementi

一九三零年香港大學委託俄羅斯藝術家安納托爾·斯托為港督任期即將屆滿的金文泰爵士繪畫肖像。卸任港督後，金文泰隨即出任海峽殖民地（包括新加坡）總督及馬來亞高級專員。同年六月二十三日《海峽時報》（第10頁）報導畫像完成的消息，並提到金文泰希望藝術家多畫一幅讓他贈送家人。第二次繪畫的畫像現懸掛於倫敦綢布商人同業公會內，紀念金文泰於一九四零年擔任該會主席。第三幅畫像由新加坡維多利亞紀念廳於一九四八年委託斯托繪畫，翌年完成。

The portrait of Sir Cecil Clementi was commissioned by the University of Hong Kong and painted by the Russian artist Anatole Shister in 1930, the year in which Clementi took up his last colonial appointment as Governor and Commander-in-Chief of the Straits Settlements (including Singapore), and High Commissioner for the Malay States. A report in *The Straits Times* dated 23rd June 1930 (p. 10) announced the completion of the portrait, and Clementi's desire for the artist to paint a copy for his family. That version now hangs in the Mercer's Guild Hall in London, as Clementi became Master of the Mercer's Company in 1940. A third version of the portrait, also painted by Shister, was commissioned in 1948 for Singapore's Victoria Memorial Hall and completed in 1949.

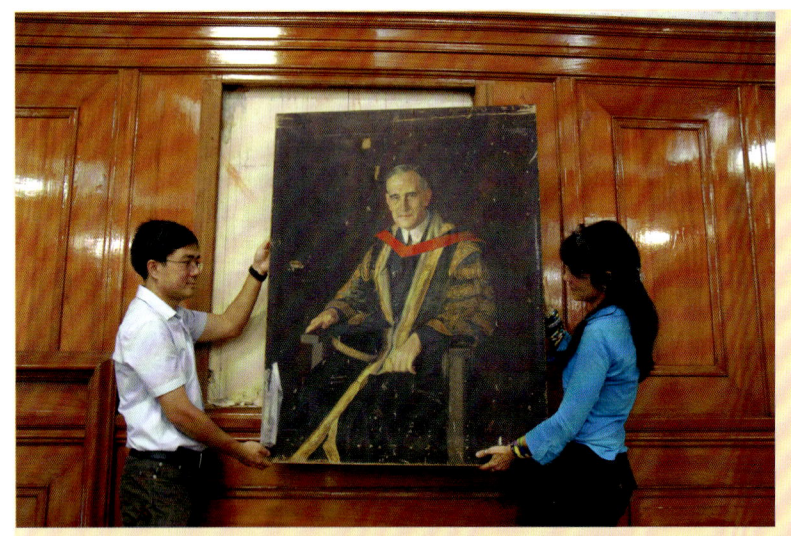

二零一一年，復修專家 Dawne Steele Pullman（右）及博物館職員合力取下懸掛於大禮堂走廊牆上的金文泰畫像
The Clementi portrait being removed from the wall of the gallery in Loke Yew Hall in 2011 by Dawne Steele Pullman and Chung Ma of the Museum

香港大學校報《交流》（第15頁）一九七五年一月號報導新加坡輔政司於一九四八年一月來函，希望借金文泰爵士的畫像讓斯托參考。'斯托先生收到畫像後感到不安，因畫作在日本侵占香港時損毀，留下彈孔和刀痕。他認為修復舊作耗費時間和金錢，故將畫作送還大學。翌年四月，畫作裝掛於陸佑堂（舊稱大禮堂）樓座。'斯托所繪相信是參照了金文泰家人收藏、一九四九年初由輔政司麥克倫爵士夫人從英國帶回亞洲的畫像。《海峽時報》（第1頁）於一九四九年三月十五日報導，斯托為了讓不同版本的畫像各具特色，他將第三次繪畫的肖像按原作縮小一吋。

It was reported in the January 1975 issue of the University's *Interflow* (p. 15), that the Colonial Secretary of Singapore wrote to borrow the painting in January 1948 for Shister to copy. 'Mr Shister upon receiving it was perturbed to see the condition it is in after its ill-treatment [having sustained damage from bullet holes and a bayonet cut during the Japanese occupation], and concluded that it would be a waste of time and money to attempt to touch it up. The painting was returned to the University in April 1949, and was fixed onto the wall in the balcony of the Loke Yew Hall.' It is believed that Shister instead copied the Clementi family's version, which was brought from England in early 1949 by Mrs. P. A. B. McKerron, the wife of the Colonial Secretary at the time. The portrait was reported in *The Straits Times* (15th March 1949, p. 1) as having been completed by Shister who made it an inch smaller than the copied version in order that they might be distinguished from one another.

金文泰爵士畫像的復修
Restoration of the Clementi Portrait

一九三零年本畫像懸掛在本部大樓大禮堂（陸佑堂）圓形大廳內校監座椅背後的位置，為第二次世界大戰以前掛於大禮堂而唯一倖存的畫像。它於日治時期獲匿名人士秘密收起，至戰後回歸港大時，已嚴重損毀，畫面留下刺刀和子彈的痕跡。一九五零年代初油畫給鑲進較小的畫框，並改掛在大禮堂唱詩班廂席的牆上。

In 1930, the portrait of Sir Cecil Clementi hung in the rotunda of the Great Hall, behind the Chancellor's Chair. It is the only surviving portrait of the pre-war period that hung in the Great Hall. It survived the Japanese occupation through the efforts of unnamed individuals, and was returned to the University after the war. It was badly damaged. In the early 1950s it was put onto a smaller set of stretchers and set into the wall of the gallery in the Great Hall.

為慶祝港大百周年誌慶，港大檔案中心特聘國際美術復修專家 Dawne Steele Pullman 回復畫像的本來面目，為期六星期的工作包括重新為畫作裝框，恢復了畫像原本較大的畫面，清除表面因污漬和霉菌引起的垢層和損壞，並填補十一個較大的孔，以及修復逾三百剝油處。畫面上的穿孔是刺刀割過和子彈穿過留下的痕跡，以往嘗試的復修反令畫作更破損，導致這次修復工作難度更高。

As part of the Centenary Celebrations, the Archives arranged for the portrait to be restored by an international fine art conservator, Dawne Steele Pullman. Over a period of six weeks, it was restretched and restored to its original larger size, cleaned of old varnish and damage caused by mould and mildew. Eleven major holes were repaired and over 300 instances of paint loss replaced. Some of the holes are rumoured to have been caused by knife, bayonet or bullet. Earlier attempts to repair the painting caused further damage and were the most difficult part of the restoration process.

二次大戰以前大禮堂校監座椅背後掛著金文泰畫像
The Great Hall before the war showing Clementi's portrait hanging above the Chancellor's chair

畫像修復前
The portrait before restoration

畫家款
The artist's signature
on the portrait

畫像修復後
The portrait after restoration

金文泰爵士畫像
安納托爾・斯托作
一九三零年
油彩
Portrait of Sir Cecil Clementi
Anatole Shister
1930
Oil on canvas
H: 128.3 cm   W: 97.8 cm

大學權杖
The University Mace

大學權杖舊稱校長權杖，主要用於畢業禮、名譽博士學位頒授典禮等重要場合，作為引領教職員出場。

原來權杖由何福（一八六三至一九二六年）出資鑄造，香港巴馬丹拿建築師樓 H. W. Bird 設計，英國謝菲爾德市皇室御用銀匠 Mappin and Webb 製造。一九一六年製成，因由英國運抵香港需時，延至一九一八年第二屆港大畢業禮時才首度使用。

一九四三年三月原來權杖曾於本部大樓圖書館漢口閱讀室展出，但日治時期已遺失。戰後大學重開時，校長賴廉士向校董會熱切陳詞募捐，得校董會成員梁燿熱心響應，於一九五一年捐贈本權杖仿製品（參看第176頁）。權杖上的校徽及校訓圖案均填琺瑯，四方杖身鑲有兩環共十六顆紅綠寶石，中間部份的雕刻紋飾，是新權杖獨有的設計。四杖面之一飾二次大戰後損毀至通頂的本部大樓，一面為致謝梁燿慷慨捐贈的題詞，一面為香港維港的景色，一面光素。權杖相當巨大（長1米、重8.5千克），持杖者必須強壯有力。最近的持杖者為生物科學院的生態與生物多樣性學系講座教授杜德俊。

The Mace is carried before the Officers of the University at every major ceremony, especially at the conferring of degrees and honorary degrees. It is sometimes referred to as the Chancellor's Mace as it is the most visible symbol of the authority of the University.

The original Mace was commissioned by Ho Fook (1863–1926), the brother of Sir Robert Ho Tung and Ho Kam Tong. It was designed by H. W. Bird, an architect with Palmer and Turner in Hong Kong, and made by Mappin and Webb Limited of the Royal Works at Sheffield in England. It was completed in 1916 but was first used at the Second Congregation of 1918 due to the time it took to ship from England.

The original Mace disappeared during the Japanese Occupation of World War II. It was last seen on display in the Hankow Room of the Library in the Main Building in March 1943. When the University re-opened Vice Chancellor Sir Lindsay Ride made an impassioned speech to the Court regarding the Mace to which Leung Yew responded by commissioning a replacement in 1951, which is the one used today. (See page 176). This Mace is a copy of the original. The University's shield and motto are decorated in enamel work, the heft inlaid with cabochons of green and red jewels in the bands above and below the lozenges. The current Mace differs from the original in having one panel decorated with the damaged and roofless Main Building, as it looked after the war, and an inscription of thanks to Leung Yew on another. A third panel has an image of Hong Kong harbour, while a fourth is empty. Because of its great size (1 metre in length) and weight (8.5 kgs), the Mace-bearer is always a faculty member of large stature. It is currently carried by David Dudgeon, Chair Professor of Ecology and Biodiversity, School of Biological Sciences.

何福與家人合照
約一九一二年
Ho Fook and his family
c. 1912

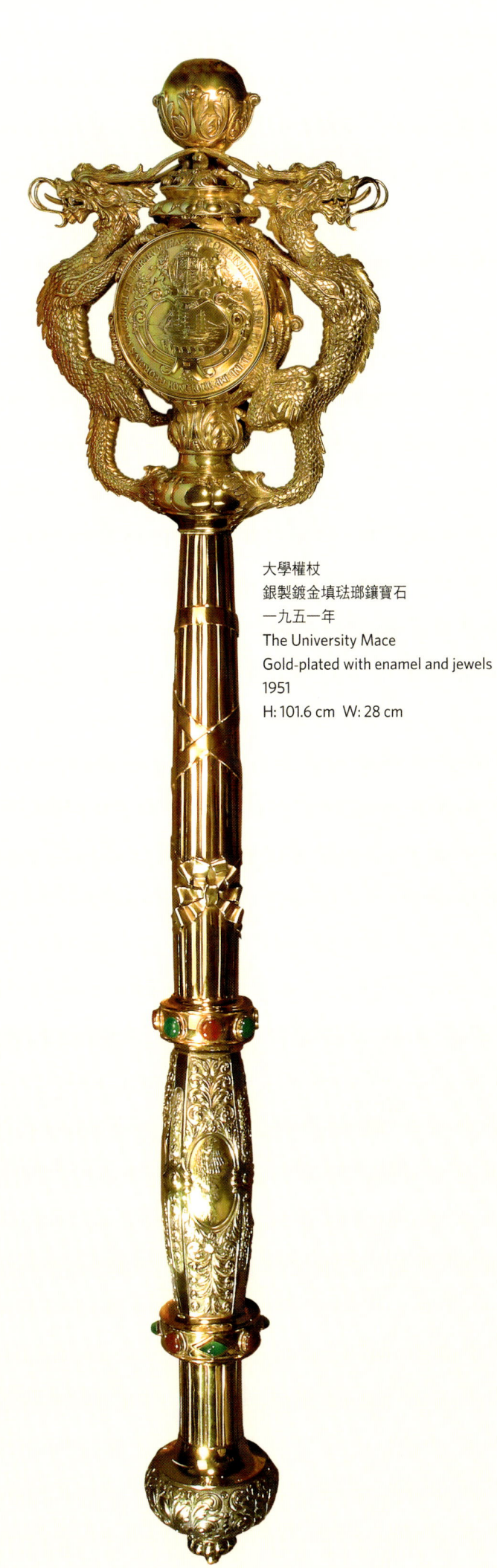

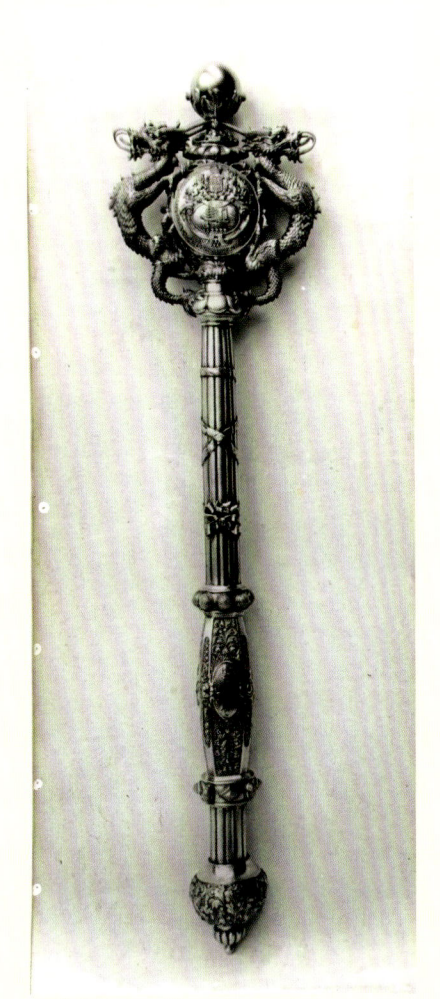

大學權杖
銀製鍍金填琺瑯鑲寶石
一九五一年
The University Mace
Gold-plated with enamel and jewels
1951
H: 101.6 cm W: 28 cm

原來大學權杖存照
Photograph of the Original Mace
H: 104 cm W: 35.7 cm

HKU Memories | from the Archives 63

香港大學與共濟會
The University and the Freemasons

共濟會是一個兄弟會組織，宣揚博愛美德的精神，鼓勵會員學習組織的秘密儀式，幫助社會上有需要的人士，特別是貧窮、醫療、教育方面的問題。共濟會只是一個聯盟，並沒有跟隨任何一個指定的信仰，會內禁談政治。傳統上共濟會只歡迎男士加入，提出申請入會必須經委員會批准。

若干共濟會會員與香港大學的創校及發展息息相關，這部份的大學歷史並不廣為人知。首先是麼地爵士本身為該會導師，其子則擔任孟買分會總導師。麼地早期的生意伙伴遮打爵士（一八四六至一九二六年）為亞美利亞裔，他出生於印度加爾各答。遮打亦於一八八二年成為香港及華南的分區總導師，直至一九一一年為止。遮打做生意長袖善舞，曾於一八八六年幫助白文信創立乳牛場，一八八九年更成立置地公司，並監督翌年開始的中環海旁填海計畫。

香港首座共濟會會所'雍仁會館'，英文名稱以泄蘭伯爵二世湯姆斯命名，一八四四至一八七零年間他出任英格蘭分支共濟會總部的總導師。原館建於一八四六年，一八六五年在泄蘭街建成較大的新館，一九四四年二戰期間遭美軍炮彈炸毀，戰後在中環半山堅尼地道重建，由利安建築師樓負責興建，該公司並建造了香港大學的本部大樓、馮平山圖書館。

現今'雍仁會館'仍是香港共濟會的總部，供各分會及團組會員聚會之用。

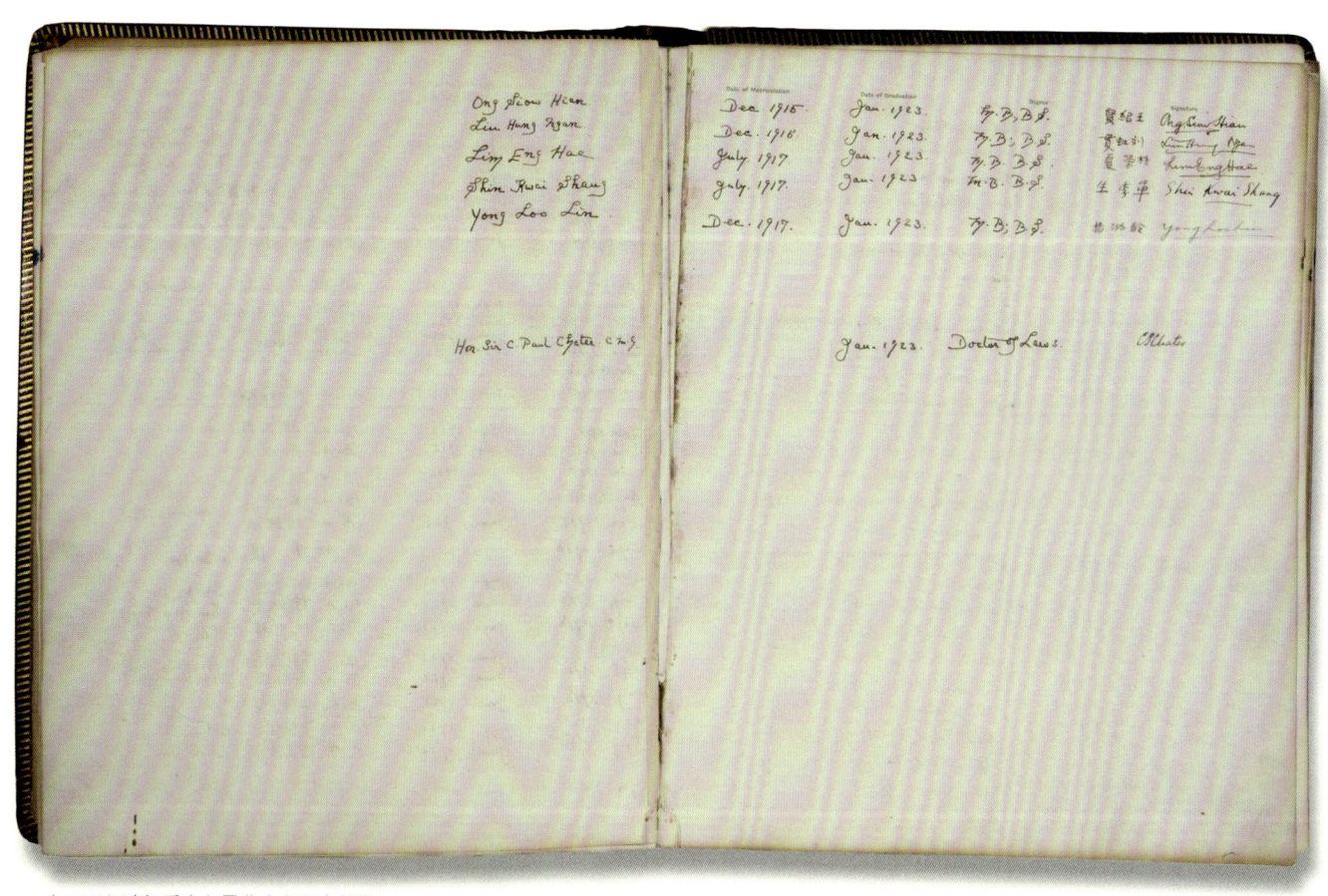

一九二三年遮打爵士在畢業生名冊上簽署
他是一九一二年香港大學捐贈基金的司庫。
Sir Paul Chater's signature in the Register of Graduates, 1923
Chater was Treasurer of the Hong Kong University Endowment Fund in 1912.

The Freemasons, or Masons, are a benevolent fraternity whose aims are to improve the moral character of their members through the study of their secret rites, and to benefit society through their charitable work, bringing relief to the poor and infirm, and promoting education for all. They have no religious or political affiliations and consider themselves a universal brotherhood. Traditionally its lodges are open only to men upon completion of a petition and approval by the lodge committee.

One of the lesser known parts of the University's history is the role of individual Freemasons in the founding and development of the University. These included Sir Hormusjee Naorojee Mody, who was a Master Mason, and his son who was Grand Master of a lodge in Bombay. Sir Mody's former business partner was Sir Catchick Paul Chater (1846–1926), who was of Armenian descent born in Calcutta. Chater was made District Grand Master of Hongkong and South China in 1882, a position that he held until 1911. A successful businessman, he helped Patrick Manson establish the Dairy Farm in 1886 and he established Hongkong Land in 1889 to oversee the Praya Reclamation Scheme of the following year.

The first Masonic Hall in Hong Kong was named after Thomas, the Second Earl of Zetland, The Grand Master of the United Grand Lodge in England from 1844 to 1870. Originally built in 1846, Zetland Hall was replaced in 1865 by a grander building on Zetland Street in Central. This building was destroyed by American bombing in 1944 during the Japanese occupation of Hong Kong. It was re-built after the war on Kennedy Road in Central Mid-levels by Leigh & Orange, the architects responsible for the Main Building and the Fung Ping Shan Library.

Zetland Hall today remains the centre of Freemasonry in Hong Kong and is open to all members of a Masonic Lodge, Chapter, or affiliated brotherhood to use.

一九四四年遭美軍炸毀的雍仁會館
Zetland Hall after the American bombing of 1944

位於中環泄蘭街的雍仁會館
相片由雍仁會館信託會提供
Zetland Hall in Zetland Street, Central
Photographs by permission of the Zetland Hall Trustees

大學分會
The University Lodge of Hong Kong

大學分會於一九一三年成立，一九二一年易名香港大學3666團。創會成員包括校董會及校務委員會成員何啟爵士，他亦是共濟會導師；校董會及校務委會員成員韋寶珊爵士；以及醫學院院長奇力加教授。一九一四年，首屆'遮打共濟會獎學金'在香港大學設立，惠澤學子。之後五十年內另頒發了九個獎學金。[1]

The University Lodge was founded in 1913. In 1921, its name was changed to University of Hong Kong Chapter No. 3666. Among the founding members were Sir Kai Ho Kai, who was a Master Mason and member of the University's Court and Council, the Honorable Wei Yuk, also a member of Court and Council, and Professor Francis Clark, Dean of Medicine. Through the Chater Masonic Scholarship Fund, the Freemasons awarded bursaries to students, the first of which was awarded in 1914. A further nine scholarships were awarded over the next fifty years.[1]

大學分會徽章 (3666團)
金、琺瑯彩
管沛德博士捐贈
University Lodge Medal (No. 3666)
Gold and enamel
H: 10 cm W: 3.7 cm
Gift of Dr Peter Cunich

[1] 如欲進一步了解共濟會在遠東地區及香港的組織和歷史，可參考：
For more on the history of the Masonic Orders in the Far East and Hong Kong see:
Christopher Haffner, *The Craft in the East* (Aberdeen, Hong Kong, Libra Press, 1977)

共濟會徽章
The Masonic Medals

這些共濟會徽章為大學物理系教授 William Faid 之物，他曾任盧吉堂舍監、文理學院院長。徽章象徵共濟會會規，並顯示他身兼共濟會導師、大學分會會員、遮打分會創辦會員等身份。一九四一年二次大戰爆發時，本部大樓設立臨時醫院，他出任院長照顧傷員，後來他和任教數學的妻子雙雙被拘留在赤柱監獄，一九四四年於獄中一次維修屋頂時不慎滑倒墜地，傷重逝世。

The Masonic Medals symbolise the Masonic order, and indicate the owner to be a Master Mason, member of the University Lodge, and a founding member of the Paul Chater Lodge. These Jewels belonged to William Faid, a professor of physics, who was also Warden of Lugard Hall and Dean of Arts and Sciences when the two were a single faculty. When war broke out in December 1941, he was Lay Superintendent of the temporary hospital set up in the Main Building. Both he and his wife, Jean, who taught mathematics at the University, were interred in Stanley Prison Camp, where he died after falling from a roof that he was repairing in 1944.

徽章的圖案富象徵意義，正方形代表恪守道德，指南針代表自我節制，眼睛是上帝之眼，守望我們的所思所行；兩個交叉十字架代表兩個學科：道德和科學，意指人類不斷追求真理，了解上帝創造世界萬物的奧妙。

Among the symbols of the Masonic order indicated by the Jewels are the square and compass, which represent living a moral life and having control over one's actions. The eye represents the all-seeing eye of the Higher Power (or of one's own God), while the crossed keys represent the Two Sciences: Moral Science and Physical Science, or the Knowledge that is sought by those interested in the 'Plan of the Great Architect'.

約一九二四年 William Faid 抵港後不久拍攝
William Faid shortly after his arrival in Hong Kong, c. 1924

約一九四一年二次大戰前 William Faid 留影
William Faid c. 1941 shortly before the outbreak of war

大學分會徽章
一九三五至一九三六年
金、琺瑯彩
管沛德博士捐贈
Medal for University of Hong Kong Chapter
1935-1936
Gold and enamel
H: 10 cm W: 4 cm
Gift of Dr Peter Cunich

創會者徽章：遮打分會任命導師（5391團）
金、琺瑯彩
管沛德博士捐贈
Medal of Founder: The Paul Chater Lodge of
Installed Masters (No. 5391)
Gold and enamel
H: 10 cm W: 3.5 cm
Gift of Dr Peter Cunich

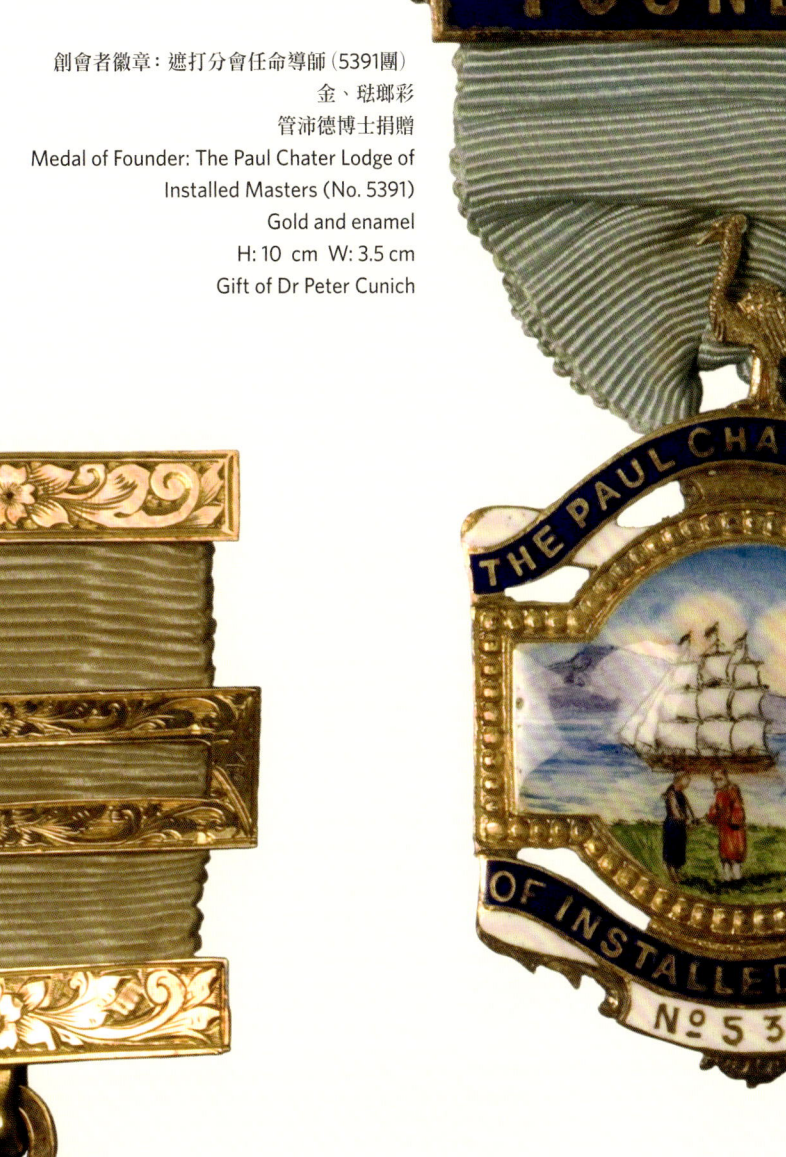

共濟會總導師徽章
金、琺瑯彩
管沛德博士捐贈
Medal for Master Mason
Gold and enamel
H: 10 cm W: 3.3 cm
Gift of Dr Peter Cunich

HKU Memories | from the Archives   69

世界大戰服務勳章
Medals from the Great War

William Faid 教授來港前曾於一次大戰期間服役，故早已受封兩枚勳章。英國戰爭勳章是頒給一九一四年八月五日至一九一八年十一月十一日期間的軍員。一九一九年訂定勳章一面刻英皇佐治五世的側照，另一面刻聖佐治的馬上英姿。圖案所見聖佐治配備短劍，象徵他以身體和精神兩股力量戰勝普魯士人；馬匹踏在普魯士人的盾牌上，勝利的光輝照射在骷髏和交叉骨頭上。

勝利勳章為鍍金銅質，正面刻勝利女神像，背面刻字'一九一四至一九一九年偉大的文明之戰'。服務及勝利二勳章常與一九一四年或一九一四至一五年的嘉許星章一起頒發。三枚勳章並分別以英國《每日鏡報》連載漫畫故事的主人翁'狗爸爸'、'企鵝媽媽'、'白兔小孩'作為暱稱。

一九一四至一九一八年世界大戰服務軍員的英國戰爭勳章
銀製
管沛德博士捐贈
British War Medal for service
in the Great War of 1914–1918
Silver
勳章 Medal H: 5.7 cm W: 3.7 cm
綬帶 Ribbon L: 22 cm W: 3 cm
Gift of Dr Peter Cunich

Professor William Faid served in World War I before he came to Hong Kong and was awarded two medals. The British War Medal was awarded to all those who served in the British or Imperial forces between 5th August of 1914 and 11th November of 1918. It was approved in 1919 and has the profile of King George V on the obverse and St George on the reverse. St George is naked on horseback and armed with a short sword symbolizing physical and mental strength over the Prussians. The horse is trampling on the Prussian shield and skull and cross bones, while the sun of victory shines over them.

The Victory Medal is made from gold-plated bronze. The Victory Medal features the figure of winged Victory on the obverse and inscribed with 'The Great War for Civilisation 1914–1919' on the reverse. The two medals were always awarded together, often along with a 1914 or 1914–15 Star. The three medals are affectionately referred to as 'Pip, Squeak, and Wilfred'.

勝利勳章
金製
管沛德博士捐贈
Victory Medal
Gold
勳章 Medal Diam: 3.5 cm
綬帶 Ribbon L: 21.8 cm W: 3.7 cm
Gift of Dr Peter Cunich

HKU Memories | from the Archives

何東爵士
Sir Robert Ho Tung

何東爵士（一八六二至一九五六年）一八七八年畢業於香港中央書院（今皇仁書院），隨即加入廣州粵海關工作，後在香港怡和洋行任職，並升為買辦之首。他是歐亞混血兒，但以中國人自居，是一位熱心公益的大企業家，在殖民地政府與華人社會兼享舉足輕重的地位。

一九一五年何東慷慨捐獻五萬元予港大作教學用途，包括資助一個臨床外科教授職位。隨著繼任盧吉的港督梅含理呼籲後，他額外捐款十萬元予香港大學捐贈基金。一九二一年再向財政緊絀的大學捐建何東機械實驗所。一九一六年獲香港大學頒授名譽法學博士。

何東的女兒何艾齡、何綺華為第二任夫人張靜蓉所生，亦是港大最早收錄的女生。一九二五年何艾齡成為首位香港出生的女畢業生，一九二六年何綺華亦成為首位女醫科畢業生。一九二三年香港大學聯會邀請孫中山到大禮堂發表歷史性演講，何東的兒子何世儉為該會主席（參看第12頁）。

戰後何東再捐贈一百萬元予大學，用作興建女生宿舍何東夫人紀念堂，以紀念一九四三年逝世的元配夫人麥秀英。

Sir Robert Ho Tung (1862–1956) was educated at Central School (Queen's College) and graduated in 1878. After working for the Chinese Imperial Maritime Customs in Guangzhou, he returned to Hong Kong and entered Jardine's, eventually becoming Head Compradore. Although Eurasian, he considered himself Chinese and as a prominent businessman and philanthropist he enjoyed equal influence in the colonial government and the local community.

Ho Tung was a generous supporter of the University donating $50,000 in 1915 towards teaching, including a professorship in Clinical Surgery. Following a personal appeal from Sir Henry May, who succeeded Lugard as Governor of Hong Kong, Ho Tung gave an additional $100,000 for the general endowment. In 1921 he made a donation of $100,000 to the struggling University for an engineering laboratory. The University awarded him an honorary Doctorate of Laws in 1916.

Sir Robert's daughters by his second wife, Clara, Irene Ho Tung (Irene Cheng) and Eva Ho Tung were among the earliest female students admitted into the University. Irene was the first Hong Kong-born woman to graduate in 1925, and her sister Eva was the earliest woman medical graduate in 1926. During the war Eva assisted at the relief hospital that was set up at the University. Ho Tung's son Edward was President of the University Union when it invited Sun Yat-sen to deliver his historic speech in the Great Hall in 1923 (see page 12).

Following the end of the war Sir Robert gave an additional $1 million to the University for the building of Lady Ho Tung Hall in memory of his first wife Margaret, who died in 1943.

何東爵士銅像
陳錫鈞（一八九三至一九五一年）作
一九三零或四零年代
Sir Robert Ho Tung
Chan Shek-kwan (Goon T. Chan)
(1893–1951)
Bronze
1930s or 1940s
H: 59 cm W: 50 cm

陳錫鈞（一八九三至一九五一年）為廣東台山人，是第一代到海外留學的華人雕塑家。一九零七年他到加拿大蒙特利爾學習英文，一九一七至一九二八年間到蒙特利爾美術學校學習藝術及雕塑。畢業後憑獎學金資助到巴黎安東尼‧布爾德爾（一八六一至一九二九年）的工作室實習。一九三一年回國後，他任教於廣州市立美術學校雕塑系，並在廣東省立勤勤大學師範學院（華南師範大學前身）擔任教授。一九三七年日本侵華，他舉家遷往香港。

如其他早期中國雕塑家一樣，陳錫鈞努力嘗試在雕刻作品中融匯中西，以西方的技巧體現中國傳統藝術的精神。在香港時，他多次受委託參與藝術項目，並獲邀請與另外四名雕塑家製作南京中山陵孫中山紀念像。一九四一年日本侵占香港，他逃難到湛江市，一九四五年返回香港繼續藝術事業，直至一九五一年去世。

Chan Shek-kwan (1893–1951), also known as Goon T. Chan, was among the first generation of Chinese sculptors to study in the West. Originally from Taishan in Guangdong province, he initially traveled to Montreal, Canada to study English, later taking up fine art and sculpture at the School of Fine Arts, Montreal from 1917 to 1928. After graduating, Chan worked as an assistant to the French sculptor Antoine Bourdelle (1861–1929). He returned to China in 1931 and taught sculpture at the Guangzhou School of Fine Arts and became a professor at Xiang Qin University, a precursor to today's South China Normal University. When war broke out in China in 1937 he moved to Hong Kong with his family.

Chan was a prolific sculptor who experimented with combining ideas of traditional Chinese art with the techniques of Western sculpture. While he was in Hong Kong, Chan received many commissions and was selected as one of the sculptors for a statue of Dr Sun Yat-sen. When Hong Kong fell to the Japanese in 1941, he fled to the city of Zhanjiang in Guangdong returning to Hong Kong after the war in 1945. He remained here until his death in 1951.

何東爵士墨水筆座
Sir Robert Ho Tung Inkstand

二次大戰後，本部大樓進行擴建修葺，同時增設教務委員會、校董會、校務委員會三間會議室。並計劃訂製三套墨水筆座分別放於三室，較大的一套放在教務委員會室，兩套較小放在其餘兩室。後來因費用高昂，終於在一九五一年決定擱置。一九五六年四月享年九十三歲的何東爵士離世，為了紀念這位校董會的終生會員，大學決定訂製一套墨水筆座以茲紀念。

When the University re-opened following the war, the Main Building was restored, and expanded to include rooms for the University Senate, Court and Council. Originally, three inkstands were designed for these rooms: a larger one for the Senate Room and two smaller versions for the rooms intended for use by the Court and Council. The price for all three was considered prohibitively expensive and the idea was abandoned in 1951. However, following the death of Sir Robert Ho Tung, a lifelong member of the Court, in April 1956 at the age of 93, it was decided to have an inkstand made in his honour.

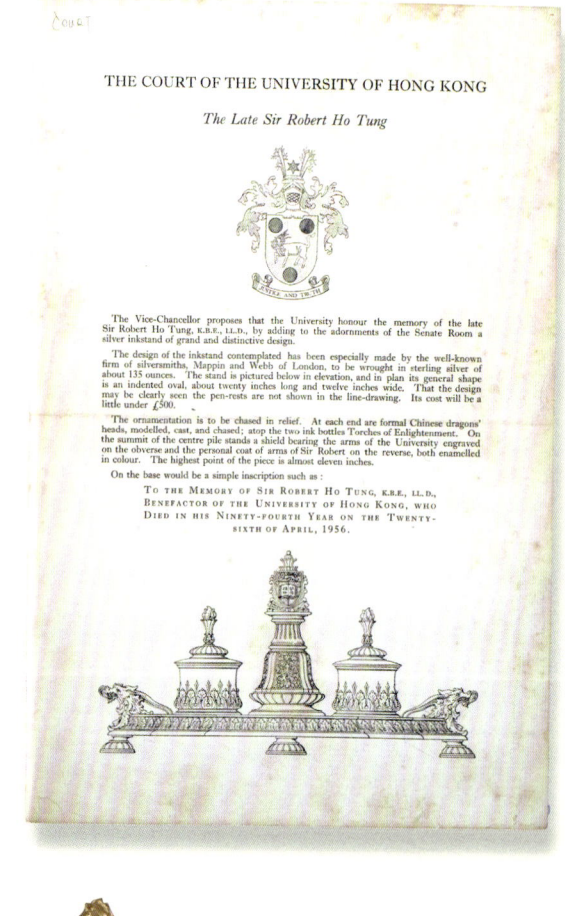

墨水筆座由英國銀匠 Mappin and Webb 製造，與大學權杖是同一商號的出品。筆座托盤左右兩端各鑲精雕龍首，猶如雙龍鎮守中央的高塔。高塔正面以琺瑯彩飾大學校徽、校訓，另一面飾何東爵士的徽號及格言'正義和真理'，兩旁的墨水瓶蓋頂飾火炬形鈕，意謂啟蒙知識，旁為筆架。原來的墨水筆早已失去，然而墨水筆座沿用至今。

The Inkstand was designed and made by Mappin and Webb, the same company that made the Mace. The ends are mounted with dragon heads guarding the tower, also known as a pile, in the centre. The pile is decorated in enamels with the University's shield and motto on one side, and Sir Robert Ho Tung's own shield and motto, 'Justice and Truth', on the other. The two inkwells are topped by a torch representing the flame of knowledge, with pen rests beside them. Although the original pens have been lost, the Inkstand continues to be used to this day.

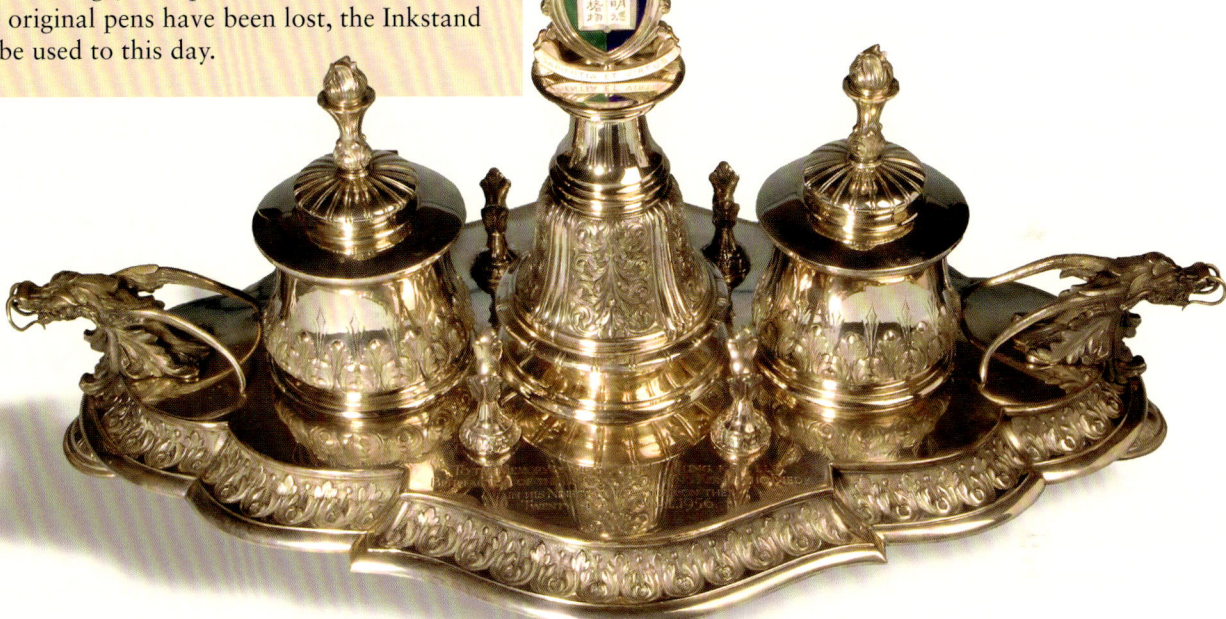

何東爵士墨水筆座
銀製
一九五六年
The Sir Robert Ho Tung Inkstand
Silver
1956
L: 51 cm W: 28 cm

HKU Memories | from the Archives   75

大學紋章
The University Coat of Arms, Letters Patent

香港大學為本地唯一擁有紋章的大學。紋章中的盾牌及校訓於一九一三年獲英國紋章院特許，其餘圖案則於一九八一年才提出申請專利，至一九八四年黃麗松出任校長後獲批准。本手寫證書即當年所發大學紋章專利特許證。[1]

一般的紋章包括四部份：盾牌、格言、頭盔、冠飾。大學紋章原來的圖案表達了對這所未來大學的眾多期望，其首要使命為融和中西，這都體現於盾牌及護盾物的設計。本紋章紅地獅紋代表英國國徽，正中一本翻開的書上寫著'明德格物'。盾牌以左綠右藍為地，違反了紋章的設計常則，應是刻意以綠藍色隱喻港大位於四面環海的香港島上。

中文校訓寫隸書'明德格物'出自儒家《禮記·大學》。'明德'就是自我修身顯德，'格物'指探究事物原理，盾牌下承拉丁文'Sapientia et Virtus'，意為'智慧和真誠'。[2]

一般紋章的盾牌上托武士頭盔，頂部飾冠冕，本章的冠冕以獅子及翻開書本為造型，與盾牌互相呼應。

兩側直立持盾的中國龍和英國獅，象徵中西融和，兩獸分別站在兩片不同草坡上，應是代表香港島，它們頸部戴著青玉環，以區別於香港殖民地區徽。

專利特許證下方有三個蠟印，分別代表嘉德(Garter)紋章官、克拉倫蘇克斯(Clarenceaux)紋章官、諾魯伊及阿爾斯特(Norroy and Ulster)紋章官，他們都是英國紋章院的高級紋章官，負責授予個人或機構紋章專利。高級紋章官下有紋章官、紋章官助理，這個體制於一四八四年三月二日成立，同日並獲英王李察三世頒發皇家御准特許。

> 本證書寫於犢皮紙上，為最上乘的羊皮紙。製造過程要把羊皮浸泡漂白，以幼細的浮石去垢磨光，製成質地柔韌的布料，用來抄寫重要文件，包括大學畢業文憑。時至今日，有些外國大學稱畢業證書為'羊皮紙'，便是基於這歷史淵源。只要妥善處理，羊皮紙可保存幾百年。
>
> The Letters Patent is on vellum, a fabric made from sheepskin that has been bleached and scraped repeatedly with pumice stones. Many important documents, including university diplomas, were written or transcribed onto vellum, which is why diplomas are often referred to colloquially as 'sheepskins'. With proper care and handling, vellum can last many hundreds of years.

---

[1] 關於大學紋章的詳情，可參考 David Wilmshurst 撰文 'The Meaning and Significance of the University's Coat of Arms'，載於 www.hku.hk/about/uid/background.html.

[2] 1912年校務委員會及校董會採納的校訓是拉丁'Auspicium Melioris Aevi'，中文翻譯為'美好年代的吉兆'，意指大學是新時代文藝興復之地，為東西方知識交流融洽之處。至一九三零年十月十七日，校務委員會議備忘錄提及當時的拉丁文校訓'Sapientia et Virtus'並未正式通過校董會的審批。因此校務委員會提議由校董會正式接納校訓，但大學檔案中心尚未發現紀錄證明校董會已正式承認新校訓。

香港大學紋章專利特許證
犢皮紙水墨設色
一九八四年十月三十日
The University Coat of Arms, Letters Patent
Ink and colour on vellum
30th October 1984
H: 40.4 cm W: 53 cm
Diameter of seals: 6.7 cm

HKU Memories | from the Archives

香港大學紋章

自上至下
嘉德紋章
克拉倫蘇克斯紋章
諾魯伊及阿爾斯特紋章

The University Coat of Arms, Seals
Diameter of seals: 6.7 cm

Top to bottom
Garter Principal King of Arms
Clarenceaux King of Arms
Norroy and Ulster King of Arms

The University of Hong Kong has the distinction of being the only university in Hong Kong to have a complete coat of arms assigned by the College of Arms in London. The shield and motto were granted in 1913 by the College of Arms, while the remaining components of a full coat of arms were applied for in 1981, under Vice-Chancellor Rayson Huang, and granted in 1984. This hand-illuminated manuscript shows the University's coat of arms (formally known as the armorial bearings) upon the letters patent issued by the College of Heralds in 1984.[1]

In heraldry, a coat of arms consists of four main elements: the shield, motto, helmet and crest and supporters. The original design of the coat of arms represents many of the aspirations for the future university, chief among them the balance of Chinese and Western elements. This is most evident in the design of the shield and its supporters. The lion against a red background refers to the coat of arms of England, while the open book at its centre is a symbol of learning used by many European universities. The juxtaposition of the colours blue and green is not ordinarily allowed in heraldry but permitted in this case to refer to the islands of Hong Kong and the surrounding sea.

The University's motto, '*ming de ge wu*', consists of two phrases taken from the Confucian classic, *The Great Learning*. The first two characters suggest the function of education 'to manifest virtue', while the second two characters mean 'to investigate things' (in the pursuit of knowledge). It is written in *lishu* or clerical script. The motto beneath the shield in Latin reads 'Sapientia et Virtus', meaning 'wisdom and virtue'. [2]

Above the shield is usually a knight's helmet topped with a crest. In this case, the crest is in the form of a lion with an open book, echoing the design of the shield.

The supporters again reflect the idea of balance between Western and Chinese elements. On the left is an upright Chinese dragon while on the other is an English lion. Each stands on a separate green mound, thought to represent the island of Hong Kong. They each wear a collar of green jade to distinguish them from the colonial arms of Hong Kong.

Three wax seals at the bottom of the Letters Patent show the individual coat of arms of the Garter Principal King of Arms, the Clarenceaux King of Arms, and the Norroy and Ulster King of Arms who have the right to confer full Armorial Bearings on people or institutions. Those who work under their signature are known as the Heralds and Pursuivants and have been an incorporated body since 2nd March 1484, when they were granted a Royal Charter by King Richard III.

---

1. For further information about the Coat of Arms refer to 'The Meaning and Significance of the University's Coat of Arms', by Dr David Wilmshurst, available at www.hku.hk/about/uid/background.html.
2. The original motto adopted by the Council and the Court in 1912 was 'Auspicium Melioris Aevi' (meaning 'An Omen of a Better Age'). This referred to the University as an omen of a new Age of Enlightenment in which Chinese and Western learning would be balanced. A memo in the minutes of the Council of 17th of October, 1930, states; 'that the present motto of the University 'Sapienta et Virtus' had never been formally sanctioned by the Court'. The Council recommended that the Court formally accept the change to the new motto but there is no evidence that it was ever accepted.

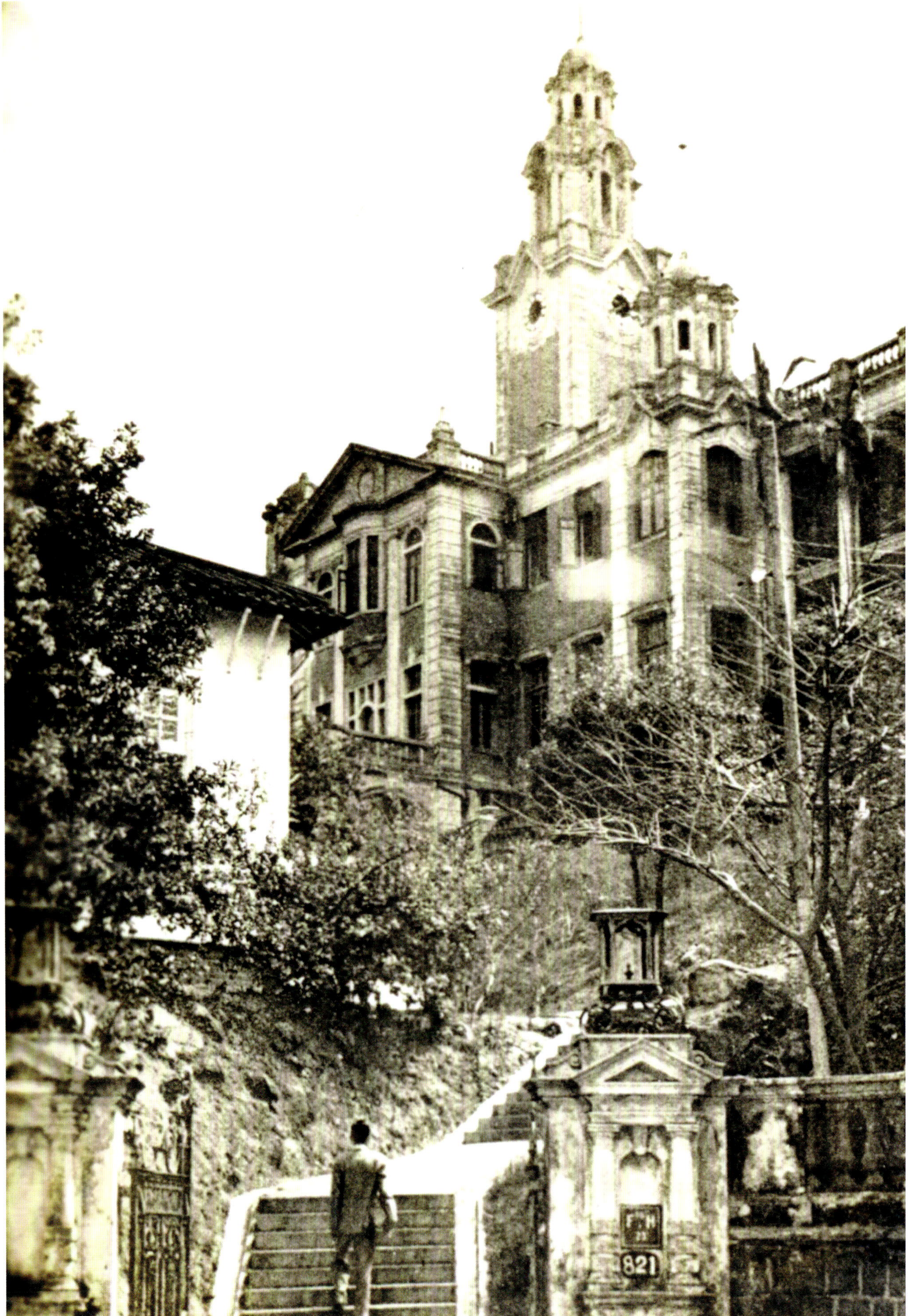
821

早期大學生生活
EARLY STUDENT LIFE

3

香港大學聯會與學生會

一九六一年學生會大樓
Student Union Building, 1961

一九一二年港大創校,同年十月十六日香港大學聯會成立,成員包括教職員及學生。大學聯會透過各式學會舉辦辯論、體育等活動,最初會址設於本部大樓,後來經遮打爵士、佐頓教授、其他善長共捐款五萬元,遂於原址對面興建獨立大樓作新會址。一九一九年二月聯會大樓啟用,由當時港督司徒拔主禮,至一九八六年改名孔慶熒樓,作為紀念大筆捐款港大的命名。

二次大戰後該址曾短暫用作行政大樓,一九六二年更擴建了東翼,一九七四年改作高級職員會所,一九九六年至二零一三年一月撥歸音樂系使用。

一九四五年香港大學聯會重組並易名為香港大學學生聯會。一九四九年正式註冊為獨立學生組織,定名香港大學學生會。

戰後大學於一九五三年的發展計劃,包括在本部大樓後面興建一幢新學生會大樓,該處原為余東璇體育館及網球場。一九六一年港大金禧校慶,新學生會大樓及時竣工,並由雅麗珊郡主揭幕啟用;當時她蒞港出任大學特別畢業禮的嘉賓,作為慶典節目之一。

一九八六年學生會大樓拆卸,以備擴建圖書館新翼,學生會則遷往徐朗星文娛中心。隨著港大百周年校園的發展,嶄新的學生會大樓亦於二零一二年落成。

現今學生會共有超過一百二十個附屬組織,分成六個組別,包括院會及學術會、獨立學社(組成學社聯會)、校園傳媒等。學生會目前架構參看附錄二。

Hong Kong University Union (1912) and Students' Union (1949)

The Hong Kong University Union (HKUU) was founded on 16th October 1912 in the same year as the University opened. Its membership was open to officers of the University, lecturers and students, as well as graduates of other universities. Its activities included debating and sports through its various societies. The Union was initially housed in the Main Building, and through a donation of $50,000 raised by Sir Paul Chater, Professor G. P. Jordan and other donors, it was able to erect a stand alone building facing the Main Building, which was opened in February 1919 by Governor Sir Reginald Stubbs. Known then as the Union Building, it was renamed the Hung Hing Ying Building in 1986 in honour of a generous benefactor to the University.

Following the war the building was briefly used for administration. It was expanded, with the addition of an east wing in 1962, and converted into the Senior Common Room in 1974. From 1996 to January 2013, it housed the University's Department of Music.

In 1945, the Union was reorganised and renamed the Hong Kong University Students' Society (HKUSS), and in 1949 it was registered as an independent student organization and known as the Hong Kong University Students' Union (HKUSU).

The 1953 development plan for the University following the war included the building of a new Student Union Building on a site behind the Main Building where the Eu Tong Sen Gymnasium and tennis courts stood. The new Student Union Building was completed in time for the University's Golden Jubilee in 1961, and officially opened by H. R. H. Princess Alexandra of Kent when she attended a special Congregation held as part of the celebrations.

In 1986, this building was demolished to make way for the Library's new wing and the Students' Union was moved to the Hsu Long Sing Amenities Centre. With the development of the University's centennial campus, this building was replaced by a new Student Union Building completed in 2012.

There are currently over 120 sub-organisations affiliated to the HKUSU, divided into six main groups: these include faculty and academic societies, independent clubs (forming the Independent Clubs Association) as well as Campus media. See Appendix II for its current organiation.

香港大學聯會委員會早期相片
香港大學聯會相簿
Early photo of the University Union Committee
Hong Kong University Union Album

香港大學聯會相簿
The Hong Kong University Union Album

本相簿收藏逾一百幅原版相片,記錄了一九一二至一九三九年二次大戰爆發前學生活動及大學典禮之點滴。其中包括一九一二年大學聯會會員合照、一九一三至一四年度學生會評議會成員合照,以及一九二三年孫中山於大禮堂演講後與學生合照(參看第12頁)。

香港大學聯會相簿
一九一二至一九三九年
香港大學檔案中心「香港大學學生會特藏」
The Hong Kong University Union Album (1912-1939)
H: 33 cm W: 44.5 cm
Collection of the Hong Kong University Students' Union, HKUA

The Union Album contains over 100 original photographs recording student activities and University ceremonies from 1912 to 1939, the eve of outbreak of World War II. The Album includes pictures of Union members in 1912 and Union Council members in 1913–1914, as well as the meeting of Sun Yat-sen with students in 1923 after his speech in the Great Hall (see page 12).

香港大學聯會委員會早期相片
香港大學聯會相簿
Early photo of the University Union Committee
Hong Kong University Union Album

學生衣飾
Student Attire

香港大學校褸
一九六零年代
張葉媛儀捐贈
HKU Jacket
1960s
L: 65 cm W: 42 cm
Gift of Mrs Grace Cheung Ip Woon-yee

香港大學領帶
一九四零年代
一九四一年工程學系畢業生凌斯駿捐贈
School Tie
1940s
L: 114 cm W: 8.5 cm
Gift of Mr Vincent Ling (BSc Eng 1941)

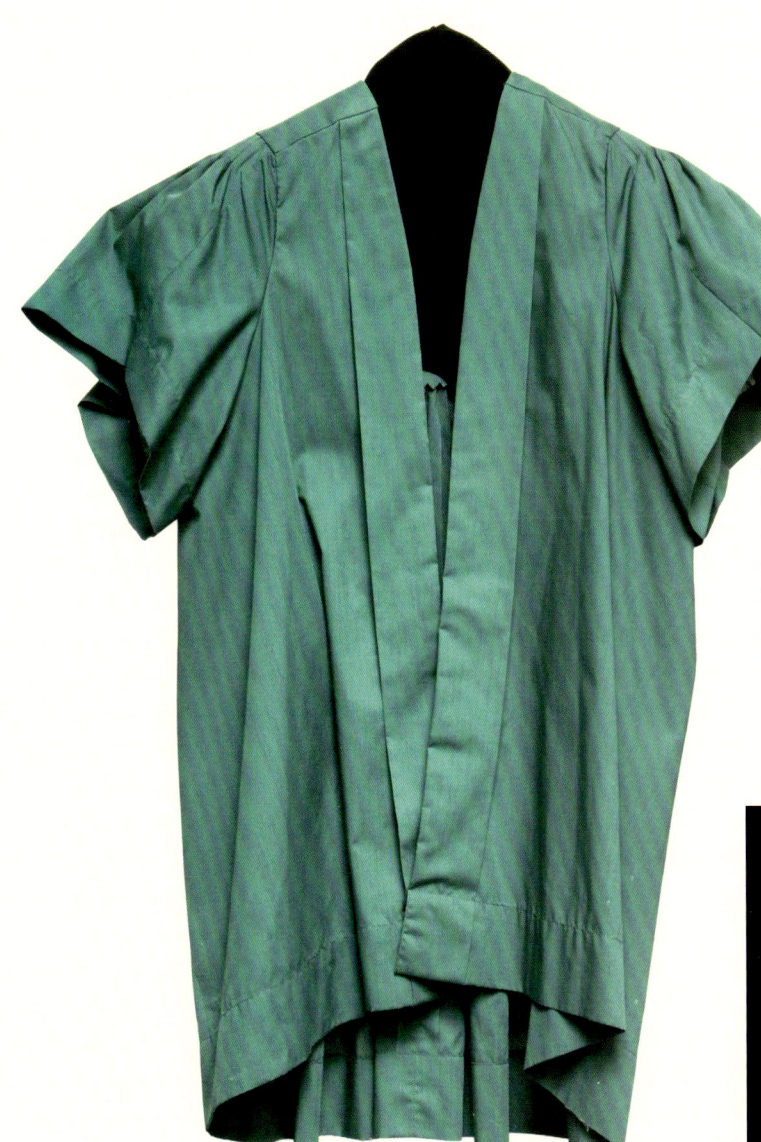

學生會幹事專用綠袍
一九六零年代
Ivan Ho 捐贈
Green Gown worn by HKUSU Committee members
1960s
L: 81 cm
Gift of Mr Ivan Ho

香港大學學生會會長披肩
香港大學檔案中心「香港大學學生會特藏」
HKUSU President's Academic Stole
L: 152 cm W: 13 cm
Collection of the Hong Kong University
Students' Union, HKUA

HKU Memories | from the Archives   87

一九一九年建成的舊香港大學聯會大樓，背景為本部大樓
View of the old University Union Building, built in 1919 with the Main Building in the background.

香港大學本部大樓、舊香港大學聯會大樓（今孔慶熒樓）
Main Building and the old University Union Building (known today as the Hung Hing Ying Building)

香港大學聯會（今孔慶熒樓）
一九一九年十一月三日開幕時港督司
徒拔主禮的銀鑰匙
葉承耀醫生珍藏
Silver key to the University Union Building (known today as the Hung Hing Ying Building) presented to Governor Sir Reginald Stubbs at its opening ceremony on 3rd November, 1919
H: 7 cm W: 9 cm
Dr S. Y. Yip Collection

背面刻字 Inscribed on the reverse:
'"PRESENTED TO HIS EXCELLENCY THE GOVERNOR OF HONGKONG AND CHANCELLOR OF THE UNIVERSITY, AT THE CEREMONY OF OPENING THE NEW BUILDINGS OF THE HONG KONG UNIVERSITY UNION."
3RD NOVEMBER, 1919.'

底部刻字 Inscribed along the base of the key:
'WANG LEE & CO CONTRACTORS',
'LITTLE, ADAMS & WOOD ARCHITECTS'
with two hallmarks

正面刻字 Inscribed on the key:
'SECURITY'

大學舍堂

一九一二年三月十一日港大創建時，原擬設立多座舍堂，每間可容納六十名學生，並由英文教授及中文助理各一名擔任舍監，可惜未能如期啟用。當時港督盧吉轉向宗教團體尋求協助，因他們熱心支持教育及培育品德，與剛成立的港大之使命一致。其中教會傳道會率先響應，在般咸道大學對面建立聖約翰堂，於一九一二年港大開校時及時啟用。至一九一三年大學堂落成，後加入儀禮堂（一九一四年）、梅堂（一九一五年），大學堂亦易名盧吉堂。一九六六年三座舍堂合併為明原堂。

第三間建成的大學舍堂位於克頓道，由倫敦傳道會興建，一九一三年九月落成，並以該會最早的傳教士之一馬禮遜命名。他是最早將聖經翻譯成中文的學者。他在中國逝世後，其藏書移送香港大會堂，一九二五年由港大圖書館購藏。戰後一九四八年馬禮遜堂重建，二十年後再關閉，直至二零零五年才復開。一九二九年座落薄扶林道的耶穌會港大舍堂落成，並以傳教士利瑪竇命名。

一九二一年大學首名女生伊惠珠入學，一九二三年聖士提反書院即興建聖士提反舍堂。一九三九年寶珊道的聖母堂啟用，只收納女生。一九五一年大學首間非教會女生舍堂建成，即何東爵士為紀念亡妻而捐款興建的何東夫人紀念堂。

港大舍堂中其中一座最古老的建築物是杜格拉斯堡，該樓原為蘇格蘭商人杜格拉斯興建之大宅，落成於一八六四年。後由法國傳道會接管，取名拿撒勒堡。一九五四年港大購置改建成大學堂。一九九五年根據香港古物及古蹟條例列為歷史建築。另外，一九五五年聖約翰與聖士提反舍堂合併，在薄扶林道成立聖約翰學院。

隨著港大擴展，本地、國際、研究院的學生數目不斷增長，大學舍堂亦陸續增建，包括太古堂（一九八零年）、李國賢堂（一九八五年）、研究生堂（一九九八年）、施德堂（二零零一年）、李兆基堂（二零零五年）、孫志新堂（二零零五年），以及沙宣道一系列的醫學生舍堂，計有利希慎堂（一九九二年）、何善衡夫人紀念堂、利銘澤堂（以利希慎兒子命名）、偉倫堂。

約一九六零年代大學徑上的職員宿舍，背景為學生舍堂
Staff accommodation on University Path, c. 1960s. Old Halls for student accommodation are in the background.

杜格拉斯堡（大學堂）
華籍畫家作
約一八六四年
紙本水彩水粉畫
香港大學美術博物館藏品 (HKU.P.2002.1430)

Douglas Castle (University Hall)
Chinese artist
c. 1864
Watercolour and gouache on paper
H: 24 cm　W: 29 cm
Collection of the University Museum and Art Gallery (HKU.P.2002.1430)

杜格拉斯堡位於薄扶林山，由蘇格蘭商人杜格拉斯・立僻（一八一八至一八六九年）興建，一八六四年落成。他逝世後由侄兒繼承，再由其子於父親一八九三年逝世後，因香港爆發瘟疫而急忙出售。一八九四年巴黎外方傳教會購入這建築物作退修用途，並易名為拿撒勒堡。一九五四年香港大學再購入作為學生宿舍，取名大學堂，一九五六年啟用。

Douglas Castle on Pokfulam Hill was built by the Scottish businessman Douglas Lapraik (1818–1869) and completed in around 1864. Following Lapraik's death in 1869, his nephew John Steward Lapraik inherited it. When he died in 1893, his son John Douglas sold it quickly due to the outbreak of bubonic plague in Hong Kong. It was purchased by the French Mission in 1894 and converted into a retreat for its missionaries known as Nazareth. The building was acquired by the University of Hong Kong in 1954, and opened in 1956 as a residential hall for students with its new name of University Hall.

約一九六六年大學三座舍堂合併為明原堂，前景為鄧志昂中文學院。
The student halls known collectively as Old Halls *c.* 1966. The Tang Chi Ngong Building is in the foreground.

University Halls

When the University opened on 11th March 1912, its own student halls had not yet been built. They were designed to house sixty students each with an English professor and Chinese assistant in residence. Governor Frederick Lugard sought the help of existing religious organisations whose interest in supporting education and promoting good moral character was in keeping with the mission of the new university. The Church Missionary Society was the first to respond by providing accommodation on Bonham Road, opposite the University, which was named St John's and was established in 1912 in time for the opening. The University Hall opened the following year in 1913. It was renamed Lugard Hall when the other halls, Eliot (1914) and May (1915) were added. These were later combined as a single residential unit in 1966 known as Old Halls. St John's College, which opened on Pokfulam Road in 1955 combined the earlier St John's and St Stephen's Halls.

The third hall of residence was built by the London Missionary Society on Hatton Road in September 1913, and named after one of its earliest missionaries, Robert Morrison, the first translator of the Bible into Chinese. Morrison's library was transferred to Hong Kong's City Hall following his death in China. It was later acquired by the University Library in 1925. Morrison Hall was restored after the war in 1948, but closed twenty years later. It was re-established in 2005. Ricci Hall, named after Matteo Ricci, was founded on Pokfulam Road in 1929 by the Jesuit order.

The University's first female student was admitted in 1921. St Stephen's Hall, established by St Stephen's College, opened shortly after in 1923 as the University's first hall exclusively for women. Like St Stephen's, Our Lady's Hall was for women only and opened on Po Shan Road in 1939. The first non-religious woman's hall did not open until 1951. It was named Lady Ho Tung Hall by its donor Sir Robert Ho Tung in honour of his late wife.

One of the oldest buildings to be converted into a residential hall is the former castle built by the Scottish businessman Douglas Lapraik, and completed in 1864. Acquired by the University in 1954 from the French Mission who had called it Nazareth House. Re-named University Hall, it opened as a residential hall in 1956. In 1995, it was declared a historical building by the Antiquities and Monuments Ordinance of Hong Kong.

Since then the number of residential halls has grown to reflect the expansion of the University, and the increase in local, international and postgraduate student numbers. These include Swire Hall (1980), Simon K Y Lee Hall (1985), Graduate House (1998), Starr Hall (2001), Lee Shau Kee Hall (2005), Suen Chi Sun Hall (2005) and a cluster of halls of residence for medical students on Sassoon Road including Lee Hysan Hall (1992), Madam S H Ho Residence, R C Lee Hall (named after the son of Lee Hysan), and Wei Lun Hall.

何東夫人紀念堂女宿生相片，刊載於 London Illustrated News
Women students in residence at Lady Hotung Hall, published in the London Illustrated News

香港大學首批學生
First Class

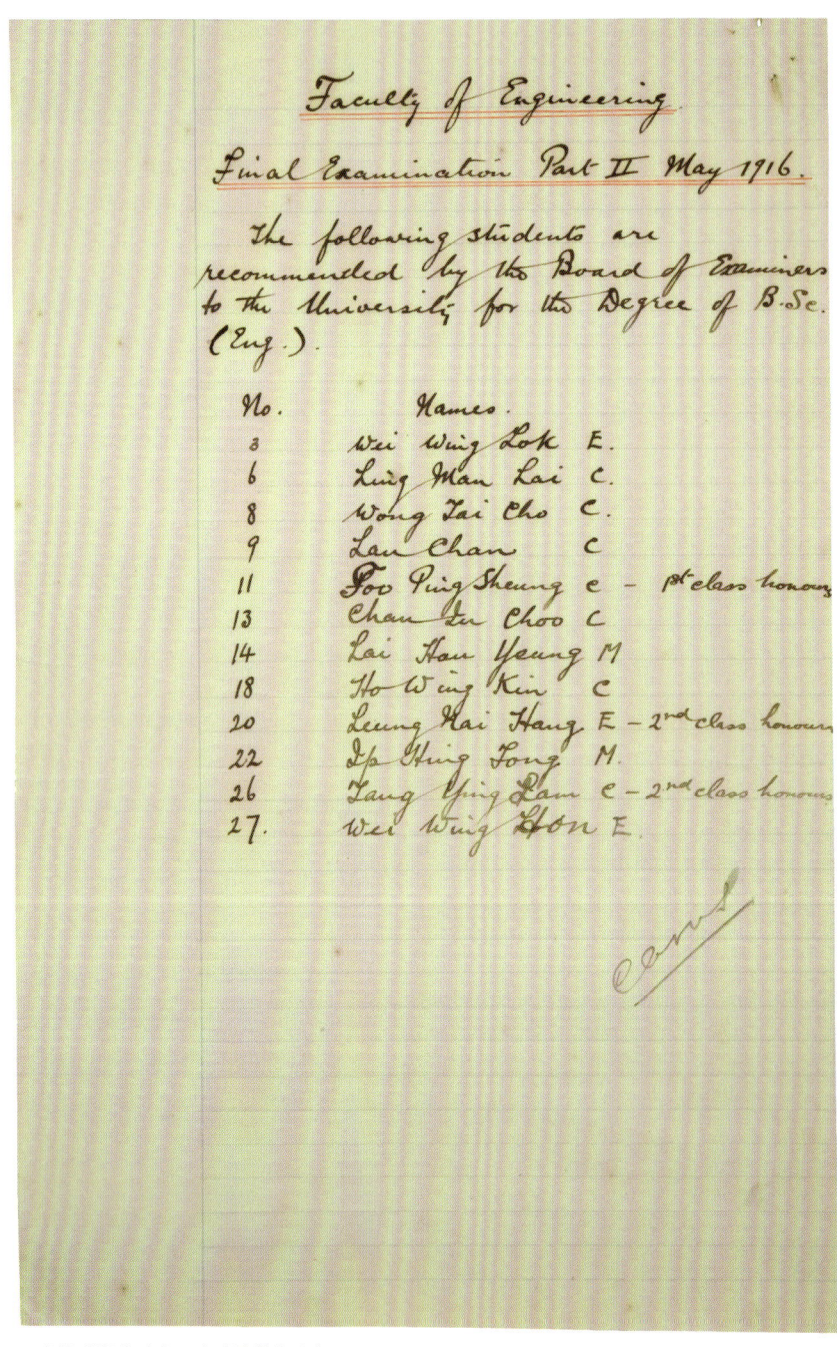

工程學院期終試卷二之成績排名公布
一九一六年
Faculty of Engineering Final Examination Part II results
1916

排名十一的傅秉常為第一批工程學畢業生，獲頒一級榮譽文憑。
No. 11 in the list, Foo Ping Sheung was one of the earliest engineering graduates, and awarded first class honours.

傅秉常（一八九五至一九六五年）出生於廣東佛山。來港就讀聖士提反書院，後考入香港大學工程學院。他是首屆香港大學工程科畢業生，畢業後一路平步青雲。他最初服務於姻親叔父輩伍廷芳的鐵路工程公司。伍廷芳（一八四二至一九二二年）是香港的首位大律師，當時為民國總統黎元洪的外交部長。一九一八至一九二四年間傅秉常成為孫中山大元帥府秘書。一九一九年他出任廣州國民政府出席巴黎和會代表團秘書，期間兼任海南島海關總督（一九一九至一九二二年）、粵海關總督及外交秘書（一九二二至一九二六年）。一九二七至一九二八年與伍朝樞到訪美國。一九二八年回國後出任外交部政務次長、國民政府首屆立法委員、立法院外交委員會委員長。一九三一年獲香港大學頒授名譽法學博士。一九三三至一九三六年間他參與中華民國憲法草案的起草及修訂。一九四三至一九四九年擔任蘇聯大使，後暫居法國。一九五六年應邀擔任台灣公務員懲戒委員會委員長及台灣司法院副院長，直至一九六五年病逝。

他幼年時得母親啟蒙，一生熱愛攝影。他的公職使他有機會拍下國民黨會員的面貌，並且於一九三零及四零年代到訪中國及蘇聯農村期間以鏡頭記錄了當地的景觀。

Foo Ping-sheung (Fu Bingchang) (1895–1965) was born in Foshan, Guangdong, and educated in Hong Kong at St Stephen's College and then the University of Hong Kong where he studied civil engineering. He was one of the University's earliest and most successful graduates. After graduation, Foo worked as a railway engineer for his uncle by marriage, Ng Choy (Wu Tingfang, (1842–1922)), Hong Kong's first Chinese barrister, and at the time Foreign Minister to Li Yuanhong. Foo served as Secretary to Sun Yat-sen from 1918 to 1924. In 1919 he was appointed Attaché to the delegation of the Canton Constitutional Government to the Paris Peace Conference and went on to hold a number of posts such as Governor of Hainan Island (1919–1922), Superintendent of Customs, and Commissioner for Foreign Affairs at Canton (1922–1926), before accompanying Wu Chaoshu to America between 1927 and 1928. Following his return to China in 1928, he was appointed a member of the Foreign Relations Committee of the National Government, member of the Legislative Yuan and Chairman of its Foreign Relations Committee. In 1931 he was awarded an Honorary Doctor of Laws by the University of Hong Kong. He helped draft the Chinese Civil Code between 1933 and 1936 and was eventually posted as Ambassador to Moscow from 1943 to 1949. He retired to Paris until 1956 when he took up the post of President of the Anti-Corruption Board and Vice-President of the Judicial Yuan in Taiwan under Chiang Kai-shek until his death in 1965.

Foo Ping-sheung was encouraged in artistic pursuits by his mother as a child and went on to become a keen and accomplished photographer. His position as a politician allowed him to capture many candid images of members of the Nationalist party, as well as record personal excursions into the Chinese and Russian countryside in the 1930s and 1940s.

Note: *Historical Photographs of China* project, Project Director: Robert Bickers, University of Bristol. www.hpc.vcea.net

早期女畢業生
The First Female Graduates

香港大學於一九二一年九月建校，十年後才首度招收女生，由當時新任校長William Brunyate爵士向教務會提出修訂校例。歸因於時任教育署長伊榮的女兒伊惠珠剛在倫敦貝德福德學院修畢社會科學證書課程，她希望在香港大學完成學位課程。一九二一年六月二十三日香港大學教務會通過決議，承認她的畢業證書等同考獲劍橋高級本地證書中級試第二部份資歷，並豁免她入住宿舍的要求。大學校務會批准教務會落實新措施，於是大學正式收納女生。

一九二一年九月伊惠珠入讀大學文學課程三年級，適逢學年改制，由五月改為十二月終結，因此當年入學的學生均延至一九二二年十二月才完成首年課程。伊惠珠亦於一九二三年五月才畢業。

何東的女兒何艾齡、何綺華均為大學最早的女生。一九二五年十二月何艾齡首先畢業。翌年何綺華亦成為首位醫科女畢業生。一九二三年一月曾廷謙入讀香港大學，成為工程系首位女生。

香港大學首位女生伊惠珠
文學院相簿
一九二三年五月
The first female student admitted to HKU was Rachel Irving
Arts Faculty Album
May 1923

Women were not admitted into the University of Hong Kong until September 1921, ten years after it was founded. The newly-appointed Vice-Chancellor, Sir William Brunyate proposed a change of policy to the University Senate when Rachel Irving, the daughter of then Director of Education, Mr E. A. Irving, who had already taken a certificate course in Social Science at Bedford College, London applied to complete her education in Hong Kong. On 23 June 1921, the Senate resolved to accept her certificate as equivalent to the Intermediate Examination Part II of the Cambridge University Higher Local Certificate, and exempt her from residency requirements. The Council subsequently confirmed the action of the Senate and began to admit women into the University.

Rachel Irving entered the University's third-year arts course in September 1921 but the end of the academic year was changed that year from May to December so students entering at this time did not complete their first year until December 1922. As a result, Rachel Irving did not graduate until May 1923.

Sisters Irene (later Cheng) and Eva Ho Tung were among the earliest Hong Kong born women to be accepted at the University with Irene being the first to graduate in December 1925. Her sister Eva became the first female medical graduate in the following year. Tseng Ting Chien, admitted in January 1923, was the first female engineering student.

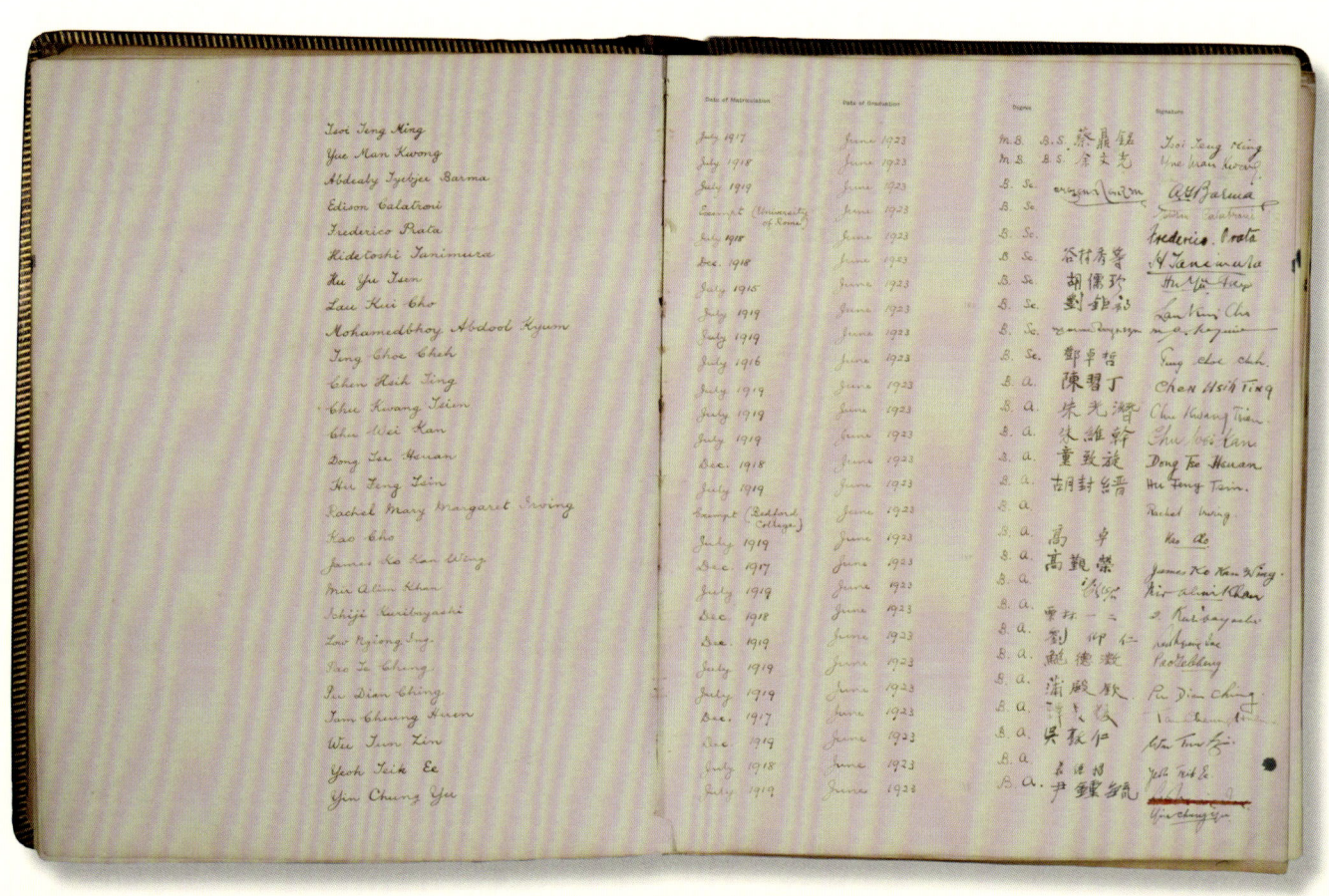

一九二三年大學畢業生名冊中伊惠珠的簽署
Rachel Irving's signature in the Register of Graduates
1923

何艾齡的學生紀錄
Irene Ho Tung's student record

一九六一年大學金禧誌慶，何艾齡在文學院相簿上親筆註明相片的內容。
In 1961, the year of the Golden Jubilee, Irene Cheng (née Ho Tung) annotated the Arts Faculty Albums, identifying many of the photographs in her own hand.

```
                    17th Congregation, January 12, 1926
                               All Faculties

       (First occasion with full Hong Kong Woman Graduate...Miss Irene Ho Tung, B.A.)

Standing (left to right) 1925 Graduates: So Pak Sui B.A.,Pun Siu Pang B.A.,Lam Choi Chiu B.A.,Tong Chun Chung, B.A.,
              Fung Yui Siu,B.A.,Lau Lai Sang B.A.,B.M.Talati B.A.,V.F. Viccajee B.A.,A.G.Botelho B.A.,N.H.F.Prew B.A.,
              Leung Lin Kee B.Sc(Eng),....?....,A.G.F.Prew B.A.,S.B.Ahmed B.Sc.(Eng).
Sitting (left to right): Ma Char Zur B.A.,N.V.Nguyen B.A.,Cheong Wai Fung B.A.,Miss I.Ho Tung B.A., Prof.Shellshear (Dean,
              Medical Faculty),Mr.(later Sir Wm) Hornell(Vice-Chancellor), Prof.Byrne(Dean,Arts Faculty),Dr.Yeo Kok
              Cheang M.B.,B.S., Dr. Tseung Fat In M.B.,B.S.,
In Absentia:  Lee Boon Choe M.B,B.S.,Leung Hsing Kuei M.B.,B.S.,Soo Hoy Mun M.B.,B.S.,Teh Yok Chee M.B.,B.S., Teo Kah Toh
              M.B.,B.S., Yuen Sze Chung, William M.B.,B.S., ?Cheng Hsu Ting B.Sc.(Eng), ?Liang Lin Kee B.Sc.(Eng),
              ?Wu Chang Ching B.Sc.(Eng), ?Yue Shui Chiu B.Sc.(Eng), ?Yui Zong Chen B.Sc.(Eng), Ban Teong Hoe B.A., Chan
              Cheuk Wa B.A.,Wong Ching Yau B.A., Leigh Byng B.A., Ooi Khay Bian B.A., C.A.Peterson B.A.,?Shu Yu Pong B.A.,
              ?Teoh Khoy Moh B.A.
```

一九二六年一月十二日大學第十七屆畢業生合照及第一位本土女畢業生何艾齡。
文學院相簿
The University's 17th Congregation with the first Hong Kong female graduate, Irene Ho Tung.
12th January 1926
Arts Faculty Album

一九六一年香港大學五十周年誌慶出版 *University of Hong Kong: The First Fifty Years 1911–1961*，包括了何艾齡撰寫文章，論述大學女生及女畢業生。

In Brian Harrison's publication *University of Hong Kong: The First Fifty Years 1911–1961*, published for the fiftieth anniversary of the University, Irene Cheng wrote an essay entitled, 'Women Students and Graduates'.

何綺華的學生紀錄
Eva Ho Tung's student record

工程學會最早的合照
一九二六年
John Rux-Burton 捐贈
Earliest photograph of the Engineering Society
1926
Gift of Mr John Rux-Burton

相片右二坐者是首位工程系的女畢業生曾廷謙。
Seated second right is the University's first female engineering graduate, Tseng Ting-chien.

首位工程系女生曾廷謙於一九二三至二四年度入學,至一九三一年初畢業。戰前大學有不少學生需要攻讀六年方完成課程,就讀理科的女生尤其普遍。同期另一位工程系女生黃越瀾則於一九三九年畢業。

Tseng Ting-chien was the first female engineering student admitted into the University between 1923 and 1924. She graduated in early 1931. During the pre-war years it was not unusual to take six years to complete one's studies, and women science students would have been particularly disadvantaged. Another female engineering student during this time was Wong Yuet-lan who graduated in 1939.

鄭兆如(左)和鄭杏如(右)的畢業相片
李景勳捐贈
Graduation photograph of
Cheng Siu-yue (left) and Cheng Hung-yue (right)
Gift of Mr Andrew K. F. Lee

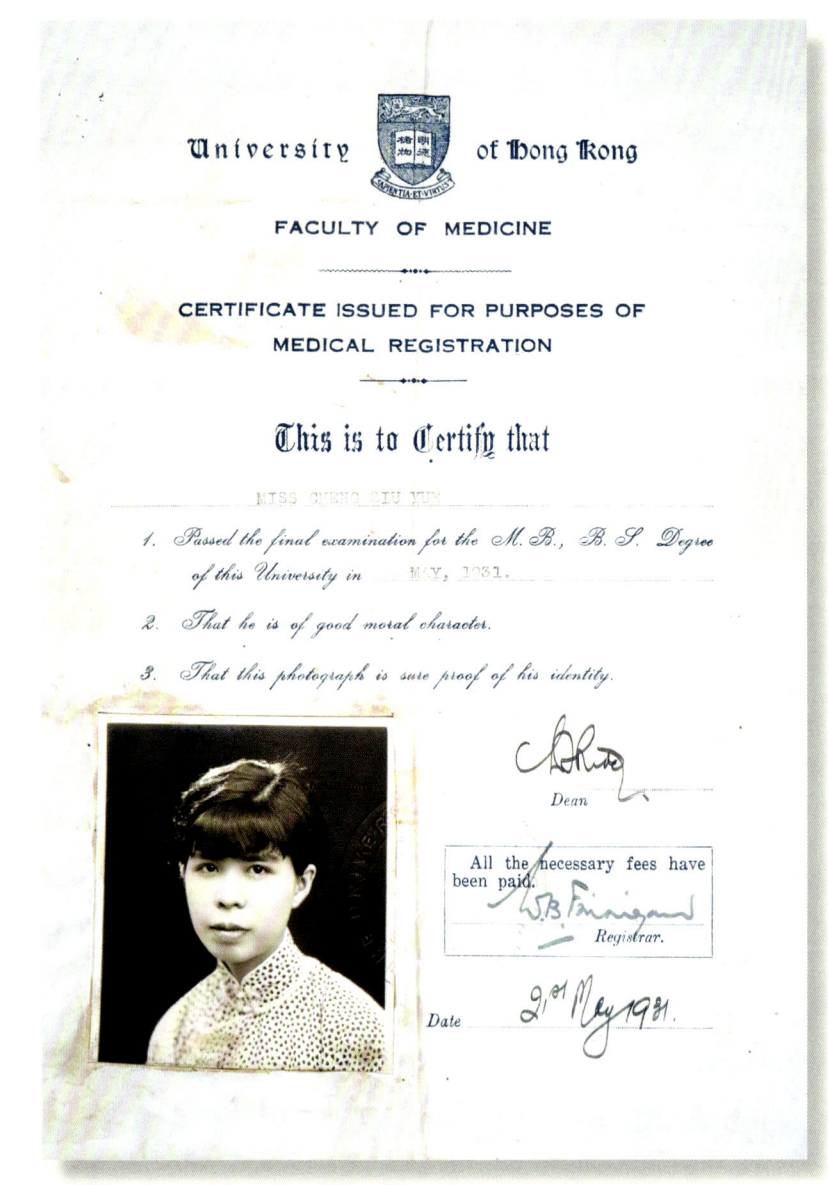

鄭兆如醫學證書
一九三一年
李景勳捐贈
Medical Registration Certificate awarded to Cheng Siu-yue
1931
Gift of Mr Andrew K. F. Lee

鄭兆如（一九零六至二零零六年）、鄭杏如（一九零八至一九七一年）均出生於廣州，一九一一年中移居香港的堅道，就讀聖士提反女子中學。姊妹二人同於一九三二年獲頒香港大學全科醫學士學位。

鄭兆如最先服務於香港政府轄下的九龍及離島診所。她初任護理科主考官，後主管助產士部門，直至一九六二年退休。退休後她在香港家庭計劃指導會服務至一九七八年。

鄭杏如則加入香港政府轄下的產科及護養院工作，一九五四年出任醫院道新建成贊育醫院院長，直至一九六四年退休。

Cheng Siu-yue (1906–2006) and Cheng Hung-yue (1908–1971) were born in Guangzhou and moved to Caine Road in Hong Kong in mid-1911 where they attended St Stephen Girls' College. Both sisters studied medicine at the University of Hong Kong, graduating with M.B.B.S (Bachelor of Medicine and Bachelor of Surgery) in 1932.

Cheng Siu-yue worked for the Hong Kong Government as a medical officer for Kowloon and Outlying Island clinics. She sat on the Nursing Examination Board and became a Supervisor of midwives until her retirement in 1962. Following retirement she continued to help the Family Planning Association until 1978.

Cheng Hung-yue joined the Hong Kong Government as a medical officer in maternity homes and hospitals and became the Medical Superintendent at the new Tsang Yuk Hospital on Hospital Road in 1954, a position that she held until her retirement in 1964.

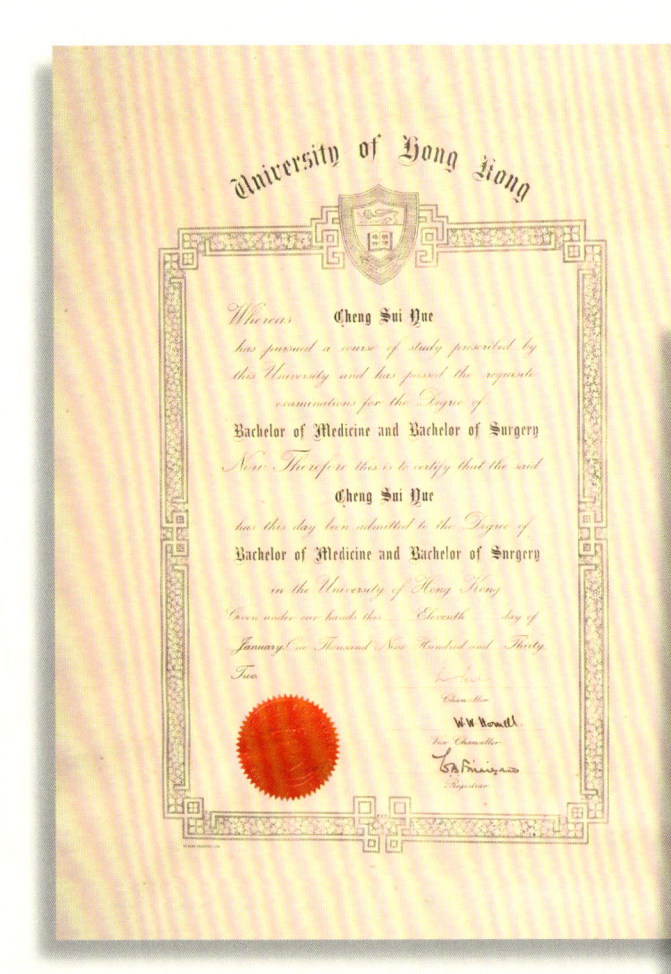

鄭氏姊妹香港大學全科醫學士畢業證書
一九三二年
李景勳捐贈
Bachelor of Medicine degree Certificates awarded to the Cheng sisters
1932
Gift of Mr Andrew K. F. Lee

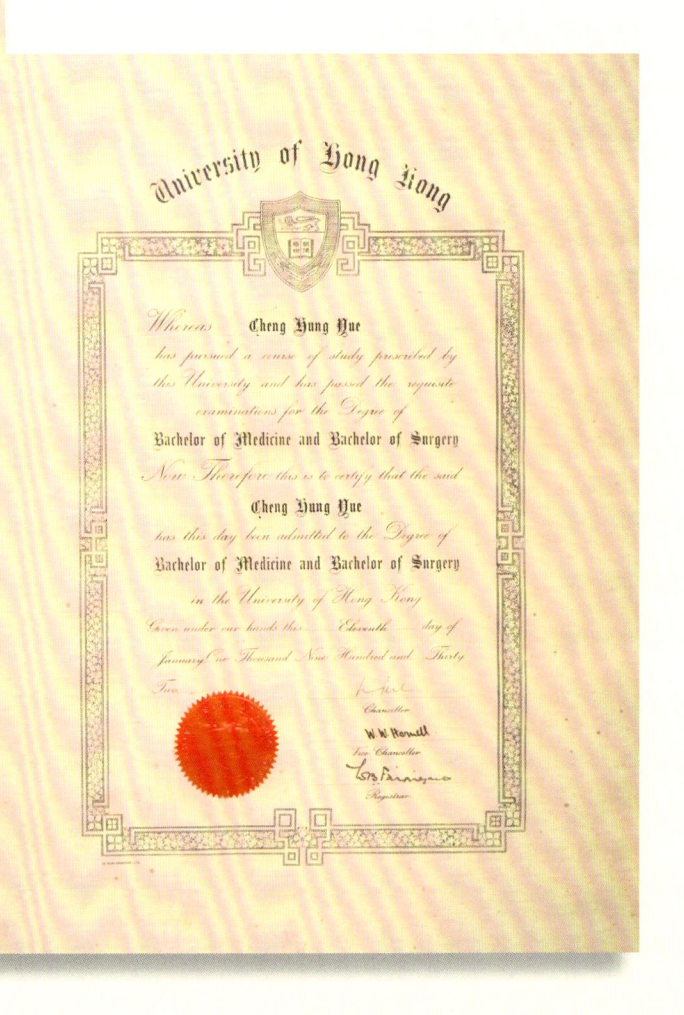

HKU Memories | from the Archives

香港大學與庚子賠款獎學金

義和團是一個民間秘密組織，成員多為流民，他們好勇鬥狠，以反外國軍國主義為口號，到處搗亂，尤其針對西方傳教士及華人基督徒。時值一連串的天災、鴉片煙禍、西方影響等令事情惡化。他們到處襲擊基督教傳教士、外國人、華人基督徒及教會，暴行自義和團之發源地山東擴散到北京。一八九八至一九零一年間發生的義和團運動，引致數以千計的人死亡，情況最嚴重時為一九零零年，北京發生外國使節、西什庫天主教堂被圍攻事件。

結果引致英、法、德、美、日、俄、意、奧八國聯軍，組成一支兩萬人的軍隊出兵中國，聯軍直駛北京，大敗清軍，佔領京師。當時執政的慈禧太后甚支持義和團。後來為平息各國的聲討，清政府被逼簽訂庚子條約，向八國賠款四億五千萬兩白銀，分三十九年償還。

後來清廷駐美公使安默斯特畢業生梁誠發現庚子賠款的金額過鉅而不合理。美國遂把索賠金額以資助中國學生留美獎學金的形式歸還中國。庚子賠款獎學金於一九零九年設立，由中國負責留學生的選拔和訓練，在北洋建立「留美預備學堂」，即清華大學的前身。一九零九至一九二九年期間，共有一千三百位學生獲取庚子賠款獎學金。這一做法也得到英國、日本、法國三國的仿效。

中英庚款留英公費獎學金的研究生考試於五個中國城市舉行，唯於一九三八年因日軍屢襲廣州，五十四名原在廣州應考的學生須轉到香港試場，參加在香港大學舉行的三天考試。

該批考生包括黃用諏教授（一九一三至二零零四年），他成為著名的幾何數學家兼教育家。一九四八至一九七三年出任香港大學數學系講座教授，一九六三至一九六六年擔任香港大學副校長。

中英庚子賠款第六屆留英公費學生出發之前在香港大學合照，相片最左方坐地者是黃用諏
一九三八年。
香港大學檔案中心「黃用諏教授特藏」
Photograph of the sixth group of British Government Indemnity Fund scholarship recipients taken at the University of Hong Kong before their departure for Great Britain. Seated first left is Wong Yung-chow.
1938
Y. C. Wong Collection, HKUA

HKU and the Boxer Indemnity Scholarship Fund

The Society of Righteous and Harmonious Fists were a secret society of disenfranchised men skilled in martial arts. They were known as the Boxers. Driven by anti-imperialist, anti-missionary and anti-Christian sentiments, their discontent was exacerbated by hardships such as poverty, natural disasters and opium addiction. Attacks targeted Christian missionaries, foreigners, Chinese Christian converts and their churches, and soon spread from the home of the Boxers in Shandong province northwards to Beijing. The rebellion lasted from 1898 to 1901 and resulted in the deaths of thousands. It culminated in the siege of foreign legations and the Northern Cathedral in Beijing in 1900.

In response, an Eight-Nation Alliance (consisting of the United States, Russia, German empire, France, Britain, Japan, Italy and the Austro-Hungarian empire) sent 20,000 troops to Beijing, defeating the Qing Imperial Army and capturing the city. The Empress Dowager Cixi and the Qing army had backed the Boxers. Under the terms of the Boxer Protocol, which marked the end of the siege, an indemnity of 450 million taels of silver (equivalent to £67 million), were to be paid in reparations to the eight nations over thirty-nine years.

When the Qing representative to the United States, Amherst-educated Liang Cheng, discovered that China had overpaid the reparations, a Boxer Indemnity Scholarship Fund was established in 1909 to compensate China. The resulting scholarships funded Chinese students to study in the US. It also included funds to establish a preparatory school in Beijing called Tsinghua College for graduates wanting to study in the US. This later became a university in its own right. Between 1909 and 1929 around 1,300 students benefitted from the fund. The United Kingdom, France, and Japan later set up similar schemes for Chinese students.

Postgraduate candidates for the Sino-British scholarships were examined in five Chinese cities, but in 1938, the 54 students who would have been examined in Canton had to travel to Hong Kong to HKU for their three-day examinations, as Canton was under seige by the Japanese.

Future HKU mathematics professor, Wong Yung-chow (1913–2004), was among this group. Wong was a leading mathematician and educator. He was head of the Department of Mathematics from 1948 to 1973, and served as Pro-Vice-Chancellor from 1963 to 1966.

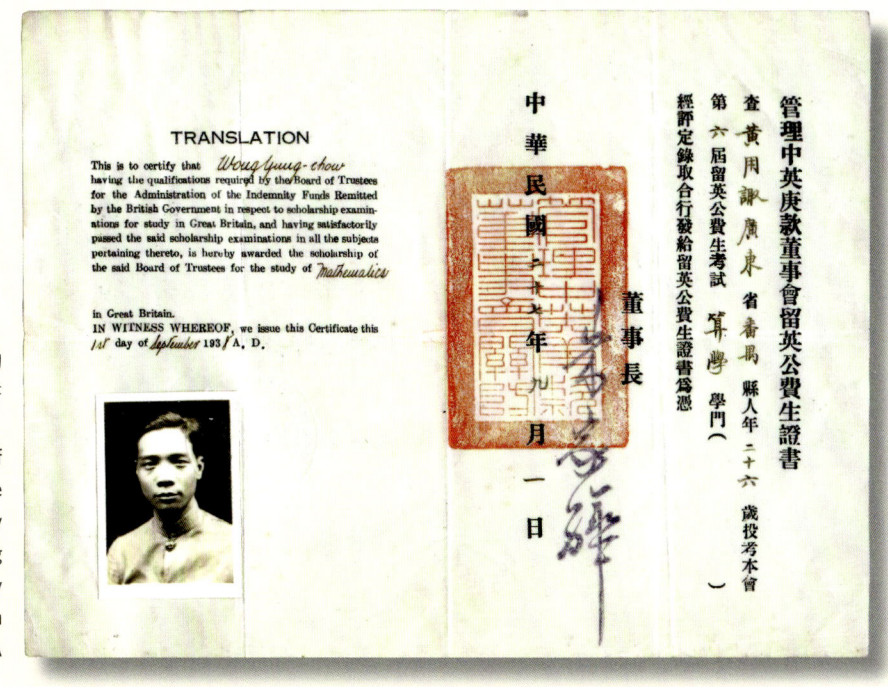

中英庚子賠款董事會簽發予黃用諏的留英公費生證書
香港大學檔案中心「黃用諏教授特藏」
Certificate issued by the Board of Trustees for Administrating the Boxer Indemnity Funds remitted by the British Government to Wong Yung-chow for a scholarship to study mathematics in Great Britain
Y. C. Wong Collection, HKUA

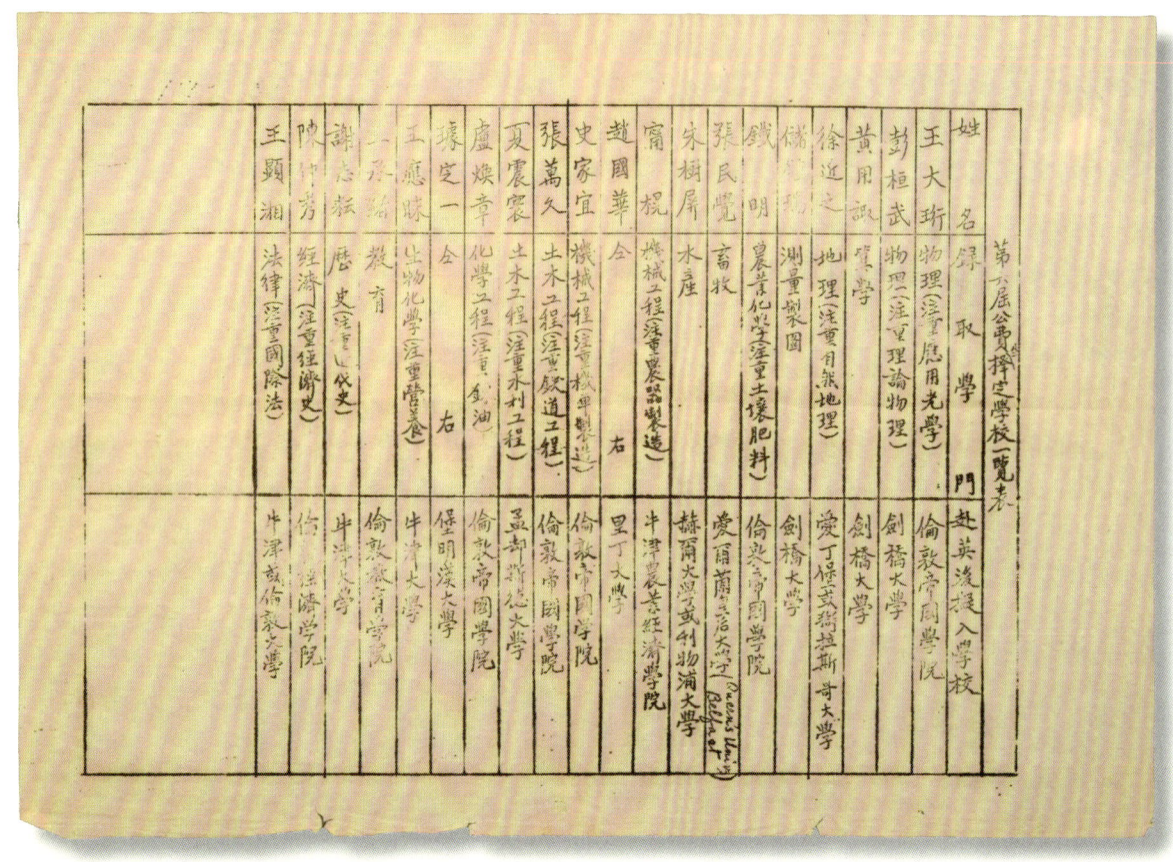

中英庚子賠款留英二十位公費學生選課及學校一覽表
一九三八年
香港大學檔案中心「黃用諏教授特藏」
Table listing the twenty British government Boxer Indemnity Fund scholarship recipients with their chosen disciplines and universities
1938
Y. C. Wong Collection, HKUA

黃用諏（右三）選往劍橋大學供讀算學。
Wong Yung-chow (third right) is listed as having chosen Cambridge University to study mathematics.
1938

黃用諏獲大學取錄的電報
香港大學檔案中心「黃用諏教授特藏」
Telegram to Wong Yung-chow informing him of his admission
Y. C. Wong Collection, HKUA

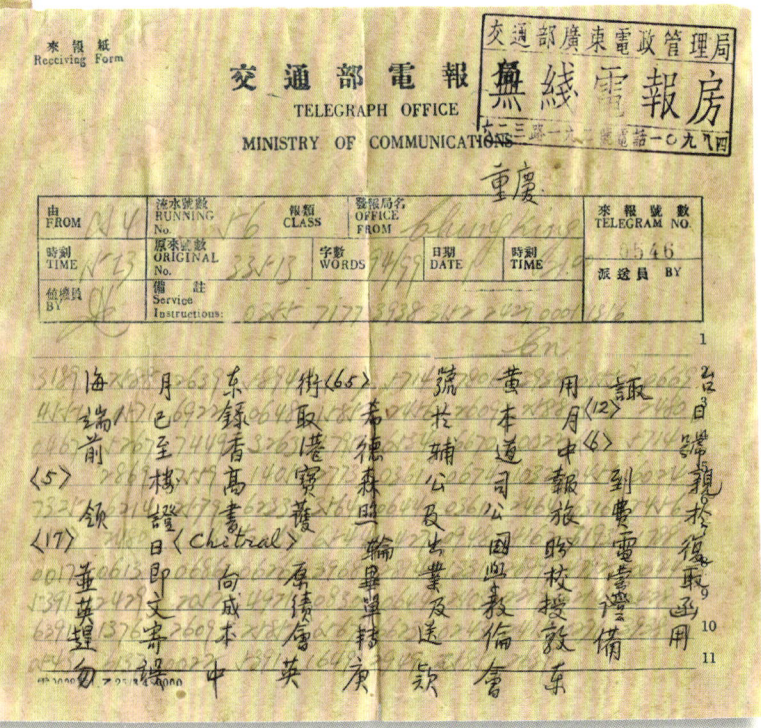

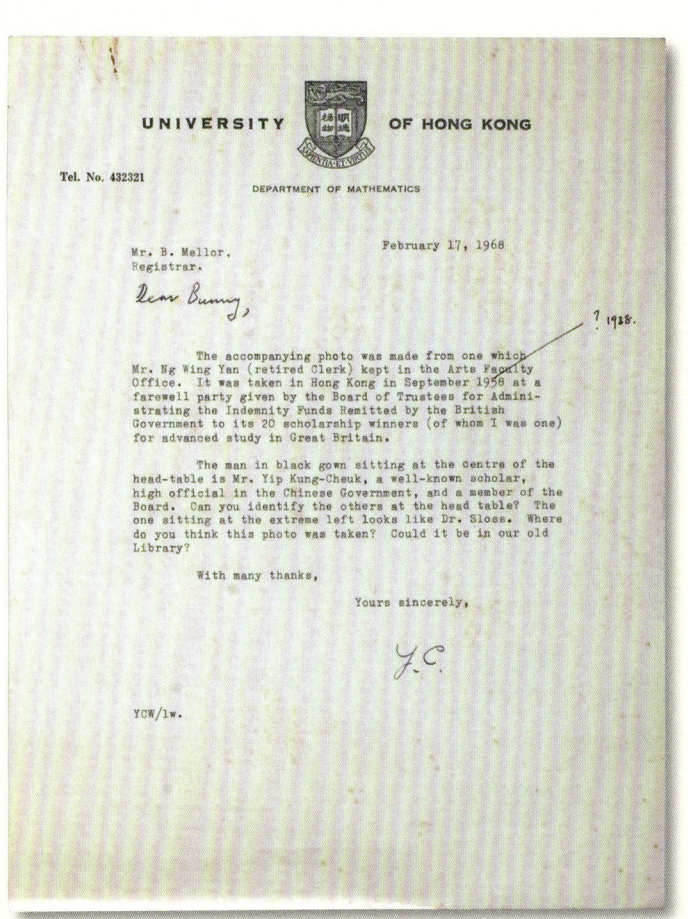

一九六八年黃用諏寫給香港大學教務長梅樂彬
的信，提及以下的相片
香港大學檔案中心「黃用諏教授特藏」
Letter written by Wong Yung-chow to the
University's Registrar, Bernard Mellor in 1968
regarding the photograph below
Y. C. Wong Collection, HKUA

```
UNIVERSITY OF HONG KONG
Tel. No. 432321
DEPARTMENT OF MATHEMATICS

Mr. B. Mellor,                          February 17, 1968
Registrar.

Dear Bunny,
                                                  ? 1928.
    The accompanying photo was made from one which
Mr. Ng Wing Yan (retired Clerk) kept in the Arts Faculty
Office. It was taken in Hong Kong in September 1938 at a
farewell party given by the Board of Trustees for Admini-
strating the Indemnity Funds Remitted by the British
Government to its 20 scholarship winners (of whom I was one)
for advanced study in Great Britain.

    The man in black gown sitting at the centre of the
head-table is Mr. Yip Kung-Cheuk, a well-known scholar,
high official in the Chinese Government, and a member of the
Board. Can you identify the others at the head table? The
one sitting at the extreme left looks like Dr. Sloss. Where
do you think this photo was taken? Could it be in our old
Library?

    With many thanks,

                                        Yours sincerely,

                                            Y.C.
YCW/lw.
```

中英庚子賠款第六屆二十位留英公費學生出發之前
在香港大學留影
一九三八年
香港大學檔案中心「黃用諏教授特藏」
Photograph of the twenty British Government
Indemnity Fund scholarship recipients taken at
the University of Hong Kong before their
departure for Great Britain
1938
Y. C. Wong Collection, HKUA

相片正中是漢學家葉恭綽，左二是黃用諏，後方最右是中文系教授馬鑑。
Seated at the head of the table is the Sinologist Yip Kung-cheuk, second left is
Wong Yung-chow. In the background far right is Chinese professor Ma Kiam.

HKU Memories | from the Archives

一九三三年出版的香港大學英文紀念刊物
Souvenir booklet, *Hongkong University, 1912-1933*

香港大學一九三零至四零年代
HKU IN THE 1930S AND 1940S

4

香港大學成長期
HKU Comes of Age

康寧爵士為香港大學第四任校長（一九二四至一九三七年）。他於一九三三年出版的香港大學紀念特刊（*Hong Kong University 1912–1933*）撰寫前言，提及成立大學時，白文信爵士和盧吉勳爵的目標十分清晰，他們均對香港充滿信心，認為香港可為中國出力，所以白文信促成香港西醫書院的建立，盧吉則設立了香港大學。當時大學仍於起步階段，財政並未穩健。康寧接受了鄧志昂和馮平山的捐獻，帶領著大學不但克服經濟方面的困難，更負起為本地華人提供高等教育及發展大學的使命。

Sir William Hornell was the University's fourth Vice-Chancellor (1924–1937). In the foreword of the University's souvenir booklet *Hong Kong University 1912–1933*, Hornell wrote of the founding of the University, 'The motives of Sir Patrick Manson and Lord Lugard were clear and straightforward. They had faith in Hong Kong and in what Hong Kong could and should do for China. Therefore one founded a Medical College; the other created a University.' The University was still in its infancy and faced many challenges in becoming financially stable. In accepting the donations from Tang Chi-ngong and Fung Ping-shan, Hornell was supporting a vision of the University that met the aspirations of the local Chinese population as well as the University's need to grow.

校長康寧爵士畫像
小磯良平（一九零三至一九八八年）作
一九三七年
油彩
Portrait of Sir William Hornell as Vice-Chancellor
Ryohei Koiso (1903-1988)
1937
Oil on canvas
H: 124 cm W: 94 cm

HKU Memories | from the Archives

香港大學中文學科的早期發展

一九一二年大學開校以後,校方聘請賴際熙、區大典兩位太史執教經史。一九二六年康寧校長與賴際熙計劃將原來一年制的經史選修課程改為學位課程,並興建獨立的中文學院校舍,內置圖書館及博物館;甚獲雅好中文的港督金文泰支持。

港大創立初年,何啟領導香港大學華人勸捐支會大力募捐,呼籲華人慈善家贊助為中國而立的香港大學,反應非常熱烈。遠在海外馬來亞的個別華人亦大力支持,包括中國駐東南亞總領事張弼士,他相信興辦大學將帶領中國走上現代化,一九一零年捐出九萬元創辦港大,一九一三至一九一九年間再捐出七萬六千元予文學院課程。另外郭春秧則特別捐款予中文教學。

一九一五年馬來亞錫礦及橡膠大王陸佑向大學提供五十萬元免息貸款,為期二十一年,令大學安然渡過財政危機。一九一八年余東璇亦捐款予大學捐贈基金。

一九二六年康寧與賴際熙到馬來亞為中文學院籌款,獲當地戴喜云之遺產捐款四萬元。大學並自行撥款一萬元購買中文書籍。再得鄧志昂、馮平山兩位慈善家慷慨捐建院舍,一九三一年鄧志昂樓啟用作為中文學院,一九三二年馮平山圖書館亦落成。兩座大樓均由港督兼大學校監貝璐爵士主持揭幕。

陸佑 Loke Yew

可惜當時馮平山已離世,未及親睹他的捐建正式啟用。其家族及其他捐贈者繼續為圖書館出力不少,開館時已共捐置逾三萬冊書籍,亦成為日後大學圖書館的發展基礎。

一九六一年大學圖書館脫離本部大樓,搬進新建樓房,並首次擴展藏書規模。馮平山圖書館則易名馮平山博物館,專門展出中國藝術文物。一九九四年,企業家、收藏家兼慈善家徐展堂博士(一九四一至二零一零年)慷慨捐獻港大,興建位於馮平山樓旁以其命名的徐展堂樓,並訂立條件必須將新樓最底三層撥作博物館新翼。一九九六年香港大學美術博物館正式開放。

一九三五年賴際熙、區大典相繼退休。許地山應聘為首位中文系教授,他是國際知名學者、精通古典文學、佛學、梵藏語文,卻於一九四一年抗戰期間突然逝世。陳寅恪繼任為中文系主任,但他因不願投誠日軍,憤而離開香港。日治時期馮平山圖書館館長陳君葆兼任大學助理講師,他致力保存館內圖書收藏,居功不少。

二次大戰後馬鑑出任中文系主任,至一九五零年退休。由萊德敖教授繼任,可惜翌年(一九五一年)他猝然離世。一九五二年林仰山教授接任為中文系主任。

賴際熙 Lai Chi-hsi

參考:C. M. Turnbull, 'The Malayan Connection', in Chan and Cunich, pp. 99–117; Frederick Drake, 'Chinese and Oriental Studies', in Harrison, pp. 142–147; Cunich, pp. 220–227; 315–317.

The early development of Chinese studies

When the University opened in 1912, two Hanlin Academy scholars, Lai Chi-hsi (Lai Jixi) and Au Tai-tin (Ou Dadian) were teaching courses in Chinese literature and history. In 1926, with the support of Chancellor Sir Cecil Clementi, himself a distinguished Sinologist, Vice-Chancellor Sir William Hornell and Lai Chi-hsi planned to turn the University's one-year elective course in Chinese literature and history into a degree-level course. The plan was ambitious and included the establishment of an independent faculty of Chinese, with its own library and museum.

Chinese philanthropists were enthusiatic supporters of the University project through the Chinese fund-raising sub-committee, chaired by Ho Kai, who advocated the benefits of the project for Chinese. It also enjoyed generous support from individual donors in Malaya including the Chinese Consul-General in South East Asia, Cheung Pat-sze (Cheong Fatt Tze), who believed that the University would help China to modernise. In 1910, he donated $90,000 towards the founding of the University, and gave a further $76,000 between 1913 and 1919 for classes in the Arts Faculty. Specific funds for the teaching of Chinese were also donated at the time by Kwok Chun-yeung. In 1915 Loke Yew, a tin and rubber magnate in Malaya, saved the University from further financial difficulties by offering an interest free loan of $500,000 for a period of twenty-one years. An additional $55,000 was given in 1918 by Eu Tong-sen towards the general endowment.

In 1926 Vice-Chancellor Hornell and Lai Chi-hsi traveled to Malaya to raise funds for the Chinese faculty. They returned with a donation of $40,000 from the estate of Tye Kee-yuen. The University itself committed $10,000 towards the purchase of Chinese books. As part of this initiative, two Chinese philanthropists, Tang Chi-ngong and Fung Ping-shan each donated funds for specific buildings. The Tang Chi Ngong building opened in 1931 as the School of Chinese while the Fung Ping Shan Library was opened in 1932. Both openings were presided over by then Governor of Hong Kong and Chancellor of the University, Sir William Peel.

Fung Ping-shan did not live to see his gift to the University completed but the Fung family and other donors contributed large collections of books for the new library so that when it opened, it already included some 30,000 volumes and was a significant contribution to the development of the University's Libraries.

In 1961, when the Library moved out of the Main Building into its own purpose-built facility, the Libraries were consolidated for the first time. The Fung Ping Shan Library building was renamed the Fung Ping Shan Museum showing exhibitions of Chinese art and archaeology. In 1994, a donation from the entrepreneur, collector and philanthropist Tsui Tsin-tong (T. T. Tsui, 1941–2010), made possible a new building named after him adjacent to the Fung Ping Shan building. One of the conditions of the donation were that the lower three floors would constitute an extension of the existing museum, which was renamed the University Museum and Art Gallery when the new extension opened in 1996.

Lai Chi-hsi and Au Tai-tin retired in 1935. Dr Hsu Ti-shan (Xu Dishan), a highly distinguished scholar

張弼士 Cheung Pat-sze

of Classical Chinese, Buddhism, Sanskrit and Tibetan, joined the University as the first Professor of Chinese. His premature death in 1941 coincided with the outbreak of war in Hong Kong. Visiting professor Chen Yinke took over briefly as head of the department but left Hong Kong during the occupation. Assistant lecturer and keeper of the Fung Ping Shan Library, Chan Kwan-po, a graduate of the department helped save many of the books in the Library from destruction.

After the war, Ma Kiam (Ma Jian) assumed the position of head until his retirement in 1950. He was succeeded by Professor J. K. Rideout who died shortly after taking up his post in 1951. In 1952, Professor Frederick Seguier Drake joined the University as the new head of the School of Chinese.

一九三一年（左二）周壽臣爵士、旭龢爵士、港督貝璐爵士、及其他賓客參加鄧志昂中文學院開幕盛會。一九三三年周壽臣爵士獲港大頒授名譽法學博士學位，但相關檔案卻遍尋不獲。

From left to right, Sir Shouson Chow (second left), Sir Robert Kotewall, Governor Sir William Peel and guests attending the opening ceremony of the Tang Chi Ngong School of Chinese in 1931. In 1933, the University awarded Shouson Chow with an honorary doctorate in law, however in common with other pre-war records, these are missing.

鄧志昂中文學院開幕典
一九三一
Alethea Rogers 夫人捐
The opening ceremony of t
Tang Chi Ngong School of Chine
19
Gift of Mrs Alethea Roge

鄧志昂中文學院
Tang Chi Ngong School of Chinese

一九三一年中文學會合照
文學院相簿
The Chinese Society in 1931
Arts Faculty Album

HKU Memories | from the Archives

馮平山與他的圖書館
Fung Ping Shan and his Library

一九二九年二月二日馮平山致康寧校長信件，內容以第三身同意捐款十萬元興建中文圖書館。可惜他於一九三二年圖書館落成前逝世，未能親睹他的捐建成真。

Correspondence dated 2nd February 1929 from Fung Ping-shan to Vice-Chancellor Hornell regarding his promised gift of $100,000 for the building of a Chinese book library. In the letter he refers to himself in the third person. Sadly, Fung Ping-shan did not live to see his plans realised when the building was opened in 1932.

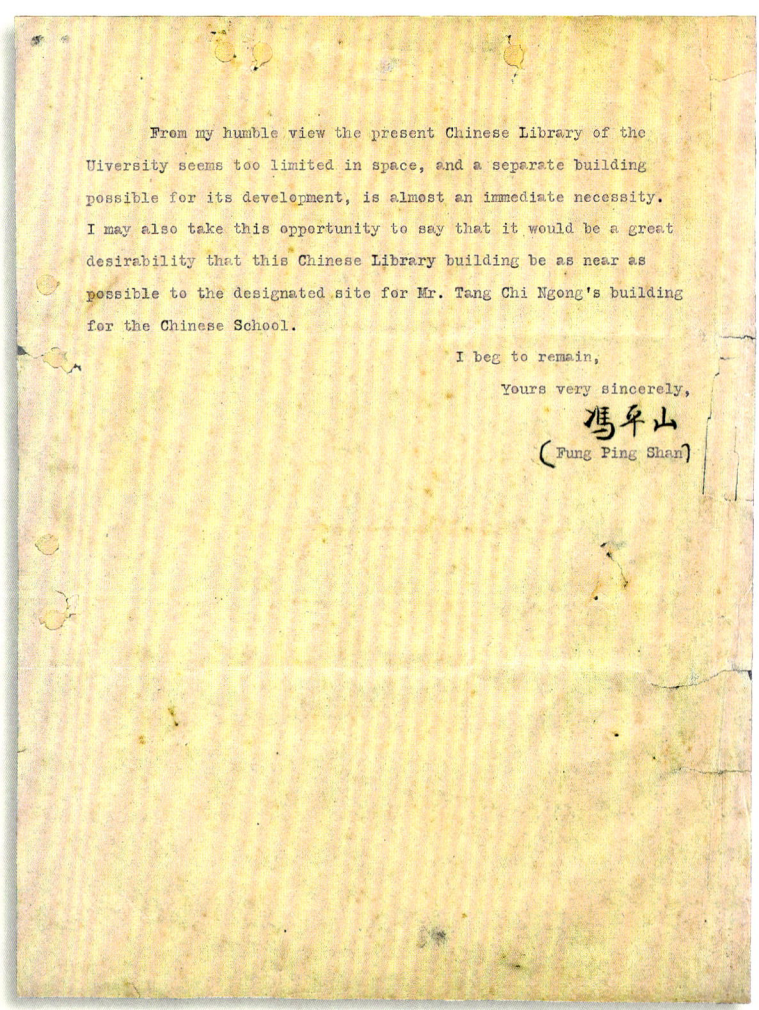

> 1, Park Road,
> February 2nd. 1929
>
> Dear Mr. Hornell,
>
> I have the pleasure to inform you that my friend who proposed to present the University a building worth $100,000 for the Chinese Library has confirmed his proposal and already deposited some money in a local bank for that purpose. I may add that I am glad to be responsible for the payment of this promised gift.
>
> Recently he returned to Hongkong for a few days and took the opportunity to look round the University site in my company. As a result we considered the foot of "Haldon" (opposite King's College) as most suitable for the site of the Chinese Library building.
>
> As you know, the only conditions he would ask for were (1) that the proposed Chinese Library should be also open to the public and for this purpose it is desirable that it should be built within the University site and also near the public road; & (2) that this building should be permanently and exclusively used to house the Chinese Library. As these conditions had been mentioned to you and met with your kind consent in our first interview on the matter, I am sure they would be agreeable to the University authorities as a whole.
>
> As to other conventional honours which the University would confer on my friend in return for this gift (such as the building would bear his name etc.), I shall be glad to have them so that I may be able to communicate to him at an early date.
>
> From my humble view the present Chinese Library of the University seems too limited in space, and a separate building possible for its development, is almost an immediate necessity. I may also take this opportunity to say that it would be a great desirability that this Chinese Library building be as near as possible to the designated site for Mr. Tang Chi Ngong's building for the Chinese School.
>
> I beg to remain,
> Yours very sincerely,
> 馮平山
> (Fung Ping Shan)

馮平山畫像
一九三零年代
油彩
Portrait of Fung Ping-shan
1930s
Oil on canvas
H: 140 cm W: 101 cm

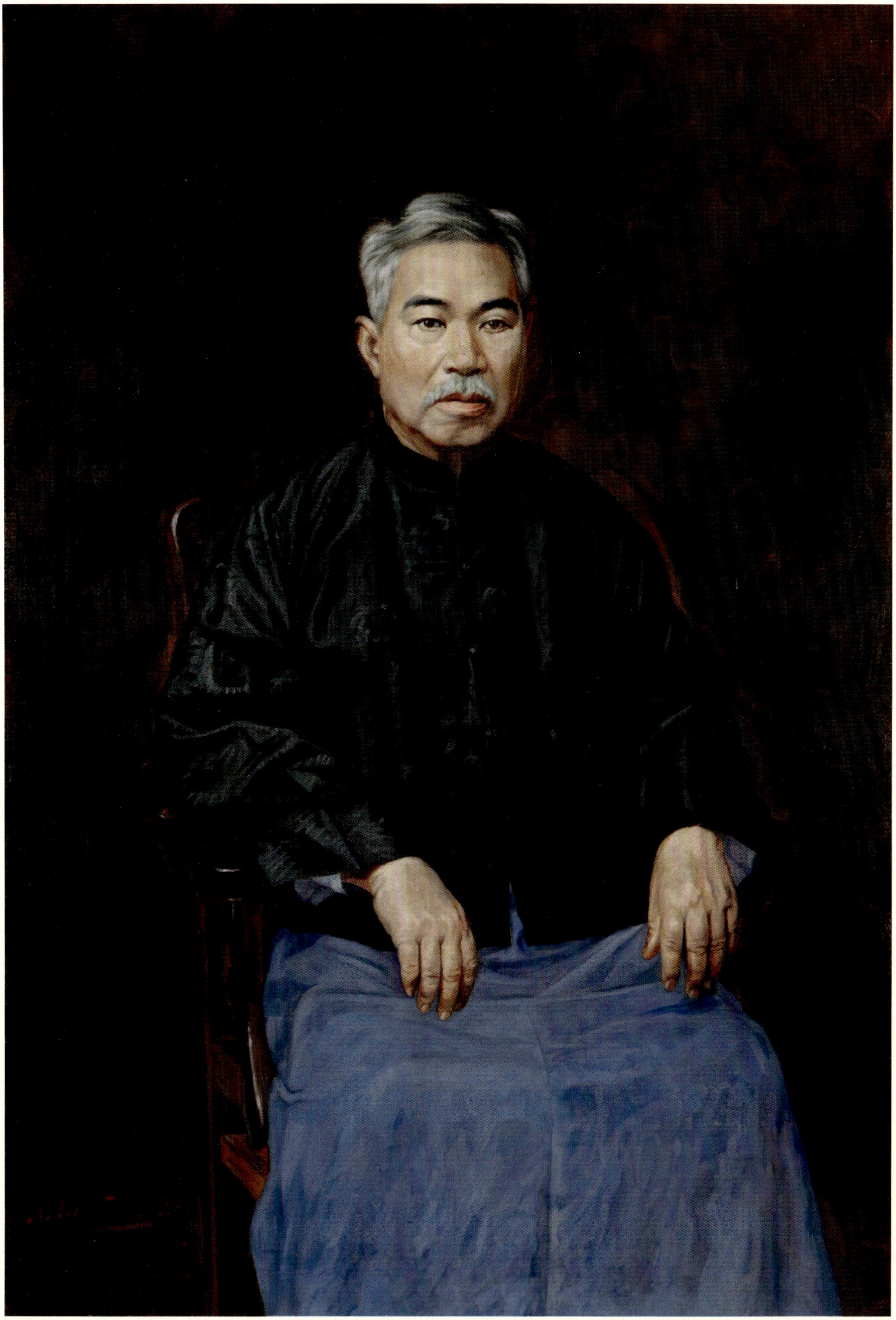

馮平山圖書館內貌，展示馮平山銅像
Interior of the Fung Ping Shan Library showing the Librarian's desk and the bust of Fung Ping-shan amid the stacks

意大利雕塑家蒙蒂（一八八八年至一九五八年）於一九三零年至一九五八年旅居菲律賓。美國殖民統治期間（一九三五至一九四六年）以及戰後，他製作了很多公共雕塑藝術。由於他早年受業於意大利皮埃蒙特裝飾藝術與科技學院、米蘭比里扎皇家藝術學院，其作品深受古典藝術以及裝飾藝術運動影響。蒙蒂於一九二八年離開意大利到各地遊歷，他在紐約結識了菲律賓建築師阿雷拉諾，獲邀前往菲律賓，開始了他餘生的旅居生涯。蒙蒂經常借鑒古典文學中的寓言典故為創作主題，並引用菲律賓文化與歷史的元素在作品中。

Francesco Riccardo Monti (1888–1958) was an Italian sculptor who lived in the Philippines from 1930 to 1958. He made many public sculptures there during the years when the Philippines was a Commonwealth of the United States (1935–1946) and during the post-war period. Monti's works have a strong classical influence, owing to his early training in Italy at the Institute of Ponzone for Decorative Arts and Technology and the Royal Academy of Breza in Milan, as well as the Art Deco movement. He left Italy in 1928 to travel. In New York he met the Philippine architect Juan M. de Guzman Arellano who invited him to the Philippines, where he spent the rest of his life. He often created allegorical works with classical allusions, making use of elements from Filipino culture and history.

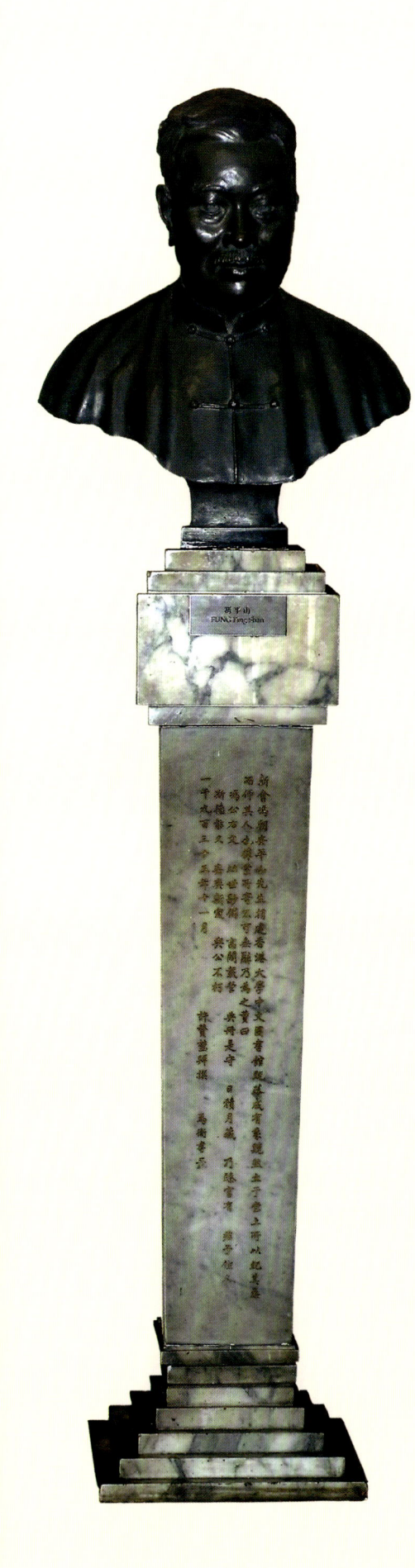

馮平山 (一八六零至一九三一年) 銅像
Bronze bust of Fung Ping-shan (1860 - 1931)
作者款 Signed 'R. Monti'

銅像 Bust: H: 60 cm W: 50 cm D: 30 cm
雲石座 Marble base: H: 122 cm W: 36 cm D: 36 cm

雲石座上題款：

新會馮朝安平山先生，捐建香港大學中文圖書館。既落成，有象巍然立于堂上，所以紀其惠而仰其人也。偉業所寄，不可無辭，乃為之贊曰：

馮公右文，竝世妙偶，高閣載營，典冊是守。日積月藏，乃臻富有，君子作

人，斯德能久。奕奕新成，與公不朽。

一千九百三十五年十一月
許贊堃 [許地山] 拜撰   馬衡 [一八八一年至一九五五年] 書丹

The translation of the inscription on the base reads:

On the completion of the Chinese Library of the University of Hong Kong gifted by Mr Fung Ping-shan, original name Chao'an, a native of Xinhui in Guangdong province, a bust of the donor was placed in the hall for people to admire his generosity. His great achievement must be acknowledged with the inscription below:

The efforts of Master Fung in promoting ancient culture are great, and unique in this world. The construction of this grand library to house valuable Chinese books will enhance the development of a rich collection generation to generation. Mr Fung's character has reached so extraordinary a level that his merits and virtues as a cultivated gentleman will be everlasting. Now with the newly completed library named after him, Mr Fung Ping-shan will become immortal.

November 1935
Composed by Xu Zankun [Hsu Ti-shan]
Calligraphy by Ma Heng [1881–1955]

港督貝璐爵士與外科系大樓金匙

一九三五年港大第二十六屆學位頒授典禮當日，港督貝璐爵士主持狄比外科系大樓開幕儀式時所用金鑰匙。貝璐爵士為一九三零至一九三五年港大校監，他在開門儀式上把金鑰匙拗曲了。

貝璐爵士在獻詞時說：'近年外科醫學進步飛快，拯救無數生命。狄比教授在這方面的貢獻勞苦功高，他對香港外科醫學的發展可算功不可抹。這幢新外科系大樓已於數月前啟用，到今天舉行開幕典禮，我在此送上祝福，希望事成功。我雖未及目睹健康學系和法律學系的開幕，但深信往後的港督一定有幸參與這些盛事。'[1]

在當天典禮上，貝璐爵士獲頒名譽法學博士學位。校長康寧爵士讚頌他：'您貴為港大的終生成員，相信絕不會忘記大學。而我們亦一樣，憑著閣下的真知灼見，促使大學跨越障礙，努力達到服務社會的使命，我們會銘記您對港大的貢獻。'[2]

外科學院

這座三層高紅磚大樓為港大首間外科學院，它位於本部大樓西閘旁邊，當時耗資二萬四千元興建，一九三五年一月七日啟用。大樓後來以狄比教授而命名，以紀念他一九一三年入職港大，並擔任外科系主任逾三十年。戰時狄比不幸被俘，戰後轉業私人行醫，後來獲聘為大學講座教授，直至一九五四年逝世為止。一九五零年外科系搬到瑪麗醫院上課，大樓便轉作骨科學系、疾病防治與社會醫藥系的校舍。大樓於一九七七年拆卸。

School of Surgery

This modest three-storey red brick building was the University's first School of Surgery. Built near the West Gate at a cost of $24,000, it opened on 7th January 1935. It was later named in honour of Professor Kenelm H. Digby, who joined the University in 1913 and served as head of the Department of Surgery for over thirty years. He was interned during the war and entered private practice following its cessation. Digby was appointed Emeritus Professor at the University, a position he held until his death in 1954. The Department of Surgery was transferred to Queen Mary Hospital in 1950. The Digby Building then housed the Departments of Orthopaedic Surgery and Preventive and Social Medicine. It was demolished in 1977.

Sir William Peel and the Golden Key to the School of Surgery Building

This golden key was used on the occasion of the inauguration of the School of Surgery Building in 1935 on the day of the 26th Congregation by Sir William Peel, Governor of Hong Kong (and Chancellor of the University) from 1930 to 1935. The building was eventually named after Professor Kenhelm H. Digby, an event foreshadowed in Peel's speech.

He had this to say upon the occasion: 'The science of surgery has advanced enormously during recent years and through it countless lives have been saved. I feel that I am not overstating facts when I say that in this work Professor Digby has played a notable part and the Colony owes him much. This new surgery block has been in use for some months though its formal opening only takes place today. I wish it every success. I would that it had fallen to my lot to open a new School of Health and a School of Law but I trust that such privileges will fall to my successor…' [1]

As Chancellor, Sir William Peel was also honoured on that day with a Doctor of Laws degree. The Vice-Chancellor, Sir William Hornell, said to him 'We do not think that you will easily forget this University of which you are now a life member. Here your name will long be valued as one who, with rare foresight, ever looked beyond our many defects and the difficulties of the moment to the greater possibilities for service towards which every University must strive or perish.' [2]

1, 2 26th Congregation, 1935, Registry Records, HKUA.

金鑰匙由 Alethea Rogers 夫人捐贈，是她送予港大百周年慶典的禮物，也為了紀念其祖父貝璐爵士。她其後從家庭相簿中送來兩幅相片，一張是貝璐爵士出席聖約翰救傷隊活動時所攝，另一張攝於四年之前的一九三一年鄧志昂中文學院開幕典禮，記錄了貝璐爵士、周壽臣爵士、旭龢爵士與其他賓客衣香鬢影參加開幕禮盛會。鄧志昂中文學院開幕之後兩年，周壽臣爵士獲港大頒授名譽法學博士學位。

The key was given to the Archives by Mrs Alethea Rogers, in honour of the Centenary and of her grandfather, Sir William Peel. Mrs Rogers later sent two photographs from the family collection: one is of Sir William Peel at a function of the St John's Ambulance Brigade and the other of him and other dignitaries, including Sir Shouson Chow and Sir Robert Kotewall, at the opening of the Tang Chi Ngong Building for Chinese Studies four years earlier in 1931 (see page 114). Two years after this picture was taken Sir Shouson Chow was given an Honorary Doctor of Laws degree by HKU.

HKU Memories | from the Archives 121

徐悲鴻與香港大學
Xu Beihong visits HKU

徐悲鴻《琵琶行》
紙本水墨設色
一九三八年繪贈香港大學中文學會
款識：廿七年歲闌悲鴻
香港大學美術博物館藏品（HKU.P.2002.1424）
Xu Beihong
Playing Pipa
Ink and colour on paper
1938
H: 87 cm W: 66 cm
Collection of the University Museum and
Art Gallery (HKU.P.2002.1424)

一九三八年徐悲鴻（左一）在馮平山圖書館大門拍攝的合照
The artist Xu Beihong (first left) at the entrance of the Fung Ping Shan Library in 1938

題款：

留得琵琶伴此身，紅綃一曲為誰陳。
同情有淚惟司馬，濕透青衫第一人。

二十七年十二月徐悲鴻先生出其所藏近人書畫陳馮平山圖書館，以供觀覽，並為中文學會作此圖，俾留紀念，畫成，適郭天祐女士以近作讀琵琶行絕句見示：余愛其饒有風致，因與商榷數字，即以題之左方。竊人之詩，污人之畫，作者見之，將毋謂此君何好事乃爾。

馬鑑於香港

The translation of the inscription reads:

I keep a pipa with me. They all award me silk for one song, but who should I play for? Bai Juyi is the only one that understands me. His are the first tears to wet his clothing.

Xu Beihong painted this painting in 1938 for the Chinese Society of the University of Hong Kong. Xu also loaned a number of his works to the Fung Ping Shan Library in December for viewing by the public. Coincidentally, Ms Kwok Tin-yau wrote a four-line poem called 'Playing Pipa'.

I liked her work, modified it and wrote it on the left of the painting. I stole a poem and ruined a painting. If the authors see them, they might say that I had done something unnecessary.

Ma Kiam in Hong Kong

HKU Memories | from the Archives

UNIVERSITY OF HONG KONG
DEPARTMENT OF CHINESE STUDIES.

Confidential
15th. August, 1940.

Vice-Chancellor.

Dear Mr. Sloss,

Acting on your instructions, I have spoken with Prof. Chen Yin-ko on your offer of a visiting professorship in this University. He expresses his keen appreciation of the offer and says nothing but the following consideration prevents him from accepting it immediately. At the Tsing-hwa University, a professor, who has completed fifteen years of service, will be entitled to pension. Prof. Chen has completed his fourteenth year and quite naturally is not prepared to forego his privileges almost earned by his service. He has therefore asked Dr. Han Lih-wu to consult the Tsing-hwa University authorities if he be allowed to accept this offer without prejudice to his privileges. So soon as he hears from Dr. Han, he will let us know his definite reply, he assures me.

With regard to his subjects, I have already explained to you Prof. Chen's position in relation to the new established tradition in Chinese universities. In the light of this consideration, it will be most convenient if he is asked to give a course on Mediaeval Chinese Literature and History, including the "Six Dynasties" and "Tang", i.e. from the 4th to the 10th Century roughly. Under that general heading, Prof. Chen can, of course, deliver a series of lectures with special relation to Chinese philosophy and the development of Chinese thought during that period. It may perhaps be pointed out that the professor's title with the Tsing-hwa University is "Research Professor of Mediaeval Chinese Literature and History".

As soon as an answer is received from Dr. Han Lih-wu, I shall arrange to accompany Prof. Chen to see you.

Yours sincerely,

Hsü Ti-shan.
Professor of Chinese.

HTS:L

一九四零年許地山向史羅司引薦陳寅恪的兩封信
Two letters from Hsu Ti-shan to Duncan Sloss recommending Chen Yinke, 1940

UNIVERSITY OF HONG KONG
DEPARTMENT OF CHINESE STUDIES.

28th. August, 1940.

Vice Chancellor,

In connection with the proposed appointment of Prof. Tschen Yin-koh as a visiting professor in this University, I beg to furnish the following particulars:

Prof. Tschen Yin-koh （陳寅恪）
b. July 3, 1890.
Native of I-ning county, Kiangsi Province.
Graduates School, Harvard University and Berlin University.
Since 1927, Professor of Chinese and History, Tsing Hwa University.
Research Fellow and Head of Historical Department, Institute of History and Philology, Academia Sinica.
Member of the National Council of Higher Learning, Academia Sinica.
Prize Winner, China Foundation.
His written works:-
1) Origin and Development of the Political Institutions of Sui and Tang.
2) A Critical Study of "Tsin Fu Yin", a Tang poem about a refugee woman from the Tsin, i.e. Shen-si Province.
3) Numerous other historical essays appearing from time to time in the Bulletins of the Institute of History and Philology, Academia Sinica, and in the Tsing Hwa Journal.
4) Various Contributions (in English) to the Harvard Journal of Asiatic Studies.
5) Articles (in Japanese) appearing in the Bulletin of Oriental Studies, published by the Societas in Memoriam Wangkwowei.

In regard to a course of lectures while he is here, I suggest the following:-
1. History of the Tang Dynasty, with special relation to the Poetry of the Middle and the Later Tang Period and its historical and social background. A series of about 20 weekly lectures or more delivered in Chinese say at 4 to 5 p.m. on a week-day to be fixed later on.
2. A Seminary course of 4 monthly professional talks of say 2 hours each. Explanation, if required, might be given in English.
Nov. A Study of the Poem: "Tsin Fu Yin".
Dec. Empress Wu Tse-tein and Buddhism.

- 2 -

Jan. 'Huai Chen Chi' the short story by Yuan Chen.
Feb. Taoism in the 'Six Dynasties'.

Yours sincerely,

Hsü Ti-shan.
Professor of Chinese.

HTS:L

一九三八至一九三九年教育系學會合照
文學院相簿
The Education Society in 1938-1939
Arts Faculty Album

前排右方為許地山
Hsu Ti-shan is seated in the front row, bottom right

許地山（一八九四至一九四一年）原名許贊堃，出生於台灣，成長於福建，筆名落花生。一九一七年考入北平燕京大學，修讀文史及神學，曾創辦文藝學會，並參加了五四運動。畢業後於一九二三年到美國紐約哥倫比亞大學的聯合宗教研究院進修碩士課程，再入讀英國牛津大學。一九二七年在母校燕京大學文學院及宗教學院任教。一九三五年出任香港大學中文系主任，他於任內革新中文系課程，加入文學、史學、哲學三科，大力提倡白話文。許地山在家因心臟病發逝世，享年四十八歲。雖然他在港大任教只有短短六年時間，但他對學生、同事以至社會影響深遠。在其喪禮上，憑弔的公眾表現極為哀傷。

Hsu Ti-shan (Xu Dishan) (1894–1941) was born in Taiwan and raised in Fujian. He is also known by his literary pen name of 'Louhuasheng', literally 'peanuts'. In 1917 he was admitted to Yenching University to study arts and theology, during which time he formed a literary society and participated in the May Fourth Movement. After graduation, Hsu went to the Union Theological Seminary at Columbia University, New York in 1923 to study for a Masters degree and later furthered his studies at Oxford University. From 1927 onwards he was a lecturer at Yenching University until he was appointed the Head of the Chinese Department of the University of Hong Kong in 1935. He reformed the curriculum to include literature, history and philosophy, and advocated the use of vernacular Chinese. He died of a heart attack at home at the age of 48. Although he was only at the University for six years he had a great influence on students, colleagues and the community. The public outpouring of grief at his funeral was immense.

陳寅恪（一八九零至一九六九年）出生於湖南長沙，為著名漢學家、歷史學家、語言學家。父親陳三立是大詩人散原老人。一九二五年陳寅恪擔任國立清華大學國學研究院導師，教授佛經翻譯文學、東方目錄學、梵文文法、碑志學、摩尼教經、回紇譯文本研究、蒙古文與滿州文研究等新課程。他與王國維、梁啟超、趙元任合稱清華四大才子。

一九三一年出任中央研究院和國立故宮博物院理事，以及清代檔案館委員。一九四一年獲香港大學許地山教授禮聘作客座教授。一九四一年許地山猝然逝世，他繼任為中文系主任，半年後日本占領香港時離開。一九四五年陳寅恪不幸失明，仍獲牛津大學聘請教授漢學，成為華人出任英聯邦大學講座教授的第一人。一九四六年回歸中國。一九四九至一九五七年任教於廣州嶺南大學。

Chen Yinke (1890–1969) was born in Changsha, Hunan province to the poet Chen Sanli. Chen was a renowned Sinologist and historian, and an accomplished linguist. Appointed to Tsinghua (Qinghua) University in 1925, he taught subjects such as Buddhist translation, oriental bibliography, Sanskrit grammar, the comparative study of inscriptions, the comparative study of Manichaean texts and the old Uighur alphabet.

In 1931, he was appointed a member of the Council of Academia Sinica, the National Palace Museum Council, and Qing dynasty Archive Committee. In 1940 he was invited to The University of Hong Kong by Hsu Ti-Shan to be a visiting professor, taking up the position of Head of the Chinese Department following Hsu's untimely death in 1941. He held this position for only half a year before the Japanese occupation. In 1945 Chen became blind but continued to teach Sinology at Oxford University, becoming the first Chinese to be appointed full professor in a university of the British Commonwealth. He returned to China in 1946. Although blind, he taught at Lingnan University from 1949 to 1957.

文學協會
約一九三四年
文學院相簿
Arts Association
c. 1934
Arts Faculty Album

前排右一為陳寅恪
Chen Yinke is seated in the front row, bottom right

戰後陳君葆攝於本部大樓
Chan Kwan-po at the entrance of the Main Building after the war

陳君葆（一八九八至一九八二年）出生於廣東中山。一九一七年獲獎學金到香港大學攻讀政治及經濟。一九三四年受聘為香港大學翻譯員，兼任馮平山圖書館館長，期間他與許地山等人合力推動新文學運動，提倡改革，並加強大學的文史學科教育。至日軍占領香港，查封港大圖書館，陳君葆為保存圖書免受破壞，自願留在圖書館整理藏書。此外，他也致力保護文獻檔案，把散落在中環郵政總局的出生註冊文件運送到圖書館保管，這些資料對戰後核實香港人身份起了很大作用。一九四七年獲英女皇頒授OBE勳銜。一九五六年從大學退休，繼續從事文學寫作。

Chan Kwan-po (1898–1982) was born in Zhongshan, Guangdong province. In 1917 he was awarded a Hewett Memorial Scholarship to study politics and economics at HKU. He returned to the University in 1934 as a Translator, and concurrently served as Librarian of the Fung Ping Shan Library. He joined Hsu Ti-shan in promoting new literary movements and advocating reform and promoted arts education at the University. During the war, the Library fell into the hands of the Japanese. Chan remained to look after the holdings under the surveillance of the occupiers. During this time he also collected discarded birth certificate documents found at the Central Post Office and kept them in the Library. He performed the work of a government archivist when the government was no longer functioning. These papers became extremely important in confirming the identities of Hong Kong citizens in the post-war period. Chan was awarded an OBE in 1947. He retired in 1956 and continued to write.

Univ. No. 250 Name Chan Kwan Po 陳君葆

BIRTH: Place, Heung Sha District. Date, / /1899   Nationality, Chinese

Parent or ~~Guardian~~ Chan Pui Chi

Home Address 5, Poh Wah Street, (2nd floor)

Local Guardian —

Address of same —

Previous Education Queen's College   (Stamped photograph)

Matric. Exam. (or equivalent) /Dec/1916

~~Equivalent~~

Registered /Feb/1917   Hall Lugard Hall

Scholarships Chamber of Commerce' & Chan Kwai Tsing
(Hewitt memorial)

Degree Examinations......First /May/1917 . Second /May/1918 .
Third /May/1919 . Fourth /May/1920 .

Graduation /5/1920

Dean's comments and Signature   The retiring Dean gave an excellent verbal
report. In my opinion a most satisfactory
student.
                                W. J. Hornell. Dean. 13/7/20

Subsequent career.

陳君葆的香港大學學生紀錄
Chan Kwan-po's student record

陳君葆戰時的日記
Chan Kwan-po's Wartime Diaries

陳君葆戰時的日記
謝榮滾伉儷珍藏
Chan Kwan-po's wartime diaries
Collection of Mr and Mrs Tse Wing-kwon

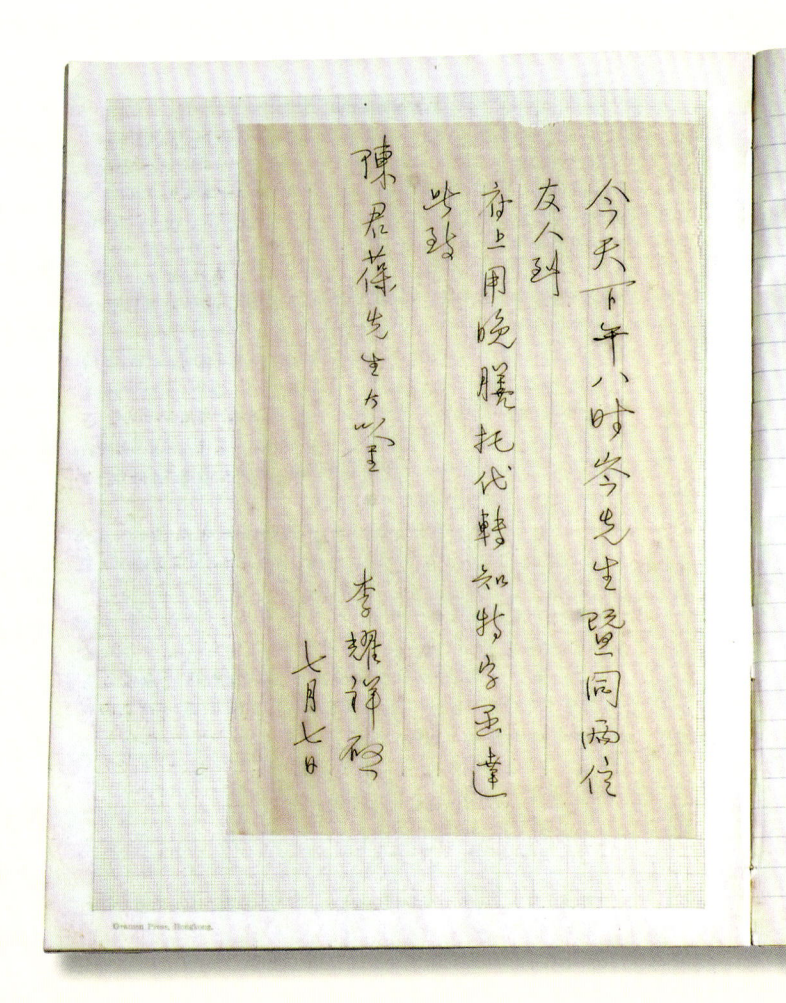

張愛玲與香港大學

大學校園文娛活動區計劃圖，內有聖母堂宿舍位置
Drawing of the proposed site for Recreation, including Our Lady's Hostel

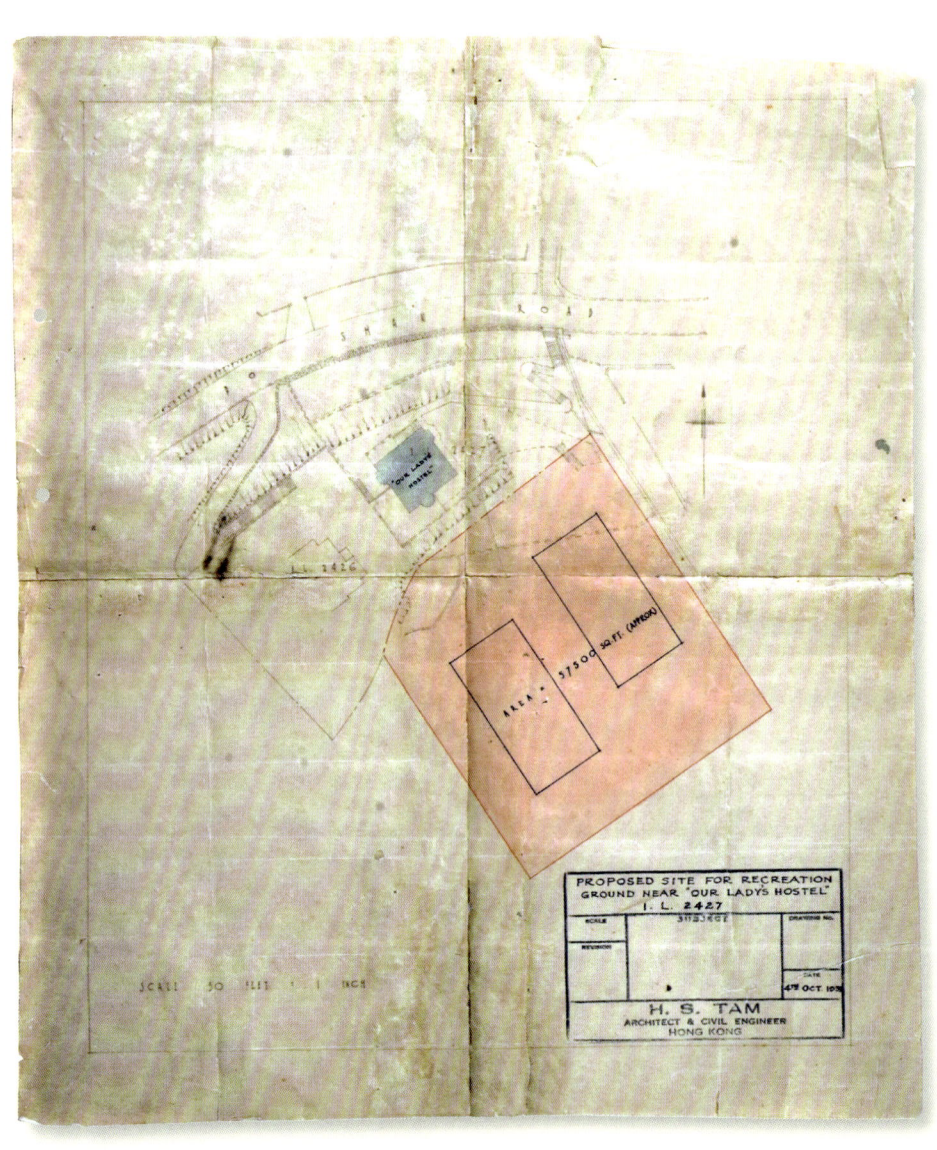

作家**張愛玲**(一九二零至一九九五年)出生於上海。童年生活並不愉快，為求離家，本擬負笈英國倫敦大學就讀，惟遭逢二次大戰爆發，致令計劃告吹，轉而投考香港大學，一九三九至一九四一年間入讀港大文學院。至日軍占領香港，未及完成學位課程而返回上海。

她在港大留學期間，憑著《天才夢》一文參加上海《西風》雜誌舉辦徵文比賽而獲獎；並開始專注英文寫作以磨礪外文。她在香港的經歷對她影響深遠，她於'爐餘錄'（首次發表於一九四五年出版張愛玲作品集《流言》）寫道：'戰時香港所見所聞，唯其因為它對於我有切身的、劇烈的影響，當時我是無從說起的。'其名作《傾城之戀》、《易經》，均取材於戰時香港。至最近她的短篇小說《色戒》由台灣導演李安拍成電影，部份影片更於本部大樓取景。

張愛玲才情橫溢，她廣泛涉獵清代文學，將傳統中國文人寫作結合現代西方感性，創作了膾炙人口的作品。

一九五二年她重回香港，在美國新聞處擔任美國文學翻譯。一九五五年移居美國，後於洛杉磯幽居避世，逝世時孑然一身。其遺產後來轉交摯友宋淇及宋鄺文美夫婦，他們的兒子宋以朗現為張愛玲遺產管理人，他並主持'東南西北'網誌。[1] 張愛玲曾結婚兩次，一九四四年她與胡蘭成結婚，婚姻只維持短暫時間。一九五六年再與編劇家賴雅（Ferdinand Reyher）結婚，至一九六七年賴雅離世。

Eileen Chang and the University of Hong Kong

Photograph by permission of Dr Roland Soong

相片由宋以朗博士提供

The writer Eileen Chang (Zhang Ailing) (1920–1995) was born and raised in Shanghai. She had an unhappy childhood and had applied to study at London University in part to escape it but her plans were curtailed by the outbreak of war. She enrolled instead at the University of Hong Kong. She studied in the Faculty of Arts from 1939 to 1941 but when Hong Kong fell to the Japanese, she returned to Shanghai without completing her degree.

During her time at the University, Chang entered her essay, 'Dream of talent' into a writing competition organised by the magazine, *West Wind* in Shanghai for which she won her first prize. She began to write exclusively in English to improve her written language skills. Chang was deeply influence by her years in Hong Kong. In her essay 'From the Ashes' (first published in a collection of essays, *Written on Water*, in 1945), she wrote that, 'The experiences of wartime Hong Kong had an acute and personal influence on me that I was not aware of at the time'. Her novels, *Love in a Fallen City*, and *The Book of Change*, were set in wartime Hong Kong. More recently one of her short stories was made into the film, *Lust, Caution* by the Taiwanese director, Ang Lee, parts of which were filmed in the University's Main Building.

Chang occupies iconic status as a writer. Her background in Qing literature contributed to her unique literary voice that combines traditional Chinese writing with a modern Western sensibility.

In 1952 she returned to Hong Kong to work for the United States Information Agency as a translator of American literature. She emigrated to the United States in 1955 and died in Los Angeles, a recluse. She left her estate to lifelong friends Mae and Stephen Soong, whose son, Dr Roland Soong, author of the *EastSouthWestNorth* blog,[1] now administers her estate. Chang married twice, once briefly in 1944 to Hu Lancheng, and later in 1956 to scriptwriter Ferdinand Reyher who died in 1967.

聖母堂宿舍
張愛玲在港大的居處
Our Lady's Hall
Eileen Chang lived here while at HKU

[1] www.zonaeuropa.com

ANNUAL REPORT 1939-40, FACULTY OF ARTS.

Univ. No. 3

Name: Miss EILEEN CHANG 張愛玲 Hall: Our Lady's

Department: Group A

Year 1	Subjects	Attendance 1st.	2nd.	3rd.	Examinations Midsessional	Degree	Class and Lab. Work	Remarks

Year 2	Subjects	Attendance 1st.	2nd.	3rd.	Examinations Midsessional	Degree	Supplementary	Remarks
					Jan. 1941.	May, 1941.		Group A
	English	94	98		89P	88P		
	History	100	98		90P	88P		
	Psychology	96	96		63P	51P		
	Chinese: Lit.	95	94		92P	69P		
	Tran.	91						

Name: Miss Eileen Chang.

(Signed) _____ Dean

張愛玲就讀香港大學的學生紀錄
Eileen Chang's student record

Univ. No. .... Name EILEEN CHANG 張愛玲	
BIRTH: Place. Shanghai .... Date, 19/ 9 /1920 .... Nationality. Chinese	
Parent or Guardian... Mr. K.D. Li Miss Yvonne Whang	
Home Address 51 Eddington House, 195 Hart Road, Shanghai	
Local Guardian... Mr. K.D. Li	
Address of same c/o Arnold Co., Holland Building, Hongkong	
Previous Education St. Mary's Hall	
(Stamped ph	
Matric. Exam. (of equivalent) London Matriculation, January/1939	
Equivalent............	
Registered............ 29/ 8 /1939 Hall Our Lady's	
Scholarships............	
Degree Examinations............ First / /19 . Second / 19 .	
Third / /19 . Fourth / 19 .	
Graduation............/ 19............	

Dean's comments and Signature

Subsequent career.

張愛玲就讀香港大學的學生紀錄
Eileen Chang's student record

香港大學的戰時畢業生
Wartime Graduates

徐家祥(一九一六至一九九四年)於一九三八年入讀香港大學,在許地山主持的中文系受業,同班還有伍冬瓊、劉殿爵。一九四一年二次大戰爆發,他還差六個月才畢業,與許多戰時大學生一樣延至一九四二年才獲頒畢業證書。日治時期他加入輔助消防隊伍,後來因此獲授保衛勳章。後來他逃往中國,加入英軍服務團。他在惠州策劃特工活動及逃亡,負責聯繫英軍服務團、中國國民黨、東江縱隊。一九四四年獲頒MBE勳銜。

一九四五年加入英軍政府,任職於新界。一九四六年十月成為首位華人保送英國牛津大學深造政務主任課程。一九四八年回港服務,成為香港首位華人政務官。一九六八年獲擢升,成為首位華人擔當署任華民政務司。同年獲頒OBE勳銜。一九七零年至一九七三年退休為止,他出任立法局議員、徙置事務處處長(一九七零年)、勞工處處長(一九七一年)。退休後,他陸續擔任廉政專員公署顧問委員會成員、明愛總幹事。一九七三年獲頒CBE勳銜。一九九四年逝世,享年七十七歲。遺下妻子Rose、十一名子女、二十一名孫兒。

Tsui Ka-cheung, Paul (1916–1994) entered the University of Hong Kong in 1938 to study Chinese Studies under Hsu Ti-shan. Among his classmates were Ng Tung-king and Lau Din-cheuk. When the war broke out in 1941, he was 6 months shy of his graduation but, in common with other wartime graduates, was awarded his degree in 1942. During the Japanese occupation Tsui worked with the auxiliary Fire Services, for which he later received a Defense Medal. He escaped to Free China where he joined the British Army Aid Group (BAAG). In Huizhou he organized field agent activities and 'runners' liaising between the BAAG and the Chinese nationalist Forces as well as the East River Column. He was made a Member of the Most Excellent Order of the British Empire (MBE) in 1944.

In 1945 Tsui joined the Civil Service working for the British Military Administration in the New Territories. In October 1946 he was the first Chinese to be sent to Oxford to train as a Civil Service Cadet Officer. Upon his return in 1948, he became Hong Kong's first Chinese Administrative Officer, and the first Chinese Deputy Secretary of Chinese Affairs in 1968. In 1968 he was made an Officer of the Most Excellent Order of the British Empire (OBE). From 1970 to his retirement in 1973, Tsui was a member of the Legislative Council and Commissioner for Resettlement (1970) and then Commissioner for Labour and Mines (1971). After retirement, he continued to serve on the advisory committee of the Independent Commission on Corruption (ICAC), and as Secretary General of Caritas, the Catholic charity. Tsui was made a Commander of the Most Excellent Order of the British Empire (CBE) in 1973. He passed away in 1994 at the age of 77, survived by his wife Rose, and their 11 children, and 21 grandchildren.

Notes: *Dictionary of Hong Kong Biography*, pp. 440–441; Records of May Hall, the Old Halls, and Student Records from the Arts Faculty, HKUA; *Growing with Hong Kong*, p. 208; Cunich, pp. 422–423.

Univ. No. .... Name ...Tsui Ka Cheung........ 徐家祥
BIRTH: Place ...Hong Kong... Date. 5/11/1916   Nationality. Chinese
Parent or Guardian ...Peter Tsui...
Home Address ...Sung Him Tong, Fanling, N.T....
Local Guardian ...Peter Tsui...
Address of same ...Sung Him Tong, Fanling, N.T....
Previous Education ...Wah Yan College...

Matric. Exam. (of equivalent) ...June / /1938
Equivalent ...
Registered ...16/9 19 38 Hall ...May...
Scholarships ...
Degree Examinations .... First / /19 . Second / 19 .
                              Third / /19 . Fourth / 19 .
Graduation ..../ 19......

Dean's comments and Signature

Subsequent career.

徐家祥就讀香港大學的學生紀錄
Student record of Tsui Ka-cheung

劉殿爵（一九二一至二零一零年）是國際知名的中國哲學家和文化學者，父親是詩人劉伯端（劉景棠）。他畢業於英皇書院，後入讀香港大學中文學院，受業於許地山和馬鑑，香港淪陷後於一九四一年獲頒戰時學位。

一九四六年劉殿爵取得獎學金到英國深造，成為戰後第一批入讀當地大學的香港留學生。他先在格拉斯哥大學主修西方哲學，獲一等榮譽學士學位；繼往牛津大學唸語言哲學。自一九五零年起，他擔任倫敦大學亞非學院講師，期間他翻譯《道德經》等中國古典作品，獲學生公認為標準範本。他也是英國歷來首位華人出任中文講座教授。

一九八零年劉殿爵返港，受聘為香港中文大學中文系講座教授，後來中文大學中國文化研究所替他出版《先秦兩漢古籍逐字索引叢刊》，這叢書獲國際漢學家視為重要參考書籍。

香港中文大學及香港大學先後於一九七五年、一九八九年頒授劉殿爵名譽博士學位，以表揚他對中國文化的貢獻。

Lau Din-cheuk (1921–2010), more commonly known as DC Lau, was a renowned scholar of Chinese philosophy and culture. He was the son of scholar and poet Lau King-tong. DC Lau attended King's College and studied in the Chinese department of the University of Hong Kong under Hsu Ti-shan and Ma Kiam. He fled to China in 1941 shortly before the outbreak of war.

In 1946 Lau was awarded a scholarship to study in Britain and became one of the first Hong Kong students to go there during the post-war era. He gained a first in philosophy at Glasgow University and went on to study language philosophy at the University of Oxford. Lau's translations of classical Chinese texts such as the *Tao Te Ching* (Daodejing) have become the standard texts of generations of students through his work at the School of Oriental and African Studies (SOAS) at the University of London where he was appointed lecturer in 1950. He became professor of Chinese at SOAS, establishing it as a world centre for the study of Chinese philosophy.

In 1980, DC Lau returned to Hong Kong where he took up the position of professor of Chinese language and literature at the Chinese University of Hong Kong where his *Ancient Chinese Texts Concordance Series*, published by the Institute of Chinese Studies, Chinese University of Hong Kong, is a standard reference work used by Sinologists worldwide.

Lau was awarded an honorary doctorate by the Chinese University of Hong Kong in 1975, and by the University of Hong Kong in 1989 in recognition of his achievements in the promotion of Chinese culture.

Note: Roger T. Ames, 'DC Lau obituary', *The Guardian*, Monday 31 May, 2010.

Univ. No. .... Name	Lau Din Cheuk 劉殿爵
BIRTH: Place ...Hongkong... Date 8/3/1921	Nationality. Chinese
Parent or Guardian ...Lau Pak Tsun...	
Home Address ...66B Bonham Rd, Hongkong...	
Local Guardian ...Lau Pak Tun...	
Address of same ...66B Bonham Rd., Hongkong...	
Previous Education ...King's College...	
Matric. Exm. (of equivalent) ...June / /1938	
Equivalent	
Registered 9 /9 1938 Hall May	
Scholarships ...H.K. Govt...	
Degree Examinations ...... First / /19 . Second / 19 .	
Third / /19 . Fourth / 19 .	
Graduation ..../ 19	

Dean's comments and Signature

Subsequent career.

劉殿爵就讀香港大學的學生紀錄
Student record of Lau Din-cheuk

伍冬瓊在一九三七年畢業於聖保羅女書院（今聖保羅男女中學）。一九三八年考進香港大學中文系。當時許地山、馬鑑、陳君葆分別教授中國歷史、中國文學、翻譯。她在就讀的最後一年，獲英國文化協會獎學金到英國求學，可惜一九四一年抗日戰爭爆發，未能成行。她當時距畢業還有六個月，後獲頒戰時學位，其他獲得同樣學位的中文系同學還有金應熙、劉殿爵、徐家祥、賴恬昌。

日治時期，陳君葆擔任馮平山圖書館館長，帶領一批如伍冬瓊等留港的大學生，整理馮平山圖書館和鄧志昂中文學院的藏書，當中包括嶺南大學和南京大學的存館圖書，這些寄存書籍後來都悉數歸還。

戰後一九四五年至一九五一年，伍冬瓊擔任高等法院的臨時翻譯工作，以及《華僑日報》的英文翻譯；後應香港大學圖書館館長施高德夫人的邀請，在圖書館任職。一九五五年伍冬瓊獲獎學金送往英國完成圖書館學位課程，一九五六回港繼任陳君葆為馮平山圖書館館長。一九五八年初美國國會圖書館亞洲部的艾允表博士造訪馮平山圖書館，引薦伍冬瓊取得洛克菲勒獎學金，補送往北美洲參觀各地東方圖書館。一九六零年伍冬瓊創辦並主理溫哥華英屬哥倫比亞大學的東亞圖書館，工作至一九八七年退休。

Ng Tung-king graduated from St Paul's Girls' College (St Paul's Co-Educational College) in 1937 and was admitted to the Chinese Department of the University of Hong Kong in 1938, where Hsu Ti-shan taught Chinese history, Ma Kiam taught Chinese literature, and Chan Kwan-po taught translation. During her final year, she received a British Council scholarship to study in the UK but the outbreak of war in 1941 interrupted this ambition. With six months remaining to graduation, she received a wartime degree alongside other Chinese Department graduates Kam Ying-hee, Lau Din-cheuk, Tsui Ka-cheung and Lai Tim-cheong.

During the Japanese occupation of Hong Kong Chan Kwan-po was detained to work at the Fung Ping Shan Library, asking Ng and others who had remained in Hong Kong to assist him there in cataloguing the books in the Fung Ping Shan Library and the Tang Chi Ngong School of Chinese (including those transferred from the libraries of Lingnan University and Nanjing University for safekeeping, all of which were returned after the war).

Following the end of the war in 1945, Ng acted as a temporary translator at the High Court and at the Wah Kiu Yat Po (Overseas Chinese Daily) until 1951, when she was asked to return to HKU as a librarian by Librarian Mrs Dorothea Scott. In 1955 she received a scholarship to study a librarianship course in the UK and in 1956 succeeded Chan Kwan-po as the Fung Ping Shan Librarian. In early 1958, Dr Edwin Beal, the chief of Orientalia (later Asian) Division of the US Library of Congress visited the Fung Ping Shan Library. He applied for a Rockefeller Foundation scholarship for Ng to visit East Asian libraries in North America. In 1960 Ng was appointed to establish an East Asian Library at the University of British Columbia where she worked until her retirement in 1987.

戰時畢業生
文學院相簿
War-time Bachelor of Arts degree graduates
Arts Faculty Album

一九五零年三月一日在大禮堂合照。立左一為徐家祥，立左三為伍冬瓊，坐左為 Simpson 教授，坐右為羅拔臣教授。
Photograph taken on 1st March 1950, in the Great Hall. Standing first left is Tsui Ka-cheung, third left is Ng Tung-king, while seated left is Professor R. K. M. Simpson and right is Professor R. Robertson.

一九四零年馮平山圖書館舉辦的廣東文物展覽，參觀人數非常可觀。
馮平山圖書館藏品
The Fung Ping Shan Library in 1940 on the occasion of the exhibition
'Cultural Relics of Guangdong'. The exhibition was visited by much of
the population of Hong Kong at the time.
Collection of the Fung Ping Shan Library

香港大學聯會日治時期之前最後一次集會，在大學運動亭慶祝該會成立二十九周年，並歡迎候任港督楊慕琦。相片前排中坐者為楊慕琦，將來第十任校長黃麗松站於第三行最左位置。
攝於一九四一年十月十六日星期四
聯會相簿，香港大學檔案中心「香港大學學生會特藏」
The Union's last meeting before the Japanese occupation was a tea party at the University Sports Pavilion to welcome the incoming governor, His Excellency Sir Mark Young, on the Union's 29th anniversary. Sir Mark Young is seated in the centre of the front row. Rayson Huang, the University's future Vice-Chancellor, stands at the far left of the third row.
Thursday 16th October, 1941
Union Album, Collection of the Hong Kong University Students' Union, HKUA

一九四一年香港開埠百周年紀念郵票，上印
英皇佐治五世肖像、香港大學圖樣
謝天錫捐贈
Two uncut sheets of the 1941 Hong Kong Centenary Stamp
featuring King George VI and the University
Gift of Mr Michael Tse

這些郵票在香港淪陷前十一個月發行，日治時期全港改用日本郵封，香港光復後再次通行。
These stamps were released eleven months before Hong Kong fell to the Japanese occupation at which time Japanese covers replaced them. They were not used again until the end of the war.

(FRENCH)

Cher Ami Francais,
Je suis un combattant allié. Je ne suis pas venu afin de vous nuire à vous, Francais qui sont mes amis. Je n'en veux qu'aux Japonais, et mon but est de les chasser d'Indochine aussi vite que possible. Si vous voulez me conduire au bureau militaire allié le plus proche, le Gouvernement de mon pays vous recompensera.

(TAMIL)

[Tamil text]

(SUMATRA)

Kepada Toean njang terima,
Saja soldadoe inggris tida datang sini boeat bikin sosoa apt-ipa kepada orang dari negeri Soematra. Saja maoe bikin sosoa kepada orang Djepan sadja, dan tekas sekali oesir dari negeri ini. Kalao Toean maoe tolong sama kita saja poenja Kompeni temtoe kasi tjoekoep persen sama tuan kapan orang Djepan soeda di-oesir.

(THAI)

[Thai text]

(SHAN & N. THAI)

[Shan text]

(W. SHAN)

[Shan text]

Dear Friend,
I am an Allied fighter, I did not come here to do any harm to you who are my friends. I only want to do harm to the Japanese and chase them away from this country as quickly as possible. If you will assist me, my Government will sufficiently reward you when the Japanese are driven away.

JAWI

[Jawi/Arabic script text]

(CHINESE)

我是同盟國的戰鬥員，馬來亞的民眾是我的朋友，我決不會來傷害你們的；我的目的是要打倒日本軍，把他們趕出馬來亞去。假使你們可以幫助我等日本兵打退以後政府一定會賞國們的。

(HAKA)　　(CHIN)

Ka Kawl,
Keimah cu Mirang ralkap kasi. Mahkah hin nanmah sifah pek ah ka ra lo, ka-hawi-kom-man si Japan ral tuk ah ka ra, Japan hi sifah pe hna ning law, nan khua ram in zok zok in thawi hna ning ti ka duh.
Zangfah nak in kan mah Mirang le American ralkap an um nak lam nal bik ah nan kan kalpi ah cun, ka sawi le nin laksawng tha mi an nin pek lai.

Khau duwa ni,
Ngai kaw inglist phenla re nga ai. Anthu kaw menmung masani dan kyaw na matu sa n rea. Aikaw Japanni pheh menmung le ko de dan kyaw stut kona matu sa re nga ai. Khauni anthe khau phenla ni, kodon i lam ko na sukun dapatang kumpraw sungul asoyani law law kyawna re nga ai.

Pemberi Tahu.　(MALAY)

Sahaya askar Pehak Berikat. Sahaya tidak datang hendak membenchanakan orang-orang di tanah Malayu. Sahaya mahu membenchanakan sahaya Jepun dan menghalaukanya keluar daripada negeri ini dengan segera-nya. Jika tuan menolong dan membantu sahaya kerajan sahaya akan membalas dengan sa-chukop-nya apabila Jepun sudah di halaukan.

(LAIZO)　(CHIN)

Ka rual,
Keimah cu Mirang ralkap kasi, Hinah nanmah zonzaih pekding ah ka ra lo, ruaipi tha nansi Japan ral hi zonzaih Pek in, nan khua ram in zamrang ten dawl hlo ka duh.
Kannah Mirang le American ralkap pawl um nak a nal bik ah zangfah ten in foh pi le, ka bawi pawl in laksawng tha an lo pe ding.

(BENGALI)

[Bengali text]

(ANNAMITE)

Tôi là một quân sĩ của Đồng-Minh. Tôi tôi đây không có muốn gì phá hại dân chúng Annam là bạn thân của tôi. Tôi chỉ muốn phá hại quân Nhật và đuổi chúng nó ra khỏi Đông-Dương cho tối đi sớm nơi trại binh của Đồng-Minh, thì chánh phủ của tôi sẽ ban thưởng cho các anh một cách rất xứng đáng.

(KAREN)

[Karen text]

(BURMESE)

[Burmese text]

軍人身份證明布條
香港大學檔案中心「賴廉士爵士特藏」
Blood chit
Sir Lindsay Ride Collection, HKUA

二次大戰與
日治時期
THE WAR YEARS

5

二次大戰與日治時期
The War Years

儘管一九三零年代世界經濟大蕭條，大學財政緊絀的陰霾深深濃罩，港大學生數目仍不斷增長，更有捐建大樓落成，包括了鄧志昂樓設立中文系，馮平山樓用作中文圖書館，以及外科醫學大樓啟用。自一九三零年代末起，很多學生及教職員意識到戰爭逼在眉睫，紛紛加入香港義勇軍及其他輔助隊伍。

一九四一年聖誕日香港淪陷後，港大師生被殺傷、拘禁的不一而足。日治時期本部大樓改作臨時醫院，由港大師生義務主理，以支援瑪麗醫院接收傷患。後來一些學生及教職員被困於明原堂，至一九四二年二月運往赤柱營囚禁。另外不少曾參與抗日或輔助隊伍的則拘留於深水埗。俘囚營房皆為臨時搭建，簡陋而衛生極差，情況每況愈下。

日治時期港大亦飽經浩劫，不但校舍遭搶掠，很多檔案被破壞。戰時校長史羅司（任期一九三五至一九四九年）領導大學渡過戰爭的艱難時期功不可沒。當時師生臨時囚禁於校內，他於一九四一年底秘密頒發戰時學位予完成大學課程的學生，以至大學教職員被拘往赤柱戰俘營後，他先後透過英軍服務團、特務、與英國政府保持秘密聯絡。早於一九四三年史羅司已向英廷提議大學未來的路向，戰後商討重建大學時他的意見仍然舉足輕重。

日治時期前後，不少港大師生逃往中國。一些學生在國內大學修畢課程。一些更攀山越嶺到印度，最後抵達英國，在當地就讀至畢業。港大教授王國棟、賴廉士最不遺餘力協助其他師生渡過難關。王國棟在中國繼續指導港大學生之學業進度。賴廉士則在香港組織英軍服務團，於日治時期協助傳遞消息，營救居民逃離香港。至於教務長 Stanley Victor Boxer 則在被囚禁集中營期間仍致力保存大學戰時檔案。

一九四五年二次大戰結束，部份教職員及學生重返大學，致力重整校業。面對校舍滿目瘡痍，一些人員曾質疑是否值得搶救倖存的校內設備。日軍占領期間馮平山圖書館館長陳君葆全力保護館藏，獲視為戰時英雄。

Although the University suffered financial setbacks during the Great Depression of the 1930s, its student body was continuing to grow steadily. There were several new buildings including the Tang Chi Ngong building for Chinese Studies, the Fung Ping Shan Library building, and the School of Surgery building. Yet, from the late 1930s onwards, the threat of imminent war loomed over the University. Many students and faculty joined the Hong Kong Volunteer Defense Force or other support services in preparation for what was to come.

When Hong Kong eventually fell to Japanese forces on Christmas Day 1941, many staff and students were killed, wounded, or captured. The Main Building became a hospital staffed by University students, staff and volunteers to relieve Queen Mary Hospital during the siege. Students and faculty were confined to Old Halls before they were transferred to the prison camp at Stanley in February 1942. Those known to have fought, or served in the support services, were sent to the prison camp at Sham Shui Po. During the interim periods they were often housed in temporary, inadequate, and unhygienic quarters and their circumstances often became worse in the camps.

The occupation wrought havoc on the University. Its buildings were ransacked and looted and many of its records were destroyed. The wartime Vice-Chancellor, Duncan Sloss (served 1935–1948), played an important leadership role throughout the war. When staff and students were temporarily interned at the University, he presided over the secret awarding of wartime degrees for those who had completed their studies at the end of 1941. Later, when staff joined the internment camp at Stanley, he maintained secret contact with British authorities through the British Army Aid Group, and later through individuals. As early as 1943 Sloss smuggled his views on the future of the University to the government in Britain. These were to prove influential in post-war deliberations on the University's future.

Many students and some faculty escaped to Free China both before and after the invasion. Of these, some students were able to complete their education in Chinese universities, while others made their way 'over the hump' to India, and from there to Great Britain where they were able to complete their education. In addition to the wartime leadership of Vice-Chancellor Duncan Sloss, several faculty and staff members in particular stood out in their efforts for the University and for others. Professor Gordon King helped many students to complete their education through the war years in Free China, Registrar Stanley Victor Boxer ensured that the University's pre-war papers were saved, and continued to act as Registrar throughout the internment. Professor Lindsay Ride founded the British Army Aide Group, smuggling both people and intelligence out of occupied Hong Kong.

When the war ended in 1945, some faculty and students returned to HKU and a great effort was made to revive the University despite the fact that much of it was in ruins and some members of the faculty questioned the viability of saving what was left. The Fung Ping Shan Librarian Chan Kwan-po was hailed as a hero for his role in safeguarding many of the Library's holdings under the Japanese.

王國棟醫生
Dr Gordon King, Lieutenant Colonel,
Royal Army Medical Corps

王國棟（一九零零至一九九一年），父親為浸信會主教，中學肆業（一九一一至一九一五年）於英國西部布里斯托爾文理學校，一九一九年入讀倫敦醫學院，一九二四年畢業，獲頒英格蘭皇家外科醫學院院士名銜。一九二六年加入浸信傳道會，到中國作為傳道醫生，後出任北京協和醫院產科醫生。一九三二年當選為英國婦產科醫學院創院院士。一九三零年成為山東濟南齊魯大學教授，兼任婦產科主管，期間認識漢學家林仰山、病理學家侯寶璋，後來相繼進入香港大學任教，成為摯友。

一九三七年日軍佔領濟南，戰情危急，王國棟遂應聘來港，出任香港大學婦產科學系主任，一九四零年更接替賴廉士成為醫學院院長。一九四一年十二月香港淪陷，王國棟在大禮堂設立救濟醫院，由 William Faid（參看第67頁）指導學生及職員充當醫護人員，幫忙照顧瑪麗醫院不能容納的傷患者。

香港淪陷時期王國棟鼓勵學生逃離，一九四二年二月他亦抵達重慶，在英國駐華大使館及中國教育部的協助下，安排香港大學學生繼續學業。當時重慶、曲江、桂林、桂陽的香港難民救濟局均協助抵華的香港大學學生，安排他們戰時就讀當地大學，346名學生中有140名醫科生，不少於一九四五年畢業。

一九七三年王國棟在香港大學第八十四屆學位頒授典禮上演說：

'一九四五年八月，戰事結束，大禮堂只剩四壁空牆，天花失去，屋樑、門窗、地板全被取走，地上滿佈瓦礫。

但很快地約六十名逃離香港的醫科生在中國完成醫學課程，他們回港後積極投入醫療重建工作。各大醫院診所的初級職位迅速恢復，大部份由這批年輕的畢業生填補。

一九四六年三月二十二日大禮堂戰後重開，三十三名畢業生獲香港大學醫科學位緊急委員會頒發學位。

當時學位頒授典禮在缺屋頂的大禮堂舉行，雖然滿目瘡痍，但卻顯露出大學即將來臨的新生曙光。'

香港重光後王國棟致力重整港大醫學院，出任兩屆醫學院院長（一九四八至一九四九年）、（一九五一至一九五四年）。一九五六年他離港就任西澳洲大學在柏斯新建的醫學院院長。一九七一年返回香港，擔任香港家庭計劃指導會總監，直至一九七三年退休。

Gordon King (1900–1991) was the son of a Baptist minister. He studied at Bristol Grammar School in the west of England (1911–1915) and began training in medicine at the London Hospital Medical College in 1919 from which he graduated in 1924 with a Fellowship of the Royal College of Surgeons. In 1926 he joined the Baptist Missionary Society to work as a medical missionary in China, joining the Peking Union Medical College as an obstetrician. He became a Foundation Fellow of the British (later Royal) College of Obstetricians and Gynaecologists in 1932. In 1930, he joined Cheeloo (Qilu) University in Jinan, Shandong province as Professor and head of Obstetrics and Gynaecology where he would meet the Sinologist Frederick S. Drake and pathologist Hou Pao-chang who would both later join King at the University of Hong Kong.

When the Japanese occupation of Jinan made it too dangerous to remain there in 1937, King left to take up the position of Professor of Obstetrics and Gynaecology at the University of Hong Kong. In 1940, he succeeded Lindsay Ride as Dean of the Faculty of Medicine. The Japanese occupied Hong Kong in December 1941, and King set up a relief hospital in the Great Hall staffed by student volunteers and staff, and administered by William Faid (see page 67), to receive the overflow of civilian patients from Queen Mary Hospital.

King encouraged students to escape when Hong Kong fell, and in February 1942 left for Chongqing, the capital of Free China, where he worked with the British Embassy and Chinese Ministry of Education to arrange for HKU students to continue their studies there. The Hong Kong Refugee Relief Board administration in Chongqing, Qujiang, Guilin and Guiyang helped arriving students to find places at Chinese universities. Many of the 346 students, 140 of whom were medical students, were therefore able to graduate in 1945.

Years later at the 84th Congregation in 1973, King recalled that:

In August 1945, when the war was over, this [Loke Yew] Hall had been reduced to its four bare walls open to the sky. The roof beams had all been removed, doors, windows, and floorboards had all gone and the ground was strewn with rubble.

But very shortly afterwards nearly 60 of the medical students who had escaped Hong Kong and completed their medical studies in China, returned to Hong Kong to play their part in the medical rehabilitation of the Colony. And the junior staff positions in the hospitals and clinics, that were rapidly being re-established, were largely filled by these young graduates.

And the first post-war use of this Great Hall (as it was then known) was on March 22nd, 1946, when 33 candidates received degrees awarded by the Hong Kong University (Medical Degrees) Emergency Committee.

The congregation took place under the open sky, amid the ruins of the Great Hall, but it was symbolic of the new life which was about to return to the University.

During the post-war reconstruction years, King was instrumental in helping re-establish the medical faculty in his role as Dean of Medicine (1948–1949) and (1951–1954). He left the University in 1956 to become Dean of a new medical school at the University of Western Australia in Perth. He returned to Hong Kong in 1971 to become Director of the Family Planning Association of Hong Kong before finally retiring in 1973.

Notes: *Dictionary of Hong Kong Biography*, pp. 226–227; 'Citations and Speeches', HKU 84th Congregation (1973).

Stanley Victor Boxer（一八九一至一九四九年）曾為香港大學教務長及工程學院講師，並兼任馬禮遜堂舍監。他任職港大前曾在中國漢口從事傳道工作十七年。[1] 他在任馬禮遜堂舍監期間，經常在舍堂招待不同的訪客，包括一九四零年八月作家兼英文系講師 Norman H. Mackenzie 及友人的到訪。[2]

一九四二至一九四五年二次大戰期間他和校長史羅司等大學職員被囚禁於赤柱拘留營，他在營中仍維持大學入學試委員會的工作，並安排上課出席率足夠的學生進行考試，更須擔任營中的膳食職務，這一切均令人津津樂道。[3] 其間他並確保大學會議能繼續舉行，以及妥善儲存其他有關紀錄。

他五十四歲時自拘留營釋放出來後，曾致力收集一九四六至一九四八年間'過渡'期的大學會議紀錄。至於倖存的戰前及日治時期資料成為了大學檔案重要的部份，他將這些資料連同一九二八至一九三九年間的備忘錄、一九一二至一九四一年間的書信和有關文件，在當時校長秘書梅‧威徹爾（後為賴廉士夫人）的幫助下編寫索引。他所編的 'Guide to Indexes' 成為了二次大戰前三十年大學紀錄的編索指南，他認為這是'從日治時期的混沌中整理和保存歷史資料的最後努力'。[4]

戰後他曾短遊澳洲及英國，返港後發現馬禮遜堂已成頹垣敗瓦，不但給流浪者佔據，室內的木樑、喉管皆被盜去。在當時資金緊絀的情況下修葺舍堂回復舊貌似乎並不可能，但他努力周旋，最後獲得財務委員會主席羅旭龢爵士協助，向港大畢業生和倫敦傳道會募捐重建經費。最終他籌得足夠的捐款及貸款去聘請建築承辦商，工程則由他的繼任人 Frank Short 牧師完成。

一九四八年初他自香港大學退休不足十八個月，在澳洲墨爾本一次帶領學生作戶外測量課時不幸被汽車撞倒，後傷重不治，終年五十八歲。

Stanley Victor Boxer (1891–1949) held the positions of Registrar of the University and Lecturer in the Department of Engineering while also acting as Warden of Morrison Hall. Before arriving at HKU he served as a missionary for seventeen years in Hankow.[1] During his time as Warden, he often hosted visitors at Morrison Hall, including the author Norman H. MacKenzie, who was a lecturer in the Department of English, along with his friends in August 1940.[2]

During the war, Boxer was detained in Stanley internment camp from 1942 to 1945 with other University colleagues including Vice-Chancellor Duncan Sloss. While there, he was responsible for maintaining the work of the University's Matriculation Board, conducting examinations for students who had taken enough classes, and was remembered for carrying out kitchen duties in addition to his University ones.[3] He ensured that the proceedings of University meetings held in the camp, as well as other related papers were saved.

Following his release at the age of 54, Boxer also collected the minutes of meetings held during the 'interim' period from 1946 to 1948. These formed a significant part of the records of the University that survived the pre-War period and the Japanese occupation. Boxer indexed these materials alongside memoranda dating from 1928 to 1939, and other correspondence and related documents dating from 1912 to 1941 with the help of the Vice-Chancellor's secretary at the time, May Witchell (later Lady Ride). His 'Guide to Indexes' was a guide to the indexes for the thirty years before the war, which he considered his 'last effort to bring order and accessibility out of the chaos of Japanese Occupation'.[4]

Following brief trips to Australia and England after the war, Boxer returned to Hong Kong and a Morrison Hall occupied by squatters and stripped of all timber and plumbing. The task of restoring the hall to a habitable state seemed insurmountable given the money needed to do so but Boxer secured the support of the Board of Control, chaired by Sir Robert Kotewall, to launch a fundraising appeal to alumni and the London Missionary Society. He raised enough funds and gained enough in loans to engage a contractor. His successor, the Reverend Frank Short, completed the work.

Less than 18 months after his retirement from the University in early 1948, Stanley Boxer was hit by a motor vehicle while leading a surveying class in Melbourne and died of his injuries. He was 58 years old.

---

1. Peter Cunich, 'Godliness and Good Learning: The British Missionary Societies and HKU', Chan and Cunich, p. 62.
2. Recorded in Norman MacKenzie, 'An Academic Odyssey: A Professor in Five Continents (Part 1),' in Clifford Matthews and Oswald Cheung (eds), *Dispersal and Renewal: Hong Kong University during War Years*, p.27; also recorded in the memoir of former Warden of Morrison Hall, S. Withers Green's, 'The Re-Opening in 1948 of Morrison Hall', http://www.morrison.hku.hk/drupal/?q=node/131.
3. Lindsay Ride, 'The Test of War', Harrison, pp. 69–70.
4. Mellor, 1980, p.177.

賴廉士上校畫像
英軍服務團桂林總部團員作
香港大學檔案中心「賴廉士爵士特藏」
Portrait of Lindsay Tasman Ride as Lieutenant Colonel painted by a member of his BAAG unit at their headquarters in Guilin
Sir Lindsay Ride Collection, HKUA

賴廉士爵士（一八九八至一九七七年）為香港大學第六任校長（一九四九至一九六四年），亦是歷來任期最長的校長。他憑著戰時的英勇功績，以及戰後在校任內領導有方，成功帶領港大重建及擴張，在大學歷史上佔一席位。

他出生於澳洲墨爾本，因應召入伍澳洲皇家空軍而放棄大學教育。第一次世界大戰時曾於伊普爾、索姆河兩地受傷，而被逼退役。惟於英國養傷期間，仍以最高榮譽通過英國軍官訓練課程。

一九一九年他返回墨爾本大學入讀醫學院。一九二二年考獲維多利亞羅德獎學金，進入牛津大學新學院。後獲倫敦皇家外科醫學院會員資格、皇家內科醫學院執照。一九二八年十月二十一日出任香港大學生理學系教授，一九三零年晉升醫學院院長。

一九三一年獲委任加入香港義勇軍，一九四一年成為野戰救護團指揮官。香港淪陷後他被扣押在深水埗戰俘營。一九四二年一月九日在東江縱隊協助下逃往重慶，成立英軍服務團，該組織的總部設於桂林，實為MI9/19軍情科的化身，專職協助平民、囚犯、間諜逃避敵軍追蹤，並為逃港難民提供醫療及人道支援。他深得同袍愛戴，贏得'笑面虎'的雅號。

戰後賴廉士返回港大，一九四九年出任校長。在任期間學生數量增至戰前三倍；校園內新建了二十二座校舍；土木、電子、機械等工程，以及建築學系，所頒學位均獲國際認可；香港大學出版社、港大校外進修部（今香港大學專業進修學院）、東方文化研究院相繼成立。一九六一年，他更統籌了港大金禧校慶。

賴廉士爵士的文獻由他的女兒 Elizabeth Ride 悉數捐贈香港大學檔案中心，她現正撰寫有關英軍服務團歷史的叢書。

Sir Lindsay Tasman Ride (1898–1977) was the University's sixth and longest-serving Vice-Chancellor (from 1949 to 1964). Ride holds a unique position in the annals of the University, in particular for his heroic actions during the war, and for his skills as an administrator presiding over the re-building and expansion of the University after the war ended.

Ride was born in Melbourne, Australia. In 1916 he eschewed university in favour of enlisting in the Australian Imperial Force as a private. He was wounded twice during the First World War at Ypres and on the Somme, which effectively ended his military career. Yet while recovering in Britain he passed the British Officers' Training Course, sharing top honours.

He returned to Australia to study medicine at the University of Melbourne in 1919 and in 1922 was elected Victorian Rhodes scholar to New College, Oxford. He later qualified as a member of the Royal College of Surgeons, and a licentiate of the Royal College of Physicians, London. On 21st October 1928, Ride was appointed Professor of Physiology at the University of Hong Kong. He became Dean of Medicine in 1930.

Ride was commissioned into the Hong Kong Volunteer Defence Corps in 1931, and made commanding officer of the Hong Kong Field Ambulance in 1941. After Hong Kong fell to Japanese occupation on Christmas Day, 1941 Ride was imprisoned at Sham Shui Po Military Camp. With the help of Hong Kong guerilla forces, he escaped to Chongqing on 9th January 1942. He formed the British Army Aid Group (BAAG), which was a covert MI 9/19 military intelligence unit to prevent the capture of civilians, prisoners and agents and aid their escape. Headquartered in Guilin the BAAG also provided medical and humanitarian aid to refugees from Hong Kong. Ride was an inspiration to those who worked with him and was known by the nickname of 'The Smiling Tiger'.

After the war ended Ride returned to HKU, succeeding Duncan Sloss as Vice-Chancellor in 1949. Under his leadership, the student body grew to three times its pre-war population and 22 new buildings were added to the campus. The University gained formal recognition of its degrees in civil, electrical, and mechanical engineering, and in architecture. The University Press, Extramural Studies Department (now HKU SPACE) as well as the Institute of Oriental Studies were established, and Ride presided over the University's Golden Jubilee Anniversary celebrations in 1961.

The Sir Lindsay Ride Collection was given to the University Archives by his daughter Elizabeth Ride who is compiling a multi-volume history of the British Army Aid Group.

Notes: *Dictionary of Hong Kong Biography*, pp. 367–369.

賴廉士爵士特藏
The Sir Lindsay Ride Collection

香港大學檔案中心「賴廉士爵士特藏」擁有非常豐富的個人物品,包括他的軍禮服及佩劍,他從深水埗集中營逃出時所穿的破損衣物。賴廉士爵士留下大量有關英軍服務團之建立及軍令文獻,悉數保存於坎培拉的澳洲戰爭紀念檔案庫。

「賴廉士爵士特藏」可分成下列組別:

1. 與香港大學相關資料。包括他的著作、教學材料,以及少量行政記錄。大部份的行政記錄仍留貯於校長辦公室轄下校務處檔案中,校務處檔案亦歸香港大學檔案中心管理。

2. 生理學研究相關資料。包括大量圖片,尤其是關於頭髮漩渦狀排列的課題。

3. 譜系分類及生物信息研究相關資料。包括一份澳門新教徒公墓研究的草稿,由賴廉士爵士與夫人梅共同寫作,他過世後由梅勒於一九九六年增訂出版。該書記載了賴廉士對澳門、香港,以及南中國歷史的重要觀點,是根據公墓下葬者的生平傳記寫成。後來賴廉士夫人將資料及版權交予謝偉德,一九九九年由他增補,費正清作序,出版了普及版。

4. 英軍服務團資料。

5. 二次大戰後、一九五零至六零年代大學重建期間之檔案紀錄。

英軍服務團徽旗。團徽居中,外圈寫拉丁文 'Spes. Salutis',代表希望及救亡
香港大學檔案中心「賴廉士爵士特藏」
British Army Aid Group flag with the BAAG logo in the centre and the Latin inscription 'Spes. Salutis' meaning 'Hope and Salvation'
Sir Lindsay Ride Collection, HKUA

The Sir Lindsay Ride Collection housed at the University Archives is particularly rich in personal artefacts, including those from Ride's military service such as his dress uniform and sword, and the clothing he wore during his escape from the Sham Shui Po prison camp. The bulk of Sir Lindsay Ride's military papers covering the foundation and command of the BAAG, are preserved in the Australian War Memorial Archives in Canberra.

The materials in the Sir Lindsay Ride Collection can be broadly grouped into the following series:

1. Materials relating to the University of Hong Kong, which include his writings, teaching materials, as well as some administrative records, although the bulk of these remain in the Registry record group relating to the Vice-Chancellor's office, now in the University Archives.

2. Records relating to his research on physiology, including many photographs, in particular of his studies of hair whorls.

3. Genealogical/ biographical research materials, including draft chapters of the book on the Protestant Cemetery in Macao, *An East India Company Cemetery*, authored with his wife Lady May Ride and published posthumously with additions by Bernard Mellor in 1996. It includes important insights on the history of Macao, Hong Kong and South China through biographical information on the men and women buried there. After Lady Ride gave the materials and the copyrights to Jason Wordie, he edited an abridged version with additional material and a foreword by John King Fairbank published in 1999.

4. British Army Aide Group (BAAG) related materials.

5. Records from the post-war years, regarding the re-building of the University in the 1950s and 1960s.

英軍服務團木製盾徽由團員梁宗義於大戰結束前畫成，團內大部份地圖均由他繪製
香港大學檔案中心「賴廉士爵士特藏」
The BAAG shield was painted by Leung Chung-yee who made most of the maps for the group at the end of the war
Sir Lindsay Ride Collection, HKUA

皇家香港義勇軍團銅製襟飾。設計成中國雙龍拱著英國皇冠，下飾彩帶，寫拉丁文 'Nulli Secundus in Oriente'，代表雄霸東方。
香港大學檔案中心「賴廉士爵士特藏」
Bronze pin of the The Royal Hong Kong Defence Force logo. The design shows the British crown supported by two Chinese dragons with claw raised facing one another. Beneath them a ribbon bears the Latin inscription, 'Nulli Secundus in Oriente', meaning 'Second to None in the Orient'.
Sir Lindsay Ride Collection, HKUA

賴廉士爵士所用行軍桌
香港大學檔案中心「賴廉士爵士特藏」
Lindsay Ride's Portable Army Desk
Sir Lindsay Ride Collection, HKUA

賴廉士爵士在深水埗集中營逃生時的便服
香港大學檔案中心「賴廉士爵士特藏」
The clothing that Lindsay Ride wore when
escaping imprisonment at Sham Shui Po
Sir Lindsay Ride Collection, HKUA

HKU Memories | from the Archives 159

賴廉士爵士所用配劍，劍鞘飾英皇七世
（在位於一九零一至一九一零年）皇印，以及都鐸皇冠
Lisa Ride Bailey 捐贈
香港大學檔案中心「賴廉士爵士特藏」
Lindsay Ride's sword with a detail of the
scabbard bearing the royal cypher of
King Edward VII (r. 1901-1910), and the Tudor crown
Gift of Ms Lisa Ride Bailey
Sir Lindsay Ride Collection, HKUA

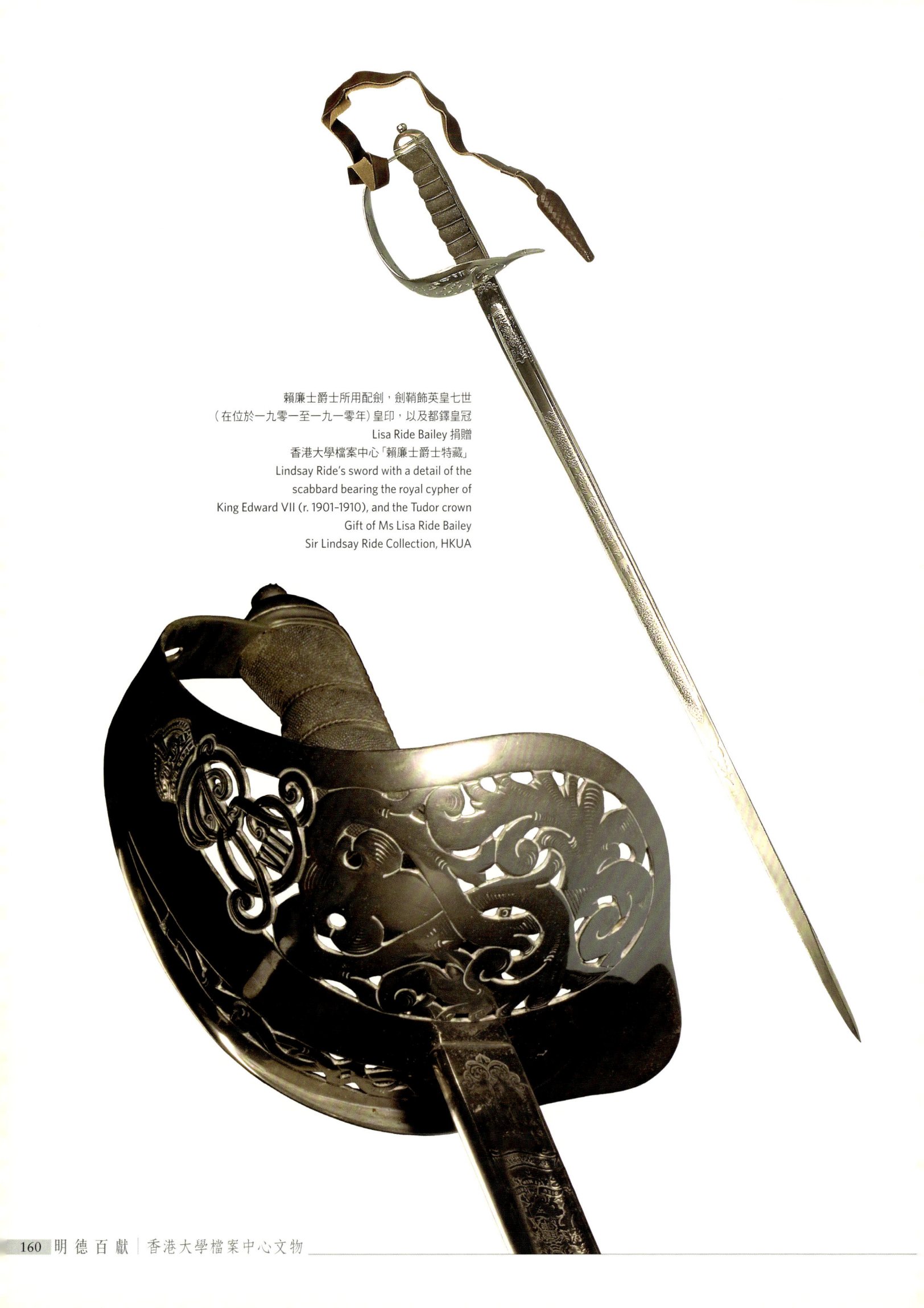

賴廉士爵士准將禮服
香港大學檔案中心「賴廉士爵士特藏」
Lindsay Ride's Uniform (Brigadier) Unique
Sir Lindsay Ride Collection, HKUA

賴廉士爵士是唯一獲擢升准將軍階的香港居民
Ride was the only Hong Kong resident
ever promoted to the Rank of Brigadier

譚藹勵戰後在英國倫敦
譚氏家族珍藏
Osler Thomas while on leave in London after the end of the war
Thomas Family Collection

譚藹勵（一九二一至二零零九年）一九三八年至一九四一年間就讀於香港大學醫學系。至戰爭逼於眉睫，港大教職員及學生紛紛加入香港義勇軍，當時賴廉士為野戰救護團指揮官，他呼籲醫學院學生包括譚藹勵加入。一九四一年年底戰爭爆發，十二月七日日軍轟炸香港前夕，香港義勇軍迅速動員起來。野戰救護團更走遍港九搶救傷患，終日閃避日軍及砲火，險象橫生。

一九四二年十二月十八日譚藹勵正在筲箕灣慈幼會執勤，陪伴傷員時遭受日軍猛襲。次日清晨他欲將醫療站傷者送往瑪麗醫院，卻被日軍突擊，全體職員被逼投降，更被帶往附近水道處決。他情急智生跳進水道，躲於其他屍體之下裝死，待入夜後才爬出逃脫，近兩星期後抵達其父家中。

他隨即經西貢及惠州逃離香港，一九四二年七月擔任英軍服務團醫務員。一九四三年他與 Francis Lee 被派返香港，成為駐西貢赤徑村隊的英軍支援隊成員，負責搜集軍情及協助難民逃亡。Francis Lee 為香港大學生理學系文員，亦是賴廉士的下屬，他是首位加入英軍服務團的香港大學成員。

一九四五年二次大戰結束時譚藹勵獲頒英帝國軍事勳銜MBE。二零零五年八月他在《南華早報》周日雜誌撰文憶述 '這事件與年青時的我有莫大關係。我知道戰爭對我而言並沒有結束。我已經歷了戰爭，所以我再沒有恐懼。'

戰後他繼續於倫敦蓋氏醫院就讀醫科。他於一九五四年回港，出任香港醫務署耳鼻喉專科醫生，直至一九六九年移居澳洲悉尼。其後每年皆出席在港的重光紀念儀式，直至二零零九離世。

二零零八年他捐贈了珍罕的歐德理著 *A Chinese-English dictionary in the Cantonese dialect (1911–1912)* 一書三冊予香港大學圖書館收藏，隨後再陸續捐贈一批戰時報章《香港新聞》及四十七幅戰時地圖。他的家人亦秉承其遺志，捐贈不少物品予香港大學檔案中心。

Osler Lister Thomas (1920–2009) studied medicine at the University of Hong Kong between 1938 and 1941. As the threat of war intensified, HKU staff and students joined the Hong Kong Volunteer Defence Corps (HKVDC). Lindsay Ride was Commanding Officer of the Field Ambulance units, and encouraged many medical students, including Osler Thomas, to join. War arrived abruptly at the end of 1941, and the HKVDC were quickly mobilised on 7th December 1941, a day before the Japanese began bombing Hong Kong. The Field Ambulance units traveled all over Hong Kong, often narrowly avoiding advancing Japanese troops and shelling.

On 18th December 1941, Osler Thomas was treating the injured at the Salesian Mission in Shau Kei Wan when it was heavily bombed. While trying to transfer patients to Queen Mary Hospital the following morning, the station was ambushed by the Japanese, and the staff forced to surrender. They were led to a nullah nearby and executed. Osler Thomas was able to survive the attack by jumping into the nullah and feigning death as bodies were piled on top of him. He crawled out after dark, and eventually arrived at his father's house almost two weeks later.

Thomas then escaped Hong Kong through Sai Kung and Waichow (Huizhou) to join the British Army Aid Group (BAAG) as a civilian medical officer in July 1942. He was sent back to Hong Kong in 1943 with Francis Lee, to establish an observation post at Post Y in Chek Keng Village in Sai Kung where they collected intelligence and helped with escape efforts. Lee had been a clerk in Lindsay Ride's Physiology department at HKU, and was among the first at HKU to join the BAAG.

Thomas was awarded a military MBE at the end of the war in 1945. In an article he wrote for the Sunday *Post Magazine* of the *South China Morning Post* in August 2005, Thomas stated that his experiences during the Japanese occupation in Hong Kong, 'had a great bearing on me as a young man. I knew the war was not over for me. I had no fear anymore since I had experienced that already.'

After the war, Thomas continued his medical studies at Guy's Hospital, London. He returned to Hong Kong in 1954 where he worked as an ear, nose and throat specialist in the Hong Kong Medical Department until he moved to Sydney, Australia in 1969. He returned to Hong Kong every year to attend the annual Liberation Day ceremony until he passed away in 2009.

In 2008 Thomas donated a rare three-volume copy of *A Chinese-English dictionary in the Cantonese dialect* by Ernest John Eitel (1838–1908) (Hong Kong, Kelly & Walsh Limited, 1911–1912) to the University Libraries collections. This was followed by a donation of a set of wartime newspapers, the *Hong Kong News* and 47 wartime maps. His family has continued a tradition of giving to the University by donating many items to the Archives.

Notes: Cunich, pp. 386–426; Charles G. Roland, 'Massacre and Rape in Hong Kong: Two Cases Studies involving Medical Personnel and Patients' in *Journal of Contemporary History* Vol. 32, No.1 (London, Sage Publications, 1997), pp. 43–61; Edwin Ride, *BAAG: Hong Kong Resistance, 1942–1945* (Hong Kong, Oxford University Press, 1981) pp. 215–216; The University of Hong Kong Libraries, *FOCUS*, New Series. Vol. 8, No. 2, Dec 2008.

'我的路線圖以東河定位。

距離以中國的里數計算,十里為一塘,是挑著擔子走一小時路的距離,但卻因地形不同而有所差別。由於我們都是徒步而走,這張地圖非常實用,它具體說明由一點到另一點所需時間。六十里或六塘代表六小時的路程。

一塘約有3.3'英'里(哩)。十塘要徒步走30哩,估計在一天內完成。我從新界到惠州就走了一天。'

My walking map I have marked in the East River.

The distances are in Chinese li, *the so-called Chinese mile. Ten* li *make up one* tong, *which is the distance walked in one hour when carrying a load, which can vary depending on the topography of the land. Since all traveling was on foot, this map was most useful as it told me how long it would take between two points. 60* li *or 6* tong *would mean a 6-hour walk.*

One tong *is roughly equivalent to 3 $^1/_3$ miles. 10* tong *would mean a 30-mile hike, which is quite good going in one day. I have made the trip from the New Territories to Waichow in one day.*

戰時譚露勵從惠陽徒步到老隆的路線圖
一九四零年代
譚氏家族捐贈
Map showing Osler Thomas' walking route from
Weiyang to Laolong
1940s
Gift of the Thomas Family

HKU Memories | from the Archives

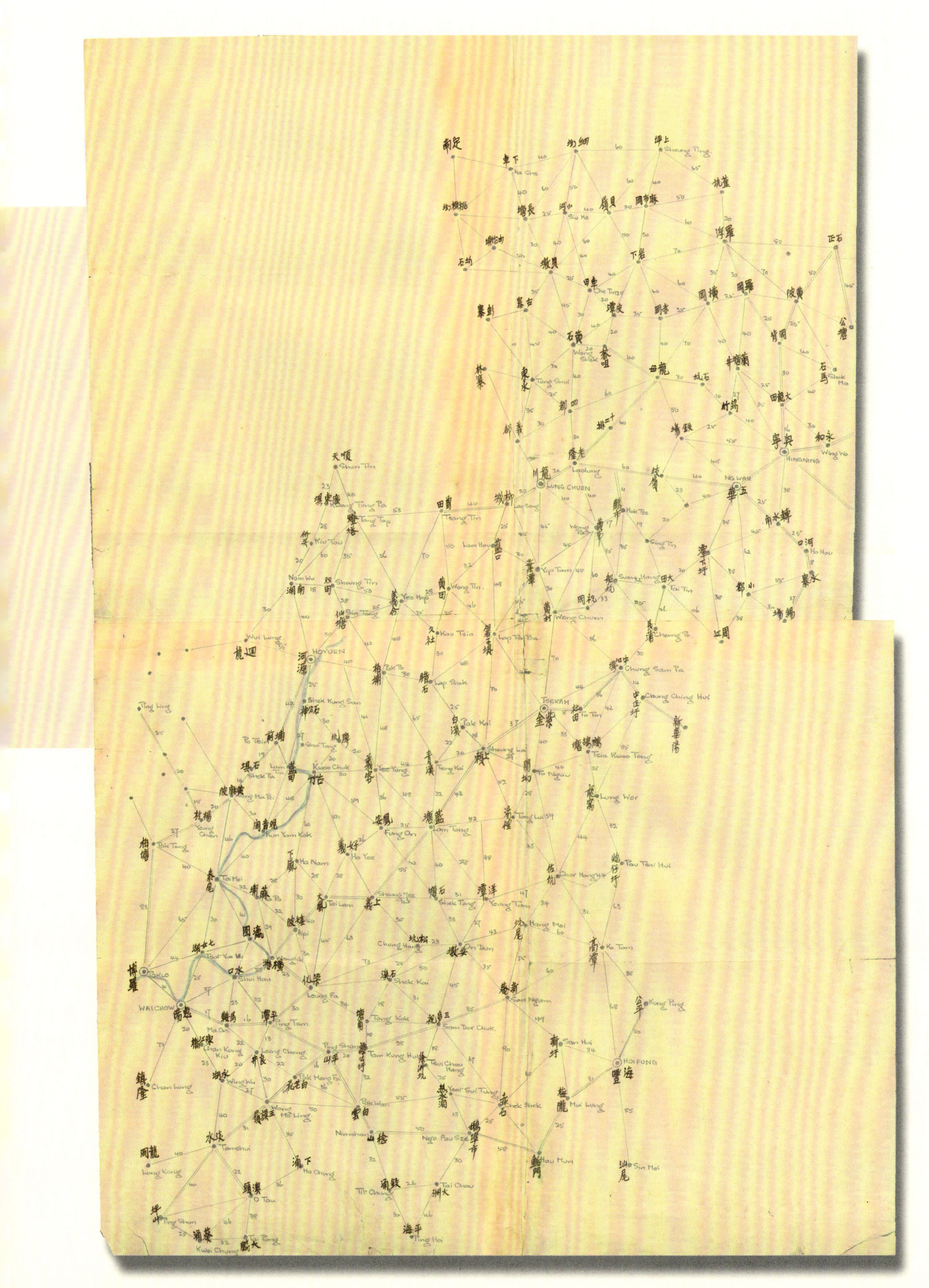

譚露勵喬裝英軍服務團間諜74號
譚氏家族捐贈
Osler Lister Thomas' disguise as BAAG Agent No. 74
Gift of the Thomas Family

DO/P/18/46.

MAIN H.Q. "E" GROUP
S.E.A. & INDIA COMMANDS
NEW DELHI GHQ APO.

12 Mar 46.

My dear Osler

    I have just written Francis and am enclosing this note to you to give you the latest information with regard to your position which, I am glad to say, is quite satisfactory.

    You were promoted to Captain w.e.f. 1 May 44, the date of your first commission, and I have pointed out that you have received no pay since November and that this is being rectified. They will also see that you are credited with your pay as a Captain for the back period. In regard to Danger Pay, I have not been able to fix this yet but hope to be able to do so within the next two or three days.

    ARMINDIA has agreed to your demobilization in England and this authority will be found in a Signal - GHQ(I) 352803/Aug.13(c) of 161230 Feb. to HQ Land Forces, copy to Force 136). This Signal should be with you by now and I hope everything will be speedily fixed up for your move to U.K.

    Please give my kindest regards to your mother and father. I hope to see you in U.K. before very long.

Yours
[signature]

Capt. Osler Thomas,
Land Forces Hong Kong.

賴廉士從印度寄信給留港的譚霭勵，提及他的升級、欠薪及稍後在英國復員
一九四六年
譚氏家族珍藏
Letter from Lindsay Ride in India to Osler Thomas in Hong Kong regarding his promotion,
backpay and subsequent demobilization in England
1946
Thomas Family Collection

戰後大學建築物外觀。馮平山圖書館絲毫無損，前方的舊水力學實驗所卻嚴重損毀，後改建成物業管理處（物業處前身），現為東閘入口

Photographs taken during a preliminary review of the University's buildings after the war show very little damage to the Fung Ping Shan Library building. The ruined buildings in the foreground are the old Hydraulics Laboratory. These were later re-purposed as the Maintenance and Premises Office (the precursor to the Estates Office) before the East Gate was built.

來源：一九四五年十二月八日《香港大學重建備忘錄》附錄二 '一九四五年十一月大學景觀'，圖二

'Memorandum on Reconstitution of the University of Hong Kong', dated 8th December, 1945. Appendix II 'Some Views of Hong Kong University, November 1945', fig. 2

戰後復元
HKU AFTER THE WAR

6

戰後重建大學

戰爭結束時，校長史羅司希望大學能迅速復校，然而校內仍百廢待興。根據一九四五年十一月大學戰後情況的評估報告，很多校舍均於戰時損毀。當學生紛紛自中國各地返港，大學亦面臨重建及復員的重大考驗。

一九四五年十二月三十一日香港大學顧問委員會成立，由郭克時擔任主席，他在一九四六年八月的最後報告書指出大學必須'盡快復校，建立穩健的財政基礎，善用職員及設施，以達到英國的學術標準，並成為中英學術交流的有效樞紐'、'港大應成為英式教育在東亞地區的典範，既盡得天時地利，可以作為中英兩大文明之間的教育融匯中心'。[1]

由於對香港憲制前景之疑問，其最終將重回中國懷抱，以及郭克時報告書所大膽建議大學復課需用的巨額資金，導致重建港大遙遙無期。這促使史羅司押後原定一九四六年十月十一日的復校計劃，縱使大學其實已開始面試收生，甚至授課。

倫敦方面的遲疑所引致的重大後果之一，是香港本土意識到大學重開為當務之急。一九四八年初香港政府撥出四百萬元用作重建港大，並將每年資助金額增加二倍至一百五十萬元，英國亦相應地出資二十五萬英鎊。

大學的校董會、校務委員會、教務委員會、學系委員會終於一九四八年初復員，標誌著港大復校。大學捐贈基金亦於一九五一年重新啟用，並於同年十二月增多一百萬英鎊。

大禮堂內部戰後的面貌，修復建築幾年後才重開
來源：一九四五年十二月八日《香港大學重建備忘錄》附錄二 '一九四五年十一月香港大學景觀'，圖六
Interior of the Great Hall after the war. It could only be used again after some years of restoration.
'Memorandum on Reconstitution of the University of Hong Kong', dated 8th December, 1945. Appendix II 'Some Views of Hong Kong University, November 1945', fig. 6

Re-establishment of the University after the War

When the war ended, wartime Vice-Chancellor Duncan Sloss hoped that the University could be re-opened quickly, but many of the conditions necessary to re-constitute the University were not yet in place. In a review of the state of the University in the immediate post-war period in November 1945, buildings were photographed in ruins, the consequence of both war damage and looting. While the student body was slowly beginning to return to Hong Kong from different parts of China, the University's financial needs for re-building of the campus, and for recruiting staff were acute.

The Hongkong University Advisory Committee, set up on the 31st December 1945 and chaired by Christopher Cox, argued in its final report of August 1946 that the University should be 're-established as soon as possible on a firm financial basis, with staff and facilities adequate to make it fully capable of reaching British academic standards and becoming an effective centre for Sino-British contact in the sphere of learning. ... The University is needed to represent British scholarship in the Far East; and to be a centre where advantage can be taken of the unique opportunities presented for cooperation between British and Chinese learning at the point of junction between the two civilizations.'[1]

Questions about the constitutional future of Hong Kong and its eventual return to China, and the significant financial investment needed if the University were to be re-opened according to the Cox report's ambitious recommendations, contributed to the lengthy delay in any formal decision to reconstitute the University. Sloss had no choice but to postpone the intended re-opening of the University scheduled for the 11th October 1946. The University was nevertheless already interviewing students and offering classes.

One of the other major consequences of the delay in London was a sense of urgency in Hong Kong that the University should be re-established as quickly as possible. Finally, in early 1948, the Hong Kong Government committed $4 million for the re-establishment, and tripled its annual grant to $1.5 million. The British responded with a grant of £250,000.

The University's Court, Council, Senate and Faculty boards were formally restored in early 1948, marking the University's official re-establishment. The University's endowment fund was reconstituted in 1951, with an additional £1 million in December of that year.

Notes: Chan Lau Kit-ching, 'The Post-war re-establishment', in Chan and Cunich, pp. 241–251; Francis Stock, 'A New Beginning', in Harrison, pp. 85–87.

1 Anthony Sweeting, 'The University by Report', Chan and Cunich, p. 236.

UNIVERSITY OF HONG KONG

26:7:46

Minutes of a meeting of the Committee on the re-opening of the University.

The first meeting of this Committee was held in the Board Room of the Hong Kong & Shanghai Bank, at 5 p.m., on Friday July 26, 1946.

Members present:-

Professor R.K.M. Simpson (Chairman)
The Hon. Mr. C. G. S. Follows
The Hon. Mr. Arthur Morse
Professor R. Robertson
Professor Gordon King

1. There was laid on the table a copy of the Colonial Secretary's letter notifying the appointment of this Committee.

2. There was appointed a sub-committee, Professor Simpson (Chairman) Professor Robertson and Professor Gordon King, to report on the results of the Entrance Examination and to make recommendations for admission of undergraduates to University courses.

3. The discussion of courses to be made available in October was left to the academic members of the Committee.

4. The Committee approved the arrangements proposed by Professor Gordon King, on attached memorandum, for the tuition and supervision of 19 Final Year Medical students.

5. Professor Gordon King, as a member of University Medical Degrees Emergency Committee indicated the arrangements that are being made for 7 graduands who are awaiting conferment of degrees.

6. The Committee approved the new form of contract, with penalty of H.K.$400 (four hundred) per day payable by contractors for each day beyond October 7, if the contractors fail to finish by that date.

7. Resolved to get a contract for grass cutting in University compound, and submit for approval to Mr. Morse.

8. Recommended that Major Meller be appointed to a lecturership in English, and posted for duty as Acting Registrar, with extra emolument for acting as Registrar.

9. Recommended early official publication through His Excellency's Public Relations Officer of the intention to re-open the University on October 11.

(1)

香港大學一九四六年七月二十六日復校會議紀錄
Minutes of the Committee on the Re-opening of the University meeting held 26th July 1946

UNIVERSITY OF HONG KONG

26:7:46

10. The Committee recommended the following financial arrangements:-
    a) That the University Accountants, Percy Smith and Fleming, should make out the amounts due monthly, as old members of the staff are re-employed or new members appointed, and cheques be countersigned by Mr. Morse and Professor Gordon King.
    b) that members of University clerical staff should be re-employed, as their services become necessary, on old pay plus increments, where such were due, plus H.C.D. allowance.
    c) Certain outstanding bills due to treasury, be sent to Percy Smith & Fleming to arrange payments.
    d) That as a temporary measure in the case of three members of the staff recently returned from United Kindgom, who are at present in Peninsula Hotel, as University has no other housing to offer them, the University will bear the actual cost of their room in the hotel up to a maxium of H.K. $12 a day.
    e) That, until living quarters are available in the University compound, the University will bear the cost of a car from month to month.

11. The Committee adjourned, with a vote of thanks to Mr. Morse for the use of this Board Room.

Note. Items 8 and 9 have since been referred to, and approved by His Excellency.

Confirmed, as Approved Aug. 19, 1946

戰時校長史羅司
Wartime Vice-Chancellor Duncan Sloss

No. 2220/45.

COLONIAL SECRETARIAT,
LOWER ALBERT ROAD
HONG KONG

9th December, 1946.

Sir,

I am directed to inform you that His Excellency the Governor has been pleased to appoint you, with effect from 7th December, 1946, to be Chairman of the University Interim Committee which is to supervise the reopening of the University of Hong Kong and to look after the current affairs of the University in the Colony, pending decisions in London about future University policy and the reconstitution of the statutory governing bodies.

The membership of the Committee is as follows:-

    D.J. Sloss, Esq., C.B.E., M.A. (Chairman)
    The Honourable Dr. Arthur Morse, C.B.E., LL.D.
    The Honourable Mr. C.G.S. Follows, C.M.G.
    The Honourable Dr. S.N. Chau, M.B.,B.S.,D.O.M.S., B.O.I.
    The Director of Education, Mr. T.R. Rowell, B.Sc.
    Professor R.K.M. Simpson, M.C., M.A.
    Professor R. Robertson, M.A.
    Mr. D.F. Davies, M.A.
    Mr. S.V. Boxer, B.Sc.Eng., Dip.Ed., (Secretary)

I am, Sir,

Your obedient servant,

Acting Colonial Secretary.

D.J. Sloss, Esq., C.B.E., M.A.
Vice-Chancellor,
University of Hong Kong.

一九四六年署理輔政司委任校長史羅司出任大學臨時委員會主席信函
Letter from the Acting Colonial Secretary appointing the Vice-Chancellor Duncan Sloss as Chairman of the University Interim Committee in 1946

賴廉士爵士主持第三十八屆學位頒授典禮，他前面放著大學權杖的空座，後來由校董梁耀捐款另造一把（參看第62至63頁）。
Sir Lindsay Ride presiding over the 38th Congregation
In front of him was the empty cradle where the original Mace would have been laid. A replacement Mace was subsequently commissioned by Mr Leung Yew, a member of the Court (see pages 62-63).

復建港大
Re-building the University

一九四八年校長史羅司最初提倡重建大學的願望終於達成，他在退休前向何東爵士募捐獲得一百萬元，興建大學首間女生舍堂，命名為何東夫人紀念堂，以紀念何東元配麥秀英夫人（卒於一九四三年），於一九五一年落成啟用。

一九四九年賴廉士繼任為港大校長。他戰時的英勇行為使他成為最佳的校長人選，而自一九二八年以來他已擔任生理學系主任，因而熟知大學內務，並協助百廢待興的港大恢復過來。

一九五零年鍾士博士、亞當斯代表殖民地大學高等教育大學校際議會訪問港大後，參考早前郭克時報告書的結論，提出應增加撥款擴建校園。[1] 首先是修建包括本部大樓在內的戰時損毀建築，以及加強教學設施，尤其是科學課程方面。本部大樓內置不少辦事處、課室、圖書館，以至職員及學生宿舍，早已不勝負荷。後來本部大樓加添了兩個方院，大禮堂亦增建了舞台，後方則另建獨立的職員宿舍。

賴廉士成為港大任期最長的校長，他見證了港大戰後的復建，到了一九六一年港大創校的金禧慶典，大學亦展現煥然一新的面貌。

In 1948, Duncan Sloss retired from the position of Vice-Chancellor knowing that his committed and early advocacy for the re-establishment of the University had succeeded. His final act before leaving office was to secure from Sir Robert Ho Tung a gift of $1 million for the building of the University's first hall of residence for women. Named in honour of his late wife Lady Margaret Ho Tung (d. 1943), Lady Ho Tung Hall was opened in 1951.

Lindsay Ride was appointed Duncan Sloss' successor as Vice-Chancellor in 1949. Ride's leadership during the war made him a popular choice and as an 'insider' who had been head of the physiology department since 1928, he represented continuity at a time of uncertainty.

Drawing upon the earlier conclusions of the Cox report, a report by Dr Mouat Jones, and Walter Adams drawn up after a visit to the University in 1950 for the Inter-University Council for Higher Education in the Colonies, recommended additional funding for the University's expansion.[1] A top priority was the repair of buildings damaged during the war, including the Main Building, and the expansion of teaching facilities, in particular those for the sciences. The Main Building had housed offices, lecture rooms, the library, as well as staff and student quarters and had long-since been operating at capacity. With the addition of two further quadrangles, the Great Hall was extended to create a stage, and new separate staff quarters were built behind the Main Building.

As the longest serving Vice-Chancellor, Sir Lindsay Ride oversaw the post-war re-building of the University, the rapid expansion of the 1960s, including the celebrations for the University's fiftieth anniversary in 1961. These were decades in which the University changed almost beyond recognition.

1 Stock, in Harrison, p. 86.

陸佑與大禮堂

大學本部大樓戰後的面貌
來源：一九四五年十二月八日《香港大學重建備忘錄》附錄二‘一九四五年十一月香港大學景觀’，圖四
The Main Building after the war
Memorandum on Reconstitution of the University of Hong Kong,' dated 8th December, 1945. Appendix II 'Some Views of Hong Kong University, November 1945,' fig. 4

一九三六年陸佑提供的貸款即將到期清還，大學的投資資本卻因中國政局動盪而大幅貶值，因此被逼向香港上海匯豐銀行貸款二萬元，以償還借款，並須根據與陸佑信託基金的部份協議，繼續為其獎學金注資。

至一九四七年大學復校，通貨膨脹導致陸佑四個獎學金的資本上升至一萬二千元，大學財政不勝負荷，因而成立委員會與陸佑信託基金展開談判，可是在史羅司校長任內不能達成協定。

一九四九年賴廉士出任校長，重申陸佑原來捐款的重要性，一九五三年陸佑兒子陸運濤（一九一五至一九六四年）接任其父之基金信託人後，與大學的關係亦大為改善。翌年雙方修訂了一九一六年的貸款協議，同意大學每年注資七千元予陸佑獎學金基金，以資助不能支付學費的清貧學生。獎學金將視乎陸佑基金的實際餘額而發放；並加入條款，大禮堂須於一九五六年命名陸佑堂，以紀念陸佑的捐獻。

在陸佑堂的命名典禮上，陸運濤亦有出席，校長賴廉士於致辭時表揚陸佑在四十年前的慷慨捐獻，幫助大學於創辦初年渡過難關，為亞洲社會培育了'逾六百名醫生、三百六十名工程師、五百七十名科學及文學系畢業生。'

Loke Yew and the Great Hall

In 1936, an interest-free loan of $500,000 made by the Malayan businessman Loke Yew in 1915 was due to be repaid. However, the value of the University's investments had plummeted due to the instability in China and the University was forced to borrow $20,000 from the Hongkong and Shanghai Banking Corporation to honour the loan. As part of the agreement with Loke Yew's trustees, the University also agreed to continue providing for the four Loke Yew scholarships established as part of the conditions of the loan.

By 1947 when the University was re-opened, inflationary pressures meant that the cost of maintaining these scholarships had risen to $12,000, which the University could no longer afford. A committee was set up to re-start negotiations between Loke Yew's trustees and the University, which had stalled under Duncan Sloss.

Assuming the role of Vice-Chancellor in 1949, Lindsay Ride was more inclined to recognise the importance of Loke Yew's original donation and relations were significantly improved when Loke Yew's son, Loke Wan Tho (1915–1964), became trustee in 1953. The following year in 1954 the 1916 agreement was amended to the effect that the University would pay $7,000 each year into a Loke Yew Scholarship Fund, which would be awarded to students without the financial means to cover the cost of education. The scholarships would be awarded according to how much was available in the fund. An additional amendment stated that the Great Hall would be re-named Loke Yew Hall in 1956 in honour of Loke Yew's donation.

At the re-naming ceremony, at which Loke Wan Tho was present, Lindsay Ride credited Loke Yew with saving the University forty years earlier thus providing the communities of Asia with 'over 600 doctors, over 360 engineers, over 570 Arts and Science graduates.'[1]

1   *University of Hong Kong Gazette*, 3/4, 1 March 1956, cited by Turnbull, 'The Malayan Connection', in Chan and Cunich, p. 115.

本部大樓大禮堂戰前的面貌
The Great Hall before the war

目標轉型

香港大學自二次大戰後因應中國形勢，導致營運的社會及教育環境與戰前截然不同。戰後至一九五四年漢布茹博士向聯合國匯報香港的政治難民情況短短十年間，本地人口增至二百萬，其中約六十六萬七千人為新移民，促使香港出現更多不同背景的學生，尋求中學及大學教育。一九四九年以前，學生如要接受中文中學或大學教育，可以前往中國內地升讀。至一九五三年中港邊境設立關卡，不但阻截了逃離共產主義統治的中國難民湧入香港，亦中斷了學生往內地求學的途徑。

以一九五一年本港中文中學及英文中學學生的數目為依據，只有半數以下的學生有望進入大學。為應付本地教育的需求，新的書院不斷成立，很多由來自中國大學的教授創辦，計有新亞書院（一九四九年）、崇基書院（一九五一年），以及一些較小型書院，稍後合併為聯合書院（一九五六年）。至一九六三年這三間書院組成香港中文大學。

由於香港政府熱衷推行普及與專業教育，促使港督葛量洪爵士成立委員會，由祁士域爵士領導進行教育情況的評估。戰前政府的教育政策，主力在發展具備雙語能力的專業階級，中文只限於小學教授，英文則是中學及大學的授課語言。祁士域委員會建議香港應在大學推行中文教育，以應付新移民的需要。港大因新近聘請了資深漢學家林仰山擔任中文系教授，教務委員會亦同意執行這些建議，但最終遭校董會否決，認為維持中英兩文的考試水平及教學語言，會超出大學現有資源的能力，大學應專注持續穩定基礎。

一九五一年港大開始重整文、理、工程等學位課程，以配合其他英聯邦國家的步伐：四年學制減為三年，醫科則需五年才畢業。自一九五四年起中學生須多讀一年預科，才能報考大學。雖然面對新中文書院林立，香港大學仍是新移民的求學首選，好讓他們進階香港專業人士的行列，亦是本地學生出國求學的最佳途徑。

至一九五三年，港大極需資金去應付不斷增長的學生人數及課程發展，港督葛量洪遂邀請律師兼錫蘭大學校長（後來出任劍橋大學校長）詹寧斯爵士與倫敦大學校長洛根爵士評估大學之財政、章程、功能各項的需要。兩人花了數天研究祁士域的建議、一九四六年的郭克時報告書，以及戰後數年的大學發展，就得出結論，並且影響深遠，成為港大日後發展的基石。詹寧斯與洛根報告書除提出增加撥款外，還建議重訂大學條例，著重校內的亞洲與中文研究，以及擴建校園。其中還包括設立大學圖書館，加入醫務所以改善學生設施。

正如普利思特利評論一九五零年的鍾士與亞當斯報告書時指出：'港大從大英帝國的裝飾品，轉變成一間優良的小型學府，努力自強不息。'[1]

Notes: Mellor, pp. 116-130; Francis Stock, 'A New Beginning,' and Kenneth Priestley, 'Changing Aims,' both in Harrison, pp. 85–102.

[1] Priestly, in Harrison, p. 96.

Changing its Purpose

Post-war conditions in China meant that the University was now operating in a substantially different social and educational environment than that before the war. In the short decade between the end of the war and Dr Edvard Hambro's report to the United Nations on Hong Kong's political refugees in 1954, the population had grown to two million, with approximately 667,000 recent arrivals. This meant more students with different needs seeking secondary and university education in Hong Kong. Before 1949 students wishing to pursue secondary or degree level education in Chinese were able to attend schools in the Chinese mainland. When the border was closed in 1953 to stem the tide of refugees leaving communist China, it simultaneously isolated those wanting an education there.

Based on the number of students enrolled in Chinese middle schools and Anglo-Chinese schools in 1951, it was clear that less than half the student population could hope to be educated at the University. Given such a climate of need, colleges began to spring up, many of them founded by professors arriving from Chinese universities. These included New Asia College (1949), Chung Chi College (1951), as well as other smaller colleges that later joined together to form Union College (1956). These three colleges would consolidate in 1963 to form the Chinese University of Hong Kong.

Government interest in general and professional education in Hong Kong led the Governor, Sir Alexander Grantham, to set up a committee headed by Sir John Keswick to review the situation. Before the war, the government's educational policy had focused on developing a bi-lingual professional class. Chinese was taught at primary school level, while English was the medium of instruction at secondary school and degree levels. Among the Keswick Committee's recommendations was that efforts should be made to introduce a degree level education in Chinese to cater to new immigrants. With the recent appointment of the experienced Sinologist F. S. Drake as Professor of Chinese, there was support in the Senate for this proposal but it was eventually rejected by the University Council who viewed the complexities of establishing equal standards of examination and teaching in both languages as beyond the University's immediate resources. It favoured instead a more measured period of consolidation.

In 1951 the University began to re-organise its degrees in arts, science and engineering to bring them more in line with other Commonwealth countries. The four-year degree was reduced to three, with medical degrees taking five years. From 1954 onwards, students were admitted to the University a year later, which meant that secondary schools were required to offer an additional senior level year. Despite the existence of the new colleges, the University remained the institution of choice for recent immigrants wishing to establish themselves professionally in Hong Kong, as well as for local students wanting to pursue opportunities elsewhere. In 2012, the University returned to a four-year curriculum.

In 1953, in light of the University's continuing financial demands, an expanding student population and curricula development, Grantham invited Sir Ivor Jennings, a lawyer and Vice-Chancellor of the University of Ceylon (later Cambridge), and Sir Douglas W. Logan, the Principal of London University, to advise on the University's financial, constitutional and functional needs. Taking into account the conclusions of the Keswick Committee, the Cox report of 1946, and developments at the University in the intervening years, the two men completed their investigations in a matter of days. Their influential report provided a road map for the University's development for years to come. In addition to the need for more funding, the Jennings-Logan Report recommended changes to the University's Ordinance, an emphasis on Asian and Chinese studies and expansion of the physical campus. Among the improvements proposed were a new Library, improved student facilities, and a health service.

As Kenneth Priestley noted in regard to the Jones-Adams report of 1950, the 'University's purposes were changing from those of an ornament in the British imperial mantel to those of a small academic institution of high quality working out its own destiny.'[1]

Univ. No .... Name RIDE EDWIN JOHN LINDSAY	
Birth Place HONG KONG Date, 12/11/31 Nationality. AUSTRALIAN	
Parent or Guardian DR L.T. RIDE	
Home Address 2 UNIVERSITY PATH H.K.	
Local Guardian "	
Address of same "	
Previous Education SCOTCH COLLEGE (Stamped p	
MELBOURNE AUSTRALIA	
Matric. Exam. (or equivalent) NOV. /1949	
Equivalent MELBOURNE UNIVERSITY MATRICULATION	
Registered March / 7 /19 50 Hall	
Scholarships	
Degree Examinations First / /19 . Second / 19 .	
Third / /19 . Fourth / 19 .	
Graduation ..../ 19	

Dean's comments and Signature

Subsequent career.

Edwin John Lindsay Ride 的香港大學學生紀錄
Edwin John Lindsay Ride's student record

本相片泛黃，是因為當時所用的膠水含硫酸引致。大學檔案中心勸喻切勿使用黏性貼紙或膠紙等物於永久留存文件。
The yellowing on the photograph is caused by the build up of acid/ sulphur in the glue used at the time. In general, the University Archives discourages the use of adhesives of any kind, including sticky notes and tape, on records that may have permanent value.

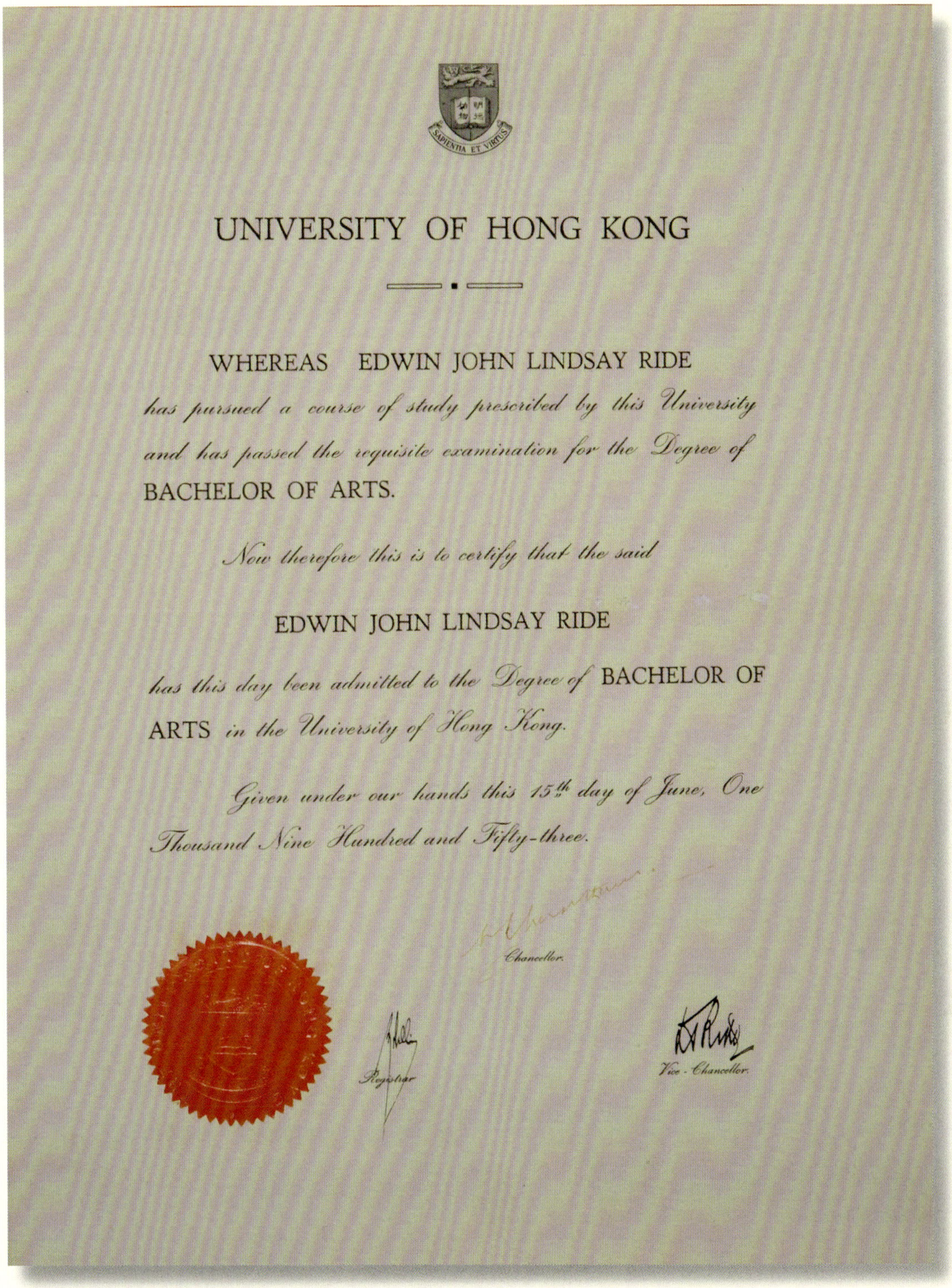

印上賴廉士爵士父子名字畢業證書
一九五三年六月十五日
David Ride 捐贈
香港大學檔案中心「賴廉士爵士特藏」

Bachelor of Arts Degree Certificate awarded to Edwin John Lindsay Ride (1931-1996)
Dated 15th June 1953
Gift of Mr David Ride
Sir Lindsay Ride Collection, University Archives

這是香港大學至今唯一父子名字同時出現的畢業證書。
This is the only known degree certificate awarded by a Vice-Chancellor to his own son.

圖書館

香港大學於一九一二年成立，同年位於本部大樓的大學圖書館啟用，為師生服務直到戰後擴充校園。今天圖書館總館與五間分館，包括余振強醫學圖書館、呂志和法律圖書館、教育圖書館、牙科圖書館、音樂圖書館遍佈大學各個校園，提供學術研究的支援。

圖書館從落成啟用至今，秉承促進學術研究的使命，在管理人員的努力及慈善家的慷慨協助下，隨著時代變遷多番擴展。

一九一二年英國殖民地官員及漢學家金文泰將康熙（一六六二至一七二二年在位）及雍正時期（一七二三至一七三五年在位）編纂、一七二五年成書的一千六百二十八卷《古今圖書集成》（又名康熙百科全書）捐贈予大學圖書館。翌年金文泰獲委派到英屬蓋亞那，其後於一九二五年回港出任香港總督（參看第7頁）。

同年，圖書館獲贈首批特藏，名為馬禮遜藏書。這批藏書以英國傳教士馬禮遜博士（一七八二至一八三四）命名，原為英國商行一八零六年於廣州建立的馬禮遜教育學會的基本館藏。一八四一年該館連同三千五百冊藏書遷到澳門，翌年遷至香港。一八六九年書籍被收歸於新建的香港大會堂圖書館。因這批書並不切合普羅大眾的需要，於是在一九一四年移送到港大新建的圖書館中寄存，至一九二五年成為永久館藏。

港大圖書館同時珍藏遮打爵士五十四本講述中國的書刊舊藏。一九二六年八十歲的遮打爵士逝世時遺下油畫、水彩畫、素描、版畫、相片、古籍。翌年，港督金文泰將遮打爵士的藏書轉贈香港大學。

一九二六年中文系教授賴際熙太史向馬來亞華僑募捐，建立中文藏書。大學將陳永等人的捐款用來購買三萬一千本中文書，並將這批藏書命名為振永書藏，置於本部大樓H教室。

其後，大學用馮平山的捐款建立中文圖書館，並增購重要中文書刊。一九三二年馮平山圖書館落成。同年港大圖書館收購了漢口總會圖書館中國部收藏，藏書量大增。漢口總會圖書館於一八七八年由英國人為外商而設，藏有約三千冊有關中國及遠東的外文古籍。當時，港大圖書館失書情況嚴重，委員會遂引入十字轉門。

港大圖書館約於一九五三年增購包括名為黃海黃氏籾學齋藏書的一萬七千六百冊中文古籍，以及吳興劉氏嘉業堂藏書。今天，這兩批藏書已然成為圖書館的中文古籍珍藏。

港大第四任校長韓惠和爵士於一九三七年離任時，亦將其收藏的一千三百本書捐贈予圖書館。

一九四一年十二月日本佔領香港時，大學藏書達九萬八千冊。當時，馮平山圖書館成為本港各學校圖書館以至個人收藏的藏書庫，保存公私文獻，由館長陳君葆負責看管整理（參看第128頁）。可惜二戰時期部份'香港圖書館'藏書被分送到東京及梅夫人婦女會。一九四四年馮平山圖書館成為日治時期的政府圖書館。一九四五年二次大戰結束，慶幸圖書館並未受戰火波及，仍然完整無缺。

香港淪陷時，大學校長史羅司於赤柱監獄拘留期間領導成立小組委員會，商討大學重建事宜。戰後重建的其中一個計劃，便是要興建一所'能夠貯藏二十萬冊書以及容立最少三百名讀者的圖書館'。[1]

此構想最終於一九六一年實現，港大圖書館趕及於大學金禧慶典前落成啟用，此為現時總館的舊翼。圖書館於一九六七年加建兩個樓層，一九八六年則落實興建毗連舊翼的圖書館大樓新翼。一九九一年新翼開幕，圖書館的藏書達一百萬冊。二零零二年圖書館貯藏的印刷及電子書突破二百萬冊，時至今日已然超過三百萬冊。

二零零六年港大圖書館聯同亞洲研究中心向香港賽馬會慈善信託基金申請五千三百萬元撥款，推行'香港記憶計劃'，建立一個收錄香港歷史和文化資料的數位圖書館。[2]

二零一一年譚華正博士捐款一千萬元，於總館三樓設立配有先進科技設備的學習共享空間，經過裝修後於二零一二年啟用。二零一一年港大圖書館獲中央政府送贈一套九千一百二十九卷的《中華再造善本》，慶祝香港大學創校一百周年。

Notes: Drake, in Harrison, p. 142–147; www.lib.hku.hk/hkul100
1 Ride, in Harrison, p. 70.
2 www.hkmemory.hk.

一九六一年圖書館大樓舊翼落成
Main Library, Old Wing, completed in 1961

圖書館館長

香港大學圖書館館長對大學的發展貢獻良多，在大學成立一百年以來，只曾聘任六位圖書館館長。

一九二一年港大聘任 Mrs Ring 為第一任圖書館館長，同年港大取錄首位女學生。Mrs Ring 憑藉豐富專業的資歷而獲聘，成為當時整間大學唯一一位全職女員工。Mrs Ring 任圖書館館長期間經歷二次世界大戰，一直堅守崗位直到一九五零年退任，其後由施高德夫人繼任館長一職。日治時期馮平山圖書館館長陳君葆邀請戰時畢業生伍冬瓊留校，協助整理馮平山圖書館的藏書。伍冬瓊於一九五一年獲施高德夫人正式聘任為館員，一九五六年接替陳君葆成為馮平山圖書館館長。

一九六一年賴定仕接替施高德夫人出任圖書館館長，適逢港大創校五十周年，校園多處進行擴展工程，包括圖書館舊翼大樓的興建。賴定仕除了帶領圖書館遷到新落成的大樓外，還統籌將馮平山圖書館的藏書運到總館。一九八三年，簡麗冰博士繼任圖書館館長，直至一九九九年。她於任內規劃興建圖書館新翼，管理並發展圖書館捐贈基金，以及推出網上目錄'DRAGON'、圖書館網頁。彭仁賢博士於二零零一至二零一零年擔任館長，期間引入用戶驅動服務，推動各項專業合作計劃，以及增加圖書館外展及籌款的機會。他促使圖書館將中文書刊加入線上電腦圖書館中心及 WorldCat 數據庫，在引入新科技的同時亦與大學電腦中心及各學院緊密合作。彭仁賢並列席最初的檔案工作小組、檔案諮詢小組。

二零一一年蘇德毅繼任圖書館館長，上任以來主持圖書館創館一百周年之一系列紀念活動，以及二零一二年總館三樓改造成創新科技空間的裝修工程。他亦列席檔案諮詢小組。

The Libraries

The University Library was established when the University was opened in 1912 and housed in two rooms of the Main Building until after the war, when the University entered a period of unprecedented expansion. Today the Libraries incorporate the Main, Medical, Law, Education, Dental and Music libraries spread across the University's various campuses.

The Library's growth and development since its foundation has largely been the result of a sense of mission, historical circumstances and the advocacy of individual administrators and philanthropists.

In 1912, Colonial Secretary and Sinologist, Sir Cecil Clementi, donated to the nascent Library a 1,628-volume edition of the *Gujin Tushu Jicheng* (known as the Imperial Encyclopedia), completed in 1725 during the reigns of the Kangxi (1662–1722) and Yongzheng emperors (1723–1735). The following year Clementi was posted to British Guiana, but would return to Hong Kong in 1925 as Governor (see page 7).

That was also the year in which the Library was gifted its first major rare book collection, known as the Morrison Collection. Originally it formed the basis of the Morrison Education Society library set up in 1806 by members of the English 'Factory' in Canton and named for the protestant missionary, Dr Robert Morrison (1782–1834). The library, consisting of 3,500 volumes, was moved to Macau in 1841, and from there to Hong Kong in 1842. In 1869 the collection became part of the newly-opened City Hall Library. Amid doubts about its usefulness to the general public, the collection was loaned to the newly-established University Library in 1914, and permanently transferred in 1925.

The Library also includes 54 rare books on China from Sir Paul Chater's collection. When he passed away in 1926 at the age of 80, the philanthropist left his collection of oil paintings, watercolours, sketches, prints and photographs, and rare books to Hong Kong. In 1927, Governor Sir Cecil Clementi presented the books to the University.

As part of an initiative to establish a separate Chinese department, donations from overseas Chinese in Malaya were solicited by professor of Chinese, Lai Chi-hsi in 1926. Mr Chan Wing and others donated funds that contributed to the purchase a collection of 31,000 volumes of Chinese books known collectively as the Chen Yung Library and housed in Room H of the Main Building.

Mr Fung Ping-shan contributed both the funds to build a Chinese book library along with a significant collection of Chinese books. The Fung Ping Shan Library opened in 1932. That year the collections of the Main Library were also substantially improved when the University purchased the 'China' section of the Hankow Club's library. Founded in 1878 by the British for the foreign concessions there, the collection contains around 3,000 volumes of rare western books on the Far East. The theft of books from the library was considered so serious that the Library Committee introduced a turnstile.

Later acquisitions around 1953 including the Huang Collection, numbering 17,600 volumes of Chinese rare books, and selections from the Liu Collection today form the core of the Chinese Rare Book Collections.

When Sir William Hornell, the University's fourth Vice-Chancellor, left the University in 1937, he also donated his collection of over 1,300 books to the Library.

At the time of the Japanese occupation in December 1941, the Libraries collections numbered 98,000 volumes. The Fung Ping Shan Library became the central repository for private and institutional libraries and its librarian, Chan Kwan-po (see page 128) remained to take care of the Library through the war. Some volumes were sent to Tokyo while others were sent to the Helena May where they were part of the City Library. In 1944, it became the Library of the Government of the Occupied Territory. When the war ended in August 1945, the Library had survived relatively intact.

Under the leadership of the wartime Vice-Chancellor, Duncan Sloss, a subcommittee on the reconstruction of the University was convened during internment at Stanley Prison Camp. Amid their post-war reconstruction plans was 'a library to house 200,000 volumes... with space for at least 300 readers.'[1]

This finally came to fruition in 1961, when the University Library was opened in time for the Golden Jubilee celebrations of the University. This is today known as the Old Wing. A further two floors were added in 1967, and in 1986 approval for a Library extension adjacent to the Old Wing was granted. The New Wing was opened in 1991, the year in which the collections reached a million in number. In 2002, the holdings passed the 2 million mark and now exceeds 3 million books in both paper and electronic versions.

In 2006, the Libraries collaborated with the Centre of Asian Studies to apply for funding of $53 million from the Hong Kong Jockey Club Charities Trust for the Hong Kong Memory Project, a web-based digital library of Hong Kong history and culture.[2]

In 2011, Dr Tam Wah-ching donated $10 million towards the establishment of a new facility on the third floor of the Main Library to provide technology rich collaborative spaces for students. This was opened in January 2012. For the centenary celebrations of the University in 2011, the Libraries received a set of 9,129 volumes of the *Zhonghua zaizao shanben* (Reproductions of Chinese Rare Editions Series) from the Central Government.

Notes: Drake, in Harrison, pp. 142–147; www.lib.hku.hk/hkul100
1 Ride, in Harrison, p. 70.
2 www.hkmemory.hk.

圖書館大樓舊翼內部及圖書館卡片目錄
Interior of the Old Library Building showing the card catalogues

The Librarians

The University's Librarians have played an important role in the development of the University, and of Hong Kong. In its first hundred years there have been only six Librarians.

The University's earliest Librarian was Mrs M. E. Ring, appointed in 1921, the year in which the first female student was admitted. She was the only full-time female staff member at the University at the time and despite her academic and professional qualifications, she experienced considerable discrimination. She served through the war until 1950 when she was succeeded by Mrs Dorothea Scott. Wartime graduate Ng Tung-king, who had remained at the University through the war to help Chan Kwan-po catalogue the Fung Ping Shan Library collection, was appointed librarian by Mrs Scott in 1951. She later succeeded Chan as the Fung Ping Shan Librarian in 1956.

In 1961 Mr H. A. Rydings succeeded Mrs Scott just as the University was celebrating its Golden Jubilee and the culmination of a period of growth and expansion. For the Libraries this meant moving into their own purpose-built building. He also presided over the move of the Fung Ping Shan Library collection to the Main Library. He was succeeded by Dr L. B Kan in 1983 who served until 1999 during which she oversaw planning, building and completion of the Library's New Wing, the growth of the Library Endowment Funds and the introduction of the online access catalogue 'DRAGON' as well as the Libraries webpage. Dr Anthony Ferguson served from 2001 until 2010, he introduced more user-centred services, and encouraged collaboration between the Libraries, Faculties and Information Technology Services. He also increased the Library's outreach and fundraising opportunities and committed the Libraries to adding a record number of Chinese works to the World Catalogue of the Online Computer Library Center (OCLC). Dr Ferguson served on the original Archives Working Group and the Archives Advisory Group.

Mr Peter Sidorko became the Librarian in 2011, and has presided over the centenary celebrations of the Library as well as the renovation of the Library's third floor and re-opening as its innovative Technology Zone in 2012. He also serves on the Archives Advisory Group.

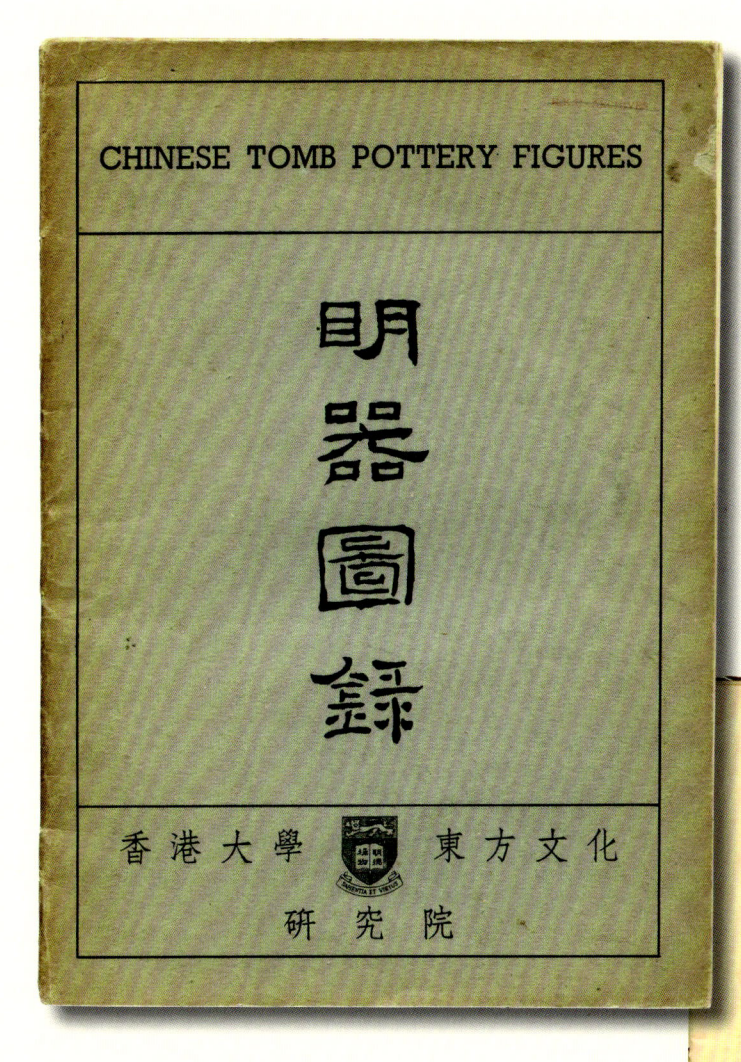

香港大學出版社首部出品：東方文化研究院
一九五三年展覽刊物《明器圖錄》
The Hong Kong University Press' first publication was a catalogue of a 1953 exhibition of *Chinese Tomb Pottery Figures*, organised by the Institute of Oriental Studies

興建中的圖書館新翼
一九八九年七月五日
Building work for the new Library extension
5th July 1989

香港大學進行擴建工程，將本部大樓前的舊學生會大樓拆卸。學生會辦事處遷到黃克競樓新址，本部大樓前則興建圖書館新翼。

As part of the University's continuing development and expansion, the old Student Union Building was demolished and the Union was re-located to the Haking Wong Building. An extension for the library was developed on the site.

HKU Memories | from the Archives

香港大學出版社

一九五一年六月大學校務委員會通過與教務委員會成立聯合出版管理局，負責監督香港大學出版社，管理局全權負責遴選會員、委任榮譽審稿人，由 J. E. Driver 教授擔任主席，一九五三年並邀得布蘭敦、林仰山加入。[1]

當時聯合出版管理局僅有一台價值不到二千元的手搖印刷機，專職印刷試卷、會議紀錄等大學印務。最早出版的是《明器圖錄》，為香港大學東方文化研究院一九五三年九月二十六至二十八日舉辦展覽之圖錄。當時在大學書店的售價是十元，同時發行海外，寄往美國連郵費售價是二美元，英國連郵費的售價是十二先令六便士。

一九五五年大學委任魏智（一八九八至一九七八年）為兼職業務經理。一九五六年轉聘他作出版社社長，合約訂明外籍僱員條件，三年半期滿可再續約。

魏智出任香港大學出版社首任社長，可算實至名歸。他在福州渡過童年，後來父母離異，他被送往塞舌耳，跟隨外祖父母生活。一九一七年到法國從軍。一九二零年復員後到天津，與父親 Francis Vetch 團聚，其父在當地經營法文書店 Librarie Française。魏智後來買下老北京飯店內的法文書店，成為著名出版商。他熱愛中國語文，因此吸引不少學者光顧書店。一九二九年他與 Elena Evreeva 成婚，育有兩名子女。一九三九年他再次到法國參軍，直至一九四一年返回中國。一九五一年他被牽涉入一宗間諜案，密謀暗殺毛澤東罪名成立，被判入獄十年，三年後卻遞解到香港。隨後他任職香港大學出版社，至一九六八年退休後，他遂與辰衝圖書公司創辦人 Rupert Li 成立出版社 Vetch & Li。[2]

第二任社長為彭傑福（一九二四至二零一零年），他一生多姿多采，從事過不同行業。他出生於湖南，父親為傳教士，後來中國排外情緒日益高漲，一九二六年舉家惟有返回英國。二次大戰時他加入公誼服務會，在四川及貴州提供救援工作，負責駕駛貨車往返昆明與重慶兩地。

後來彭傑福返回英國，進入劍橋大學修讀東方語言，主修中國古文，一九五四年取得碩士學位。他曾短期擔任倫敦大學亞非學院圖書館助理館長，負責日本藏書。一九五五年他應聘成為港大圖書館副館長。

彭傑福深受父親 B. S. Bonsall 博士熱愛中國的影響，其父曾將《紅樓夢》、《戰國策》翻譯成英文版。《紅樓夢》之翻譯原文雖未經出版，仍為大英圖書館收藏。[3]

彭傑福擔任香港大學圖書館副館長任內，負責監督興建新圖書館大樓，一九六一年該樓啟用。一九六八年他獲夏威夷大學頒發圖書館學碩士學位。一九六九年獲委任香港大學出版社秘書，後進升總監，直至一九八零年為止。二零零六年他憶述香港大學出版社社長的生涯：

'一九六八年我接手管理時，出版社仍設於馮平山樓內……，職員只得一人，我一手包辦設計封面、編版，對我來說卻是絕佳的訓練。'[4]

彭傑福對香港歷史認識極深，一九五九年皇家亞洲學會香港分會重組時，他是創辦會員之一。他亦是研究戰時一度遺失之遮打爵士香港繪畫珍藏的專家，並為畫家錢納利所使用葛爾內速記法之公認權威。

他亦是著名業餘作家，兼職香港電台播音員，其藝名 Charles Weatherill，取自母親姓氏，他並擅長代寫名人或政治家演辭，包括賭場大亨何鴻燊。他在友儕眼中為人睿智、打扮時髦、愛科技、談笑風生。[5]

---

1. 'Minutes of the Senate and the Court,' The University of Hong Kong.
2. *Dictionary of Hong Kong Biography,* pp. 445–446.
3. It is also available digitally at www.lib.hku.hk/bonsall/hongloumeng/index1.html.
4. Annemarie Evans, 'Fifty years of history rolls off the press', *Sunday Morning Post,* Sunday 31 December 2006.
5. 'Obituary: Geoffrey Bonsall/ Charles Weatherill', Annemarie Evans, *South China Morning Post,* 25 July 2010; Dr Dan Waters, 'Geoffrey Bonsall (Charles Wetherill)[sic], 1924–2010', *Journal of the Royal Asiatic Society Hong Kong Branch,* Vol. 50, pp.418–421.

歷任香港大學出版社社長
Hong Kong University Press Publishers

Mr Henri Vetch（魏智）1955–1968
Mr Geoffrey Bonsall（彭傑福）1970–1980
Mr Ken Toogood 1981–1985
Mr Leon Comber（梁康柏）1986–1991
Ms Barbara Clarke 1991–1999
Dr Colin Day 2000–2009
Mr Michael Duckworth 2009–2013

"Elliot House"
1929.

一九二九年 Elliot House 舊貌。隨著大學百周年校園發展而修復，並命名邵逸夫樓，現為香港大學出版社辦事處。
Elliot House as it was in 1929. It has since been restored as part of the Centennial Campus development, and renamed Run Run Shaw House. It now houses the Hong Kong University Press.

The University of Hong Kong Press

In June 1951, the University Council approved the formation of a Joint Publications Board of the Council and the Senate to manage the University of Hong Kong Press, with the power to co-opt members and appoint readers in an honorary capacity. The Board was chaired by Professor J. E. Driver; Edmund Blunden and Frederick Drake were appointed to the Board in 1953.[1]

Equipped with a hand-printing press costing less than $2,000, the Board was responsible for the printing of examination papers, minutes and other University work. The first publication of the Hong Kong University Press was *Chinese Tomb Pottery Figures*, the catalogue of an exhibition arranged by the Institute of Oriental Studies from the 26th to 28th September 1953. It was sold in the University Bookstore at a cost of HK $10.00, but also had international distribution as it is listed for the USA at US $2.00 postage paid and for the United Kingdom, at twelve shillings and six pence, postage paid.

In 1955, the University appointed Henri Vetch (1898–1978) to the position of part-time Business Manager. In 1956, this contract was changed to that of Publisher on a three-and-a-half year renewable contract on expatriate terms.

Vetch was uniquely qualified to be the University's first Publisher. His earliest childhood years were spent in Fuzhou until his parent's divorce in 1907 when he moved to the Seychelles where he was brought up by his maternal grandparents. In 1917 he joined the French army. After he was demobilised in 1920, he joined his father Francis Vetch in Tianjin where he was running the Librarie Française. Henri later purchased the French bookshop in the Grand Hôtel de Pékin and became a well-known publisher and bookseller. His interest in the Chinese language attracted many scholars to his store. He married Elena Evreeva in 1929, and together they had two children. In 1939, he joined the French army again, serving until 1941. In 1951, he was accused with others of espionage and plotting to assassinate Chairman Mao, serving three years of a ten-year sentence. In 1954 he was deported to Hong Kong. He served at the Hong Kong University Press until his retirement in 1968. Later he established a publishing company with Rupert Li, the founder of the Swindon Book Company, known as Vetch & Li.[2]

The University Press' second publisher was Geoffrey Bonsall (1924–2010) who had an unusually rich and varied life that included several very different careers. Born in Wuhan, Hubei province, into a missionary family, anti-foreign sentiment forced the Bonsalls to return to England in 1926. During the war Geoffrey joined the Friends Ambulance Unit to provide relief work in Sichuan and Guizhou, driving trucks between Kunming and Chongqing.

Bonsall returned to England to study oriental languages, specifically Classical Chinese at the University of Cambridge, following with a Masters degree in 1954. He worked briefly as assistant librarian, in charge of the Japanese collection at the School of Oriental and African Studies, University of London before taking up the position of Deputy Librarian at the University of Hong Kong in 1955.

In his choices Bonsall was no doubt influenced by his father's love of China. Dr B. S. Bonsall had translated both the *Dream of the Red Chamber* and the *Records of the Warring States* from Chinese to English. Although unpublished, Bonsall's original translation of *Dream of the Red Chamber* is in the collection of the British Library in London.[3]

While Deputy Librarian, Bonsall was largely responsible for overseeing the construction of the new library building completed in 1961. In 1968, he earned his Master of Library Science from the University of Hawaii, and in 1969 he was appointed Secretary, then Director of the HKU Press, a post that he held until 1980. In 2006, recalling his tenure as Publisher, he said, 'When I took over the Press in 1968 it was based in the

Fung Ping Shan Building… It was very much a one-man band. I designed the covers, paginated the books – but it was extremely good training.' [4]

Bonsall had a great interest in local history and was a founding member of the Hong Kong Branch of the Royal Asiatic Society when it was reconstituted in December 1959. He was an expert on the Sir Paul Catchick Chater Hong Kong Collection of Paintings, lost during the war, and was widely recognised as one of the leading authorities on the Gurney shorthand used by the artist George Chinnery.

A well-known freelance writer and broadcaster on RTHK, under the pseudonym of Charles Weatherill, his mother's maiden name, he was also a speech writer for prominent Hong Kong figures including the casino mogul Stanley Ho Hung-sun. Bonsall is remembered among his friends for his keen intelligence, sartorial elegance, love of technology, and wit.[5]

---

1   'Minutes of the Senate and the Court,' The University of Hong Kong.
2   *Dictionary of Hong Kong Biography*, pp. 445–446.
3   It is also available digitally at www.lib.hku.hk/bonsall/hongloumeng/index1.html.
4   Annemarie Evans, 'Fifty years of history rolls off the press', *Sunday China Morning Post*, Sunday 31 December 2006.
5   'Obituary: Geoffrey Bonsall/ Charles Weatherill,' Annemarie Evans, *South China Morning Post*, 25 July 2010; Dr Dan Waters, 'Geoffrey Bonsall (Charles Wetherill) [sic], 1924–2010,' *Journal of the Royal Asiatic Society Hong Kong Branch*, Vol. 50, pp. 418–421.

彭傑福的圖書證
Geoffrey Bonsall's Library card

賴廉士以港大校長身份出席愛丁堡國際節，
會上與英聯邦國家大學代表合照
一九五五年
香港大學檔案中心「賴廉士爵士特藏」
Lindsay Ride as Vice-Chancellor of the
University of Hong Kong visiting the Edinburgh International
Festival with other university representatives, 1955
Sir Lindsay Ride Collection, HKUA

THE PRINCIPALS, VICE-CH

CAMPBELL HARPER

Back Row: Dr A.-M. PARENT   Prof. B. MAZAR   Dr
               (Laval)   (Jerusalem)

Middle Row: Mr W. HUGHES   Prof. Dr
          (Lord Provost of Dundee)
                                      Don

Front Row: Rector P. DAURE   Dr JOSÉ COELHO
            (Caen)   (Lisbon)

RGH INTERNATIONAL FESTIVAL, 1955

VISIT OF

ORS, PRESIDENTS, AND RECTORS OF THE UNIVERSITIES OF THE WORLD

Dr F. Cyril James (McGill)	Prof. Dr Hans Sittner (Vienna Academy of Music and Drama)	Prof. Dr Frede Castberg (Oslo)	Prof. Dr B. Helferich (Bonn)	Prof. Thrasivoulos Vlesidis (Athens)
Dr T. Djuricic (Belgrade)	Dr Duncan Baxter (Cape Town)	Prof. Ch. Fragistas (Thessaloniki)		
...	Prof. Dr J. N. Bakhuizen van den Brink (Leyden)	Principal Sir Thomas M. Taylor (Aberdeen)	Prof. Dr A. Marchionini (Munich)	Prof. Dr H. M. Hansen (Copenhagen)
orcoyen	Dr A. J. McConnell (Dublin)	Dr Nathan M. Pusey (Harvard)	Mr George Stephen (Lord Provost of Aberdeen)	
art ... Perth	Dr A. H. Smith (Oxford)	Principal Sir Edward Appleton (Edinburgh)	Rt. Hon. John G. Banks (Lord Provost of Edinburgh)	Dr T. J. Honeyman (Glasgow)	Dr Antonio Tovar (Salamanca)
... Lord Provost of Glasgow	Mr A. Hood	Principal T. M. Knox (St. Andrews)	Prof. Dr W. Kuhn (Basel)		

林仰山與中文系師生在南丫島考古，中立者為林仰山。
Frederick Drake with students and staff of the Chinese department on an archaeological expedition on Lamma Island. Drake stands in the centre.

林仰山與香港大學美術博物館的成立

林仰山（一八九二至一九七四年）出生於中國山東，其家族在英國甚有名望。他為出色的委任牧師、傳教士、神學家、漢學家，後因考古研究而到中國各地遊歷，並執教多年，曾於山東濟南齊魯大學出任神學院院長。一九五零年代中國內戰時期被逐出境，曾短居英國。

林仰山與香港大學的淵源始於一九三零年代，他有豐富的教學經驗，並富於改革的理想，當時香港大學正步向中文教學現代化，欲委任他出任中文系教授，後更獲校外人士提議設立中文系講座教授一職，由他擔任，然而他卻未能應邀。著名學者兼外交官胡適與港大關係密切，遂推薦曾留學美國的燕京大學教授許地山出任。許地山亦成功在港大力推行白話文教學。[1]

一九五二年林仰山雖居退休之齡，卻再度獲邀出任港大中文系講座教授，最終就職。他在任期間購藏一批中國藝術及考古學之教學文物，並於一九五五年成功帶領大學考古隊發掘李鄭屋古墓。

該批教學藏品後來成為馮平山圖書館大樓內考古陳列所的庋藏基石，由他領導首任館長 Mary Tregear 主理，後成立馮平山博物館。[2] 他擔任文學院院長時，替大學延攬了饒宗頤等中國學者出任大學教席。他並致力研究中國藝術及考古，發表大量文章包括 *The Background of Chinese Civilisation* 系列，以及論述大學重要藏品景教銅十字的專文。一九六一年大學金禧誌慶，著名德國漢學家兼人類學家艾伯華教授（一九零九至一九八九年）主持研討會，發表論文後來編印成書，由林仰山擔任編輯。[3]

一九六零年一月他獲頒英帝國民事勳銜OBE，表揚他在香港大學出任中文系教授及東方研究學院總監。[4] 一九六四年他正式退休，曾共事的大學職員、學生及友人發起募捐並設立了林仰山基金。隨後他的舊學生王梁潔華博士更捐出一筆巨款，讓大學博物館購得四十幅中國油畫，命名為林仰山基金中國油畫藏品。[5]

劉唯邁博士後來繼 Mary Tregear 掌管博物館，並出任總監至一九九七年退休為止，共服務逾三十年。其繼任人楊春棠則於任內將徐展堂樓最底三層納歸博物館使用。

---

1 Mellor, 1980, pp. 82–83.
2 Mary Tregear 出生於中國武昌，後來轉職英國牛津大學博物館 Ashmolean Museum，最後出任該館東方藝術部館長。
3 F. S. Drake, *The Background of Chinese Civilization* (in three series) (Hong Kong Institute of Oriental Studies, 1954); second series on *China and Central Asia*, 1954; third series on *Tibet in History and Travel*, 1956. 'Nestorian Crosses and Nestorian Christians in China under the Mongols', *Journal of The Hong Kong Branch of the Royal Asiatic Society*, Vol. 2, 1962, pp.11–25. *Symposium on Historical, Archeological and Linguistic Studies on Southern China, South-East Asia and the Hong Kong Region* (Hong Kong University Press, 1967).
4 Supplement of the *London Gazette*, 1st January 1961, p. 24.
5 Michael Lau, 'Foreword', *Contemporary Chinese Oil Paintings* (University Museum and Art Gallery, The University of Hong Kong, 1995).

林仰山及馬鑑於馮平山圖書館主持《漢畫石刻拓本展覽》開幕禮。
Professor Frederick Drake opening an exhibition of rubbings from private collections in the Fung Ping Shan Library. Just behind him is Ma Kiam.

Frederick Drake and the beginnings of the Museum

Frederick Seguier Drake (1892–1974) was born in Shandong province in China to a distinguished English family. He was an ordained minister, missionary, theologian and Sinologist. Drake traveled extensively across China as an archaeologist, and spent many years teaching there, culminating in the position of Dean of the Faculty of Divinity at Cheeloo (Qilu) University in Jinan, Shandong. In 1950, during the Chinese Civil War, he was expelled from the country and went briefly to England.

Drake's relationship with the University of Hong Kong began in the 1930s when his extensive experience as a teacher, and sympathy for the reform movement attracted the interest of the University just when it was attempting to modernise its teaching of Chinese. He was offered the position of Reader in Chinese, and later that of a newly-created position of Chair of Chinese established in response to external recommendations. However he was unable to take up either post at the time and the renowned scholar, diplomat and friend of the university, Hu Shih, proposed the hiring of Hsu Ti-shan, a US-educated professor at Yenching (Yanjing) University who successfully introduced teaching in vernacular Chinese.[1]

Although Drake had already reached retirement age, he was again offered the Chair of Chinese in 1952 and this time was able to accept. Among Drake's greatest achievements were the establishment of a teaching collection of Chinese art and archaeology, and in the supervising of a team from the University in the excavation of the Lei Cheng Uk Han tomb in Hong Kong in 1955.

The teaching collections formed the basis of a museum housed in the Fung Ping Shan Library building, which later became a dedicated museum with Mary Tregear as its first curator under Drake.[2] As Dean of the Faculty of Arts, Drake was also responsible for recruiting a number of Chinese scholars to the University including Jao Tsung-I. He researched and published extensively on Asian art and archaeology including his series, *The Background of Chinese Civilisation*, and an article on the University's important collection of Nestorian crosses. He also edited a volume of papers presented at a symposium chaired by the distinguished German Sinologist and anthropologist Wolfram Eberhard (1909–1989) during the University's 1961 Golden Jubilee celebrations.[3]

In January 1960, he was made an Ordinary Officer of the Civil Division of the Most Excellent Order of the British Empire (OBE) in recognition of his services as Professor of Chinese and Director of the Institute of Oriental Studies at the University.[4] He retired in 1964. At the time of his retirement, the F. S. Drake Foundation was founded with donations from colleagues, students and friends. Following a generous donation to that fund by his former student Dr Annie Wong Leung Kit-wah, the Museum acquired forty Chinese oil paintings, named the F. S. Drake Memorial Collection of Chinese Oil Paintings, in his honour.[5] Tregear was succeeded by Dr Michael Lau, who held the positions of curator, and subsequently director for over thirty years. After Dr Lau's retirement in 1997, Yeung Chun-tong assumed the position, expanding the museum into the lower three floors of the T T Tsui Building.

---

1   Mellor, 1980, pp. 82–83.
2   Tregear was born in Wuchang, China and went on to have a distinguished career at the Ashmolean Museum, Oxford, where she eventually became Keeper of Eastern Art.
3   F. S. Drake, The Background of Chinese Civilization (in three series) (Hong Kong Institute of Oriental Studies, 1954); second series on China and Central Asia, 1954; third series on Tibet in History and Travel, 1956. 'Nestorian Crosses and Nestorian Christians in China under the Mongols', *Journal of The Hong Kong Branch of the Royal Asiatic Society*, Vol. 2, 1962, pp.11–25. *Symposium on Historical, Archeological and Linguistic Studies on Southern China*, South-East Asia and the Hong Kong Region (Hong Kong University Press, 1967).
4   Supplement of the *London Gazette*, 1st January 1961, p. 24.
5   Michael Lau, 'Foreword', *Contemporary Chinese Oil Paintings* (University Museum and Art Gallery, The University of Hong Kong, 1995).

布蘭敦（一八九六至一九七四年）出生於倫敦，[1] 在牛津大學修讀古典文學及英國語文，集詩人、記者、文學編輯、傳記作者及教育工作者於一身。一九一六至一九一八年他服役於第一次世界大戰，後所寫大戰詩集最廣為人知。在當時的著名作家圈子中，布蘭敦與薩松（Siegfried Sassoon）成為摯交，同期還有格雷夫斯（Robert Graves）。戰後他留在英國工作，至一九二四年獲濟慈學者齊藤孝邀請到東京大學出任英國語文系教授，一九二七年返英，一九四七年擔任英國文化使節團顧問再度赴日。布蘭敦於兩次世界大戰中的經歷，讓他明白到衝突的禍害，他的反戰立場促使他到歐洲和亞洲四處遊歷，他相信文學能彌補政治不足之處。

一九三一至一九四二年間布蘭敦擔任牛津大學研究員兼導師，後離職成為《泰晤士報文學增刊》撰稿員。一九五零年他從日本返英，翌年獲頒英帝國勳銜CBE，以表揚他在日本工作的貢獻。一九五三年布蘭敦獲舊學生香港大學教務長梅樂彬（任期一九四八至一九七四年）邀請出任香港大學校長一職，但他只答應作為英文系講座教授，直至一九六四年回國。

一九五六年布蘭敦獲頒英女王英詩金章。他於香港大學工作期間的著作包括 *Poems by Ivor Gurney*（一九五四年出版）、*Charles Lamb*（一九五四、一九六四年出版）、*Poems of many Years*（一九五七年出版），以及 *War Poets 1914–1918*（一九五八、一九六四年出版）。他的最後重要詩集 *A Hong Kong House: Poems 1951–1962* 亦於一九六二年出版。一九六六年他接替格雷夫斯成為牛津大學英詩教授。

梅樂彬在二冊著作 *The University of Hong Kong: An Informal History* 首卷的序言中提及對布蘭敦非常感激，一九五零年代他倆開始籌劃編寫香港大學校史，最終雖未能實現，卻促成 Brian Harrison 出版著作 *The First 50 Years*。[2]

1　有關布蘭敦詳細的生平和著作，可瀏覽其家人所設立的網址 http://www.edmundblunden.org
2　Mellor, 1980, p. xiii; pp. ix–xi 及 Harrison, pp. ix–xi.

本肖像畫的作者為香港畫家杜格拉斯・白連（一九二三至一九七五年），他出生於愛爾蘭，肄業於牛津魯斯金繪畫學院。一九四二年加入英國皇家海軍，駐守地中海及印度洋。一九四六年離職，轉往中國海關擔任水道測量員。一九四八年加入香港九龍碼頭貨倉有限公司，擢升至商業經理，可惜英年早逝。他早期的畫作多為具象水彩畫，至一九五零年代末起實驗油彩創作。一九五九年可算是其藝術生涯之里程碑，風格開始深受中國篆刻、甲骨文、書法影響，一直持續至離世為止。他作畫雖勤，卻對自己要求甚高，曾將不少認為稍遜的作品毀棄。

This portrait was painted by the Hong Kong based artist Douglas Bland (1923–1975). Born in Ireland, Douglas Bland studied at the Ruskin School of Drawing at Oxford. In 1942 he joined the Royal Navy stationed in the Mediterranean and Indian Ocean. He left the service in 1946 to join the Chinese Maritime Customs Service as a hydrographer. In 1948 he joined the Hong Kong and Kowloon Wharf and Godown Co. Ltd, where he was commercial manager at the time of his early death. His early paintings were figurative watercolours but he had been experimenting with oils in the late 1950s. In 1959, his work reached a turning point and from then until his death, they were intense works inspired heavily by Chinese seals, oracle bones, and calligraphic forms. A prolific artist, he was nevertheless known for being an uncompromising critic, destroying many works with which he was unhappy.

梅勒著'前言'，載於《白連的世界》，香港藝術館，一九七五年
Bernard Mellor, 'Introduction', *The World of Douglas Bland* (Hong Kong Museum of Art, 1975).

杜格拉斯・白連《布蘭敦畫像》
油彩布本
一九五七年
Portrait of Edmund Blunden
Douglas Bland
Oil on canvas
1957
H: 88 cm W: 100 cm

'UNDERGRAD' Page 5

man...poet...critic...oxford professor of poetry
EDMUND BLUNDEN

The election to the post of Professor of Poetry at the University of Oxford is one of the highest honours accorded to a man of letters in the English-speaking world. The Professor is elected by senior members of the Oxford University and holds office for five years, during which his duty is to give eight lectures annually. These are the famous Oxford Lectures. Mr. Robert Graves is the previous Professor. Mr. Blunden was proposed by Enid Starkie, authority on French poetry, and on February 5 was hailed to the seat of honour, defeating the American poet, Robert Lowell, in a straight contest.

The news occasioned no surprise to those who knew him, either personally or through his works. It is 52 years from now since he first published two volumes of poetry at his own expense when he was 18. All this long period of time, with only occasional interruptions, he devoted faithfully to carrying on and bringing alive the tradition of English literature to the world. At school he won prizes for Greek and Latin verse. He gained the senior classics scholarship at the Queen's College. The effect of the First World War on his sensitivity he recorded in his war poems and in *Undertones of War*, his most famous prose work. He served as assistant editor to the *Anthenaeum*, the *Nation* and the *Times Literary Supplement*. The Hawthorden Prize was awarded to him in 1922 for his collection of poems "*The Shepherd*".

Japan

In 1924 he was invited to take up the Professorship of English Poetry at Tokyo University and thus began his immense impact on Japan as scholar, poet and man. Later in 1947 he returned there as Cultural Liasion Officer to the British Mission. During these years he lectured at many Japanese universities and won great veneration. "He is Japan's best friend: he brings out the best in us," said the Japanese novelist Tomoji Abe. In 1950 Japan paid him the great tribute of electing him a member of the Japanese Academy. Fourteen years later the Japanese Government conferred on him the highest honour, the Medal of the Rising Sun, in acknowledgment to his contribution to fostering understanding between the two nations.

As a scholar and critic, Prof. Blunden illuminated the vista of English literature with his sincerity and wide sympathy. He is one of the leading authorities on the Romantic poets and writers. Together with Mr. Alan Porter, he rediscovered John Clare. He brought to life again some less well known literary figures, John Taylor, Kirke White, to name only two.

A Hong Kong House

In 1953 he took up the Chair of English at the University of Hong Kong, a post he held until 1964. He celebrated the University in describing her beautiful setting. He put it into verse. In Hong Kong he also took up his long cherished sport, cricket, and played for the University. The Masquers, that once active dramatic group of the English Department, flourished under his encouragement. The English Society of Hong Kong University came into being in April, 1960 under his patronage. He is now permanent patron to that society. It was in Hong Kong too that he celebrated his sixtieth birthday and in the same year received the Queen's Gold Medal for Poetry. In 1964, "with sad but loving adieus" he left Hong Kong for his English home "Mill House" in Sudbury, Suffolk to continue his energetic poetic career.

As Others See Him

Seen from the eyes of fellow staff members in this University, Prof. Blunden is revealed to us in a very interesting and varied light.

"Kind" is the word Mrs. Helen Kwok (one of his past students) used to describe Prof. Blunden. She said that he was "a very kind tutor and a very interesting lecturer." He would always find something good in his students' essays to praise and encourage. When there were faults, he would 'suggest that you think it over again,' but he never scolded. His most interesting lectures, said Mrs. Kwok, "were those on Keats, Milton and Shakespeare's King Lear."

As Teacher

Mrs. Mary Visick, who was also his previous student, said that he could not be called a poor 'lecturer'. The word 'teacher' would fit him more since even he himself felt that he was someone "who passes on a collection of knowledge", and not someone who "lectures". Besides, added Mrs. Visick, he could never lecture well to a large crowd. He was at his best when facing a small tutorial group where there were responses to his statements.

It was also in a lecture that Miss Margaret Yu first came across Prof. Blunden personally. It was in 1949 when he passed through Hong Kong to give a lecture. He impressed Miss Yu at that time with his "genuineness as a literary man". Later contacts with him when he came again to Hong Kong confirmed that impression. She said that he was a "poetic man" in that he had a "personal, emotional approach to life, and that he had a "deep erudition". He loved books and was always fingering them. Miss Yu said that she had once witnessed him writing a short poem as rapidly and as spontaneously as we would write a short business letter.

As Writer

However, Miss Yu said that she preferred his prose style. This opinion seems to be shared by many of the other staff members. Mr. W. I. McLachlan finds his poetry a bit "out of touch" with modern times, that he still seems to be living in the World War I period. He considers him more interesting as a prose writer than as a poet, but says even his prose is of an indecisive style. Prof. A.W.T. Green said that his vocabulary is World War I vocabulary and it hasn't changed much since then. Mrs. Visick considers him a "traditionalist" in the sense that he takes up and enlarges poetic forms and interests which had been previously developed. She prefers his prose style and especially likes his "Undertones of War". But she adds that his poetry will always be read because they "have a certain delicate flavour that appeals to readers." Prof. Green and Miss Yu also find his poetry impressive to listen to.

As Critic

As a critic, Prof. Blunden emphasized literary history. Mrs. Visick said that "his main strength as a critic is that he could reconstruct with his marvellous historical imagination the period of the author." Prof. Green finds him "penetrating and well informed." Mr. McLachlan commends him on his biographical criticism, but adds that he is not really in touch with the modern development in analytical criticism.

As Man

Personally, all the staff members interviewed find him charming and easy to get along with. Prof. Green said that he was a good talker and listener, had an interest in people and was "a good cricket player." Miss Yu described him as "intensely human and abstract at the same time". "Abstract" in the sense that there is a touch of elusiveness somewhere. Mr. McLachlan also has the same opinion: He is a charming man, a good host, but sometimes one had the feeling that he was not involved in the conversation, so it was hard to really get down to know him. He was a gentle, easy going man who never told anyone to do anything. This, perhaps, was overdone. As Miss Yu put it, "He never allowed himself to say, 'No! I don't think so.' This may be due to his sensitive nature which dislikes the possibility of hurting anyone."

This same quality can be found in his attitude to his children and students. He is a proud and affectionate father, kind and gentle tutor, always ready to help. And, as Mrs. Visick informed us, this resulted in his often bringing his students home for their tutorials and their going away with at least some of his books.

Views on HKU

Writing for the 1st Conference on Commonwealth Literature held in September, 1965, at the University of Leeds, Professor Blunden considered the cultural role of the university, drawing from his experience in Hong Kong University.

"When I was called on to give lectures in the town, tho' I often found the room well filled and the audience encouraging, I could not but admit to myself at last that certain classes of Hong Kong society never came."

There were difficulties too trying to win support for notions which would increase the pleasures and benefits of culture here, especially in the younger generation. Various projects were tried, "But want of time or faith, or conception of a university's privilege and mission in a busy modern world, narrowed the prospects. I could use harsher expressions but will add no others except indolence and dullness of soul."

On the Students

Prof. Blunden carried away tender thoughts of the students here. "Culture comes most gently to them when it does not seem impersonal. The word or two of simple respect and tutorial watchfulness may inspire remarkably... In Eastern universities and colleges, wherever I have had opportunities to look and think, a student is more apt to view his or her perceptor as guide, philosopher, and friend then students whom I have known in England. Eastern students have a particular insight into the private minds of their tutors, and speedily discern, or decide upon, the true attitude of these incomers towards them and the East. They may be young but are not easily deceived."

This is Prof. Blunden's idea of the HKU students. And the students' idea? Here is Miss Irene C. Djao, his former pupil, speaking of him, "Professor Blunden is a favourite among his students and all readily take him for their friend outside lecture hours. He greets you with a smile, stops to ask how you feel, and shows interest in what you say or how you are getting along."

Finale

Perhaps no tribute of ours can surpass that of Prof. Earl Miner, American poet, which runs: "I cannot think of another who excites in me the desire to give public tribute. It is not that he (Prof. Blunden) has so successfully harmonized four careers: poetry, teaching, scholarship, and review criticism. But it is the fact that all four careers are based upon a rare, essential goodness that leads me to praise."

Allow us to wish, then, Prof. Blunden, that across the miles you will meet with every success that deservedly belongs to you.

A Portrait of Prof. Blunden, painted by Mr. Lo King Man, his former pupil, now working in the Registry, HKU.

一九六六年三月一日《學苑》刊登布蘭敦專版
A full page tribute to Edmund Blunden in *Undergrad*, 1st March 1966

傳為盧景文所繪的布蘭敦畫像。盧景文曾素描布蘭敦的辦公室，後登載於香港大學出版社2001年出版布蘭敦詩集 *A Hong Kong House: Poems 1951-1961*。
The portrait was erroneously attributed to Mr Lo King-man, who did however make a drawing of Blunden's office reproduced in the 2001 edition of Blunden's *A Hong Kong House: Poems 1951-1961*, published by Hong Kong University Press.

Edmund Charles Blunden[1] (1896–1974) was born in London in 1896. He studied Classics and English at the University of Oxford and was a renowned poet, journalist, literary editor, biographer and educator, known in particular for his poetry about the First World War in which he served between 1916 and 1918. Blunden was part of a group of leading writers of his time including Robert Graves and Siegfried Sassoon with whom he developed a lifelong friendship.

After the war Blunden worked in England until 1924 when he was invited by the scholar of Keats, Takeshi Saito to take up the post of Professor of English at the University of Tokyo. He returned to England in 1927, but in 1947 was appointed Cultural Advisor with the UK Liaison Mission to Japan. Blunden's experiences of both wars convinced him of the futility of armed conflict. His anti-war stance also accounted in part for his travels to Europe and Asia as he believed that literature could heal where politics failed.

Between 1931 and 1942, Blunden held the positions of Fellow and Tutor at the University of Oxford. He left Oxford to become a writer at *The Times Literary Supplement*. After returning from Japan in 1950, Blunden was awarded a CBE the following year for his work there. In 1953, at the urging of Bernard Mellor, a former student of Blunden's at Oxford, he took up the position of Professor of English, which he held from 1953 to 1964, when he retired to England.

In 1956 Blunden was awarded the Queen's Gold Medal for Poetry. While at the University of Hong Kong his publications included *Poems by Ivor Gurney* (1954), *Charles Lamb* (1954/ 1964), *Poems of Many Years* (1957), and *War Poets 1914 –1918* (1958/ 1964)). His last major poetry collection *A Hong Kong House: Poems 1951–1962* was published in 1962. In 1966, he was elected Professor of Poetry at Oxford, succeeding Robert Graves but retired two years later due to ill health.

Bernard Mellor, in his acknowledgements to the first of the two-volume *The University of Hong Kong: An Informal History*, acknowledged the debt that he owed to Blunden with whom he had begun planning a history of the University in the 1950s. These efforts were superseded by the publication of *The First 50 Years*, edited by Brian Harrison.[2]

---

1 Further details of Edmund Blunden's life and work are available on a website set up by his family at http://www.edmundblunden.org
2 Mellor, 1980, p. xiii; See also Harrison, pp. ix–xi.

香港大學美術學會金禧美術展覽海報
Poster of The HKU Art Club Golden Jubilee Exhibition at Loke Yew Hall
11th to 14th October 1961

金禧誌慶
CELEBRATING THE FIRST 50 YEARS

香港大學金禧誌慶
The Jubilee Celebrations

一九六一年一月九日,香港大學舉行第五十四屆學位頒授典禮,為金禧紀念慶典揭開序幕。一連串的活動除了慶祝創校六十周年外,同時慶祝校園的擴建,包括學生會及圖書館大樓的落成。金禧慶典以校長賴廉士爵士主持的第五十七屆學位頒授典禮為壓軸項目,並特別邀請到獲頒名譽法學博士的雅麗珊郡主出席。

為期一年的慶祝活動包括一九六一年九月一日至十六日舉行的六場研討會,分別為 David Barker 教授籌劃的‘肌肉受體’研討會、H. R. Arthur 先生籌劃的‘植物化學’研討會、Sean Mackey 教授籌劃的‘高樓的設計’研討會、S. G. Davis 教授籌劃的‘香港與南中國的土地運用和礦床’研討會、E. F. Szczepanik 博士籌劃的‘東亞的經濟社會問題’研討會、林仰山教授籌劃的‘中國南部、東南亞及香港地區的歷史、考古及語言學研究’研討會。大學之友及舊生均收到慶典活動的回條,以回覆所欲參加的項目(參看第220頁)。

The University's Golden Jubilee Year began with the 54th Congregation on 9th January 1961. The celebrations were the culmination of an unprecedented period of physical development and expansion for the University, which could boast new Student Union and Library buildings. It ended with a special 57th Congregation presided over by Vice-Chancellor Sir Lindsay Ride at which an Honorary Doctor of Laws was conferred on Queen Elizabeth's representative, Her Royal Highness Princess Alexandra Helen Elizabeth Olga Christabel of Kent.

The year-long celebrations included six symposia held from 1st to 16th September 1961. These were on 'Muscle receptors', organised by Professor David Barker; 'Phytochemistry', organised by Mr H. R. Arthur; 'The design of high buildings', organised by Professor Sean Mackey; 'Land use and mineral deposits in Hong Kong and South China', organised by Professor S. G. Davis; 'Economic and social problems of the Far East', organised by Dr E. F. Szczepanik, and 'Historical, archaeological and linguistic studies on Southern China, South-east Asia, and the Hong Kong region', organised by Professor F. S. Drake. Friends and alumni were sent details of the celebration activities with a reply slip on which they could indicate the functions that they wished to attend (see page 220).

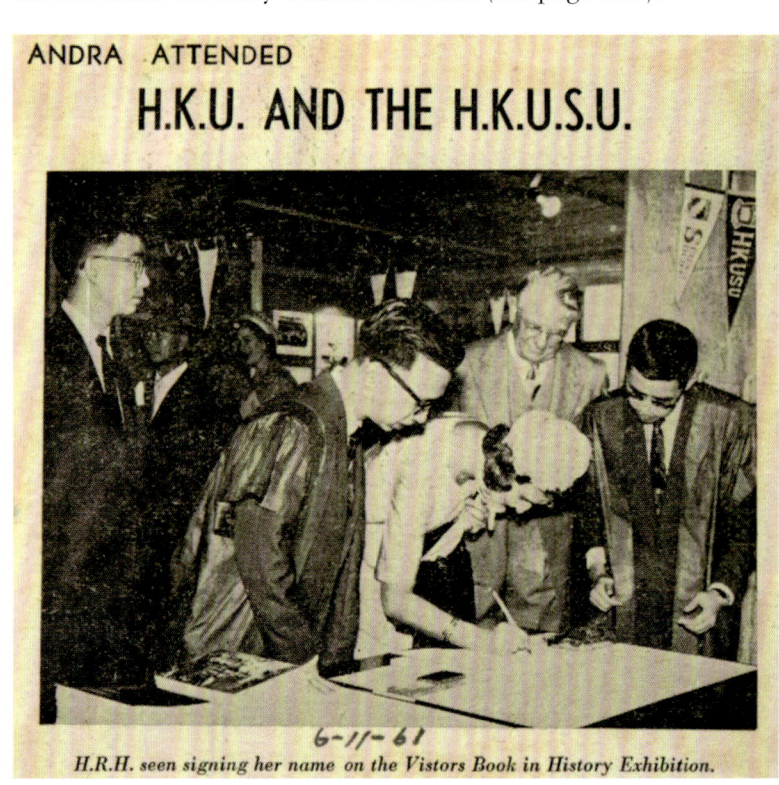

雅麗珊郡主參觀香港大學歷史展覽
文學院相簿
Her Royal Highness, Princess Alexandra Helen Elizabeth Olga Christabel of Kent visiting an exhibition on the history of the University
Arts Faculty Album

香港大學金禧
University
Golden Jubilee 1911-1961

一九六一年香港大學金禧誌慶，十一月雅麗珊郡主來港
主禮，由香港大學校長賴廉士爵士陪同
文學院相簿
Her Royal Highness, Princess Alexandra Helen Elizabeth
Olga Christabel of Kent visiting the University in
November 1961 with Vice-Chancellor Sir Lindsay Ride
Arts Faculty Album

一九六一年十一月六日第五十七屆學位頒授典禮上，香港大學校監柏立基爵士頒發名譽法學博士學位予雅麗珊郡主

Chancellor Sir Robert Brown Black conferring the Doctor of Laws on her Royal Highness, Princess Alexandra of Kent at the 57th Congregation
6th November 1961

UNIVERSITY OF HONG KONG

THE CHANCELLOR'S ADDRESS

Fifteen years ago, this Hall like many other buildings in Hong Kong, lay in ruins. It seems almost inconceivable to us now that, at that particular time, there were doubts about whether our University should be re-established at all.

It was in 1948 that the decision was taken to restore this University to life, and by 1950 its student population had come to number five hundred. Today, there are at least three times as many as that number, and we are in the middle of a seven-year expansion programme designed to bring the number of students to about two thousand in the year 1965. Progress at this speed is something, of course, with which Hong Kong is familiar. In so many ways, we have travelled a great distance since Captain Elliot raised the flag on an island inhabited by a handful of farmers and fishermen, since the days when 'Go to Hong Kong' was a euphemism for consignment to everlasting torment.

While, this year, we in the University have been celebrating our Golden Jubilee with pride, it must not be thought that we have spent the time looking over our shoulder with nostalgic longing to 'days that are dead'. On the contrary, we have been looking ahead to the future.

This seven-year plan on which we have embarked means doubling the number of students and this, in turn, calls for the provision of more accommodation and equipment. We are considering new halls of residence. We have had to build a new library to house our collection of a quarter of a million books, and, at the same time, to see that there is room for more. We are planning a new pre-clinical building for the Medical Faculty. We have extended the engineering laboratories with the resumption of full courses in electrical and mechanical as well as in civil engineering in mind.

Later this morning we hope that Your Royal Highness will formally open our new Students' Union. We are not sitting with folded hands, brooding dreamily on the past. We are on our feet and moving with purpose towards the future.

While, in this year of celebration, we are naturally sorry that Her Majesty the Queen, our Patron, has not been able to honour this Jubilee with Her presence, we are greatly privileged and delighted to welcome Your Royal Highness. As the Public Orator has declaimed, Your Royal Highness's visit marks the climax of our Jubilee celebrations.

Since this Congregation is Your Royal Highness's first public engagement during your visit to Hong Kong, there falls upon the University the pleasant duty of greeting Your Royal Highness, and we are especially proud and pleased that we are able to express this welcome to you at a stage when you have become an Honorary Graduate of our University.

The Hong Kong University Press has made its contribution to the Jubilee in the publication of a reprint of James Legge's Translation of the Chinese Classics, the first volume of which was originally published in Hong Kong one hundred years ago. While the work of later scholars has, to some extent, superseded that of Legge, it remains true to say that it was largely through this monumental treatise, undertaken incidentally in his spare time, that the Chinese Classics were made known to the West in the nineteenth century. Legge's achievement is a bridge between East and West; it is furthermore a bridge between Hong Kong and the United Kingdom, and it remains our duty here to maintain and strengthen this link, as our founder, Lord Lugard, intended.

It has, therefore, seemed most fitting to us that we should request Your Royal Highness to accept, on behalf of Her Majesty The Queen, these volumes, as a token of our dutiful allegiance to Her Majesty.

We should like to make a further request to you and that is to accept an ivory powder box as a small token of our respect and regard for Your Royal Highness, and to say that we all hope that you will enjoy your visit to Hong Kong, which is such a memorable occasion for all of us here in this Colony.

一九六一年十一月六日賴廉士爵士於第五十七屆學位頒授典禮之演辭
Sir Lindsay Ride's address at the 57th congregation, 6th November 1961

UNIVERSITY OF HONG KONG

HER ROYAL HIGHNESS PRINCESS ALEXANDRA'S ADDRESS

First of all, it is with very real pleasure that I thank you, Mr. Chancellor, for the welcome which you have just given to me on behalf of this great University. My visit, coming as it does in the year during which the University is celebrating its fiftieth anniversary, is one to which I have eagerly looked forward; it is, indeed, a happy chance that has brought me here, for Hong Kong is a place which I have always longed to see.

Of course I had heard much about Hong Kong; about its beauty, about its bustling activity, and above all about its wonderfully friendly people, from my mother - and also from my brother - who, some of you may remember, spent some very happy days here nine years ago. My friends, too, who have learned to know and to love Hong Kong have taught me some of that affection and told me something of what I should expect. Let me say at once that my hopes have been exceeded during the two most enjoyable days which I have already spent here. And may I add that I am looking forward to the remainder of my stay and to all the chances I am to be given of meeting, and talking to, representatives of this thriving community, and also of seeing for myself a few of the many remarkable achievements which have been accomplished here since the war.

The honour which the University has done me by conferring upon me its Honorary Degree of Doctor of Laws is one which I shall remember with pride throughout my life. It is indeed a privilege to be associated in this way with a university which has made for itself, in a comparatively short period of time, a fine and well deserved reputation.

It is thanks to Lord Lugard's vision that we are able to celebrate this Jubilee. It would seem that in Lugard, that wise and experienced administrator, there was also something of the artist and it was surely that quality in him which flourished while he was here as Governor of Hong Kong and impelled him to envisage the scheme from which this University sprang and to strive for it with all his heart and soul in the face of the most vigorous and critical opposition both here and at home. And when the time came at last, that the battle was won and the foundation stone laid, that moment - in the words of his biographer - 'was, perhaps, Lugard's most important moment in Hong Kong'.

Since those days, the University has grown in size and stature. And the ambitious plans to which you, Mr. Chancellor, have referred, show that you intend to continue with this policy of development and to provide Hong Kong with a University that recognizes the needs of the community which it exists to serve.

Hong Kong is unique. There is nowhere quite like it. We at home have heard a lot about you in recent years and we cannot but admire the energy with which you have tackled the problems that have beset you since the liberation in 1945. Hong Kong had set an example to the world in the way in which people of all races have worked hard here and have worked in harmony together.

It will be a very great pleasure for me, Mr. Chancellor, to convey to the Queen the gift which the University has presented to Her Majesty. You may be sure, too, that your gift to me will be a lasting reminder of this memorable day; and for your kindness I cannot be sufficiently grateful.

Finally, may I offer my congratulations to you all and indeed to all those who have served the University in the past? You must indeed feel a sense of pride and achievement; may long years of creative work and fruitful development lie ahead. Whatever befalls, I feel sure that your graduates, as they leave these calm and pleasant surroundings for the turmoil of the world outside, will be worthy of their responsibilities; and that they will look back to the days they spent here with affection and gratitude.

一九六一年十一月六日雅麗珊郡主於第五十七屆學位頒授典禮之演辭
Her Royal Highness, Princess Alexandra Helen Elizabeth Olga Christabel of Kent's address at the 57th Congregation, 6th November 1961

University
Golden Jubilee 1911-1961

香港大學金禧

Mr. Chancellor,

    I have received with great pleasure your address on the occasion of the Golden Jubilee of the University of Hong Kong and I am glad to have this opportunity of congratulating the University on the attainment of its fiftieth anniversary.

    Your celebrations have been attended by many representatives of universities throughout the Commonwealth, thus further strengthening the links that bind us together.

    It is a matter of regret for me that I have not yet been able to visit Hong Kong. I have, however, heard much about the charm of the place and the achievements of its people. I am very glad that it has been possible for Princess Alexandra to visit you and to take part in the celebrations of your Jubilee and I look forward to hearing her account of it all on her return.

    I have learned with great sympathy and admiration of the way in which Hong Kong has tackled the many problems with which it has been faced in recent years. The resolution and resilience of its people have not only enabled them to withstand the difficulties with which they have been beset; they have earned for themselves a remarkable and sustained degree of prosperity. It is my earnest hope that this prosperity will increase and that the energy of the people will continue to be used to promote welfare and social security in Hong Kong. In such a task as this a well established University has a great part to play, and I am confident that in the years to come the University of Hong Kong will not only consolidate its own development, but will also extend and enrich its contribution to the life of the whole community.

Elizabeth R

25th October, 1961.

一九六一年十月二十五日英女皇伊利莎伯二世致函香港大學校長祝賀金禧慶典
Letter from Queen Elizabeth II to the Chancellor of the University on the occasion of the Golden Jubilee
25th October 1961

HKU Memories | from the Archives

香港大學金禧賀辭
Congratulatory messages for the Golden Jubilee

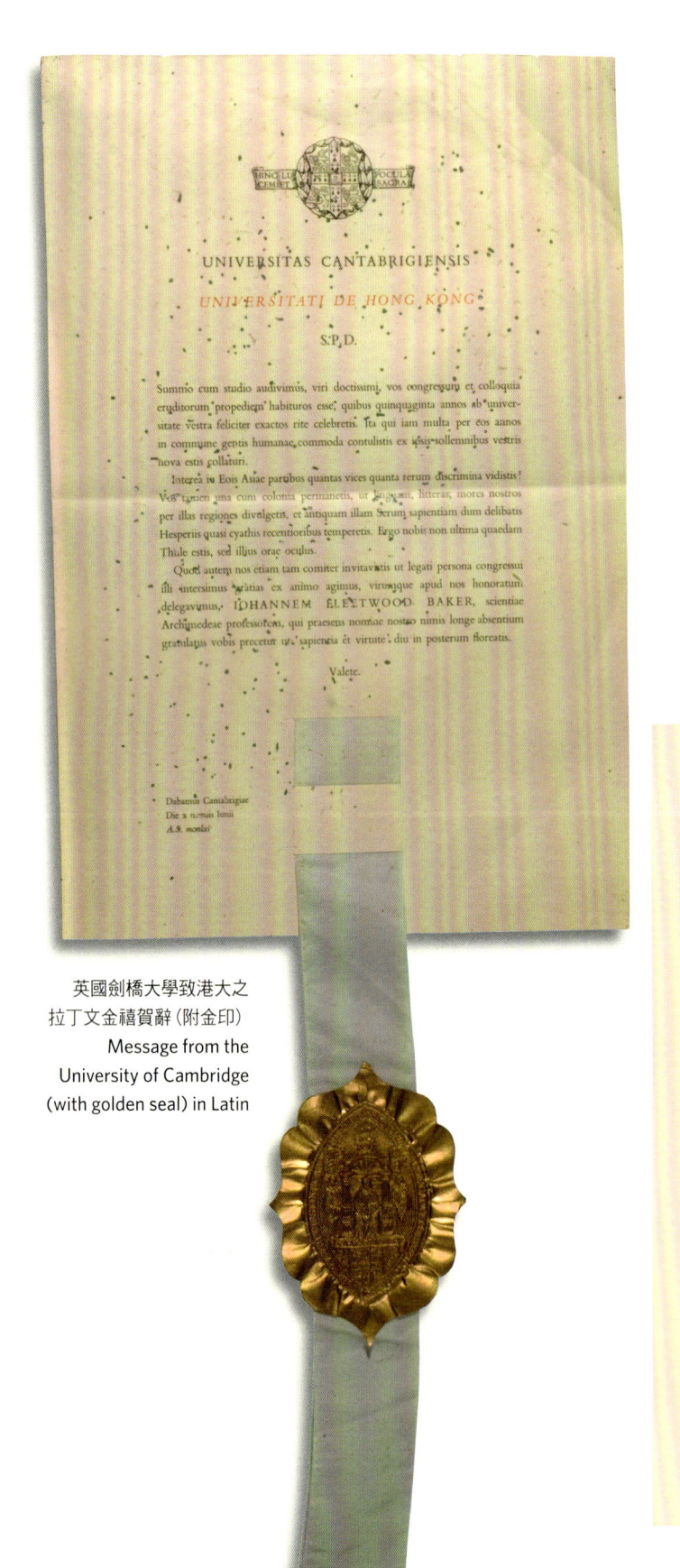

英國劍橋大學致港大之
拉丁文金禧賀辭（附金印）
Message from the
University of Cambridge
(with golden seal) in Latin

保存檔案文件的三大忌為疏忽、展露、侵蝕。疏忽包括儲存環境惡劣或不當，以至意外損毀。展露包括處於自然或人造燈光、溫度及濕度的變化，以及過量觸摸。侵蝕則指蟲、鼠、鳥類的侵害。以上問題皆能迅速摧毀文件。本信函顯示出蟲蛀的嚴重後果，導致表面穿孔，紙質韌度減弱。

There are three enemies in the preservation of archival documents. These are neglect, exposure and attack. Neglect can include everything from poor or inadequate storage to accidental destruction. Exposure includes exposure to natural and artificial light, fluctuations in temperature and humidity, and too much handling. Attack can come from insects, rodents and birds, all of which can destroy documents quickly. This congratulatory letter shows the dramatic consequences of attack by insects that has resulted in holes across much of the surface and has weakened its structural integrity.

VNIVERSITATI APVD HONG KONG FVNDATAE CANCELLARIVS MAGISTRI SCHOLARES VNIVERSITATIS OXONIENSIS S.D.P.

CELEBRANTIBVS vobis, viri doctissimi, annum disciplinae vestrae quinquagesimum ex animo gratulamur; quod nos participes esse gaudii vestri voluistis, maximas gratias agimus; ut colloquiis ludisque vestris intersit hasque litteras perferat, virum egregium Ewart Jones, Chemiae Professorem, Collegii Beatae Mariae Magdalenae Socium, Societati Regali adscriptum, libentissime mittimus. cognovimus vos inter tantas insularum amoenitates versatos, quamquam finitimis parum benignis interdum impeditos, summa constantia liberales artes scientiasque exercuisse, nec minime iis, qui honestum coloniae nomen ut inique ita stupide in peius deflectunt, quantopere prosit ut Occidens et Oriens mutuo fruantur auxilio, clare indicavistis. ipsam originem vestram debetis partim studio viri Australiani, partim munificentiae Indi, partim auctoritati legatorum Britannorum, partim Sinensium voluntati. nec praetermittendos censeo alios duos, Patricium Manson, Equitem Auratum, qui Collegium Medicinae apud vos feliciter condidit, torridae zonae morbos sollerter investigavit, summo denique iure Societatis Regalis Socius factus est, et Sun Yat-sen, inter primos alumnos vestros insignem, patriae suae ministrum amantissimum. quod superest, omnibus votis optamus ut vobis aurea haec sollemnia prosecutis saecula aurea succedant, utque nobiscum ceterisque academicis artius in dies coniuncti doctrinae, veritati, paci sicut antea inserviatis. valete.

Datum Oxonii Kal. Sept. A.S. MCMLXI.

英國牛津大學致港大之拉丁文金禧賀辭（附紅印）
Message from the University of Oxford (with red seal) in Latin

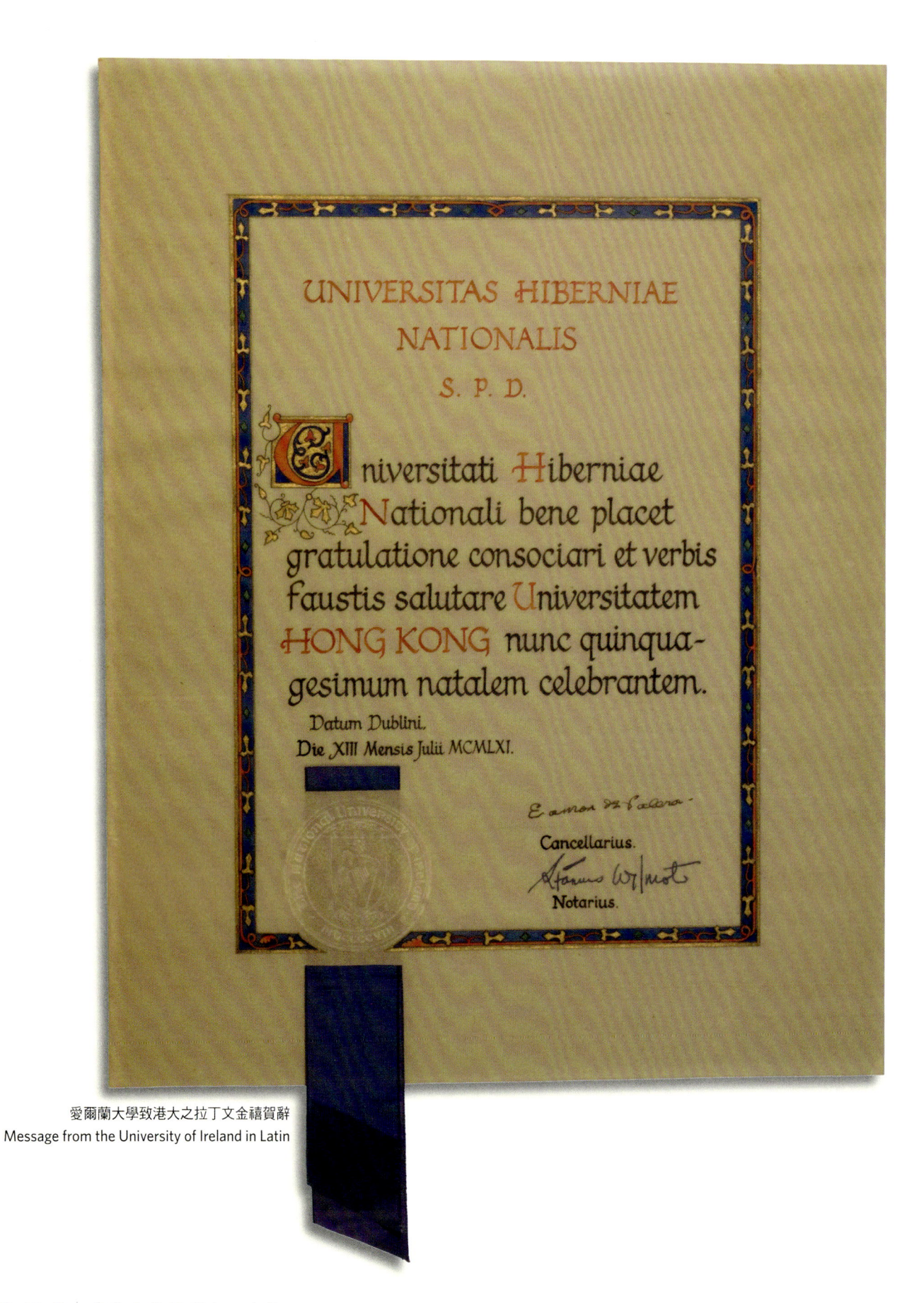

愛爾蘭大學致港大之拉丁文金禧賀辭
Message from the University of Ireland in Latin

香港大學金禧
University
Golden Jubilee 1911-1961

FROM THE BRITISH COUNCIL TO THE UNIVERSITY OF HONG KONG

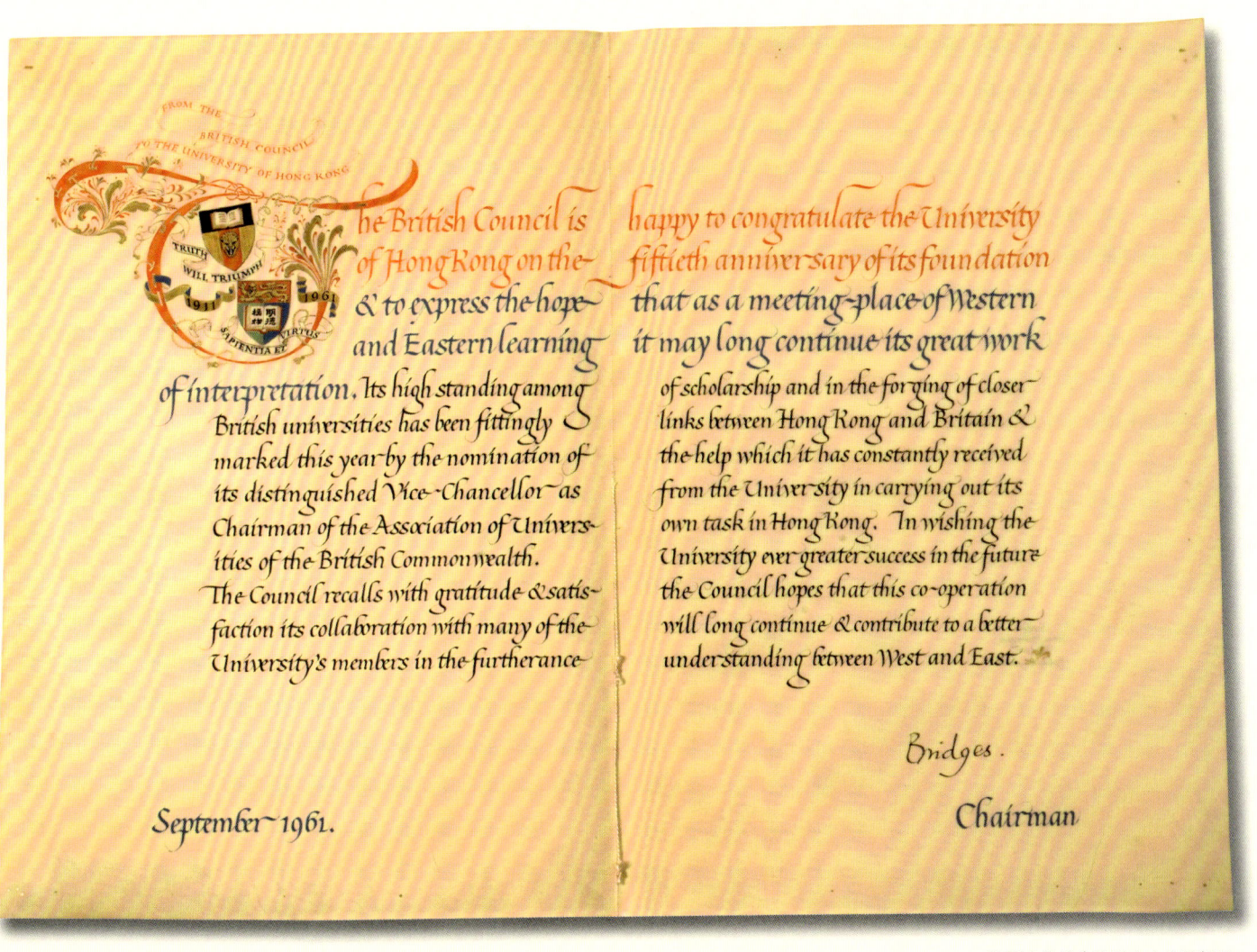

The British Council is happy to congratulate the University of Hong Kong on the fiftieth anniversary of its foundation & to express the hope that as a meeting-place of Western and Eastern learning it may long continue its great work of interpretation. Its high standing among of scholarship and in the forging of closer British universities has been fittingly links between Hong Kong and Britain & marked this year by the nomination of the help which it has constantly received its distinguished Vice-Chancellor as from the University in carrying out its Chairman of the Association of Univer- own task in Hong Kong. In wishing the sities of the British Commonwealth. University ever greater success in the future The Council recalls with gratitude & satis- the Council hopes that this co-operation faction its collaboration with many of the will long continue & contribute to a better University's members in the furtherance understanding between West and East.

September 1961.

Bridges.
Chairman

英國文化協會致港大之金禧賀辭
Message from the British Council

HKU Memories | from the Archives 215

香港大學金禧誌慶學位
Jubilee Honours

Fifty-fourth Congregation, 9th January 1961

Doctor of Laws

Edward Bridges, The Lord Bridges, PC, GCB, GCVO, MC, MA, HON D.CL, HON LL.D, HON D.LITT, FRS
Chairman of the British Council and Chancellor of Reading University

Sir Douglas William Logan, MA, D.PHIL, HON D.CL. HON LL.D
Principal of the University of London, Co-author of the Jennings-Logan Report of 1953

Sir Arcot Lakshmanaswami Mudaliar, BA, MD, LL.D, D.SC, HON.DCL, FRCOG, FACS
Vice-Chancellor of the University of Madras

The Honourable Douglas James Smyth Crozier, CMG, BA
Director of Education, Hong Kong

Dr Yung Chi-tung (容啟東), B.SC, PH.D
President of Chung Chi College

Doctor of Letters

Professor Herbert Butterfield, MA, HON.D.LIT, HON. LL.D, HON.D.LITT, HON.LITT.D
Professor of Modern History, Master of Peterhouse, and Vice-Chancellor of the University of Cambridge

Doctor of Science

Professor Hou Pao-chang (侯寶璋), MD
Emeritus Professor of Pathology

Dr Alexander Oppenheim, Knight, OBE, MA, DSC, PH.D, FRSE
Vice-Chancellor of the University of Malaya

Fifty-fifth Congregation, 16th March 1961, Foundation Day

Doctor of Laws

The Hon. Sir Sik-nin Chau (周錫年), CBE, MB, BS, DOMS, DLO, JP
Unofficial Member of the Legislative and Executive Councils of the Hong Kong Government

The Hon. Sir Tsun-nin Chau (周埈年), CBE, MA, JP
Unofficial Member of the Legislative and Executive Councils of the Hong Kong Government

Dr Li Shu-fan (李樹芬), MB, CH.B, FRCS, JP
Chairman of the Board of Directors and Superintendent of the Hong Kong Sanatorium and Hospital

Dr Mustapha Bin Osman, CBE, MD
Pathologist, Chief Medical Officer, Kedah, Federal Legislative Council, Malaya

Mr Tang Shiu-kin (鄧肇堅), CBE, JP
Son of Tang Chi Ngong, Founder of Kowloon Motor Bus Company, University Court Member and Philanthropist

Mr Tay Gan-tin (鄭彥珍), MBE, B.SC (ENG), AMI.MECH.E, JP
Mechanical Engineer, President of the University's Pan Malayan Alumni Association

Dr Doraisamy Kumara Samy, MD
Professor Obstetrics and Gynaecology, University Council Member

Dr George Harold Thomas, OBE, MD, FRCS
Surgeon, Tung Wah Hospital, University teacher

Fifty-sixth Congregation, 18th September 1961

Doctor of Laws

Sir Christopher William Machell Cox
Chair of the Cox report of 1946

Mr Leo D'Almada E Castro, CBE

Sir Ivor Jennings
Co-author of the Jennings-Logan Report of 1953

Mr Lawrence Kadoorie, CHEV. LÉG. HON, JP
Chairman China Light and Power Company, Philanthropist, Founder, New Territories Benevolent Society, Kadoories Agricultural Aid Association

Doctor of Letters

Professor Ch'en Ta-tsi (陳大齊), BA
Professor, Research Institute of National Political University of Taiwan, President of the Confucius and Mencius Society

Doctor of Science

Professor Ragnar Arthur Granit, MAG.PHIL, MD, HON. MD, HOND.SC, FOR.MEM.RS
Neurophysiologist

Dr Robert Lim Kho-seng (林可勝), MB, CH.B, PH.D, D.SC
Director, Medical Sciences Research Laboratory of Miles Laboratories, Eikhart, Indiana

Fifty-seventh Congregation, 6th November 1961

Doctor of Laws

Her Royal Highness, Princess Alexandra Helen Elizabeth Olga Christabel of Kent

Note: Harrison, 'Jubilee Honours', in Harrison, pp. 171–212.

在金禧慶祝晚宴上，港督兼香港大學校監柏立基爵士代表英女皇發表賀辭。接著是校長賴廉士爵士代表大學捐助人及畢業生致詞，其後由名譽博士李樹芬醫生（參看第14頁）與 Mustapha bin Osman 醫生作回應。

Mustapha bin Osman 醫生於一九一七年入讀香港大學，是早期來自馬來亞的非華人醫科畢業生。畢業後，他獲洛克菲勒獎學金赴愛丁堡、倫敦及巴爾的摩約翰‧霍普金斯大學留學一年。一九二五年他回到香港大學病理學系任教。一九三零年成為首位出任吉打州政府病理學家的馬來人。一九四九年成為首席醫療官，並於一九五五年退休時獲頒大英帝國司令勳章CBE。

At the Golden Jubilee Commemoration Dinner, a toast to Her Majesty the Queen was delivered by the Chancellor Governor Sir Robert Brown Black. This was followed by the Vice-Chancellor of the University, Sir Lindsay Ride with a toast to the University's benefactors and graduates. Dr Li Shu-fan (see page 14) and Dr Mustapha bin Osman, both medical doctors and recent honorary graduands, delivered the replies.

Dr Mustapha bin Osman entered the University in 1917, and became one of the earliest non-Chinese medical graduates from Malaya. On graduation he was awarded a Rockefeller scholarship to study in Edinburgh and London as well as at Johns Hopkins in Baltimore for a year. He returned to the University as a teacher in the Pathology Department in 1925, and after receiving his MD in 1930 became the Government Pathologist in Kedah State, the first Malay to do so. He became Chief Medical Officer in 1949, and was made a Commander of the Most Excellent Order of the British Empire (CBE) in 1955 when he retired.

香港大學金禧晚宴菜單
Golden Jubilee Commemoration Dinner menu

香港大學金禧議會節目單
The University of Hong Kong
Golden Jubilee Congress programme booklet

UNIVERSITY OF HONG KONG

1911-1961 GOLDEN JUBILEE CONGRESS

HISTORICAL, ARCHÆOLOGICAL AND LINGUISTIC STUDIES ON SOUTHERN CHINA, SOUTH-EAST ASIA AND THE HONG KONG REGION

Organizer

Professor F. S. Drake (University of Hong Kong)

THE AIM of this symposium is to draw together in a connected series the findings of modern scholarship on the historical development of the racial groups included in the Southern China and South-east Asia region (roughly southwards from the Nan-ling in South China to Indonesia; and eastwards from Burma and the Tibetan borderland to Fukien, Taiwan and the Philippines) in relation to one another and in the light of Chinese, Japanese, and Western scholarship.

The subject will be divided into the following five sections, each of which will be the topic for the sessions of one day; a Chairman will be appointed for each day.

1. *Archæology and pre-historic migrations in S.E. Asia:*

   This section will include comparative studies of the stone and pottery artifacts of the region; with particular attention to those of the region as a whole in contrast to those of North China and to those of other parts of the Pacific Basin; leading to a consideration of the prehistoric migrations of people from the Mainland, to the Islands, or *vice versa;* and a discussion of the ethnography of S.E. Asia.

2. *The racial groups of South China and S.E. Asia, their languages and their movements.*

   This section will include a consideration of the major racial groups at present represented in South China and S.E. Asia, their distribution and their affinities; their movements in historic times; their social structure; their religions; their languages and dialects, and the present condition of linguistic studies with reference to them.

3. *The Southward expansion of the Han Chinese in historic times.*

   This section will include an outline of Chinese military conquests in Southwest, South, and Southeast China and beyond, from the Ts'in-Han period to recent times; a study of racial infiltration in the border regions, movements of population, changes in frontiers, and cultural expansion.

4. *The sea-routes between India, S.E. Asia and China, and the origin and development of the S.E. Asian states.*

   This section will include the history of navigation in the South China seas; sea-communications between India, S.E. Asia and China from Han times to the Ming; on the one hand the advance of Indian trade, civilization and religion into S.E. Asia, and the founding of the Indianized states in Indo-China,

許伯眉（一九零六至一九六八年）一九二六年十二月畢業於皇仁書院；一九二七年一月十五日註冊成為香港大學梅堂本科生。他於一九三零年畢業，獲頒文學士學位。一九三三年他在物理系擔任助教，隨後協助該系於一九三九年歸入新成立的理學院名下。

二次大戰期間，許伯眉與家人避往澳門，戰後於一九四八年休假往英國倫敦大學攻讀博士課程。一九五一年畢業後回港大任職物理系助理講師；其後出任物理系高級講師。他對香港大學物理系建樹良多，至一九六七年退休。

一九六四年許伯眉獲頒授大英帝國員佐勳章MBE，退休後更獲委任為物理系名譽研究員。家人成立許伯眉紀念獎學金至今。

Hui Pak-mi (1906–1968) Graduated from Queen's College in December 1926, registering as a student at the University on 15th January 1927. He graduated with a Bachelor of Arts degree in 1930. In 1933, he was appointed as a Demonstrator in Chemistry becoming part of a team that formed the Physics Department of the new Science Faculty in 1939.

During the war, Hui escaped with his family to Macau, where he stayed until its cessation. He went to study for a Ph.D. at the University of London in 1948, and returned to the University in 1951 to take up the position of Assistant, and eventually Senior, Lecturer. Hui was a pivotal figure in the Department of Physics until his retirement in 1967.

Hui was awarded an M.B.E. in 1964, and appointed as an Honorary Research Fellow in the Department on his retirement. The P. M. Hui Memorial Scholarship in the Faculty perpetuates his memory.

許伯眉就讀香港大學的學生紀錄及金禧節目回條
Hui Pak-mi's student record and reply slip regarding Golden Jubilee activities

許慧嫻（一九一零至二零一零年）一九二七年十二月畢業於庇理羅士女子中學，獲香港大學取錄，一九二八年一月六日註冊成為香港大學本科生。一九三二年大學畢業，獲文學士學位。自一九三四年二月九日起獲委任為科學學院助教，自此便在香港大學執教，直至一九七三年七月退休。許慧嫻桃李滿門，學生中包括香港大學前任校長黃麗松博士。

日佔時期，許慧嫻留居香港，並在新亞藥廠兼職，為本地市場製藥。戰後更協助重建香港大學化學系，積極支持該學系的發展。一九五四年她以'番石榴的三萜系化合物成份'的研究論文為題，獲頒理學碩士學位。

一九六八年許慧嫻獲頒授大英帝國員佐勳章MBE，肯定她在學術和教學上的成就。一九八一年再獲香港大學頒授理學院名譽研究員和法學博士的名銜。許慧嫻在一九九零年以其父之名成立許磐卿基金，資助香港大學化學系、圖書館以及研究生獎學金。

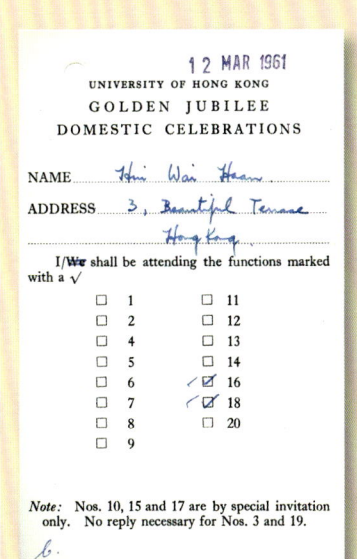

許慧嫻就讀香港大學的學生紀錄及金禧節目回條
Hui Wai-haan's student record and reply slip regarding Golden Jubilee activities

Hui Wai-haan (1910–2010) Graduated from Belilios Public School in December 1927, and registered at the University on 6th January 1928 as an undergraduate. She graduated with a Bachelor of Arts degree in 1932 and was initially appointed as a Demonstrator in Chemistry in 1934. She taught the subject almost continuously until her retirement in July 1973. Her students included the former Vice-Chancellor, Dr Rayson Huang.

During the Japanese occupation, she remained in Hong Kong working part-time as a chemist in the New Asiatic Chemical Works, making drugs for the local market. When the war ended she helped to re-establish the Chemistry Department. In 1954, she was awarded a Master of Science degree for a thesis entitled 'Triterpenoid Constituents of Psidium Guaiva. L.'

She was awarded an M.B.E. (Honorary) in the New Year's Honours List of 1968 and appointed as Honorary Research Fellow of the Faculty of Science following her retirement. She was later conferred an honorary Doctor of Laws in 1981. In 1990, Dr Hui established the Hui Pun Hing Endowment Fund in her father's honour to support the Department of Chemistry, the Library and postgraduate studies.

香港郵局一九六一年發行港大金禧紀念郵票版票
One Sheet of Golden Jubilee stamps issued by Hongkong Post
1961

一九一二年港大建校籌款義賣會成立臨時郵局戳印'香港大學'。一九四一年曾發行印上本部大樓及英皇佐治六世肖像的郵票，以紀念香港開埠百周年。一九六一年港大金禧誌慶，再次發行郵票印上大學校徽

At the University's opening Bazaar in 1912 a temporary post office was erected to frank mail with a special Hongkong University post mark. The relationship between historical landmarks and the Hongkong Post continued in 1941, when it issued a stamp featuring the University's Main Building and a portrait of King George VI in celebration of the centenary of Hong Kong. This stamp, issued in honour of the Golden Jubilee in 1961, features the shield and motto of the University's Coat of Arms.

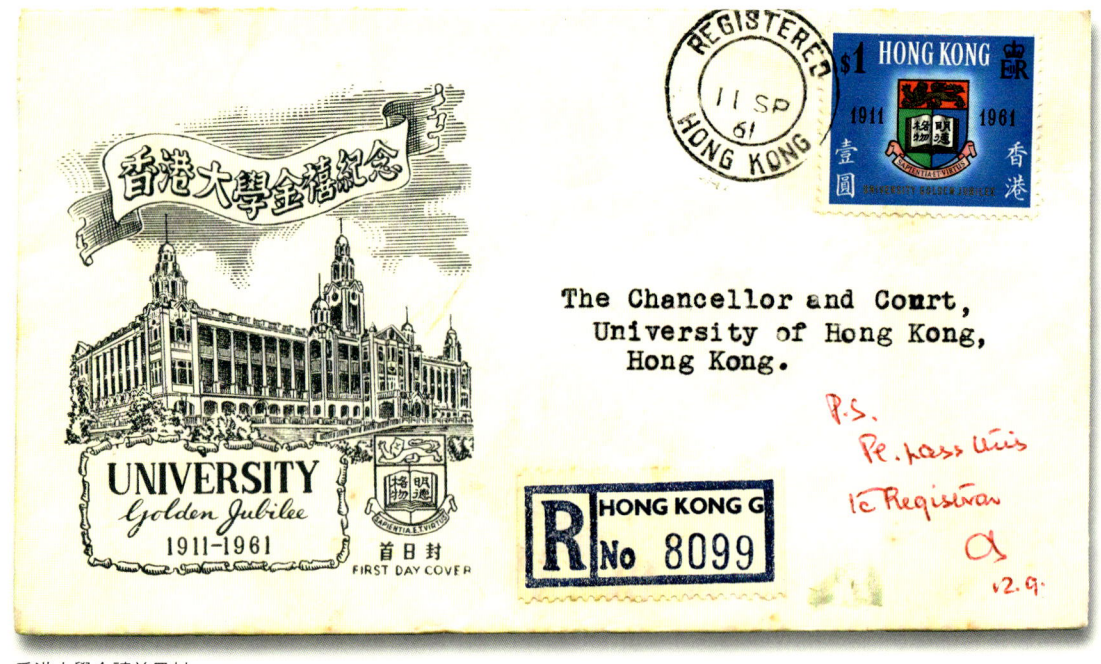

香港大學金禧首日封
First day cover with the Golden Jubilee stamp

222 明德百獻 | 香港大學檔案中心文物

香港大學金禧
University
Golden Jubilee 1911-1961

THE ARMS

The blazon of the shield of Arms of the University, featured centrally on the stamp, was assigned by Letters Patent on May 13, 1913, and described *per pale vert and azure an open book proper bound and edged or inscribed with Chinese characters sable on a chief gules a lion passant guardant or*; and the Motto is *Sapientia et Virtus*.

The Chinese characters appearing on the two pages of the open book have from time to time brought comment, two of them being of somewhat unusual form. They are a combination of two phrases in the Confucian classic *The Great Learning*, which indicate broadly the Western concepts of moral and intellectual training; *ming-tê* 明德 (bright virtue) and *kê-wu* 格物 (the investigation of things). The characters are written in the old *li-shu* style of script in vogue during the Han Dynasty, still favoured for the writing of inscriptions. There is a number of variants in this style for the two characters *ming* and *tê*; the forms used are taken from some of most highly-regarded Han inscriptions.

THE UNIVERSITY OF HONG KONG
Golden Jubilee 1911-1961

The University was incorporated in 1911, with Sir Frederick (later Lord) Lugard, then Governor of Hong Kong, its first Chancellor. Amalgamated with it was the Hong Kong College of Medicine founded by Patrick Manson in 1887, one of whose earliest graduates was Dr. Sun Yat Sen, first President of the Republic of China. Her Majesty Queen Elizabeth II is its Patron.

There are Faculties of Arts, Science, Medicine, and Engineering and Architecture. The buildings are set in a 40-acre site on a beautiful hillside on Hong Kong island. The accessions in its general library number 110,000 volumes and in its Chinese library 115,000 volumes. The students number some 1,500 and expansion plans are laid for over 2,000 within five years; most are locally-born Chinese, but many come from a score of countries overseas. The teachers, over half of whom are Chinese and one quarter British, come from many parts of Europe, Asia, and North America. Since the establishment of the Association of Universities of the British Commonwealth the University has been a member, and follows in general the pattern and standards of the Home Universities.

THE COMMEMORATIVE STAMP
Its Date of Issue

The one dollar stamp displayed on this envelope commemorates the Golden Jubilee of the University of Hong Kong, 1911-1961. The first day of a limited issue was September 11, 1961, being the first day of a Congress of six Learned Symposia convened at the University, attended by scholars from many parts of the world, to present and discuss their researches in the fields of the history, archaeology, and languages of Southern China, South-east Asia, and the Hong Kong region; the design of high buildings; economic and social problems of the Far East; phytochemistry; muscle-receptors; and land use and mineral deposits in South-east Asia. This Congress is one of a series of events throughout the year in celebration of the University's fiftieth birthday.

224 明德百獻 | 香港大學檔案中心文物

收藏香港大學的歷史檔案
COLLECTING HKU HISTORY FOR THE FUTURE

8

大學檔案中心成立之前……
教務處在保存大學歷史所擔當的角色

二次大戰前後、日治時期等艱苦歲月中，香港大學教務處及教務長對保存大學的記錄不遺餘力，近年更大力推動成立大學檔案中心及執行檔案管理方案。

配合大學九十周年誌慶出版的 An Impossible Dream 書中，編者提到香港大學早期保存記錄的工作，因人力資源不足而受阻，導致校長辦公室及各院系均自行儲存記錄，與大學行政辦公室及教務處所存資料脫節。[1] 但若干卓越人士甚有遠見，他們洞悉整頓無系統記錄儲存之逼切，使得校內不少重要記錄保存了下來。

值得一提幾位教務長，他們對現存大學文獻均有特殊貢獻。Stanley Boxer 自戰前即收集及整理大學記錄，日治及戰後過渡時期更盡力保存檔案。戰後他聯同校長秘書梅‧威徹爾（後為賴廉士夫人）將記錄整頓分類，保留不少當時百分之八十被斷定為'多餘'的資料。若不是他堅持保存，就沒有今天的大學檔案。他的繼任人梅樂彬，是大學任期最長的教務長（一九四八至一九七四年）。梅樂彬個人對大學歷史素有濃厚的興趣，他不但採用專業方法去儲存記錄，並在大學內部刊物 Interflow、Bulletin 多次發表研究文章，一九八零年他更出版了兩冊著作 The University of Hong Kong: An Informal History。

至於一九八零至一九八五年的教務長王蕙，她捐贈英文學會期刊 Pandora 予大學檔案中心，並鼓勵其他人捐獻。她又參與口述歷史訪問，分享她於港大就讀及任職時期之回憶錄。

大學檔案中心對現任教務長韋永庚更是感激萬分。二零零一年他構思並發起成立檔案中心，繼而出任檔案行動組的創辦成員，二零零六年中心開啟後，該組改名檔案諮詢組。他藉著教務長兼檔案諮詢組成員的職務，一直指導及宣揚大學檔案中心的工作。

1 'A Note on Sources', in Chan and Cunich, pp. xvii–xx.

歷任教務長	Registrars
1911	Edwin A. Irving (伊榮)
1912	J. R. Wood, MA
1912–1913	Wilfred J. Hinton, MA (軒頓)
1913–1918	A. C. Franklin, FIC
1919–1924	N. T. Macintosh, MA
1924–1926	Lancelot Forster (佛斯特), MA
1926–1940	W. B. Finnigan, OBE
1940–1948	Stanley Victor Boxer, BSc
1948–1974	Bernard Mellor (梅樂彬), OBE, MA, DLitt, JP
1975–1980	D. M. Dudgeon (杜德俊), MA, MEd, JP
1980–1985	(Mrs) Ellie L. Alleyne (王蕙女士), MBE, BA, MLitt, JP
1986–1992	N. J. Gillanders (紀朗達), MBE, LLB, FCIS, FCMA, FSCA, JP
1992–1996	M. G. Spooner (史賓南), BSc
1996–1998	Y. K. Cheung (張佑啟), OBE, BSc, PhD, DSc, DE, FEng, CEng, FICE, FIStructE, FIE, FHKIE, FIACM (署理 Acting)
1999–2000	William Ian Rees Davies (戴義安), BDS, MSc, Dip in Periodontics, FDS RCS, FDS RCSEd, FHKAM (Dental Surgery), FCDSHK, JP
2000–2002	Henry W. K. Wai (韋永庚), MA, FCIS (署理 Acting)
2002–	Henry W. K. Wai (韋永庚), MA, FCIS

Before the University Archives...
The Role of the Registry in Saving the History of the University

Over the years, the University of Hong Kong's Registry, and its Registrars have taken an active role in implementing better record-keeping practices, particularly during the chaotic years during and after World War II and the Japanese occupation of Hong Kong. More recently it has been a staunch advocate for the establishment of a University Archives and Records Management Programme for the University.

In *An Impossible Dream*, published on the occasion of the University's 90th anniversary, the editors noted that attempts at early record keeping at HKU were hampered by a lack of support staff. This resulted in the Vice-Chancellor's office and individual faculties implementing their own record-keeping systems, separate from those of the University's administrative offices and the Registry.[1] However, through the office of the Registry, and through the efforts of a number of outstanding individuals who recognised the need to impose some order on such an unsystematic approach to records management, many of the University's important records have survived.

A few of the Registrars deserve mention by name for their particular contributions to preserving the University's records for today. Stanley Victor Boxer collected and organised records from before the war, and rescued what he could during internment under the Japanese occupation and in the subsequent 'interim' period. After the war, he and the Vice-Chancellor's secretary, Miss May Witchell (later Lady May Ride), sorted and indexed the papers. What remains today is what was left after some 80% of the material was judged to be 'redundant'. Nevertheless, were it not for Boxer, very little of this period might have survived. Stanley Boxer was succeeded by Bernard Mellor who became the University's longest serving Registrar (1948–1974). Mellor's personal interest in the history of the University and professional approach to record keeping resulted in well-researched articles for the University's internal publications: *Interflow*, the *Bulletin*, and his two-volume history, *The University of Hong Kong: An Informal History*, published in 1980.

More recently, Mrs Ellie Alleyne, Registrar from 1980 to 1985, has personally donated many items to the University Archives, including issues of *Pandora*, the English Society publication, as well as facilitating donations by others. She has also shared her memories of life at the University as a student, and later staff member through an oral history interview.

The University Archives owes a very particular debt to the current Registrar, Mr Henry Wai who has championed the idea of a University Archives since it was first proposed in 2001. He was a founding member of the Archives Working Group, which became the Archives Advisory Group (AAG), following the formal establishment of the University Archives in late 2006. As Registrar, and a member of the AAG, he has contributed to, guided and promoted the work of the University Archives since its inception.

1 'A Note on Sources', in Chan and Cunich, pp. xvii–xx.

香港大學百周年校園智華館的面貌
Courtyard of the Chi Wah Learning Commons, HKU Centennial Campus

香港大學檔案中心募捐
Giving to the University Archives

香港大學檔案中心收納有關大學歷史的文獻、相片、底片、錄製影音、電子檔案、回憶錄、剪貼簿、口述歷史、文物、藝術品等藏品，歡迎香港大學畢業生、各大院系、教職員和支持者捐贈記錄資料。

檔案或文物一般只由家屬保存，往往因存放不當而令狀況惡化。個人遺物經歷一代的收藏後，相關資料如照片、檔案及文物多會隨逝者而去，令物件原來的內涵及歷史價值大減。事實上，凡是與香港大學歷史或人事相關的材料，均符合檔案中心的收藏標準。閣下將個人或家庭的檔案贈予中心，將確保資料妥善保存，可供後世使用。

檔案中心亦有賴各界捐款，以執行多項計劃：包括儘快處理檔案藏品以供研究；將部份藏品數碼化；發展電子搜尋工具；加強校外推廣；以及舉辦展覽，增加藏品的使用率及用途。

由於處理檔案的工作，需要人力資源及專門訓練，費用高昂，中心亟需資金支持運作及實施計劃。任何人士對這方面工作有興趣，歡迎聯絡我們。

如閣下有興趣支持香港大學檔案中心，無論餽贈資料或贊助捐款，請電郵 hkua@hku.hk 或致電 2219-4191 預約檔案管理主任面談。

The University Archives collects any materials that have relevance to the history of HKU. The Archives welcomes gifts of records in the form of documents, photographs, film, recordings of all kinds, electronic records, memorabilia, scrapbooks, oral history interviews, artefacts and art objects.

Often records or artefacts are accessible only to family members and stored in places that may increase the rate of their deterioration. Sadly, after a generation passes, much of the knowledge about those pictures, records and artefacts passes with them, and the contextual and historical value is lessened, if not lost altogether. Giving one's personal or family records to the University Archives is a good way to ensure that these records are preserved for future generations.

In addition to building its physical collections, the University Archives is also in need of funds to support projects that include processing archival collections to make them available to researchers, digitization of content in the case of some collections, the creation of finding aids, as well as outreach and educational programmes that broaden access to, and use of the collections.

Because archival work is labour intensive and requires special training, there is often a need for suitably skilled volunteers or student interns. If you are interested in learning about this type of work experience, please contact us.

If you wish to support the University Archives with a gift of materials for the collections, or with a gift of financial support, please contact the University Archives at hkua@hku.hk or call 2219-4191 to set up an appointment to meet with one of the archivists.

香港大學堂路牌
Hong Kong University Road Plaque
H: 41.5 cm W: 86 cm

附錄
Appendices

I 「呈盧督頌詞」華人捐獻名冊
A Profile of the Donors Listed on the Lugard Tribute

Name in English	Chinese Name	Background of Donor	HKU Fund-Raising Sub-Committee	Personal Donation (HK$)
Au Chak Man	區澤民	Proprietor, A Tack 昭隆泰 (Furniture & photo goods importer & dealer firm 洋貨傢私及影相藥料行)	Member	10,000
Chan Cheuk Hing	陳綽卿	Managing Director, Chinese Chamber of Commerce 華商總會 Director, Po Leung Kung Kuk (Chinese Reformatory 保良公局) Managing Proprietor, Chin Cheung 千祥 (Foreign goods & kerosene oil store 洋貨火水辦館) Proprietor, Kwong Yu Wing 廣裕榮 (Shanghai silk & piece goods firm 上海綢緞布疋庄)	Member	500
Chan Chik Yue	陳席儒	Comprador, Douglas Lapraik Steamship Company 德忌利士輪船公司	Treasurer	2,000
Chan Chun Chuen	陳春泉	Manager, Yuen Fat Hong 元發行 (Importer & exporter, southern & northern ports 南北行) Director, Chun On Fire Insurance Company Limited 全安保火險有限公司 Managing Director, Man On Insurance Company Limited 萬安保險有限公司 Proprietor, Man Fat Cheong 萬發祥 (Rice importer, exporter & dealer firm 米行)	Vice-Chairman	100
Chan Din San	陳殿臣	Manager, Yu Tack Shing 裕德盛 (Importer & exporter, southern & northern ports 南北行)		500
Chan Dit Yue	陳秩如	Manager, Ming Yu Tai 鳴裕泰 (Importer & exporter, southern & northern ports 南北行)	Member	
Chan Fung Toi	陳鳳臺	Managing Proprietor, Queen's Dispensary 威建藥房		200
Chan Hau Hing	陳厚卿	Accountant, Kwong On Tai 廣安泰 (Importer & exporter of yarn, Patna & Malwa opium 花紗公白出入口商店)		
Chan King Yu	陳賡虞	Director, Chinese Chamber of Commerce 華商總會 Director, Heung Shan Club 香山會所 Director, The Christian Mutual Alliance 基督教培道聯愛會 Comprador, Douglas Lapraik Steamship Company 德忌利士輪船公司 Proprietor, Ching Wo Tong 正和堂 (Chemist and druggist's store 藥材行)	Vice-Chairman	2,000
Chan Lok Chuen	陳洛川	Director, Chinese Chamber of Commerce 華商總會 Managing Partner, King Wo Hong 敬和行 (Importer & exporter, southern & northern ports 南北行) Manager, Tien Fat 天發 (Yunnan tin firm 雲南錫庄) Managing Director, Kwan On Fire Insurance Company Limited 均安火險有限公司	Member	500
Chan Suet Ngam	陳說巖	Managing Director, Chinese Chamber of Commerce 華商總會 Manager, Yan On Marine & Fire Insurance Company Limited 仁安燕梳保險有限公司		
Chan Wan Sau	陳雲繡	Proprietor, Yuen Loong Chang 源隆棧 (Exporter to California 金山庄) Managing Director, Chinese Chamber of Commerce 華商總會		

Chau Cheuk Fan	周卓凡	Manager, Shiu On Steamship Company Limited 兆安輪船有限公司 Director, Yuen On Steamship Company Limited 元安輪船有限公司 Director, Hong Kong & Kowloon Land & Loan Company Limited 香港九龍置業按揭有限公司 Assistant Manager, Chuen On Fire Insurance Company Limited 全安保火險有限公司 Treasurer, Chinese Chamber of Commerce 華商總會		500
Chau Siu Ki	周少岐	Director, Po Leung Kung Kuk (Chinese Reformatory 保良公局) Chairman, Shiu On Steamship Company Limited 兆安輪船有限公司 Manager, Yuen On Steamship Company Limited 元安輪船有限公司 Manager, Hong Kong & Kowloon Land & Loan Company Limited 香港九龍置業按揭有限公司 Manager, Chuen On Fire Insurance Company Limited 全安保火險有限公司 Manager, Man On Insurance Company Limited 萬安保險有限公司 Managing Director, Tai Foong Bank 泰豐銀行 Managing Director, Chinese Chamber of Commerce 華商總會	Vice-Chairman	1,000
Chau Yu Ting	周雨亭	Comprador, Jebsen & Company 捷成洋行 Proprietor, Yuen Cheong Lee 源昌利 (Steamship company 輪船公司) Comprador, Osaka Shosen Kaisha Steamship Company 大阪商船公司	Member	500
Cheung Si Kai	蔣士楷	Director, Tung Wah Hospital 東華醫院	Member	
Chui Chung Chak	崔仲崿	Comprador, Shewan, Tomes & Company 新旗昌洋行		
Fung Wah Chuen	馮華川	President, Chinese Chamber of Commerce 華商總會	Vice-Chairman	
Ho Fook, alias Ho Chak Sang	何福 (何澤生)	Comprador, Jardine, Matheson & Company 渣甸 (怡和) 洋行 Managing Director, Hong Kong Telegraph Managing Director, Dai Yow Bank 大有銀行 General Manager, Wing Mow Sang Kee 永茂生記 (Steamship company 輪船公司) Proprietor, Fook Kee 福記 (Coal importer and exporter firm 洋煤商店) Comprador, International Banking Corporation 萬國普通銀行	Vice-Chairman	1,000
Ho Ngok Lau	何蕚樓	Eminent medical, legal and legislative leader of the community	Member	500
Ho Kai	何啟	Unofficial member of the Legislative Council (1890 – 1914) Founder of the Alice Memorial Hospital (1886) Founder of the Hong Kong College of Medicine for the Chinese (1887) Founder of the Alice Memorial Maternity Hospital (1903)	Chairman	500
Ho Kom Tang, alias Ho Tai Sang	何甘棠 (何棣生)	Director, Chinese Chamber of Commerce 華商總會 Comprador, Jardine, Matheson & Company 渣甸 (怡和) 洋行 Managing Director, Dai Yow Bank 大有銀行 Proprietor, Shun Kee 順記 (Soochow, Hongchow & European goods dealer firm 蘇杭洋貨商店行)	Vice-Chairman	500

Ho Tung	何東	Merchant, financier, property-owner and benefactor Former Chief Comprador of Jardine, Matheson & Company 渣甸(怡和)洋行 (1894-1900)		10,000
Jiu Chau Sam	招畫三	Director, Chinese Chamber of Commerce 華商總會 Director, Po Leung Kung Kuk (Chinese Reformatory 保良公局) Manager, Kwong Mow Tai 廣茂泰 (Importer & exporter, southern & northern ports 南北行) Director, Shiu On Steamship Company Limited 兆安輪船有限公司 Director, Yuen On Steamship Company Limited 元安輪船有限公司	Member	500
Jiu Chung Hau	招頌侯	Director, Shiu On Steamship Company Limited 兆安輪船有限公司 Director, Yuen On Steamship Company Limited 元安輪船有限公司 Director, Man On Insurance Company Limited 萬安保險有限公司		200
Jiu Seung Sang	招湘生	Proprietor, Nam Shing Cheung 南盛祥 (Importer & exporter, southern & northern ports 南北行)		200
Jiu Yu Tien	招雨田	Director, Chinese Chamber of Commerce 華商總會 Proprietor, Kwong Mow Tai 廣茂泰 (Importer & exporter, southern & northern ports 南北行) Director, Tai Foong Bank 泰豐銀行 Director, Hong Kong & Kowloon Land & Loan Company Limited 香港九龍置業按揭有限公司 Director, Chun On Fire Insurance Company Limited 全安保火險有限公司	Vice-Chairman	10,000
Ku Fai Shan	古輝山	Proprietor, Bo Loong 寶隆 (Exporter to California 金山莊)	Member	200
Kwok Siu Lau	郭少流	Managing Director, Chinese Chamber of Commerce 華商總會 Comprador, Banque de l'Indo-Chine 法蘭西銀行	Member	1,000
Lai Kwai Pui	黎季裴	Chun On Fire Insurance Company Limited 全安保火險有限公司 (no information on position in company)	Vice-Chairman	
Lam Sau Ting	林壽廷	Managing Partner, Lai Yuen Bank 麗源銀號		
Lau Chu Pak	劉鑄伯	Chief President, Chinese Chamber of Commerce 華商總會 Unofficial member of the Legislative Council (1913 - 1922) Director, Po Leung Kung Kuk (Chinese Reformatory 保良公局) President, Confucian Association 孔聖會 Comprador, A.S. Watson & Company 屈臣氏大藥房 (General chemists manufacturer) Managing Director, Dai Yow Bank 大有銀行	Vice-Chairman	500
Lau Pun Chiu	劉伴樵	Comprador, Hongkong & Shanghai Banking Corporation 香港上海匯豐銀行	Member	1,000
Lau Siu Cheuk	劉少焯	Kung Yuen Hong 公源行 (no information on nature of business and position in firm)	Member	2,000
Law Suet Po	羅雪甫	Managing Director, Fook Wa & Company 福華公司 (Banking & insurance) Managing Proprietor, Cheong Lee 昌利 (Mattress exporter & dealer store 蓆莊商店)		
Leung Bing Nam	梁炳南	(No information available)		
Leung Kin On	梁建安	Comprador, Netherlands Trading Society Bank 荷蘭銀行	Member	500

Leung Pui Chi	梁培之	Director, Po Leung Kung Kuk (Chinese Reformatory 保良公局)		500
		Director, Heung Shan Club 香山會所		
		Managing Proprietor, Seu Cheong Bank 肇昌銀號		
		Managing Director, Tung On Fire Insurance Company Limited 同安火燭保險燕梳有限公司		
Li Bao Kwai	李葆葵	Treasurer, Chinese Chamber of Commerce 華商總會		500
		Vice-President, Confucian Association 孔聖會		
		Managing Proprietor, Bao Hing Tai 寶興泰 (Rice importer, exporter & dealer firm 米行)		
Li Chok Yu	李竹如	Managing Proprietor, Kum Lun Cheong 錦綸昌 (Shanghai silk & piece goods firm 上海綢緞布疋庄)		
Li Sau Hin	李秀軒	Proprietor, Kwan Mow 昆茂 (Tea importer, exporter & dealer firm 茶葉行)	Vice-Chairman	
		Proprietor, Sang Mow 生茂 (Tea importer, exporter & dealer firm 茶葉行)		
Li Sui Kum	李瑞琴	Director, Chinese Chamber of Commerce 華商總會		2,000
Li Wing Kong	李榮光	Director, Wing Hing Bank 榮興銀行		
		Managing Proprietor, Kwong Wing Cheong 廣永昌 (Importer & dealer of European goods 泰西貨物商店)		
		Proprietor, Shun Lee Wing 順利榮 (Leather dealer store 皮料商店)		
Li You Chuen	李右泉	Director, Chinese Chamber of Commerce 華商總會	Member	500
		Director, Po Leung Kung Kuk (Chinese Reformatory 保良公局)		
		President, Nam Yop Club 南邑工商總局		
		Managing Proprietor, Wing Fung Yuen 永豐源 (Exporter & importer, southern & northern Ports 南北行)		
		Proprietor, Fou On 阜安, Hang Lee 恒利, Kee Hing 其興, Kee Sang 其生, Kee Yuen 其源, Tai Sang 大生, Yuen Hang 源亨 (Pawn shops 押行店)		
Li Yiu But	李翹拔	Managing Proprietor, Tack Loong 德隆 (Shanghai silk & piece goods firm 上海綢緞布疋庄)	Member	
Lo Chung Kui	盧頌舉	Managing Director, Chinese Chamber of Commerce 華商總會		
		Director, Po Leung Kung Kuk (Chinese Reformatory 保良公局)		
		Comprador, Hong Kong & Whampoa Dock Company Limited 香港黃埔船公司		
Lo Kit Ping	老潔平	Treasurer, Nam Yop Club 南邑工商總局	Member	700
		Managing Proprietor, Wang Hing 宏興 (General exporter, gold & silver ornaments, ivory & silk dealer & maker store 洋庄金銀首飾象牙器絲髮商店)		
Lo Koong Ting	盧冠廷	Director, Chinese Chamber of Commerce 華商總會	Member	500
		Director, Heung Shan Club 香山會所		
		Director, The Christian Mutual Alliance 基督教培道聯愛會		
		General Manager, China Merchant's Steam Navigation Company 招商局輪船公司		
		Managing Proprietor, Kwong Wing Sang 廣永生 (Importer & exporter of Japanese goods 日本庄)		
		Managing Proprietor, Teung Sang Wo 東生和 (Exporter to California 金山庄)		
		Managing Director, Tung On Fire Insurance Company Limited 同安火燭保險燕梳有限公司		

Ma Hing Chau	馬杏巢	Manager, Tung Hing Loong 同興隆 (Importer & exporter, flour & sugar dealer firm 麵粉糖品出入口商行)		
Mok Yeuk Lim	莫若廉	Comprador, Butterfield & Swire Company 太古洋行	Member	250
Ng Hon Che	伍漢墀	Director, Chinese Chamber of Commerce 華商總會	Hon Secretary	500
		Manager, Yuen Fat Hong 元發行 (Importer & exporter, southern & northern Ports 南北行)		
Ng Li Hing	吳理卿	Leader of the Fukienese business community in Hong Kong	Vice-Chairman	50,000
		Proprietor, Ng Yuen Hing 吳源興 (Importer & exporter, southern & northern ports 南北行)		
Poon Wai Suen	潘維宣	Manager, Wui Loong Bank 匯隆銀行		
She Tat Choi	佘達材	Manager, Hong Kong, Canton & Macao Steam Boat Company Limited 省港澳輪船公司		250
Sum Pak Ming	岑伯銘	Managing Director, Chinese Chamber of Commerce 華商總會		300
		Comprador, Russo Chinese Bank 華俄道勝銀行		
Sin Tak Fan	冼德芬	Director, Chinese Chamber of Commerce 華商總會	Vice-Chairman	1,000
		Chief Interpreter, Ewens & Needham Solicitors Firm 伊尹氏及彌咸律師行		
Siu Yun Fai	蕭遠輝	Managing Proprietor, Ming Shun Hong 明順行 (Importer & exporter, southern & northern ports 南北行)	Member	1,000
Tam Hok Boh	譚鶴坡	Managing Proprietor, Yut On Bank 鎰安銀號	Member	500
		Managing Proprietor, Ku On Bank 鉅安銀號		
		Managing Director, Tung On Fire Insurance Company Limited 同安火燭保險燕梳有限公司		
		Director, Kwong Sun Knitting Factory Company 廣新織造局		
Tang Chi Ngong	鄧志昂	Managing Director, Chinese Chamber of Commerce 華商總會		500
		Managing Proprietor, Tien Fook Bank 天福銀行		
		Managing Director, I On Marine & Fire Insurance Company Limited 宜安洋面兼火燭保險有限公司		
Tang Kam Che	鄧鑑之	Managing Proprietor, Ching Seung Company 振商公司 (Importer & dealer of European goods firm 泰西貨物用品商店行)		
Tong Lai Chuen	唐麗泉	Managing Director, Chinese Chamber of Commerce 華商總會	Member	500
		Director, Heung Shan Club 香山會所		
		Comprador, Holland–China Trading Company 好時洋行		
		Comprador, Shewan, Tomes & Company 新旗昌洋行		
		Director, Bank of Canton Limited 廣東銀行有限公司		
Tsang Bing Kwun	曾秉鈞	Managing Director, Chinese Chamber of Commerce 華商總會		
		Managing Proprietor, Kwong Tack Fat 廣德發 (Importer & exporter, southern & northern ports 南北行)		
		Managing Director, Yan On Marine & Fire Insurance Company Limited 宜安燕梳保險有限公司		
Tsang Wai Him	曾維謙	Manager, Yue Wo Lung 裕和隆 (Importer & exporter, southern & northern ports 南北行)	Member	
		Managing Director, Man On Insurance Company Limited 萬安保險有限公司		

Name	中文	Description	Position	Amount
Tso Seen Wan	曹善允	Solicitor and community leader Founder of St. Stephen's College (1903) & St. Stephen's Girls College (1905) Unofficial member of the Legislative Council (1929 - 1937)	Secretary	500
Tsoi Hiu Lam	蔡曉嵐	(No information available)	Member	
Tsui Ngoi Tong	徐愛堂	Proprietor, Hang Sang 恆生 & Kee Yuen 其源 (Pawn shops 押行店)		
Wei Yuk, alias Wei Boshan	韋玉 (韋寶珊)	Unofficial member of the Legislative Council (1896 - 1914) Director, Po Leung Kung Kuk (Chinese Reformatory 保良公局) Former comprador of the Mercantile Bank of India Limited 有利銀行 (1872 - 1908)	Vice-Chairman	
Wong Fa Lung	黃花農	Managing Director, Sui Kut Bank 瑞吉銀行 Chun Cheung Wing 俊昌榮 (no information on nature of business and position in firm)	Member	500
Wong Lai Chuen	黃麗川	Managing Director, Chinese Chamber of Commerce 華商總會 Managing Director, Yu Tack & Company Limited 裕德有限公司 (Importer & exporter, flour & sugar dealer firm 麵粉糖品出入口商行)		500
Wong Tak Tai	黃德泰	Managing Proprietor, Tack Cheong Hong 德昌行 (Importer & exporter, southern & northern ports 南北行)	Member	
Wong Yiu Tung	黃耀東	Director, Chinese Chamber of Commerce 華商總會 Managing Proprietor, Chuen Shing 全盛 (Gold leave dealer firm 金葉行) General Manager, Fook Wa & Company 福華公司 (Banking & insurance) Proprietor, Fook Tai 福泰 (Shanghai silk & piece goods firm 上海綢緞布疋庄) Managing Director, Yu Tack & Company Limited 裕德有限公司 (Importer & exporter, flour & sugar dealer firm 麵粉糖品出入口商行)	Member	500
Wu Chue Wan	胡著雲	Managing Director, Chinese Chamber of Commerce 華商總會 Director, Po Leung Kung Kuk (Chinese Reformatory 保良公局) Assistant Treasurer, Sze Yap Chamber of Commerce 四邑工商總局 Po On Marine Insurance Company Limited 普安保險有限公司 (no information on position in company)	Member	100
Wu Ting Sam	胡鼎三	General Manager, Chui Tack Loong 聚德隆 (Importer & exporter, southern & northern ports 南北行) General Manager, Yek Tong Lin Fire & Marine Insurance Company Limited 益同人保險有限公司 Proprietor, Sam Miu 三妙 (Chinese stationery store 中式文具商店)		
Wu Hoi Chau	胡海籌	Director, Chinese Chamber of Commerce 華商總會 Director, Heung Shan Club 香山會所 Comprador, Skott & Company 新中和洋行 Manager, Hop Wo 合和 (Confectionary, bakery & European cakes dealer store 中西餅食糖果商店) Sui Li Hong 瑞利行 (no information on nature of business and position in firm)	Member	
Wu Wun Chor	胡蘊初	Managing Proprietor, Wai Sang Hong 衛生行 (General chemist & perfume manufacturer 藥房香水製造行) Managing Director, Kwong Hung Fat 廣鴻發 (Importer & exporter, flour & sugar dealer firm 麵粉糖出入口商行)		

Yiu Ku Yuen	姚鉅源	Comprador, International Banking Corporation 萬國寶通銀行	Member	500
Yu Bun Nam	余彬南	Proprietor, Yu Kwong Cheong 余廣昌 (Land investment firm 置業公司)	Member	600
Yu To Sang	余道生	Managing Director, Chinese Chamber of Commerce 華商總會 Managing Proprietor, Cheong Shing Bank 昌盛銀庄 Managing Director, Fook On Fire and Marine Insurance Company Limited 福安洋面及火燭保險有限公司		
Yu Yat Cho	余日初	(No information available)		
Yuen Lai Chuen	阮荔村	Man Cheung Yuen 萬祥源 (no information on nature of business and position in firm)	Member	600
Yuen Wan Yiu	源雲翹	Director, Po Leung Kung Kuk (Chinese Reformatory 保良公局) Manager, Kwong On Wing 廣安榮 (Importer & exporter, southern & northern ports 南北行)	Member	500
Yung Kin Bong	容建邦	Comprador, Deutsch Asiatische Bank 德華銀行	Member	600
Yung Siu Po	容兆譜	Director, Po Leung Kung Kuk (Chinese Reformatory 保良公局) Comprador, Hutchison & Company 和記洋行	Member	100
Yung Yik Ting	容翼廷	Comprador, Chartered Bank of India, Australia & China 渣打銀行	Member	

Source:

'Ho Kai to May' and 'Enclosed list of Chinese recommended' (6 February 1909) in *The Conception and Foundation of the University of Hong Kong: Miscellaneous Documents, 1908–1913* (S.l.: s.n., 1974?), nos. 88 & 88a.

University of Hongkong: List of Subscriptions to the Endowment Fund (Hong Kong: Noronha, 1911), pp. 1–25.

Zheng Zican (Jan, George Chance) 鄭紫燦: *Xianggang Zhonghua shangye jiaotong renming zhinanlu* 香港中華商業交通人名指南錄 [The Anglo-Chinese Commercial Directory] (Hong Kong: no press, 1915?), [38], 828, [80]

Alfred H.Y. Lin 連浩鋈

Honorary Associate Professor,
School of Humanities (History)
The University of Hong Kong

II 香港大學學生會組織架構
The Hong Kong University Students' Union Organizational Chart

The Hong Kong University

General Meeting 全民大會

Union C...

Faculty/Academic Societies 院會/學術會	**Hall Students' Associations** 舍堂學生會/宿生會	**Sports Assoc...** 體育聯...
Architectural Society 建築學會 　Architectural Students' Association 建築學生會 　Surveying Society 測量學會 Arts Association 文學院學生會 　Chinese Society 中文學會 　English Society 英文學會 　Fine Arts Society 藝術史學會 　French Society 法文學會 　German Association 德文協會 　History Society 歷史系學會 　Japanese Society 日文學會 　Linguistics Society 語言學學會 　Music Society 音樂學會 　Society of Comparative Literature 比較文學學會 Business and Economics Association 經濟及工商管理學會 　Business Association 商學會 　Economics and Finance Society 經濟金融學會 　Information Systems Association 資訊系統學會 Dental Society 牙醫學會 Education Society 教育學會 Engineering Society 工程學會 　Civil Engineering Society 土木工程學會 　Computer Science Association 計算機科學學會 　Electrical and Electronic Engineering Association 電機電子工程學會 　Mechanical Engineering Society 機械工程學會 　Medical Engineering Society 醫學工程學會 Law Association 法律學會 Medical Society 醫學會 　Chinese Medicine Society 中醫藥學會 　Nursing Society 護理學會 　Pharmacy Society 藥劑學會 Science Society 理學會 　Biochemistry Society 生物化學學會 　Biological Sciences Society 生物科學學會 　Chemistry Society 化學學會 　Environmental Life Science Society 環境生命科學學會 　Food and Nutritional Science Society 食物及營養學學會 　Mathematics Society 數學學會 　Statistics and Actuarial Science Society 統計及精算學會 Social Sciences Society 社會科學學會 　Geographical, Geological and Archaeological Society 地理地質及考古學會 　Politics and Public Administration Association 政治及公共行政學會 　Psychology Society 心理學學會 　Social Work and Social Administration Society 社會工作及社會行政學會 　Sociology Society 社會學學會	Duchess of Kent Hall SA 根德公爵夫人堂學生會 Hornell Hall SA 康寧堂學生會 Lady Ho Tung Hall SA 何東夫人紀念堂宿生會 Lee Chi Hung Hall SA 李志雄紀念堂學生會 Lee Hysan Hall SA 利希慎堂學生會 Lee Shau Kee Hall SA 李兆基堂宿生會 Morrison Hall SA 馬禮遜堂宿生會 R.C. Lee Hall SA 利銘澤堂宿生會 Ricci Hall SA 利瑪竇宿舍宿生會 Simon K.Y. Lee Hall SA 李國賢堂學生會 St. John's College SA 聖約翰學院學生會 Starr Hall SA 施德堂學生會 Suen Chi Sun Hall SA 孫志新堂宿生會 Swire Hall SA 太古堂宿生會 University Hall SA 大學堂宿生會 Wei Lun Hall SA 偉倫堂學生會	Archery Club 射箭會 Athletics Club 田徑學會 Badminton Club 羽毛球會 Basketball Club 籃球學會 Chinese Martial A... 中國武術學會 Dragon Boat Clu... 龍舟會 Fencing Club 劍擊會 Football Club 足球學會 Handball Club 手球學會 Hockey Club 曲棍球學會 Judo Club 柔道會 Karate Club 空手道會 Kendo Club 劍道會 Lacrosse Club 棍網球學會 Netball Club 投球學會 Rowing Club 划艇學會 Rugby Football C... 欖球學會 Softball Club 壘球學會 Sport Climbing C... 運動攀登會 Squash Rackets C... 壁球學會 Swimming Club 游泳學會 Table Tennis Clu... 乒乓球會 Taekwondo Club 跆拳道會 Tennis Club 網球學會 Volleyball Club 排球學會

ents' Union 香港大學學生會

General Polling 全民投票

il 評議會

Union Executives 學生會幹事

President 會長
Vice-President (Internal) 內務副會長
Vice-President (External) 外務副會長
General Secretary 常務秘書
Financial Secretary 財務秘書
2 University Affairs Secretaries 大學事務秘書 2 名
3 External Affairs Secretaries 外務秘書 3 名
Student Welfare Secretary 學生福利秘書
Publications Secretary 出版秘書
Social Secretary 康樂秘書
Current Affairs Secretary 時事秘書
Administrative Secretary 行政秘書
President of Sports Association 體育聯會會長
President of Independent Clubs Association 學社聯會會長
President of Cultural Association 文化聯會會長

Cultural Association 文化聯會	Independent Clubs Association 學社聯會	Campus Media 校園傳媒	Popularly Elected Union Councilors 普選評議員
Animation and Comics Association 動漫聯盟 Art Club 美術學會 Bridge Club 橋牌學會 Chess and Boardgames Club 棋會 Dancing Club 舞蹈學會 Debating Society 演辯學會 Drama Society 戲劇社 Film Society 電影學會 Literature Association 文社 Magic Club 魔術學會 Music Club 音樂社 Photographic Society 攝影學會 Union Choir 合唱團 Union Philharmonic Orchestra 管弦樂團 Youth Literary Awards Association 青年文學獎協會	AIESEC-LC-HKU 國際經濟商管學生會 Astronomy Club 天文學會 Buddhist Studies Society 佛學會 Catholic Society 天主教同學會 China Education Association 中國教育小組 China Study Society 國事學會 Christian Association 基督徒團契 Christian Choir 基督徒詩班 Computer Society 電腦學會 Golden Z Club 崇德青年社 Greenwoods 常綠林 Hong Kong Award for Young People 香港青年獎勵計劃 Investment Society 投資學會 LifePlanet 生命村 Ramblers' Club 行社 Rotaract Club 扶輪青年服務團 Social Service Group 社會服務團 Weapons and Tactics Association 槍會 World Collegiate Association for the Research of Principles - Hong Kong 世界大學原理研究會 World University Service HKUB 世界大學服務社	Campus TV 校園電視 Undergrad 學苑	Popularly Elected Union Councilor (I) 普選評議員（一） Popularly Elected Union Councilor (II) 普選評議員（二） Popularly Elected Union Councilor (III) 普選評議員（三） Popularly Elected Union Councilor (IV) 普選評議員（四） Popularly Elected Union Councilor (V) 普選評議員（五）

III 香港大學校長名錄及簽署
Vice-Chancellors' Signatures and Sources

1912–1918 Sir Charles Eliot	13 August 1912, Letter to W. H. Hewitt B.D. University Document 1912
1918–1921 (Acting) Professor G. P. Jordan	Pre-war Loke Yew loan-payment (1)
1921–1924 Sir William Brunyate	Pre-war Files Series Gr- H: Ho Tung, Including Workshop
1924–1937 Sir William Hornell	31 January 1929 meeting Minutes of Senate Meetings
1937–1949 Dr Duncan Sloss	21 February 1948 meeting, 1948(1) Senate Minutes 1948–1949
1949–1964 Sir Lindsay Ride	10 January 1950 meeting, 1950(1) Senate Minutes 1950-1952

Sir Charles Eliot, K.C.M.G. *[signature]* Pre-war Loke Yew loan-payment (1)	
[signature] Vice-Chancellor 25th June, 1923. Pre-war Files Series E-F: Fenwick A. H.	
W.W.H. Vice-Chancellor. Pre-war Loke Yew loan-payment (3)	W.W Howell Vice-Chancellor. (Chop) Pre-war Loke Yew loan-payment (3)
[signature] 5 October 1948 meeting, 1948(3) Senate Minutes 1948–1949	*[signature]* 11 September 1948 meeting, 1948 (3) Senate Minutes 1948–1949
[signature Ride] 1 June 1950 meeting, 1950(2) Senate Minutes 1950–1952	

1964–1965
Dr W. C. G. Knowles

[signature] W.C.G. Knowles (Chairman)

1965
Professor A. J. S. McFadzean

[signature] Vice-Chancellor

30 July 1965, 93/765
Council Minutes 1965

1965–1972
Dr Kenneth E. Robinson

[signature] (K.E. Robinson) Vice-Chancellor.

3 July 1968, 204/668
Council Minutes 1968

1972–1986
Dr Rayson Huang Li-sung

[signature] CHAIRMAN

6 March 1973 Minutes, 6-3-73
Senate Minutes January–June 1973

1986–1995
Professor Wang Gungwu

[signature] Professor Wang Gungwu, Vice-Chancellor

The Review 1994 P.2

CHAIRMAN

12 January 1965 meeting
Senate Minutes 1965

A.J.S. McFadzean
Vice-Chancellor

2 September 1965, 53/965
Council Minutes 1965

A.J.S. McFadzean

CHAIRMAN

30 September 1971 meeting, 38/1071
Council Minutes 1971

K. E. ROBINSON
Vice-Chancellor

February 1971, 202/271
Council Minutes 1971

Vice-Chancellor

5 April 1973, 84/473
Senate Minutes Jan-Jun 1973

1996–2000 Professor Y. C. Cheng	Professor Y C Cheng Vice-Chancellor The University of Hong Kong *The Review* 1996 P.3
2000–2002 Professor W. I. R. Davies	Professor W I R Davies Vice-Chancellor The University of Hong Kong *The Review* 2000 P.3
2002– Professor Lap-Chee Tsui	Professor Lap-Chee Tsui Vice-Chancellor *The Review* 2007 P.2

IV 學位、文憑及證書
List of Degrees

100 Years of Degrees Offered by HKU

Architecture, Faculty of (1951–59, 1984–)

1950–51	BArch	Bachelor of Architecture 建築學學士
1950–51	MArch	Master of Architecture 建築學碩士
1978–79	BSc (Building Studies)	Bachelor of Science in Building Studies 建造學理學士
1981–82	MSc (Urban Planning)	Master of Science in Urban Planning 理科碩士(城市規劃學)
1985–86	MSc (Const Project Man)	Master of Science in Construction Project Management 理科碩士(建築策劃管理學)
1988–89	MUrbanDesign	Master of Urban Design 城市設計碩士
1988–89	BSc (Surv)	Bachelor of Science in Surveying 理學士(測量學)
1991–92	MSc (RealEstDev)	Master of Science in Real Estate Development 理科碩士(房地產發展)
1992–93	MHousMan	Master of Housing Management 房屋管理碩士
1993	MLA	Master of Landscape Architecture 園境碩士
1997–98	MA (TranspPol&Plan)	Master of Arts in Transport Policy and Planning 文科碩士(運輸政策與規劃)
1997–98	MSc (RealEst)	Master of Science in Real Estate 理科碩士(房地產)
1999–2000	BHouMan	Bachelor of Housing Management 房屋管理學士
2001–02	MSc (Conservation)	Master of Science in Conservation 理科碩士(建築文物保護)
2002–03	MSc (IDM)	Master of Science in Interdisciplinary Design and Management 理科碩士(跨領域設計與管理學)

Architecture, School of (1978—1984)

1978–79	BBuilding	Bachelor of Building 建造學學士
1984–85	BSc (QS)	Bachelor of Science in Quantity Surveying 測量學理學士

Arts, Faculty of (1913–)

1913–14	BA	Bachelor of Arts 文學士
1915–16	MA	Master of Arts 文科碩士
1957–58	MA(Ed)	Master of Arts in Education 文科碩士(教育)

1966–67	DLitt	Doctor of Letters 文學博士
1971–72	MA	Master of Arts in Twentieth Century Western Literature & Thought 文科碩士
1971–72	MA	Master of Arts in Chinese Literary Studies 文科碩士
1971–72	MPhil	Master of Philosophy 哲學碩士
1973	MA	Master of Arts in Chinese Historical Studies 文科碩士
1973	MA	Master of Arts in Chinese and Comparative Literary Studies 文科碩士
1974	MA	Master of Arts in Language Studies 文科碩士
1974	MA	Master of Arts in Comparative Asian Studies 文科碩士
2002–03	MGIS	Master of Geographic Information Systems 地理信息系統碩士
2008–09	BA&Bed (LangEd)	Bachelor of Arts and Bachelor of Education in Language 文學士及教育學士(語文教育)
2010–11	MFA	Master of Fine Arts 藝術碩士

Business and Economics, Faculty of (2002–)

2001–02	MFE	Master of Financial Engineering 金融工程碩士
2001–02	BBA (IS)	Bachelor of Business Administration in Information Systems 工商管理學學士(資訊系統)
2002–03	MFin	Master of Finance 金融學碩士
2006–07	BBA (IBGM)	Bachelor of Business Administration in International Business and Global Management 工商管理學學士(國際商業及環球管理)

Dentistry, Faculty of (1982–)

1980–81	BDS	Bachelor of Dental Surgery 牙醫學士
1982–83	MDS	Master of Dental Surgery 牙醫碩士
1997–98	MOrth	Master of Orthodontics 矯齒學碩士
2004–05	MSc (DMS)	Master of Science in Dental Materials Science 理科碩士(牙科材料科學)
2006–07	MSc (ImplantDent)	Master of Science in Implant Dentistry 理科碩士(植齒學)
2009–10	MDS (Prostho)	Master of Dental Surgery in Prosthodontics 牙醫碩士(修復學)
2009–10	MDS (Perio)	Master of Dental Surgery in Periodontology 牙醫碩士(牙周病學)
2009–10	MDS (PaedDent) / MDS (PaediatrDent)	Master of Dental Surgery in Paediatric Dentistry 牙醫碩士(兒童齒科)

2009–10	MDS (Endo)	Master of Dental Surgery in Endodontics 牙醫碩士(牙髓病學)	
2010–11	MSc (General Dent)	Master of Science in General Dentistry 理科碩士(全科牙醫學)	
2010–11	MSc (Community Dent)	Master of Science in Community Dentistry 理科碩士(社會牙醫學)	

Education, Faculty of (1984–   )

1988–89	BSc(Sp & HearSc)	Bachelor of Science in Speech and Hearing Sciences 理學士(語言及聽覺學)
1991–92	BEd	Bachelor of Education 教育學士
1994–95	BEd (PrimaryEd)	Bachelor of Education in Primary Education 教育學士(小學教育)
1994–95	BEd (LangEd)	Bachelor of Education in Language Education 教育學士(語文教育)
1997–98	MA (Applied Linguistics)	Master of Arts in Applied Linguistics 文科碩士(應用語言學)
1997–98	MSc (Audiology)	Master of Science in Audiology 理科碩士(聽覺學)
1999–2000	BSc (SSLM)	Bachelor of Science in Sports Science and Leisure 理學士(運動科學及康樂管理)
2000–01	MSc (Sports Science)	Master of Science in Sports Science 理科碩士(運動科學)
2001–02	MSc (ITE)	Master of Science in Information Technology in Education 理科碩士(教育應用資訊科技)
2003–04	EdD	Doctor of Education 教育博士
2004–05	MSc (LIM)	Master of Science in Library and Information Management 理科碩士(圖書館及資訊管理)
2006–07	BSc (IM)	Bachelor of Science in Information Management 理學士(資訊管理)
2009–10	BSc (Exercise & Health)	Bachelor of Science in Exercise and Health 理學士(運動及健康)

Education, School of (1978–1984)

1977–78	MEd	Master of Education 教育學碩士

Engineering and Architecture, Faculty of (1958–1978)

1961–62	PhD	Doctor of Philosophy 哲學博士
1969–70	BA(Arch)/BA(ArchStud)	Bachelor of Arts in Architectural Studies 建築學文學士

Engineering, Faculty of (1912–1958, 1978–)

1913–14	BSc (Eng)	Bachelor of Science in Engineering 工學士	
1915–16	MSc (Eng)	Master of Science in Engineering 工程學碩士	
1982–83	BSc (CompStud)	Bachelor of Science in Computer Studies 電子計算學理學士	
1988–89	BSc (CompSc)	Bachelor of Science in Computer Science 理學士(計算機學)	
1989–90	BEng	Bachelor of Engineering 工學士	
1991–92	MSc (CompSc)	Master of Science in Computer Science 理科碩士(計算機科學)	
1992	BEng (CSE)	Bachelor of Engineering in Civil and Structural Engineering 工學學士(土木及結構工程)	
1992	BEng (Civ - EnvE)	Bachelor of Engineering in Civil Engineering (Environmental Engineering) 工學學士(土木工程 - 環境工程)	
1992	BEng (CE)	Bachelor of Engineering in Computer Engineering 工學學士(計算機工程)	
1992	BEng (EEE)	Bachelor of Engineering in Electrical and Electronic 工學學士(電機電子工程)	
1992	BEng (IMMSE)	Bachelor of Engineering in Industrial Management and Manufacturing Systems Engineering 工學學士(工業管理及製造系統工程)	
1992	BEng (ME)	Bachelor of Engineering in Mechanical Engineering 工學學士(機械工程)	
1993	MSc (Eng)(MEC)	Master of Science in Engineering (Mechanical Engineering) 工學碩士(機械工程)	
1993	BEng (EESE)	Bachelor of Engineering in Electrical Energy Systems 工學學士(電能系統工程)	
1993	BEng (MEEP)	Bachelor of Engineering in Mechanical Engineering (Environmental Engineering) 工學學士(機械工程 - 環境工程)	
1993	BEng (ME(IA))	Bachelor of Engineering in Mechanical Engineering (Industrial Automation Programme) 工學學士(機械工程 - 工業自動化)	
1993	MSc (Eng)(ELE) / MSc (Eng)(EEE)	Master of Science in Engineering (Electrical and Electronic Engineering) 工學碩士(電機電子工程)	
1993	MSc (Eng)(CSE)	Master of Science in Engineering (Civil and Structural) 工學碩士(土木及結構工程))	
1993	BEng (CEEP)	Bachelor of Engineering in Civil and Structural Engineering (Environmental Engineering) 工學學士(土木及結構工程 - 環境工程)	
1993	MSc (Eng)(BLD)	Master of Science in Engineering (Building Services) 工學碩士(屋宇設備工程)	
1993	MSc (Eng)(CIM)	Master of Science in Engineering (Computers in Manufacturing) 工學碩士(電腦應用與工業製造)	
1998–99	BSc (CSIS)	Bachelor of Science in Computer Science and Information Systems 理學士(計算機科學及資訊系統)	
1999–2000	MSc (Eng)(IEIM)	Master of Science in Engineering (Industrial Engineering and Industrial Management) 工學碩士(工業工程及工業管理)	

1999–2000	BEng (CIV)	Bachelor of Engineering in Civil Engineering 工學學士(土木工程)
1999–2000	MSc (Eng)(GEO)/ MSc (Eng)(GeoE)	Master of Science in Engineering (Geotechnical Engineering) 工學碩士(岩土工程)
1999–2000	MSc (Eng)(CIV)	Master of Science in Engineering (Civil Engineering) 工學碩士(土木工程)
2000/01	MSc (ECom&IComp)	Master of Science in Electronic Commerce and Internet 理科碩士(電子商貿及互聯網工程)
2000–01	MSc (Eng)(CommE)/ MSc (Eng)(CommEng)	Master of Science in Engineering (Communication Engineering) 工學碩士(通訊工程)
2000–01	MSc (Eng)(CompIT)	Master of Science in Engineering (Computer and Information Technology) 工學碩士(計算機及資訊科技)
2000–01	MSc (Eng)(ECOM)	Master of Science in Engineering (Electronic Commerce) 工學碩士(電子商業)
2000–01	MSc (Eng)(ICOM)	Master of Science in Engineering (Internet Computing) 工學碩士(互聯網資訊工程)
2001–02	BSc (BioInf)	Bachelor of Science in Bioinformatics 理學士(生物訊息學)
2001–02	MSc (GBM&ECom)	Master of Science in Global Business Management and E - Commerce 理科碩士(全球商業管理及電子商貿)
2001–02	BEng (InfoE)	Bachelor of Engineering in Information Engineering 工學學士(訊息工程)
2002–03	BEng (SE)	Bachelor of Engineering in Software Engineering 工學學士(軟件工程)
2002–03	BEng (EComE)	Bachelor of Engineering in Electronic and Communications Engineering 工學學士(電子及通訊工程)
2003–04	MSc (Eng)(TranspE)	Master of Science in Engineering (Transportation) 工學碩士(運輸工程)
2003–04	MSc (Eng)(StruE)	Master of Science in Engineering (Structural Engineering) 工學碩士(結構工程)
2003–04	BEng (BSE)	Bachelor of Engineering in Building Services Engineering 工學學士(屋宇設備工程)
2003–04	BSc (Eng)(BSE)	Bachelor of Science in Engineering (Building Services Engineering) 理學士(機械工程 - 屋宇設備工程)
2003–04	MSc (Eng)(EnvE)	Master of Science in Engineering (Environment Engineering) 工學碩士(環境工程)
2003–04	MSc (Eng)(IPM)	Master of Science in Engineering (Infrastructure Project Management) 工學碩士(基建項目管理)
2003–04	BEng (IETM)	Bachelor of Engineering in Industrial Engineering and Technology Management 工學學士(工業工程及科技管理)
2003–04	MSc (Eng)(ME)	Master of Science in Engineering (Mechanical Engineering) 工學碩士(機械工程)
2003–04	BEng (LESCM)	Bachelor of Engineering in Logistics Engineering and Supply Chain Management 工學學士(後勤工程及物流管理)
2004–05	BEng (EE)	Bachelor of Engineering in Electrical Engineering 工學學士(電機工程)
2004–05	BEng (MedE)	Bachelor of Engineering in Medical Engineering 工學學士(醫學工程)
2005–06	MSc (Eng)(IELM)	Master of Science in Engineering (Industrial Engineering and Logistics Management) 工學碩士(工業工程及物流管理)

2005–06	BEng (CivE - Law)	Bachelor of Engineering in Civil Engineering (Law) 工學學士(土木工程(法學))
2006–07	BEng (CompSc)	Bachelor of Engineering in Computer Science 工學學士(計算機科學)
2007–08	BEng (ME - BSE)	Bachelor of Engineering in Mechanical Engineering (Building Services Engineering) 工學學士(機械工程－屋宇設備工程)

Law, Faculty of (1984–)

1986–87	LLM	Master of Laws 法學碩士
1998–99	MCL	Master of Common Law 普通法碩士
1998–99	LLM (PRCCommL)	Master of Laws in Chinese Commercial Law 法學碩士(中國商法)
1998–99	LLM (ChineseLaw)	Master of Laws in Chinese Law 法學碩士(中國法)
1999–2000	LLM (CFL)	Master of Laws in Corporate and Financial Law 法學碩士(公司法與金融法)
1999–2000	LLM (HR)	Master of Laws in Human Rights 法學碩士(人權法)
1999–2000	SJD	Doctor of Legal Science 法律學博士
2002–03	LLM (ITL)	Master of Laws in Information Technology Law 法學碩士(資訊科技法)
2002–03	LLM (IT&IPL)/ LLM (ITIP)	Master of Laws in Information Technology and Intellectual Property Law 法學碩士(資訊科技及知識產權法)
2007–08	LLM (Arb&DR)	Master of Laws in Arbitration and Dispute Resolution 法學碩士(仲裁及排解爭端)
2009–2010	JD	Juris Doctor 法律學碩士

Medicine, Faculty of (1912–)

1913–14	MBBS	Bachelor of Medicine and Bachelor of Surgery 內外科醫學士
1913–14	MD	Doctor of Medicine 醫學博士
1916–17	MS	Master of Surgery 外科碩士
1977–78	MMedSc	Master of Medical Sciences 醫療科學碩士
1981–82	BSc (BiomedSc)	Bachelor of Science in Biomedical Sciences 理學士(生物醫學)
1994–95	BSc (NursStud)	Bachelor of Science in Nursing Studies 理學士(護理學)
1997–98	BNurs	Bachelor of Nursing 護理學學士
1999–2000	BTCM	Bachelor of Traditional Chinese Medicine 中醫全科學士
1999–2000	BPharm (ChinMed)	Bachelor of Pharmacy in Chinese Medicine 中醫藥劑學學士

2001–02	BSc (AppMedSc)	Bachelor of Science in Applied Medical Sciences 理學士(應用醫療科學)
2001–02	MN	Master of Nurse in Advanced Practice 深造護理學碩士
2001–02	MResMed	Master of Research in Medicine 醫學研究碩士
2001–02	BSc (BioInf)	Bachelor of Science in Bioinformatics 理學士(生物訊息學)
2001–02	MTCM	Master of Traditional Chinese Medicine in Acupuncture and Moxibustion 中醫學碩士(針灸學)
2002–03	MChinMed (Acup&Mox)	Master of Chinese Medicine in Acupuncture and Moxibustion 中醫學碩士(針灸學)
2002–03	BChinMed/BTCM	Bachelor of Chinese Medicine 中醫全科學士
2002–03	MNurs	Master of Nursing 護理學碩士
2004–05	MPH	Master of Public Health 公共衛生碩士
2007–08	MChinMed	Master of Chinese Medicine 中醫學碩士
2010–11	MScChinMeds	Master of Science in Chinese Medicines 理科碩士(中藥學)

Science, Faculty of (1939–)

1938–39	BSc	Bachelor of Science 理學士
1951–52	DSc	Doctor of Science 科學博士
1951–52	MSc	Master of Science 理科碩士
1959–60	BSc (Gen)	Bachelor of Science (General) 理學士
1959–60	BSc (Sp)	Bachelor of Science (Special) 理學士(深造課程)
1989–90	MSc (EnvMan)	Master of Science in Environmental Management 理科碩士(環境管理學)
1994–95	BSc (ActuarSc)	Bachelor of Science in Actuarial Science 理學士(精算學)

Social Sciences and Law, Faculty of (1972–1978)

1969–70	LLB	Bachelor of Laws 法學士
1971–72	LLD	Doctor of Laws 法學博士
1974–75	MSW	Master of Social Work 社會工作學碩士
1977–78	MBA	Master of Business Administration 工商管理學碩士

Social Sciences, Faculty of (1967–74, 1978–)

1967–68	BSocSc	Bachelor of Social Sciences 社會科學學士
1967–68	MSocSc	Master of Social Sciences 社會科學碩士
1967–68	DSocSc	Doctor of Social Science 社會科學博士
1986–87	BSW	Bachelor of Social Work 社會工作學學士
1988–89	BBA	Bachelor of Business Administration 工商管理學學士
1988–89	MPA	Master of Public Administration 公共行政學碩士
1991–92	BEcon	Bachelor of Economics 經濟學學士
1991–92	MEcon	Master of Economics 經濟學碩士
1993	MStat	Master of Statistics 統計學碩士
1994–95	BFin	Bachelor of Finance 金融學學士
1994–95	BBA (Acc&Fin)	Bachelor of Business Administration in Accounting and 工商管理學學士(會計及財務)
1995–96	BCogSc	Bachelor of Cognitive Science 認知科學學士
1999–2000	BSocSc (Govt&Laws)	Bachelor of Social Sciences in Government and Laws 社會科學學士(政治學與法學)
1999–2000	BMS	Bachelor of Management Studies 管理學學士
1999–2000	BEcon&Fin	Bachelor of Economics and Finance 經濟金融學學士
1999–2000	IMBA	Master of Business Administration (International) 工商管理學碩士(國際課程)
1999–2000	BBA (Law)	Bachelor of Business Administration in Law 工商管理學學士(法學)
1999–2000	BAcc	Bachelor of Accounting 會計學學士
2000–01	MJ	Master of Journalism 新聞學碩士
2000–01	MIPA	Master of International and Public Affairs 國際關係學碩士
2001–02	MSSM	Master of Social Service Management 社會行政管理碩士
2001–02	BCJ	Bachelor of Criminal Justice 刑事司科學士
2002–03	MBuddhStud	Master of Buddhist Studies 佛學碩士
2004–05	BJ	Bachelor of Journalism 新聞學學士
2004–05	PsyD	Doctor of Psychology 心理學博士
2007–08	MAChDS	Master of Arts in China Development Studies 文科碩士(中國發展研究)

Honorary Degrees

1916	Hon LLD	Doctor of Laws honoris causa 名譽法學博士
1961	Hon DLitt	Doctor of Letters honoris causa 名譽文學博士
1961	Hon DSc	Doctor of Science honoris causa 名譽科學博士
1965	Hon DD	Doctor of Divinity honoris causa 名譽神學博士
1969	Hon DSocSc	Doctor of Social Sciences honoris causa 名譽社會科學博士

This list is arranged by faculty in alphabetical order, and within each faculty in chronological order based on a survey and research conducted by the University Archives between 2011 and 2012.

The degrees, dates, and existing translations into Chinese were all taken from University publications of the Congregation and the Calendar.

Should any reader have information that will assist the staff in correcting or updating this information please contact the University Archives via email at hkua@hku.hk or telephone at 2219–4191.

香港大學歷史的參考資料
Selected reading on the history of the University of Hong Kong

《明德百獻：香港大學檔案文物》展覽主要的資料均源自大學檔案中心、香港大學美術博物館，以及下列歷年出版的港大歷史研究著作。本書目以作者姓氏排序，惟未能盡錄，個別參考資料將另外註明。除這些主要參考書籍外，香港大學各學院、舍堂、學系亦已出版或陸續出版其他歷史刊物、回憶錄。

Most of the research for the publication *HKU Memories from the Archives* was conducted in the collections of the University Archives and the Museum and also relies on the published research of scholars of the history of the University listed below. The list is not comprehensive and is organised in alphabetical order. Other sources used are referenced separately. In addition to the following titles, it is also worth noting that many faculties, halls and departments have published, or are in the process of publishing, histories of their own.

Bard, Solomon
Voices from the Past: Hong Kong 1842–1918 (Hong Kong University Press, 2002)

Chan Lau Kit-ching and Cunich, Peter (eds)
An Impossible Dream: Hong Kong University from Foundation to Re-Establishment, 1910–1950 (Hong Kong University Press, 2002)

Cunich, Peter
A History of the University of Hong Kong, vol. 1, 1911–1945 (Hong Kong University Press, 2012)

Development & Alumni Affairs Office, The University of Hong Kong
Growing with Hong Kong: The University and Its Graduates – The First 90 Years (Hong Kong University Press, 2002)

Evans, Daffyd Emrys
Constancy of Purpose: Faculty of Medicine, University of Hong Kong (Hong Kong University Press, 1987)

Harrison, Brian
The University of Hong Kong: The First Fifty Years (Hong Kong University Press, 1962)

Holdsworth, May and Munn, Christopher (eds)
Dictionary of Hong Kong Biography (Hong Kong University Press, 2012)

HKU Libraries Special Collections
Selected booklist on the history of the University of Hong Kong (The University of Hong Kong Libraries, Special Collections, 2001)

Huang, Rayson
A Lifetime in Academia (Hong Kong University Press, 2000)

Lam, Susan Y. Y. and Sze, Jane (eds)
Past Visions of the Future: Some Perspectives on the History of The University of Hong Kong (University Museum and Art Gallery, The University of Hong Kong, 2001)

Matthews, Clifford and Cheung, Oswald
Dispersal and Renewal: Hong Kong University During the War Years (Hong Kong University Press, 1998)

Mellor, Bernard
The University of Hong Kong: An Informal History (in two volumes) (Hong Kong University Press, 1980)

~ *Lugard in Hong Kong: Empires, Education, and a Governor at Work (1907–1912)* (Hong Kong University Press, 1992)

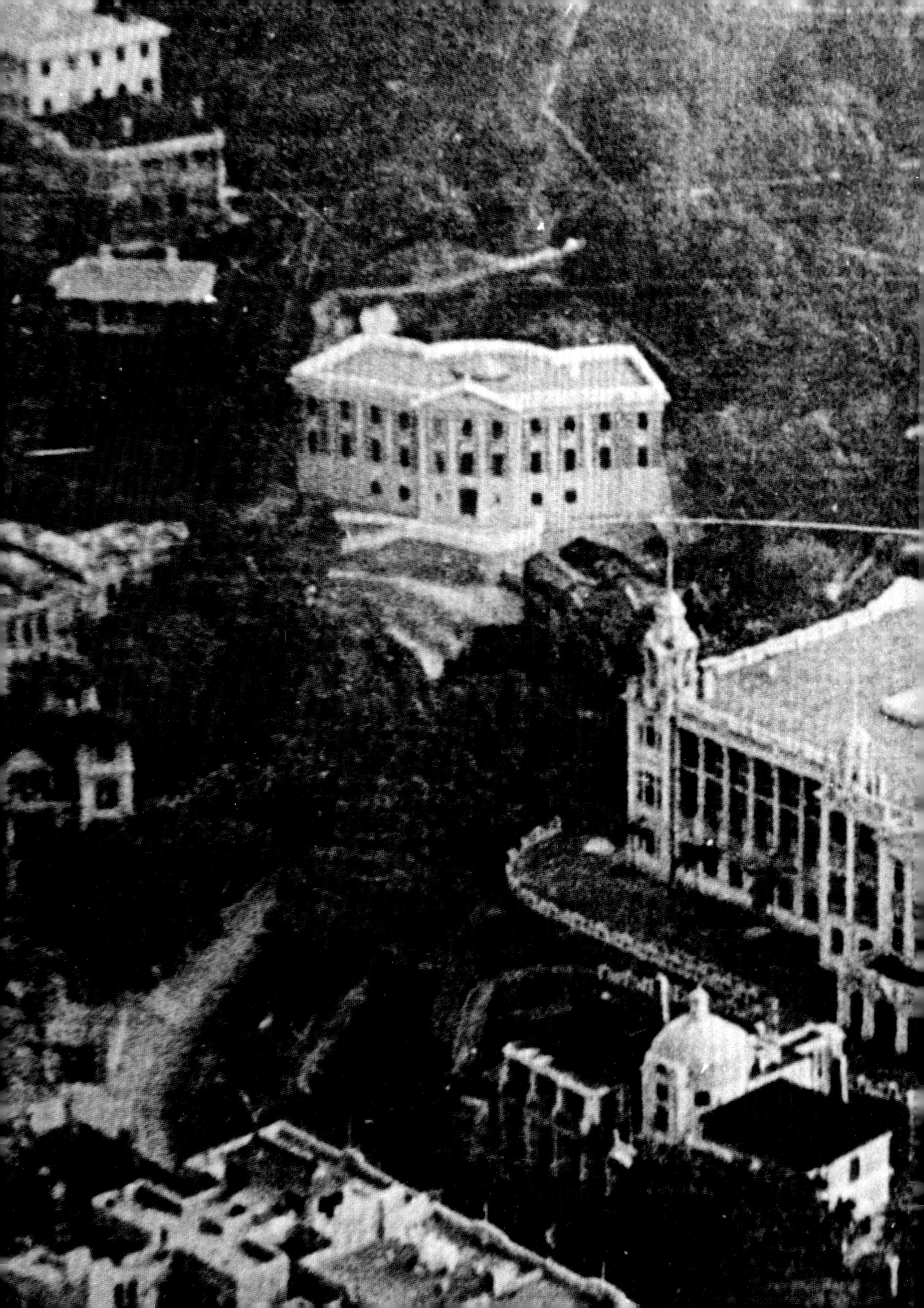